Full Color on Every Page!

America Online Simplified™

IDG's 3-D Visual™ Series

From maranGraphics™

IDG Books Worldwide, Inc.
An International Data Group Company
Foster City, CA • Indianapolis • Chicago • Southlake, TX

America Online Simplified™

Published by
IDG Books Worldwide, Inc.
An International Data Group Company
919 E. Hillsdale Blvd., Suite 400
Foster City, CA 94404
(650) 655-3000

Copyright© 1998 by maranGraphics Inc.
5755 Coopers Avenue
Mississauga, Ontario, Canada
L4Z 1R9

All rights reserved. No part of this book, including interior design, cover design, and icons, may be reproduced or transmitted in any form, by any means (electronic, photocopying, recording, or otherwise) without prior written permission from maranGraphics.

Library of Congress Catalog Card No.: 97-81242

ISBN: 0-7645-6033-6

Printed in the United States of America

10 9 8 7 6 5 4 3 2

Distributed in the United States by IDG Books Worldwide, Inc.

Distributed by Transworld Publishers Limited in the United Kingdom; by IDG Norge Books for Norway; by IDG Sweden Books for Sweden; by Woodslane Pty. Ltd. for Australia; by Woodslane Enterprises Ltd. for New Zealand; by Longman Singapore Publishers Ltd. for Singapore, Malaysia, Thailand, and Indonesia; by Simron Pty. Ltd. for South Africa; by Toppan Company Ltd. for Japan; by Distribuidora Cuspide for Argentina; by Livraria Cultura for Brazil; by Ediciencia S.A. for Ecuador; by Addison-Wesley Publishing Company for Korea; by Ediciones ZETA S.C.R. Ltda. for Peru; by WS Computer Publishing Corporation, Inc., for the Philippines; by Unalis Corporation for Taiwan; by Contemporanea de Ediciones for Venezuela; by Computer Book & Magazine Store for Puerto Rico; by Express Computer Distributors for the Caribbean and West Indies. Authorized Sales Agent: Anthony Rudkin Associates for the Middle East and North Africa.

For corporate orders, please call maranGraphics at 800-469-6616.
For general information on IDG Books Worldwide's books in the U.S., please call our Consumer Customer Service department at 800-762-2974.
For reseller information, including discounts and premium sales, please call our Reseller Customer Service department at 800-434-3422.
For information on where to purchase IDG Books Worldwide's books outside the U.S., please contact our International Sales department at 650-655-3200 or fax 650-655-3295.
For information on foreign language translations, please contact our Foreign & Subsidiary Rights department at 650-655-3021 or fax 650-655-3281.
For sales inquiries and special prices for bulk quantities, please contact our Sales department at 650-655-3200.
For information on using IDG Books Worldwide's books in the classroom or for ordering examination copies, please contact our Educational Sales department at 800-434-2086 or fax 817-251-8174.
For press review copies, author interviews, or other publicity information, please contact our Public Relations department at 650-655-3000 or fax 650-655-3299.
For authorization to photocopy items for corporate, personal, or educational use, please contact maranGraphics at 800-469-6616.

© 1998 maranGraphics, Inc.
The animated characters are the copyright of maranGraphics, Inc.

LIMIT OF LIABILITY/DISCLAIMER OF WARRANTY: AUTHOR AND PUBLISHER HAVE USED THEIR BEST EFFORTS IN PREPARING THIS BOOK. IDG BOOKS WORLDWIDE, INC., AND AUTHOR MAKE NO REPRESENTATIONS OR WARRANTIES WITH RESPECT TO THE ACCURACY OR COMPLETENESS OF THE CONTENTS OF THIS BOOK AND SPECIFICALLY DISCLAIM ANY IMPLIED WARRANTIES OF MERCHANTABILITY OR FITNESS FOR A PARTICULAR PURPOSE. THERE ARE NO WARRANTIES WHICH EXTEND BEYOND THE DESCRIPTIONS CONTAINED IN THIS PARAGRAPH. NO WARRANTY MAY BE CREATED OR EXTENDED BY SALES REPRESENTATIVES OR WRITTEN SALES MATERIALS. THE ACCURACY AND COMPLETENESS OF THE INFORMATION PROVIDED HEREIN AND THE OPINIONS STATED HEREIN ARE NOT GUARANTEED OR WARRANTED TO PRODUCE ANY PARTICULAR RESULTS, AND THE ADVICE AND STRATEGIES CONTAINED HEREIN MAY NOT BE SUITABLE FOR EVERY INDIVIDUAL. NEITHER IDG BOOKS WORLDWIDE, INC., NOR AUTHOR SHALL BE LIABLE FOR ANY LOSS OF PROFIT OR ANY OTHER COMMERCIAL DAMAGES, INCLUDING BUT NOT LIMITED TO SPECIAL, INCIDENTAL, CONSEQUENTIAL, OR OTHER DAMAGES. FULFILLMENT OF EACH COUPON OFFER IS THE RESPONSIBILITY OF THE OFFEROR.

Trademark Acknowledgments

maranGraphics Inc. has attempted to include trademark information for products, services and companies referred to in this guide. Although maranGraphics Inc. has made reasonable efforts in gathering this information, it cannot guarantee its accuracy.

All brand names and product names used in this book are trade names, service marks, trademarks, or registered trademarks of their respective owners. IDG Books Worldwide and maranGraphics Inc. are not associated with any product or vendor mentioned in this book.

FOR PURPOSES OF ILLUSTRATING THE CONCEPTS AND TECHNIQUES DESCRIBED IN THIS BOOK, THE AUTHOR HAS CREATED VARIOUS NAMES, COMPANY NAMES, MAILING ADDRESSES, E-MAIL ADDRESSES AND PHONE NUMBERS, ALL OF WHICH ARE FICTITIOUS. ANY RESEMBLANCE OF THESE FICTITIOUS NAMES, COMPANY NAMES, MAILING ADDRESSES, E-MAIL ADDRESSES AND PHONE NUMBERS TO ANY ACTUAL PERSON, COMPANY AND/OR ORGANIZATION IS UNINTENTIONAL AND PURELY COINCIDENTAL.

maranGraphics has used their best efforts in preparing this book. As Web sites are constantly changing, some of the Web site addresses in this book may have moved or no longer exist. maranGraphics does not accept responsibility nor liability for losses or damages resulting from the information contained in this book. maranGraphics also does not support the views expressed in the Web sites contained in this book. Screen shots displayed in this book are based on pre-release software and are subject to change.

Permissions

AltaVista
Digital, AltaVista and the AltaVista logo are trademarks or service marks of Digital Equipment Corporation. Used with permission.
Evian
© 1998 Great Brands of Europe Inc.
HotBot
Copyright © 1996-1998 Wired Digital, Inc. All rights reserved.
Infoseek
Reprinted by permission. Infoseek, Infoseek Ultra, Ultrasmart, Ultraseek, Ultraseek Server, Infoseek Desktop, iSeek, Quickseek, Imageseek, Ultrashop, the Infoseek logos and the tagline "Once you know, you know." are trademarks of Infoseek Corporation which may be registered in certain jurisdictions. Other trademarks shown are trademarks of their respective owners. Copyright © 1994-1998 Infoseek Corporation. All rights reserved.
Microsoft Corporation
Screen shots reprinted by permission from Microsoft Corporation.
Movie Critic
Movie Critic, a patented, artificial intelligent piece of software, was developed by Songline Studios, Inc., a major content provider on the World Wide Web. Songline Studios is an affiliate of O'Reilly and Associates, and has received a minority investment from America Online.
Saturn Corporation
© Saturn Corporation, used with permission.
Smithsonian Institution
Copyright 1995 by Smithsonian Institution.
Spiegel
© Spiegel, Inc. Used by permission.
Sportsline USA
Copyright © 1996 Sportsline USA, Inc. http://www.sportsline.com
All Rights Reserved.
Ticketmaster
Copyright © 1998 Ticketmaster Corporation.
Trimark Pictures
Copyright Trimark Pictures, 1996.
USA Today
Copyright 1996 USA TODAY Online.
Wal-Mart
Copyright © 1998 Wal-Mart Stores, Inc.
Xerox Corporation
Xerox, The Document Company and the digital X are trademarks of Xerox Corporation.
Yahoo
Text and artwork copyright © 1996 by YAHOO!, Inc. All rights reserved. YAHOO! and the YAHOO! logo are trademarks of YAHOO!, Inc.
The following screens have been used with permission:

America Online	Dupont	New Balance
Best Western	Flower Stop	Sunkist
Campbell's Soup	IDG Books	Whitehouse
Discovery Channel	Minolta	

Welcome to the world of IDG Books Worldwide.

IDG Books Worldwide, Inc., is a subsidiary of International Data Group, the world's largest publisher of computer-related information and the leading global provider of information services on information technology. IDG was founded more than 25 years ago and now employs more than 8,500 people worldwide. IDG publishes more than 270 computer publications in over 75 countries (see listing below). More than 90 million people read one or more IDG publications each month.

Launched in 1990, IDG Books Worldwide is today the #1 publisher of best-selling computer books in the United States. We are proud to have received eight awards from the Computer Press Association in recognition of editorial excellence and three from Computer Currents' First Annual Readers' Choice Awards. Our best-selling ...For Dummies® series has more than 25 million copies in print with translations in 30 languages. IDG Books Worldwide, through a joint venture with IDG's Hi-Tech Beijing, became the first U.S. publisher to publish a computer book in the People's Republic of China. In record time, IDG Books Worldwide has become the first choice for millions of readers around the world who want to learn how to better manage their businesses.

Our mission is simple: Every one of our books is designed to bring extra value and skill-building instructions to the reader. Our books are written by experts who understand and care about our readers. The knowledge base of our editorial staff comes from years of experience in publishing, education, and journalism - experience which we use to produce books for the '90s. In short, we care about books, so we attract the best people. We devote special attention to details such as audience, interior design, use of icons, and illustrations. And because we use an efficient process of authoring, editing, and desktop publishing our books electronically, we can spend more time ensuring superior content and spend less time on the technicalities of making books.

You can count on our commitment to deliver high-quality books at competitive prices on topics you want to read about. At IDG Books Worldwide, we continue in the IDG tradition of delivering quality for more than 25 years. You'll find no better book on a subject than one from IDG Books Worldwide.

John Kilcullen
President and CEO
IDG Books Worldwide, Inc.

IDG Books Worldwide, Inc., is a subsidiary of International Data Group, the world's largest publisher of computer-related information and the leading global provider of information services on information technology. International Data Group publishes over 276 computer publications in over 75 countries. Ninety million people read one or more International Data Group publications each month. International Data Group's publications include: Argentina: Annuario de Informatica, Computerworld Argentina; Australia: Australian Macworld, Client/Server Journal, Computer Living, Computerworld, Computerworld 100, Digital News, IT Casebook, Network World, On-line World Australia, PC World, Publishing Essentials, Reseller, WebMaster; Austria: Computerwelt Osterreich, Networks Austria, PC Tip; Belarus: PC World Belarus; Belgium: Data News; Brazil: Annuário de Informática, Computerworld Brazil, Connections, Super Game Power, Macworld, PC Player, PC World Brazil, Publish Brazil, Reseller News; Bulgaria: Computerworld Bulgaria, Networkworld/Bulgaria, PC & MacWorld Bulgaria; Canada: CIO Canada, Client/Server World, ComputerWorld Canada, InfoCanada, Network World Canada; Chile: Computerworld Chile, PC World Chile; Colombia: Computerworld Colombia, PC World Colombia; Costa Rica: PC World Centro America; The Czech and Slovak Republics: Computerworld Czechoslovakia, Elektronika Czechoslovakia, Macworld Czech Republic, PC World Czechoslovakia; Denmark: Communications World, Computerworld Danmark, Macworld Danmark, PC Privat Danmark, PC World Danmark Supplements, TECH World; Dominican Republic: PC World Republica Dominicana; Ecuador: PC World Ecuador; Egypt: Computerworld Middle East, PC World Middle East; El Salvador: PC World Centro America; Finland: MikroPC, Tietoverkko, Tietoviikko; France: Distributique, Golden, Hebdo-Distributique, Info PC, Le Guide du Monde Informatique, Le Monde Informatique, Reseaux & Telecoms; Germany: Computer Partner, Computerwoche, Computerwoche Extra, Computerwoche Focus, I/M Information Management, Macwelt, PC Welt; Greece: GamePro, Multimedia World; Guatemala: PC World Centro America; Honduras: PC World Centro America; Hong Kong: Computerworld Hong Kong, PCWorld Hong Kong, Publish in Asia; Hungary: ABCD CD-ROM, Computerworld Szamitastechnika, PC & Mac World Hungary, PC-X Magazine; Iceland: Tolvuheimur/PC World Island; India: Information Systems Computerworld, PC World India, Publish in Asia; Indonesia: InfoKomputer PC World, Komputek Computerworld, Publish in Asia; Ireland: ComputerScope, PC Live!; Israel: People & Computers; Italy: Computerworld Italia, Computerworld Italia Special Editions, Macworld Italia, Networking Italia, PC Shopping, PC World Italia, PC World/Walt Disney; Japan: DTP World, HP Open World Japan, Macworld Japan, Nikkei Personal Computing, Open World Japan, OS/2 World Japan, SunWorld Japan, Windows World Japan; Kenya: East African Computer News; Korea: Hi-Tech Information/Computerworld, Macworld Korea, PC World Korea; Macedonia: PC World Macedonia; Malaysia: Computerworld Malaysia, PC World Malaysia, Publish in Asia; Mexico: Computerworld Mexico, Macworld, PC World Mexico; Myanmar: PC World Myanmar; Netherlands: Computer! Totaal, LAN Magazine, LanWorld Buyers Guide, Macworld, Net Magazine, Totaal! Beurskrant; New Zealand: Absolute Beginner's Guide, Computer Buyer, Computer Industry Directory, Computerworld New Zealand, MTB, Network World, PC World New Zealand; Nicaragua: PC World Centro America; Nigeria: PC World Nigeria; Norway: Computerworld Norge, Computerworld Privat (Datamagasinet), CW Rapport Norge, IDG's KURSGUIDE, Macworld Norge, Multimediaworld, PC World Ekspress, PC World Nettverk, PC World Norge, PC World's Produktguide, Windows World Spesial; Pakistan: Computerworld Pakistan, PC World Pakistan; Panama: PC World Panama; P. R. of China: China Computer Users, China Computerworld, China Infoworld, China Telecom World Weekly, Computer & Communication, Electronic Design China, Electronics Today, Electronics Weekly, Game Camp, Game Soft, Network World China, PC World China, Popular Computer Weekly, Software Weekly, Software World, Telecom World; Peru: Computerworld Peru, PC World Profesional Peru, PC World Peru; Poland: Computerworld Poland, Computerworld Special Report, Macworld, Network, PC World Komputer; Philippines: Computerworld Philippines, PC World Philippines, Publish in Asia; Portugal: Cerebro/PC World, Computerworld/Correio Informático, Dealer World Portugal, Mac*In/PC*In, Multimedia World Portugal; Puerto Rico: PC World Puerto Rico; Romania: Computerworld Romania, PC World Romania, Telecom Romania; Russia: Computerworld Russia, Mir PK, Sety; Singapore: Computerworld Singapore, PC World Singapore, Publish in Asia; Slovenia: MONITOR; South Africa: Computing S.A., InfoWorld S.A., Network World S.A., Software World; Spain: Computerworld Espa-a, COMUNICACIONES WORLD, Dealer World, Macworld Espa-a, PC World Espa-a; Sweden: CAP&Design, Computer Sweden, Corporate Computing, MacWorld, Maxi Data, MikroDatorn, Natverk & Kommunikation, PC/Aktiv, PC World, Windows World; Switzerland: Computerworld Schweiz, Macworld Schweiz, PCtip; Taiwan: Computerworld Taiwan, Macworld Taiwan, PC World Taiwan, Publish Taiwan, Windows World; Thailand: Thai Computerworld, Publish in Asia; Turkey: Computerworld Turkiye, MACWORLD Turkiye, PC WORLD Turkiye; Ukraine: Computerworld Kiev, Computers & Software, Multimedia World Ukraine, PC World Ukraine; United Kingdom: Acorn User, Amiga Action, Amiga Computing, Appletalk, Computing, GamePro, Macworld, Network News, Parents and Computers, PC Advisor, PC Home, PSX Pro UK, The WEB; United States: Cable in the Classroom, CD Review, CIO Magazine, Computerworld, Computerworld Client/Server Journal, Digital Video Magazine, DOS World, Federal Computer Week, GamePro, InfoWorld, I-Way, JavaWorld, Macworld, Multimedia World, Netscape World Online, Network World, PC Entertainment, PC World, Publish, SunWorld Online, SWATPro Magazine, Video Event, WebMaster; Uruguay: PC World Uruguay; Venezuela: Computerworld Venezuela, PC World Venezuela; and Vietnam: PC World Vietnam.

**Every maranGraphics book represents
the extraordinary vision and commitment of a unique family:
the Maran family of Toronto, Canada.**

Back Row (from left to right): Sherry Maran, Rob Maran, Richard Maran, Maxine Maran, Jill Maran.
Front Row (from left to right): Judy Maran, Ruth Maran.

Richard Maran is the company founder and its inspirational leader. He developed maranGraphics' proprietary communication technology called "visual grammar." This book is built on that technology—empowering readers with the easiest and quickest way to learn about computers.

Ruth Maran is the Author and Architect—a role Richard established that now bears Ruth's distinctive touch. She creates the words and visual structure that are the basis for the books.

Judy Maran is the Project Manager. She works with Ruth, Richard, and the highly talented maranGraphics illustrators, designers, and editors to transform Ruth's material into its final form.

Rob Maran is the Technical and Production Specialist. He makes sure the state-of-the-art technology used to create these books always performs as it should.

Sherry Maran manages the Reception, Order Desk, and any number of areas that require immediate attention and a helping hand.

Jill Maran is a jack-of-all-trades who works in the Accounting and Human Resources department.

Maxine Maran is the Business Manager and family sage. She maintains order in the business and family—and keeps everything running smoothly.

Oh, and three other family members are seated on the sofa. These graphic disk characters help make it fun and easy to learn about computers. They're part of the extended maranGraphics family.

Credits

Author & Architect:
Ruth Maran

Copy Editors:
Kelleigh Wing
Jill Maran

Project Manager:
Judy Maran

Editors:
Raquel Scott
Jason M. Brown
Janice Boyer
Cathy Benn
Michelle Kirchner
Vicki Harford
James Menzies
Frances LoPresti

Layout Designer:
Treena Lees

Illustrators:
Russ Marini
Jamie Bell
Peter Grecco

Screens & Illustrations:
Jeff Jones

Indexer:
Raquel Scott

Post Production & Screen Captures:
Robert Maran

Editorial Support:
Michael Roney

Acknowledgments

Thanks to the dedicated staff of maranGraphics, including Jamie Bell, Cathy Benn, Janice Boyer, Jason M. Brown, Francisco Ferreira, Peter Grecco, Vicki Harford, Jeff Jones, Michelle Kirchner, Wanda Lawrie, Treena Lees, Frances LoPresti, Michael W. M^{ac}Donald, Jill Maran, Judy Maran, Maxine Maran, Robert Maran, Sherry Maran, Russ Marini, James Menzies, Raquel Scott, Roxanne Van Damme, Paul Whitehead and Kelleigh Wing.

Finally, to Richard Maran who originated the easy-to-use graphic format of this guide. Thank you for your inspiration and guidance.

Table of Contents

CHAPTER 1

GETTING STARTED

Introduction to AOL	4
What You Can Do With AOL	6
Connect to AOL	8
The AOL Screen	10
View the Online Clock	11
Maximize a Window	12
Minimize a Window	13
Move a Window	14
Size a Window	15
Scroll Through a Window	16
Switch Between Windows	17
Getting Help	18

CHAPTER 2

FIND INFORMATION ON AOL

View the AOL Channels	22
The AOL Channels	24
Using the Channel Guide	30
Using Keywords	32
Keyword Examples	34
Find Information on AOL	38

CHAPTER 3

BROWSE THE WEB

Introduction to the Web	42
Display a Specific Web Page	44
Select a Link	46
Stop Transfer of Information	47
Move Through Web Pages	48
Refresh a Web Page	49
Find Web Pages	50
Display and Change Your Home Page	52
Cool Web Pages	54

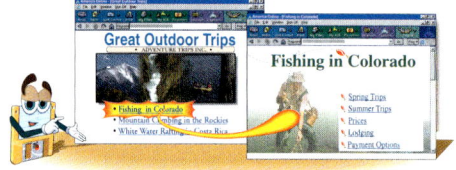

CHAPTER 4

READ AND COMPOSE E-MAIL

Introduction to E-mail 62
Read Messages 64
Send a Message 66
Reply to a Message 68
Forward a Message 70
Add a Name to the Address Book.........72
Add a Group to the Address Book 74
Select a Name from the Address Book....76
Find an E-mail Address 78

CHAPTER 5

WORK WITH E-MAIL

Print a Message..............................82
Save a Message 83
Delete a Message 84
Mark Read Message as New 85
Attach a File to a Message 86
Download an Attached File 88

Spell Check a Message......................90
Change Font and Font Size 92
Bold, Italic and Underline 94
Change Text Alignment 95
Change Text Color 96
Change Background Color...................97
Request Return Receipt 98
Add Favorite Place to Message 99
Send a Message Later......................100
Unsend a Message..........................102
Change How Long AOL Keeps Read
    Messages 103

CHAPTER 6

USING MESSAGE BOARDS

Introduction to Message Boards 106
Read Messages 108
Print a Message.............................110
Mark Message Board as Read 111
Reply to a Message 112
Add a Message 114

Table of Contents

CHAPTER 7

USING NEWSGROUPS

Introduction to Newsgroups 118
Search for Newsgroups 120
Subscribe to a Newsgroup Quickly 124
Unsubscribe from a Newsgroup 125
Read Messages 126
Print a Message 128
Mark Newsgroup as Read 129
Reply to a Message 130
Send a New Message 132

CHAPTER 8

CHAT WITH OTHER AOL MEMBERS

Introduction to Chat 136
Find a Chat Room 138
Send a Comment 140
Play Sounds in a Chat Room 141
View Member Profile Information 142
Ignore a Chat Member 143
Create a Private Chat Room 144
Send an Instant Message...................146
Reply to an Instant Message...............149

CHAPTER 9

ATTEND LIVE EVENTS

View AOL Live Events 152
Enter an Auditorium 154
Turn Chat Off 155
Send Messages 156

CHAPTER 10

FIND AOL MEMBERS

Search the Member Directory 160
Enter Member Profile Information 162
Locate an AOL Member.....................164
Add Members to a Buddy List..............166
View Buddy Lists 168

CHAPTER 11

DOWNLOAD FILES

Introduction to Downloading Files 172
Find Files to Download 174
Download a File 178
Using the Download Manager 180

CHAPTER 12

KEEP TRACK OF FAVORITE PLACES

Add a Favorite Place 184
Change Order of Favorite Places 186
Delete a Favorite Place 187
Add a Favorite Places Folder 188

CHAPTER 13

AOL FEATURES

Create a Screen Name 192
Change Your Password 196
Change Parental Controls 198
Switch Screen Names Without
   Signing Off 200
Using the Personal Filing Cabinet 202
Create a Stock Portfolio 204
Add Item to Stock Portfolio 206
Display and Print a Stock Portfolio 208
Create a News Profile 210
Manage News Profiles 214
Using the Reminder Service 216

CHAPTER 1

GETTING STARTED

What is America Online? In this chapter you will learn all about America Online, what it has to offer and how to explore its wide range of online services.

Introduction to AOL 4

What You Can Do With AOL 6

Connect to AOL 8

The AOL Screen 10

View the Online Clock 11

Maximize a Window 12

Minimize a Window 13

Move a Window 14

Size a Window 15

Scroll Through a Window 16

Switch Between Windows 17

Getting Help 18

INTRODUCTION TO AOL

America Online (AOL) is a graphical, easy-to-use online service that offers a wide range of information and features.

AOL is the largest online service, with over 10 million members. You can be informed, entertained and get to meet new people on AOL.

AOL and the Internet

AOL has many advantages over the Internet.

- AOL is easy to set up and use.

- AOL provides an enormous amount of well-organized information that is easy to find.

- AOL is an online community where you can attend live events with celebrities and chat with other members to discuss ideas and make new friends.

- AOL provides controls for parents worried about the information their children can access.

Screen Names

When you set up an account with AOL, you must specify your screen name. This is the name people will use to identify you. You can create up to five screen names to place different members of your family or company on one AOL account.

GETTING STARTED

WHAT YOU NEED

AOL Software

You need to install AOL's software to access AOL. You can get the AOL software and a free trial membership at major software retailers and bookstores or by calling 1-800-466-5463. In addition, new computers may come with the AOL software. If you have access to the Internet, you can download the software from the AOL Web site at www.aol.com

Modem

You need a modem to exchange information between your computer and AOL's computer system. A modem transmits information over telephone lines. A modem can be a circuit board inside your computer or a small box that plugs into the back of your computer. Most modems today have a speed of 28.8 Kbps or 33.6 Kbps. Faster modems transfer information more quickly to your computer.

Sound

You need a sound card and speakers to hear sound when using AOL. If your computer can play sound, you will hear sounds such as "Welcome" when you connect to AOL and "Goodbye" when you sign off.

WHAT YOU CAN DO WITH AOL

Find Information on AOL
AOL offers an enormous amount of information organized into channels such as computing, entertainment, games, health, news, personal finance, sports and travel.

Browse the Web
You can use AOL to browse through the vast amount of information available on the World Wide Web. The Web is part of the Internet and consists of a huge collection of documents stored on computers around the world.

Exchange Electronic Mail
You can exchange electronic mail (e-mail) with other AOL members and people on the Internet. E-mail provides a fast, economical and convenient way to send messages to family, friends and colleagues.

Message Boards and Newsgroups
You can use message boards to exchange information with other AOL members who share your interests. Each message board discusses information on a specific topic, such as animals, books, budgeting, games, hardware, health care issues, parenting and travel destinations. AOL also allows you to join newsgroups on the Internet so you can exchange information with people around the world.

6

GETTING STARTED

Chat With Other AOL Members
You can instantly exchange text messages with other members of AOL. Chatting is a great way to meet other AOL members, exchange ideas and ask questions.

Attend Live Events
AOL offers many live, interactive events where you can exchange comments and questions with special guests, including athletes, movie stars, musicians, politicians and writers.

Download Files
AOL offers thousands of files that you can transfer to and then use on your computer. You can get files such as documents, games, images, sounds and videos.

AOL Features
AOL offers many features that you may find useful.

- You can create a portfolio to track stocks and mutual funds of interest.

- You can use the free reminder service to ensure that you never forget an important occasion.

- You can create a news profile to search AOL's news sources for articles of interest. Articles that match your interests will be sent to your mailbox.

7

CONNECT TO AOL

You can connect to AOL at any time to access the information and features offered.

CONNECT TO AOL

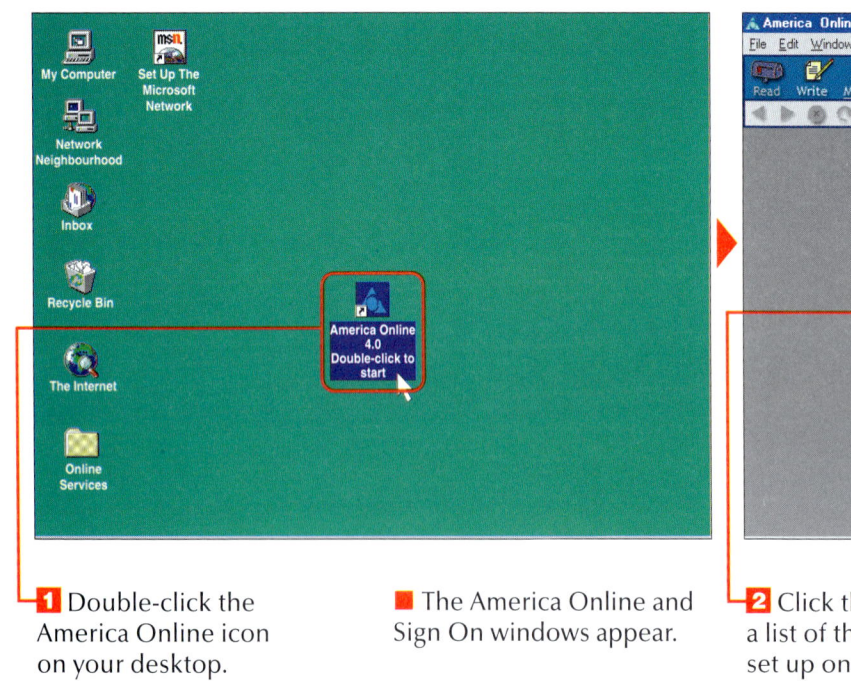

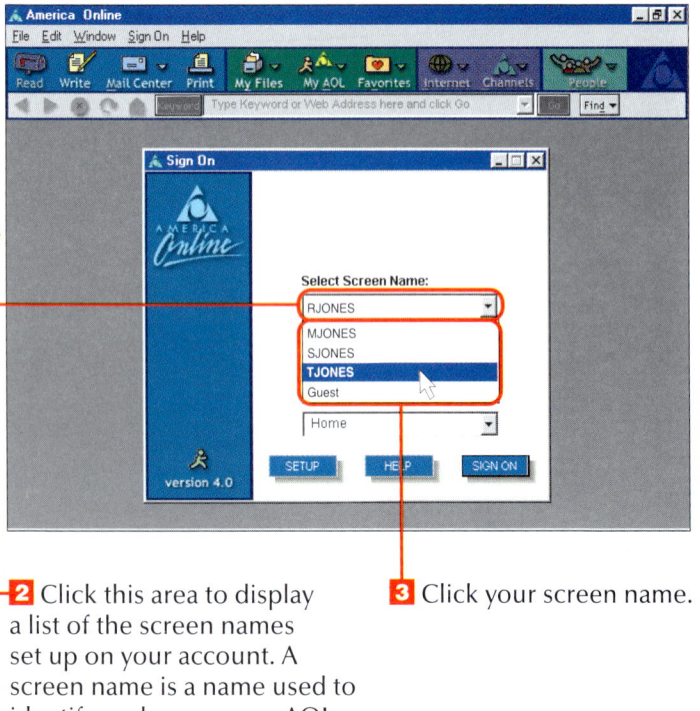

1 Double-click the America Online icon on your desktop.

■ The America Online and Sign On windows appear.

2 Click this area to display a list of the screen names set up on your account. A screen name is a name used to identify each person on AOL.

3 Click your screen name.

8

GETTING STARTED

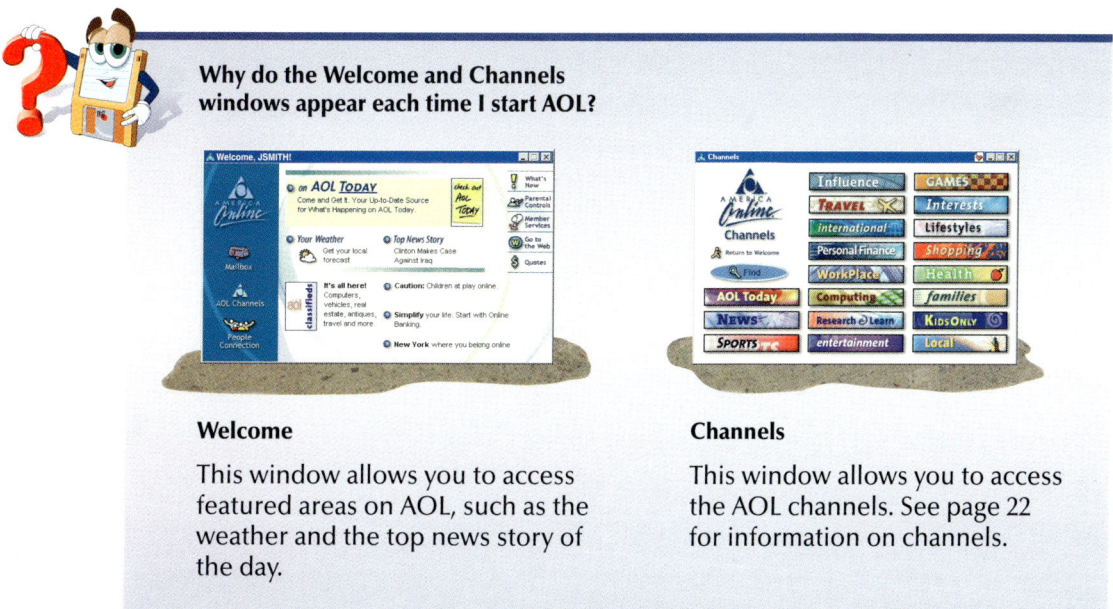

Why do the Welcome and Channels windows appear each time I start AOL?

Welcome

This window allows you to access featured areas on AOL, such as the weather and the top news story of the day.

Channels

This window allows you to access the AOL channels. See page 22 for information on channels.

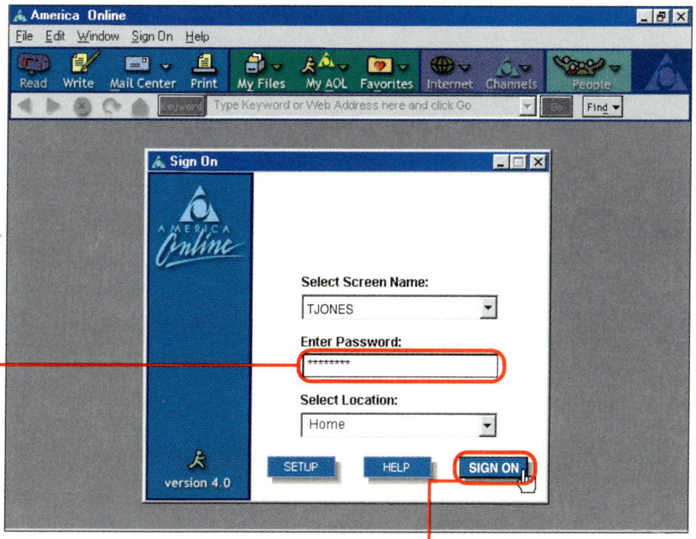

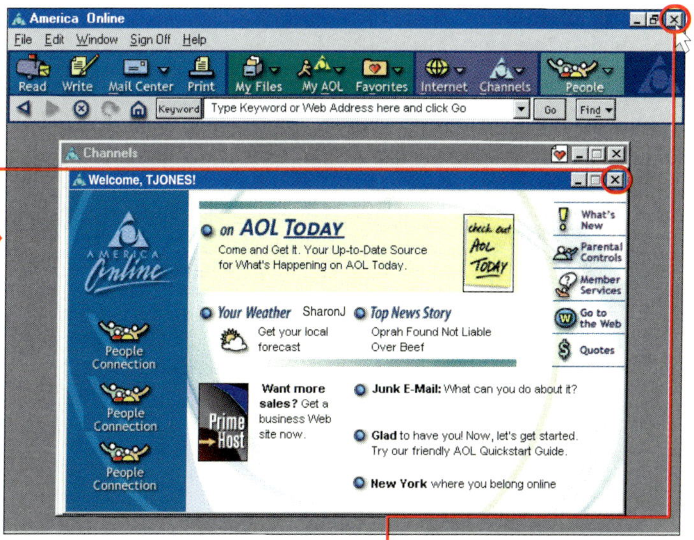

◢ **4** Click this area and type your password. An asterisk (*) appears for each character you type to prevent others from seeing your password.

5 Click **Sign On** to connect to AOL.

■ The Welcome and Channels windows appear. If your computer can play sound, you will hear "Welcome."

Note: Other windows may appear.

■ You can click ☒ to close a window to unclutter your screen.

EXIT AOL

1 Click ☒ to exit AOL.

■ If your computer can play sound, you will hear "Goodbye."

9

THE AOL SCREEN

The AOL screen displays many items to help you access information and use the features offered on AOL.

Menu Bar

Provides access to commonly used commands.

Toolbar

Contains buttons that provide access to commonly used commands and features. You can determine what a button does by positioning the mouse over the button.

Window

AOL displays information in windows.

MOUSE POINTER

The mouse pointer allows you to select and move items on your screen. When you move the mouse on your desk, the mouse pointer on your screen moves in the same direction.

The mouse pointer assumes different shapes, such as and , depending on its location on your screen and the task you are performing.

MOUSE TERMS

Click

Press and release the left mouse button.

Double-click

Quickly press and release the left mouse button twice.

Drag

When the mouse pointer is over an object on your screen, press and hold down the left mouse button. Still holding down the left button, move the mouse to where you want to place the object and then release the button.

VIEW THE ONLINE CLOCK

GETTING STARTED

You can view the current time and date, as well as an estimate of the amount of time you have spent online.

VIEW THE ONLINE CLOCK

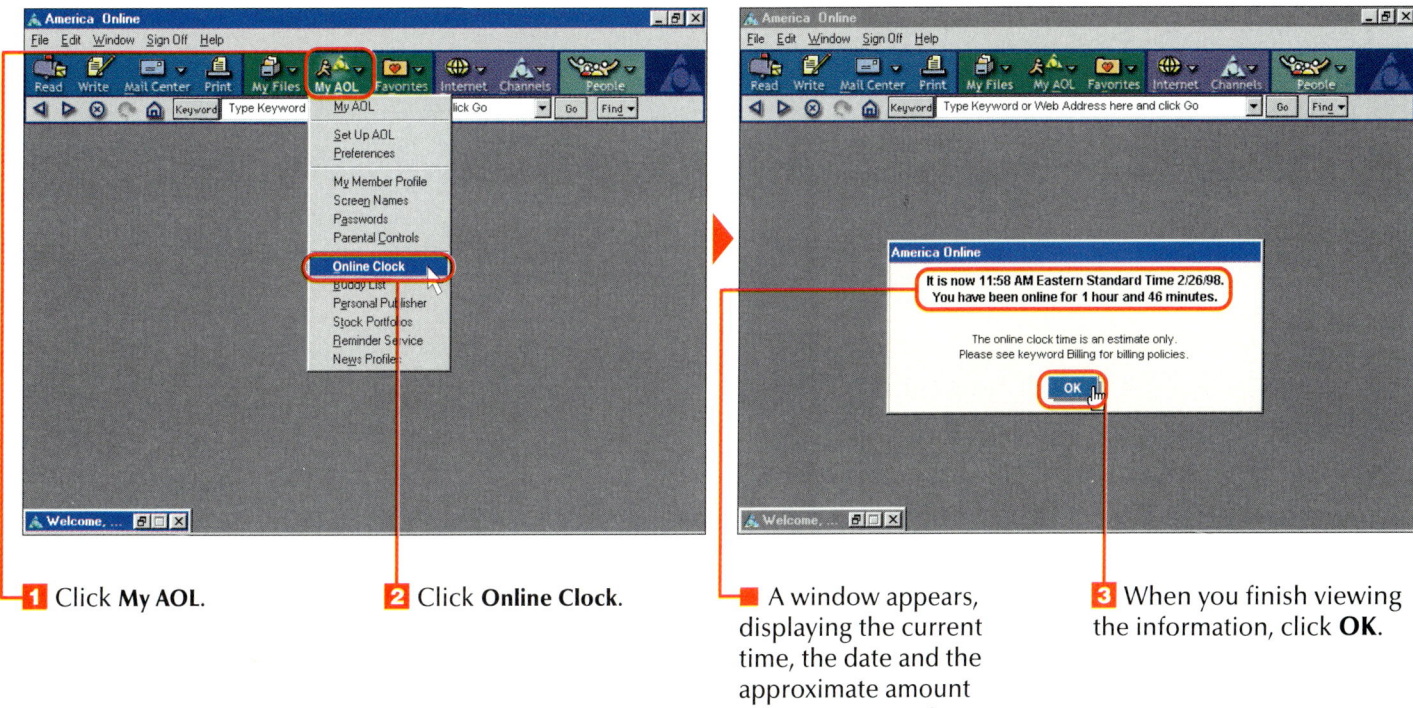

1 Click **My AOL**.

2 Click **Online Clock**.

■ A window appears, displaying the current time, the date and the approximate amount of time you have been online.

3 When you finish viewing the information, click **OK**.

MAXIMIZE A WINDOW

You can enlarge a window to fill your screen. This lets you view more of the window's contents.

MAXIMIZE A WINDOW

■ Click ◻ in the window you want to maximize.

Note: You cannot maximize some windows.

■ The window fills your screen.

■ To return the window to its previous size, click ◳.

MINIMIZE A WINDOW

GETTING STARTED

If you are not using a window, you can minimize the window to temporarily remove it from your screen. You can redisplay the window at any time.

MINIMIZE A WINDOW

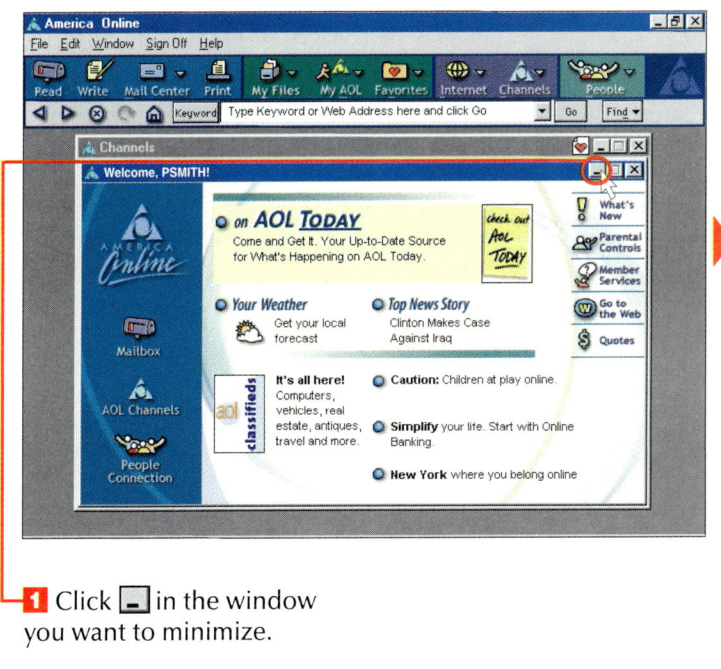

■ Click ▬ in the window you want to minimize.

■ The window appears as a bar at the bottom of your screen.

■ To redisplay the window, click 🗗.

13

MOVE A WINDOW

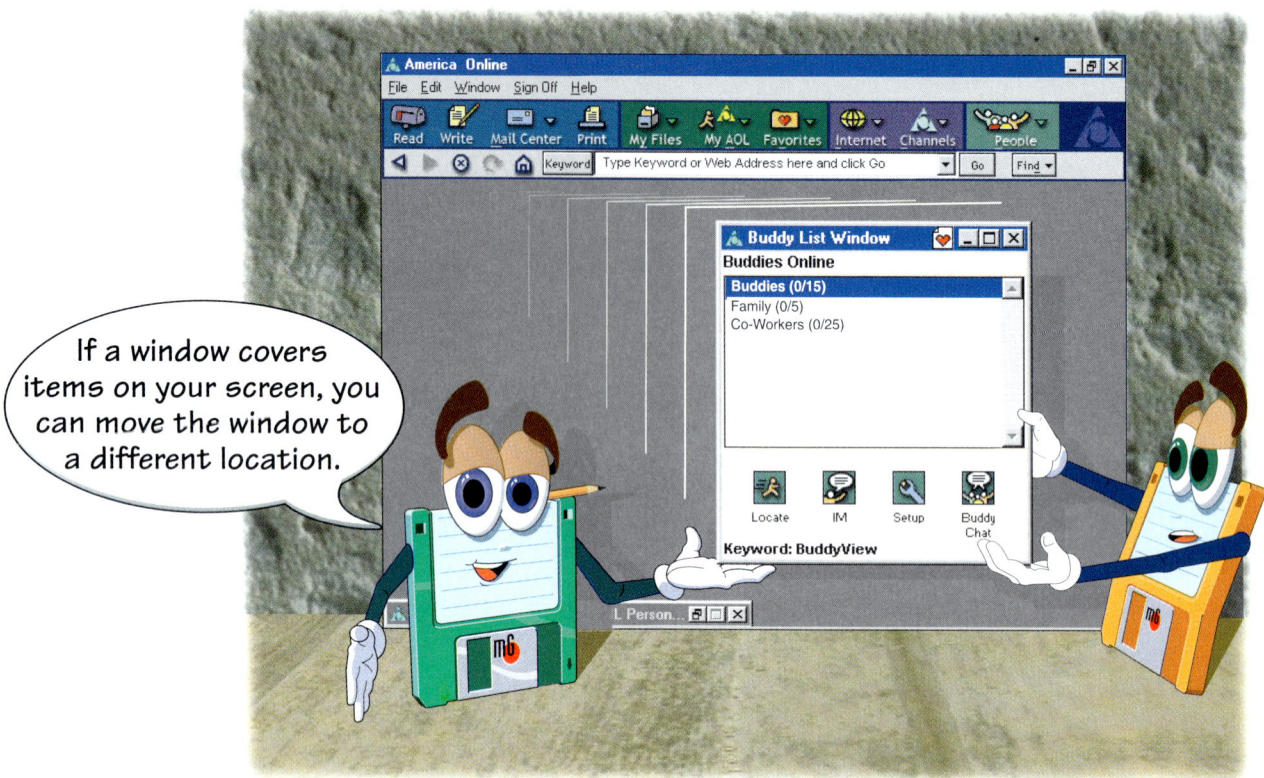

If a window covers items on your screen, you can move the window to a different location.

MOVE A WINDOW

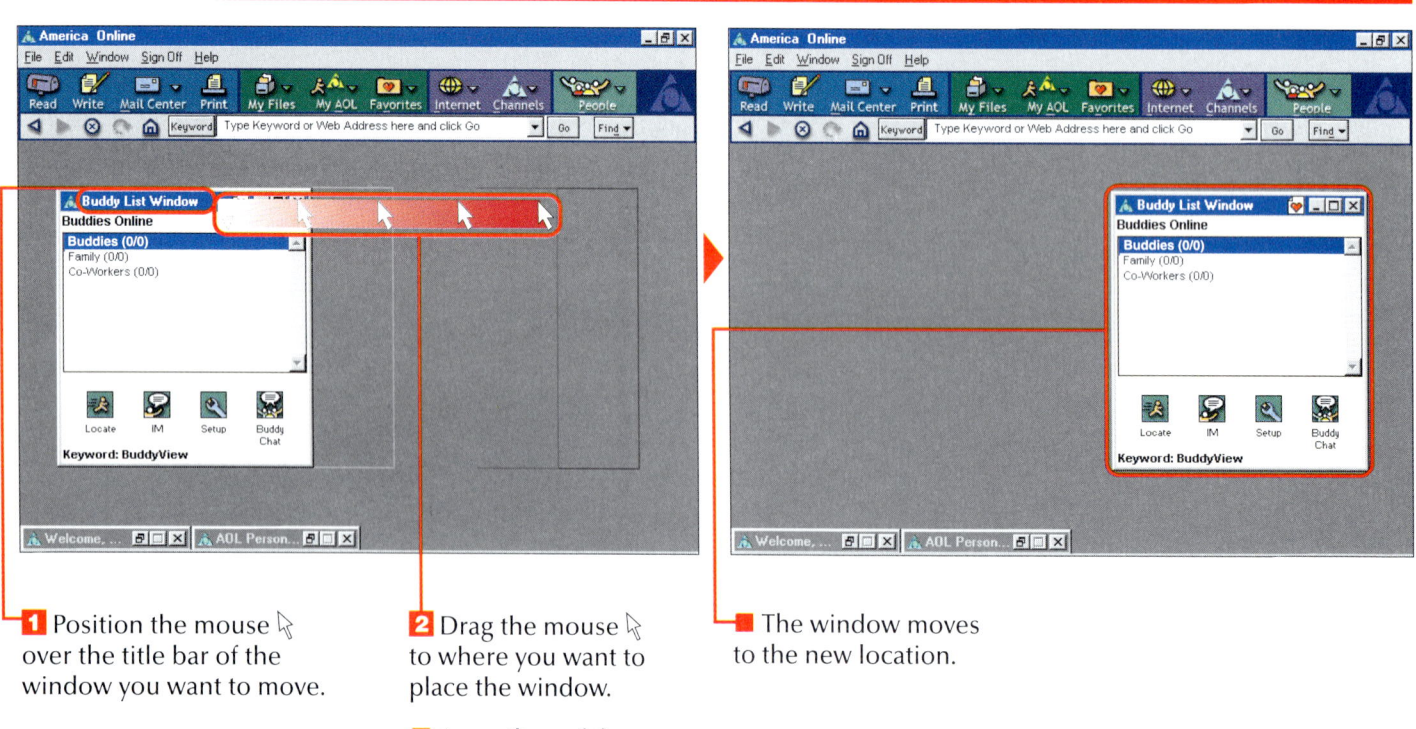

1 Position the mouse over the title bar of the window you want to move.

2 Drag the mouse to where you want to place the window.

■ An outline of the window indicates the new location.

■ The window moves to the new location.

14

SIZE A WINDOW

GETTING STARTED

You can change the size of a window displayed on your screen.

Enlarging a window lets you view more of its contents. Reducing a window lets you view items covered by the window.

SIZE A WINDOW

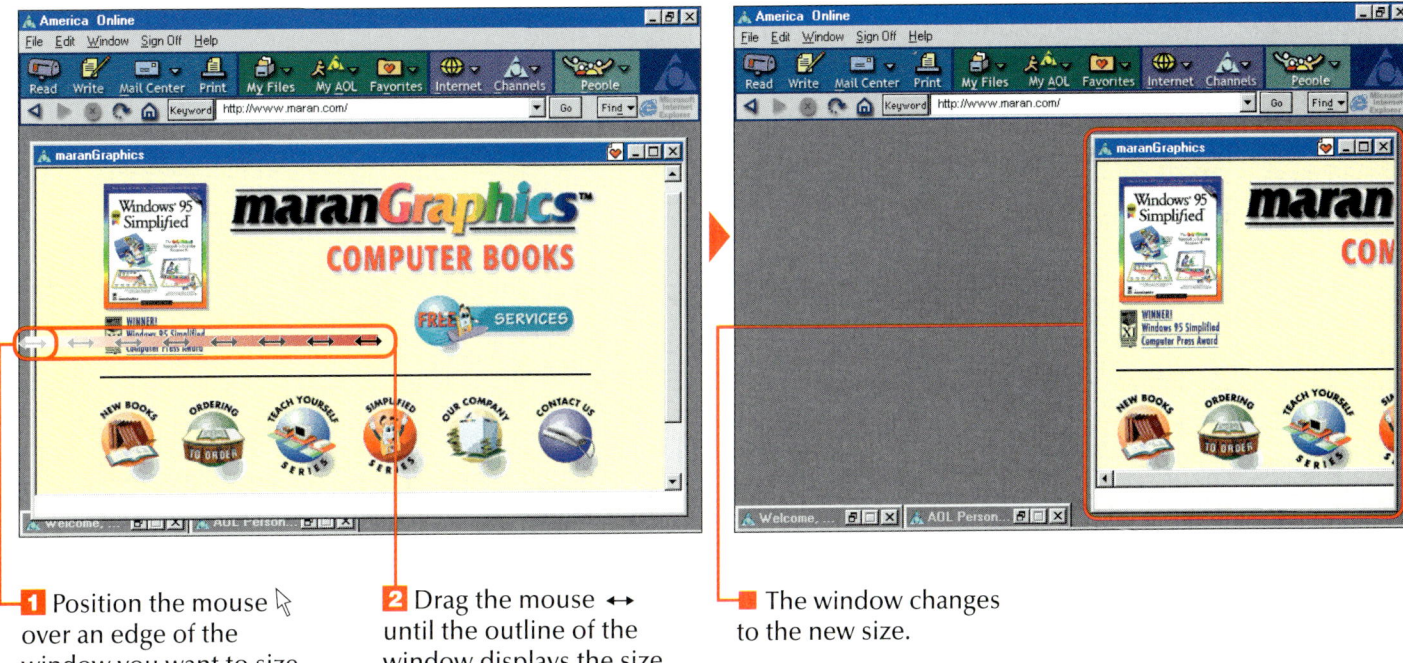

1 Position the mouse over an edge of the window you want to size (changes to ↔, ↕ or ↘).

Note: You cannot change the size of some windows.

2 Drag the mouse ↔ until the outline of the window displays the size you want.

■ The window changes to the new size.

15

SCROLL THROUGH A WINDOW

A scroll bar lets you browse through information in a window. This is useful when you cannot see all the information in a window.

SCROLL THROUGH A WINDOW

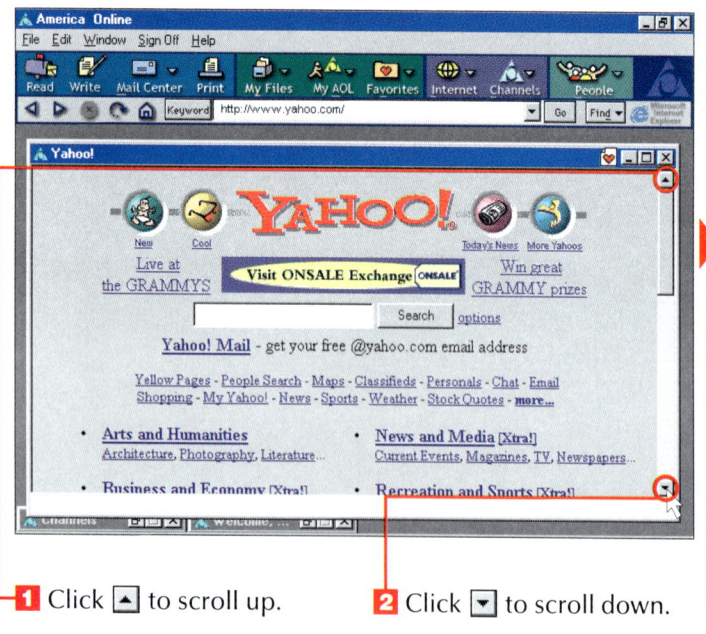

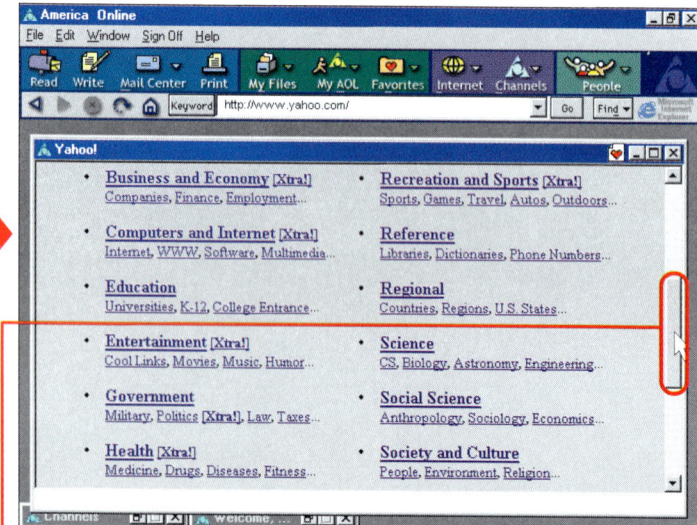

1 Click ▲ to scroll up.

2 Click ▼ to scroll down.

3 To scroll to a specific location in a window, drag the scroll box up or down the scroll bar.

■ The location of the scroll box indicates which part of the window you are viewing. To view the middle of the window, drag the scroll box halfway down the scroll bar.

16

SWITCH BETWEEN WINDOWS

GETTING STARTED 1

You can have more than one window open at a time. You can easily switch from one open window to another.

SWITCH BETWEEN WINDOWS

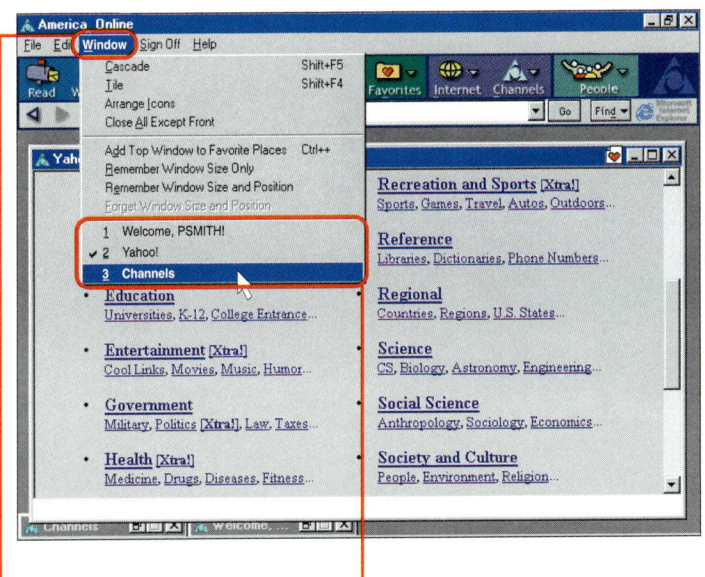

■ **1** To display a list of all open windows, click **Window**.

■ **2** Click the window you want to display.

■ A check mark (✔) indicates which window currently appears in front of all other open windows.

■ The window you selected appears in front of all other open windows.

■ To close a window to remove it from your screen, click ⊠.

■ You can also click any part of an open window to place it in front of all other open windows.

17

GETTING HELP

GETTING HELP

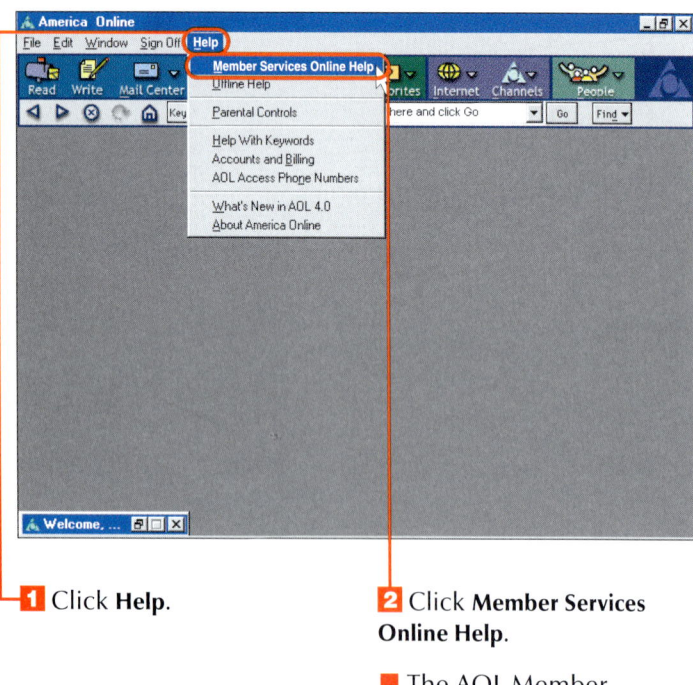

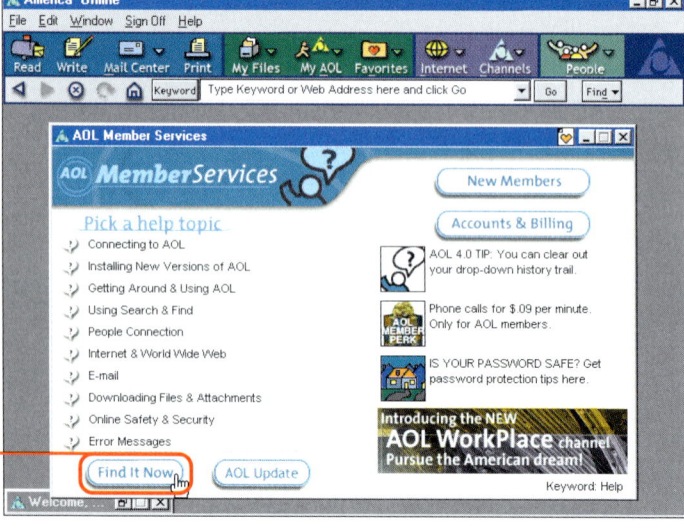

1 Click **Help**.

2 Click **Member Services Online Help**.

■ The AOL Member Services window appears.

3 Click **Find It Now** to search for a help topic of interest.

■ The Search window appears.

GETTING STARTED

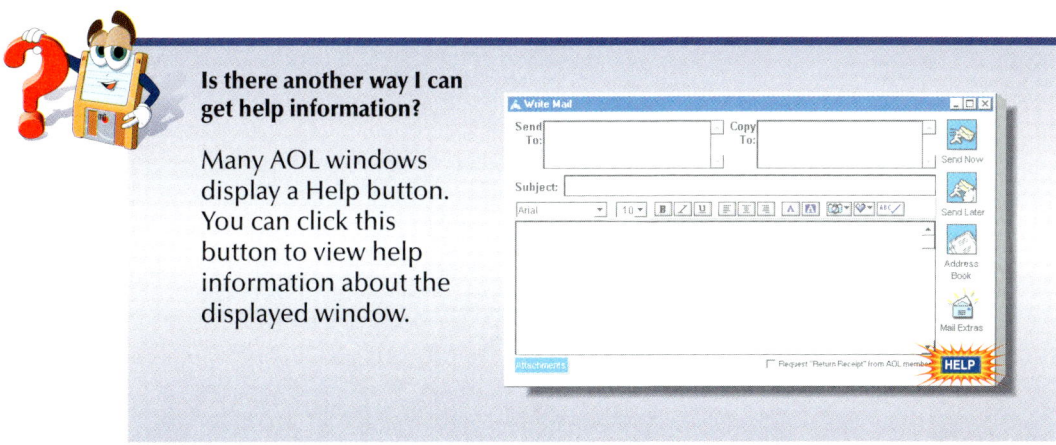

Is there another way I can get help information?

Many AOL windows display a Help button. You can click this button to view help information about the displayed window.

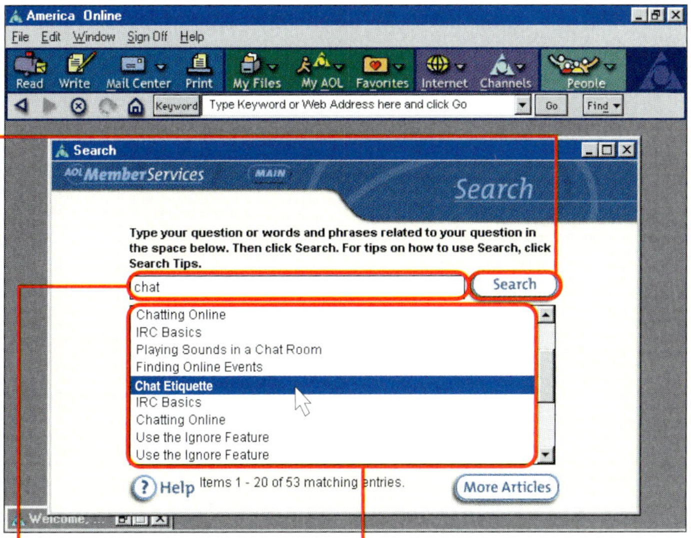

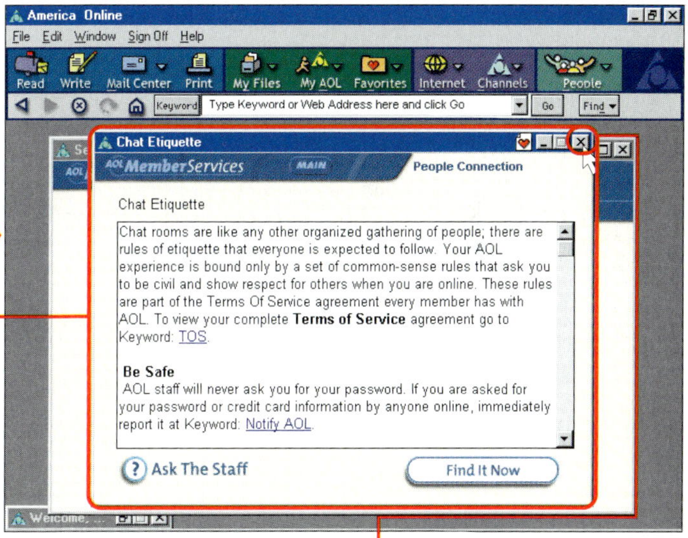

■ **4** Type a word or phrase that describes the information you want help on.

■ **5** Click **Search** to start the search.

■ This area lists the topics related to the text you typed.

■ **6** Double-click a topic of interest.

■ A window appears, describing the topic you selected.

■ **7** When you finish viewing the information, click ☒ to close the window.

19

CHAPTER 2

FIND INFORMATION ON AOL

Wondering how to sift through the vast amount of information offered by America Online? In this chapter, you will learn about the different channels and how to use keywords to find topics that interest you.

View the AOL Channels 22

The AOL Channels 24

Using the Channel Guide 30

Using Keywords 32

Keyword Examples 34

Find Information on AOL 38

VIEW THE AOL CHANNELS

AOL constantly changes the information offered on each channel. Make sure you revisit channels to view the latest information on topics of interest.

VIEW THE AOL CHANNELS

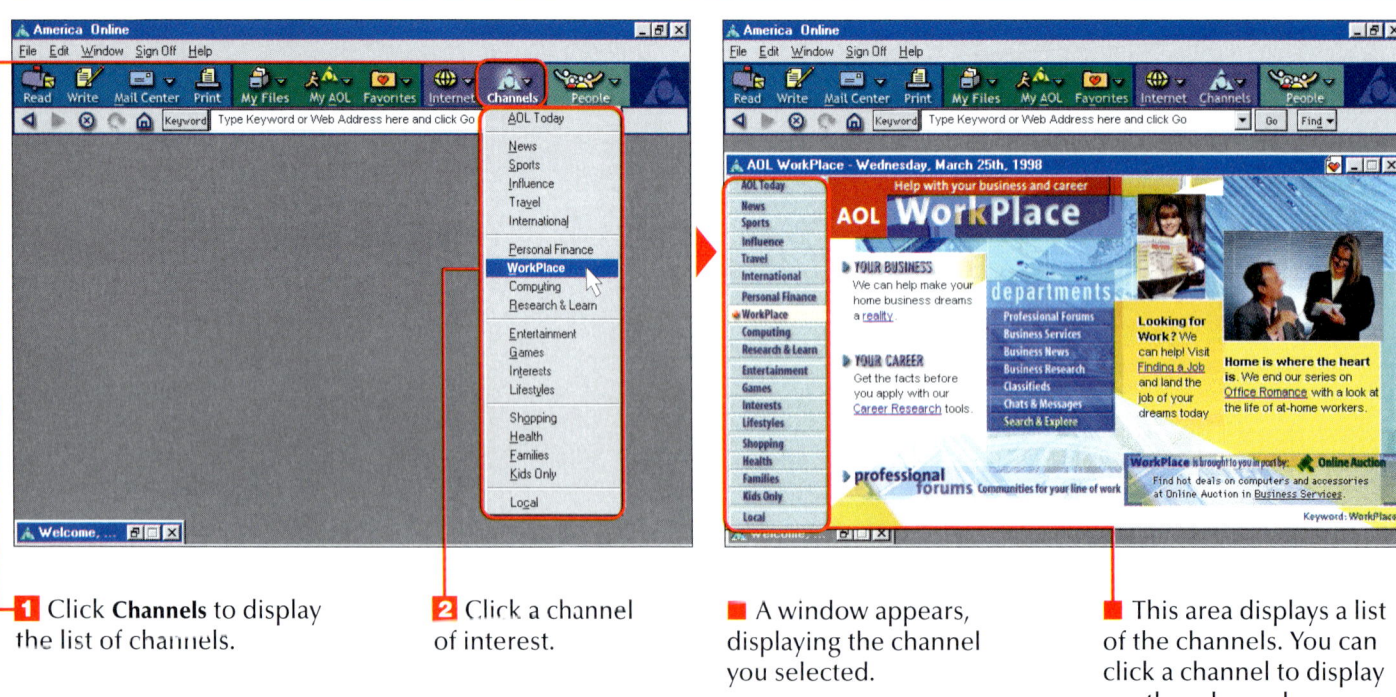

■ Click **Channels** to display the list of channels.

■ Click a channel of interest.

■ A window appears, displaying the channel you selected.

■ This area displays a list of the channels. You can click a channel to display another channel.

22

FIND INFORMATION ON AOL

Why do the graphics take a while to appear?

When viewing information on channels, text transfers quickly to your computer so you can start reading the text right away. Graphics transfer more slowly. You may have to wait a moment to clearly view the graphics.

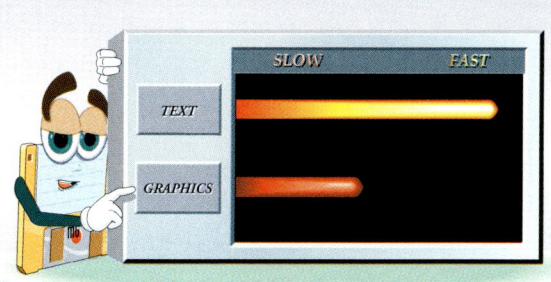

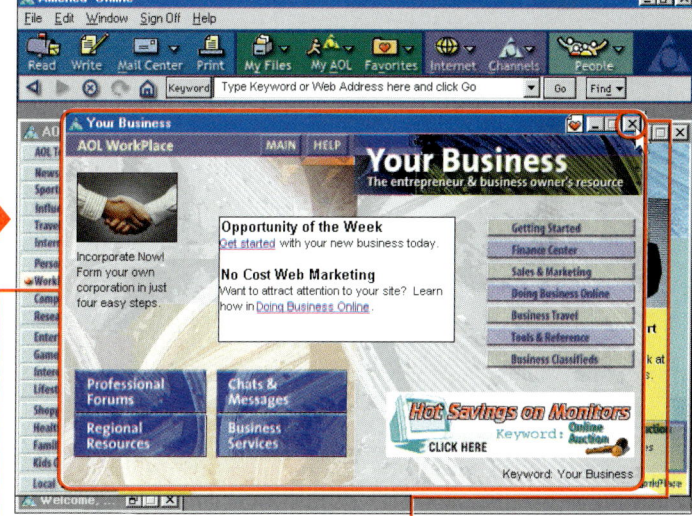

■ The channel offers information on various topics that may be of interest to you.

4 When you position the mouse over a topic, the mouse changes to a hand. Click the topic to view information on the topic.

■ A window appears, displaying information on the topic you selected.

■ You can continue to click topics of interest to browse through the information offered on the channel.

4 When you finish viewing the information in a window, click ☒ to close the window.

23

THE AOL CHANNELS

AOL Today

This channel focuses on today's best information on AOL. You can get the top news stories, as well as other featured information on AOL.

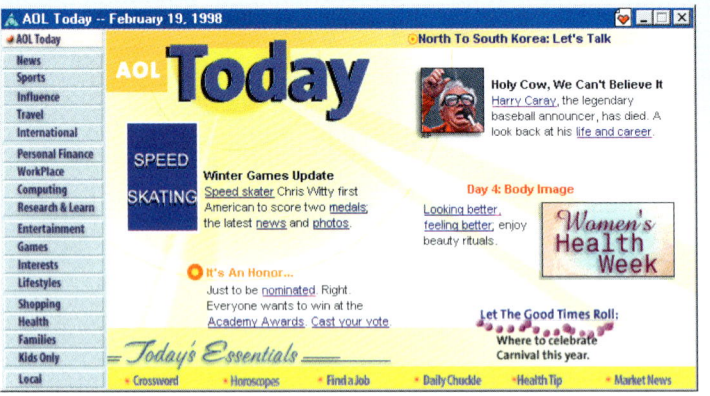

News

This channel provides the latest headlines on various topics, such as U.S. and world news, business, sports and weather.

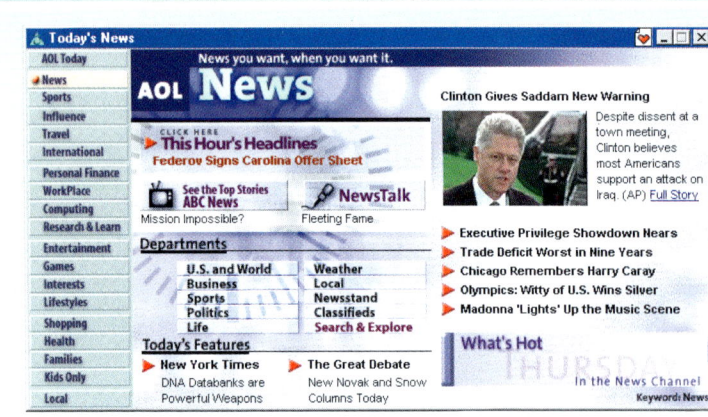

Sports

This channel offers sports fans in-depth information on various sports such as baseball, basketball, football, golf, hockey and tennis.

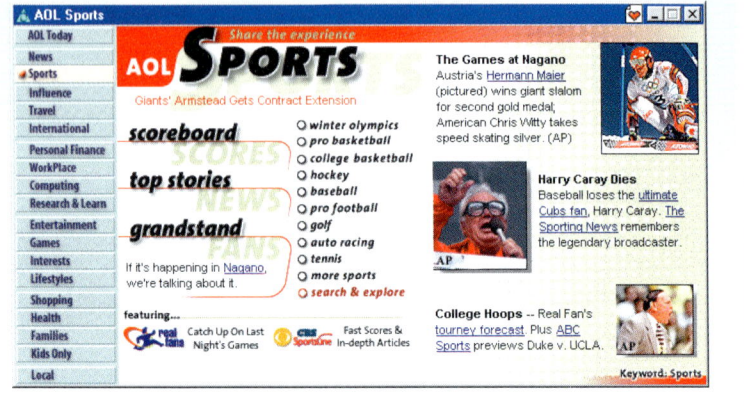

24

FIND INFORMATION ON AOL

Influence

This channel explores current issues, book and movie reviews, fashion, the latest gossip and more.

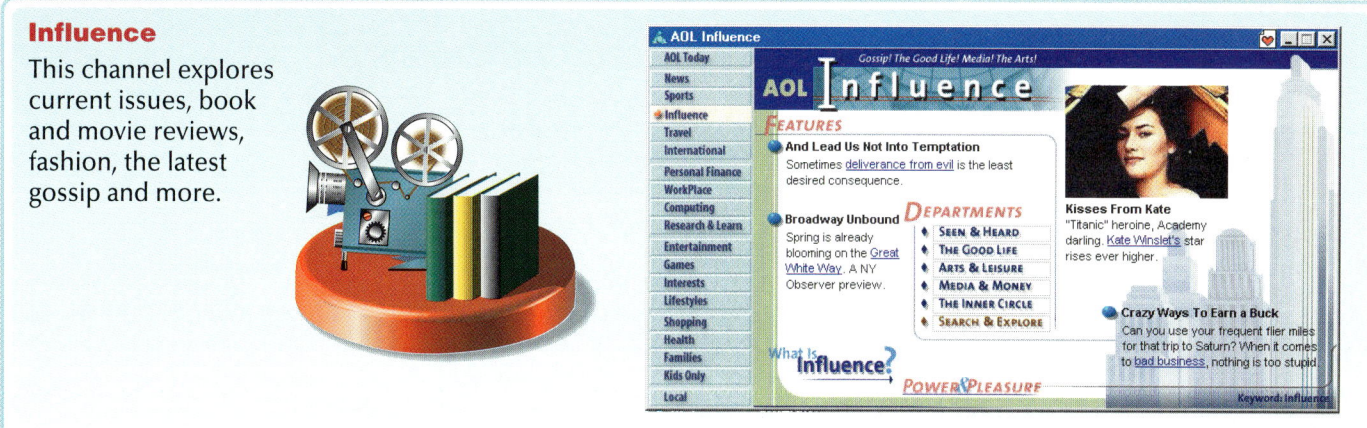

Travel

This channel offers information on travel, such as bargain airfares, destinations and an online reservation center.

International

This channel gives you access to the current news, business and cultural information on places around the world.

25

THE AOL CHANNELS

Personal Finance
This channel provides information on topics such as stocks, business news, investment research, tax planning and online banking.

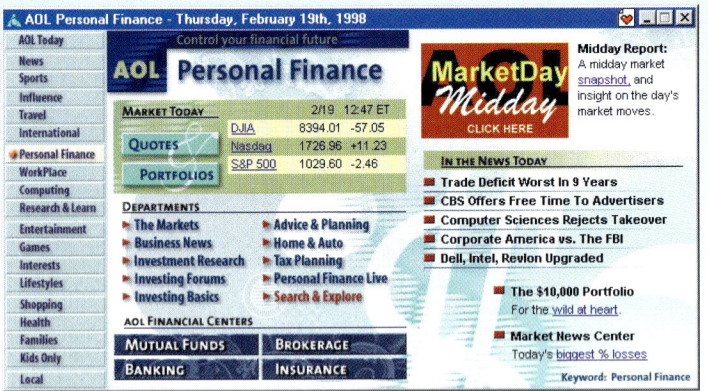

WorkPlace
This channel offers many resources to help your business and career. You will find business news, classifieds and discussions about various professions.

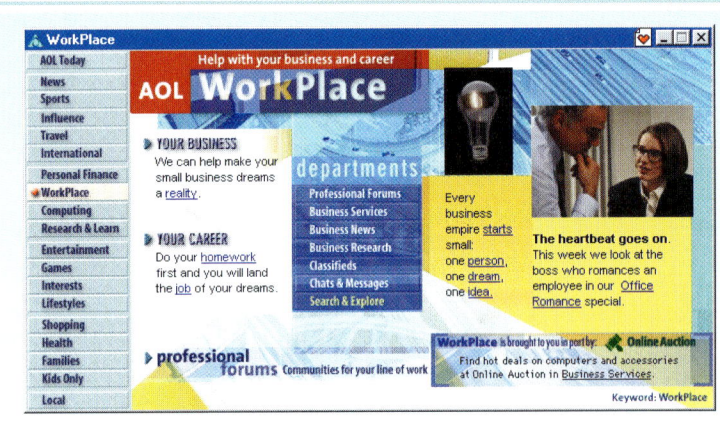

Computing
This channel is a good resource for those who want to learn more about computers. You can download software, research companies, read hardware and software reviews, join an online classroom and review popular computer magazines.

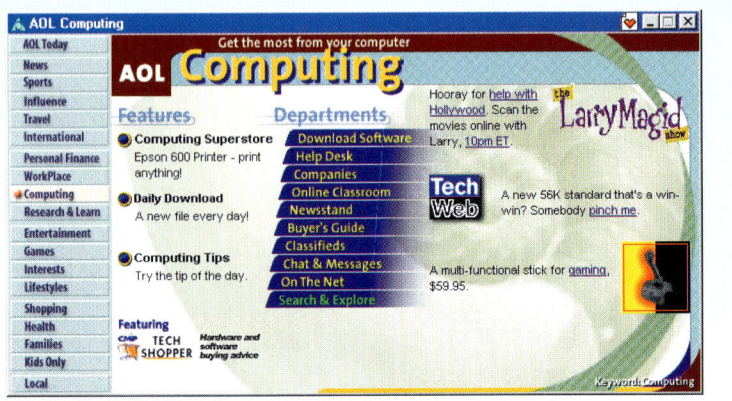

FIND INFORMATION ON AOL

Research & Learn

This channel is a great resource center for students and those looking to expand their knowledge. Find information on history, science, health and geography, as well as a reference section with online encyclopedias.

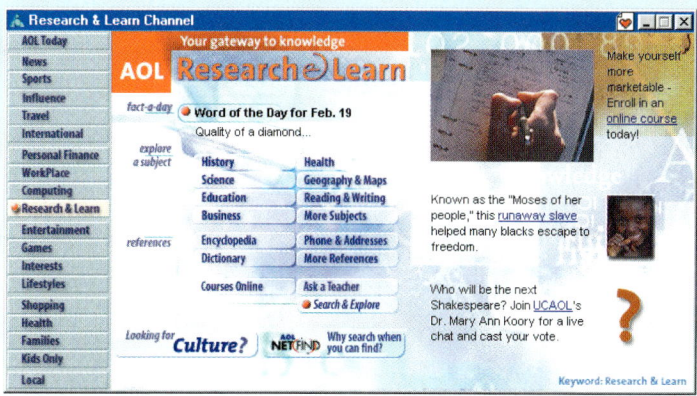

Entertainment

This channel offers information on television shows, movies, books and music.

Games

This channel provides access to many of the popular computer and video games available today. You can read reviews of new games, play games, find tips on how to improve your gaming skills and more.

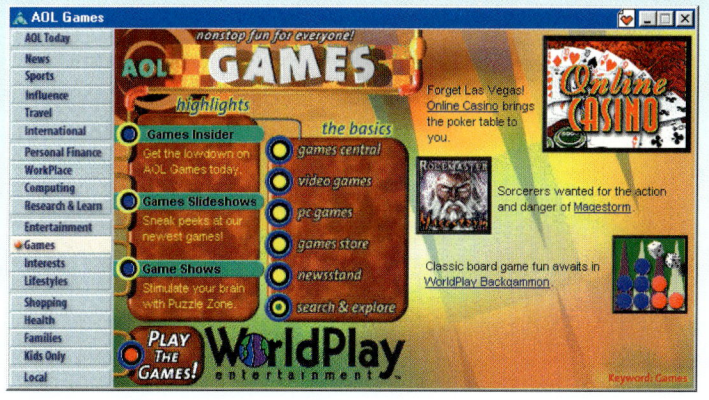

27

THE AOL CHANNELS

Interests

This channel explores a wide variety of interests and hobbies, such as pets, home improvement, photography, food, cars and more.

Lifestyles

This channel explores topics such as self improvement, women's issues, ethnicity and romance.

Shopping

This channel offers information and savings on a wide variety of products and services. You can browse through the various departments such as jewelry, electronics, flowers, home office, sports and toys.

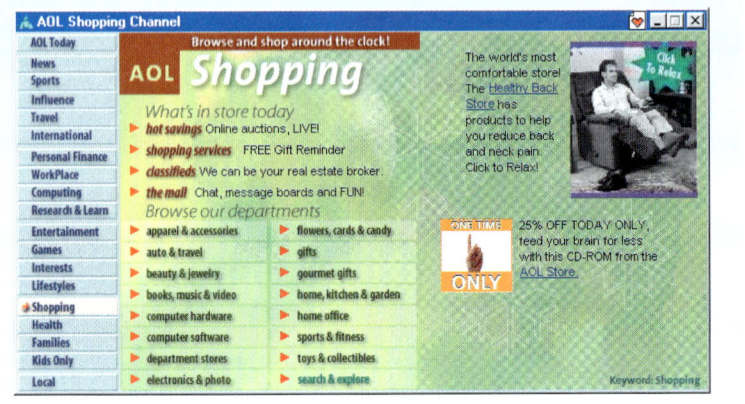

FIND INFORMATION ON AOL

Health
This channel offers information on illnesses and treatments, support groups, healthy living, a medical reference section and more.

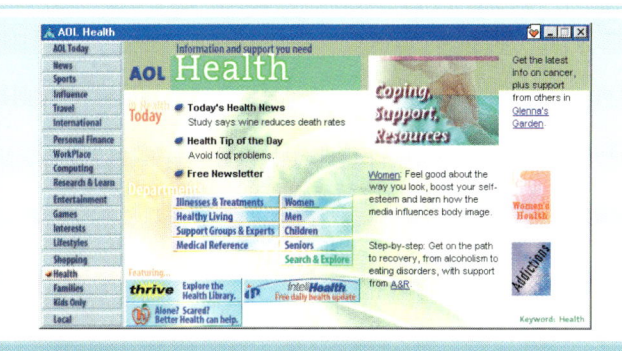

Families
This channel provides information and advice on parenting children of all ages, family activities, time-saving tips, ideas for improving your home and much more.

Kids Only
This channel is geared towards children's interests and hobbies. Children can find information on sports, games, television shows and even get help with their homework.

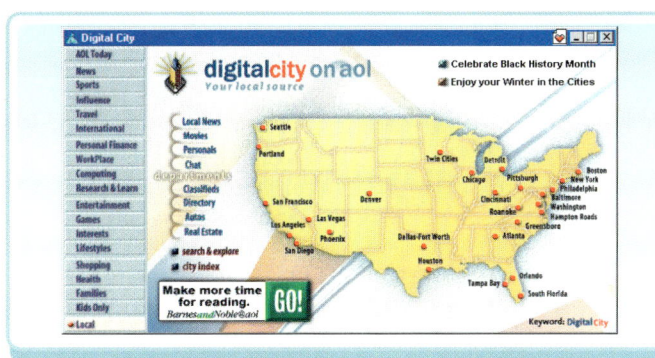

Local
This channel offers local information for many cities, including local news, movie listings, restaurants, classifieds and real estate.

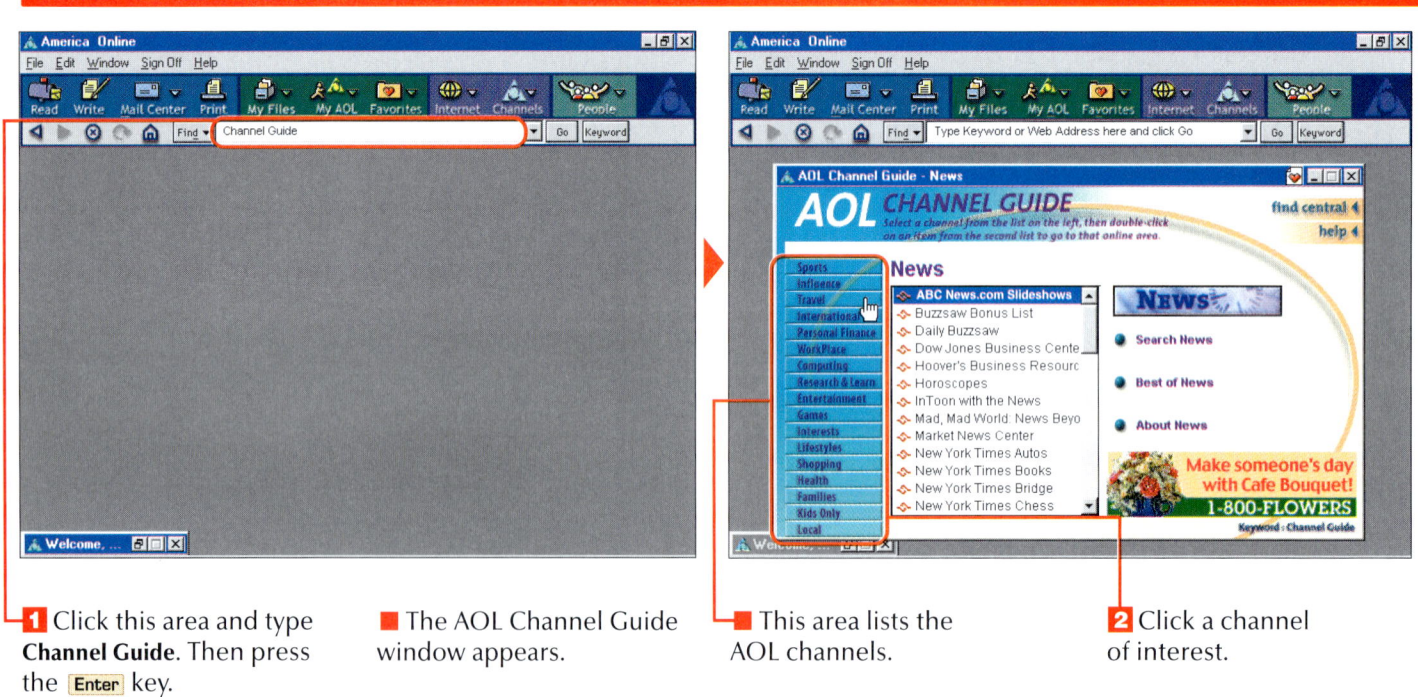

USING THE CHANNEL GUIDE

> You can use the Channel Guide to see a list of areas offered on each channel. You can then instantly go to the area of interest.

USING THE CHANNEL GUIDE

1 Click this area and type **Channel Guide**. Then press the Enter key.

■ The AOL Channel Guide window appears.

■ This area lists the AOL channels.

2 Click a channel of interest.

30

FIND INFORMATION ON AOL

What are some areas the Channel Guide can take me to?

The News Channel

Market News Center

New York Times Front Page

Sports

Today's Weather

US and World News

The Entertainment Channel

Celebrities

Movie Main Screen

MTV Online

Soap Opera Digest

Television Main Screen

The Interests Channel

Auto Center

Civil War

Home & Garden

Pets

Photography Forum

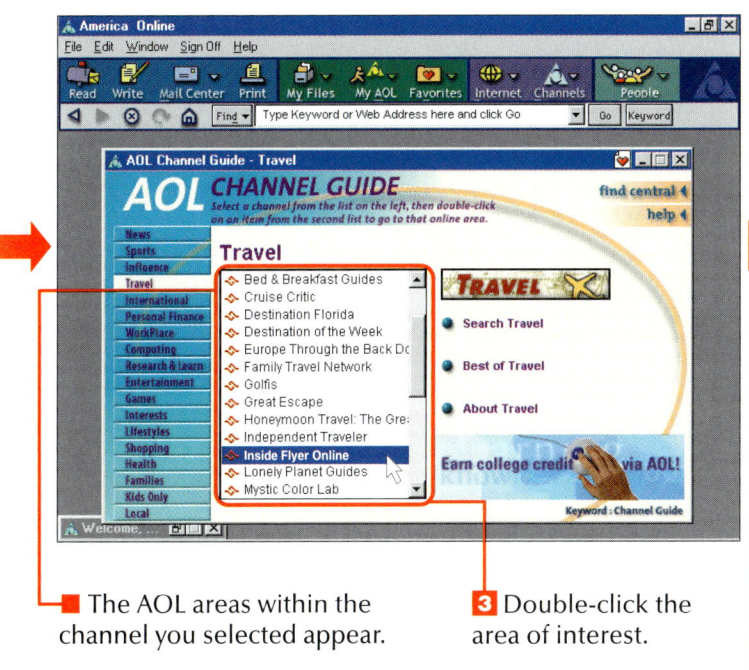

■ The AOL areas within the channel you selected appear.

3 Double-click the area of interest.

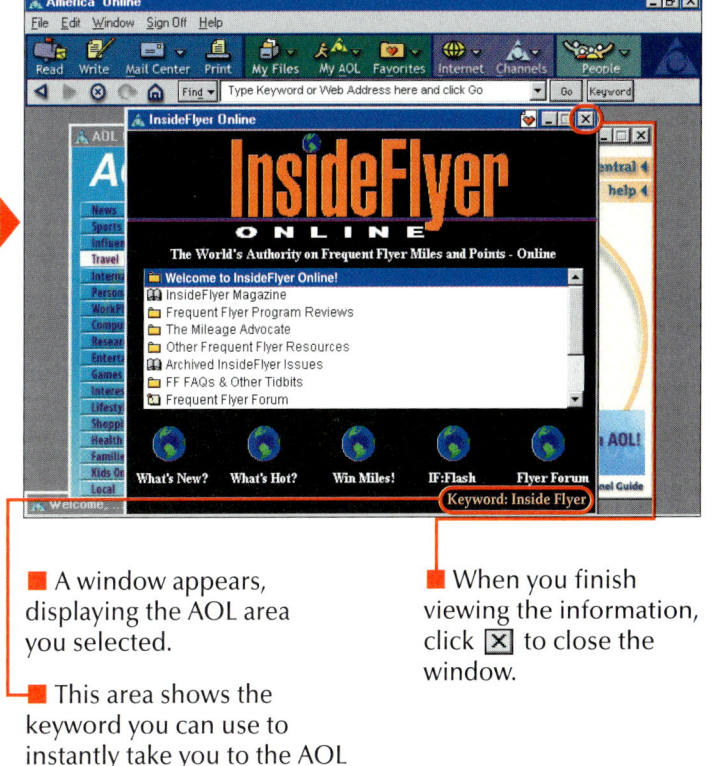

■ A window appears, displaying the AOL area you selected.

■ This area shows the keyword you can use to instantly take you to the AOL area at any time. See page 32 for information on keywords.

■ When you finish viewing the information, click ⊠ to close the window.

31

USING KEYWORDS

You can type a keyword that will instantly take you to an area on AOL. A keyword exists for almost every AOL area.

USING KEYWORDS

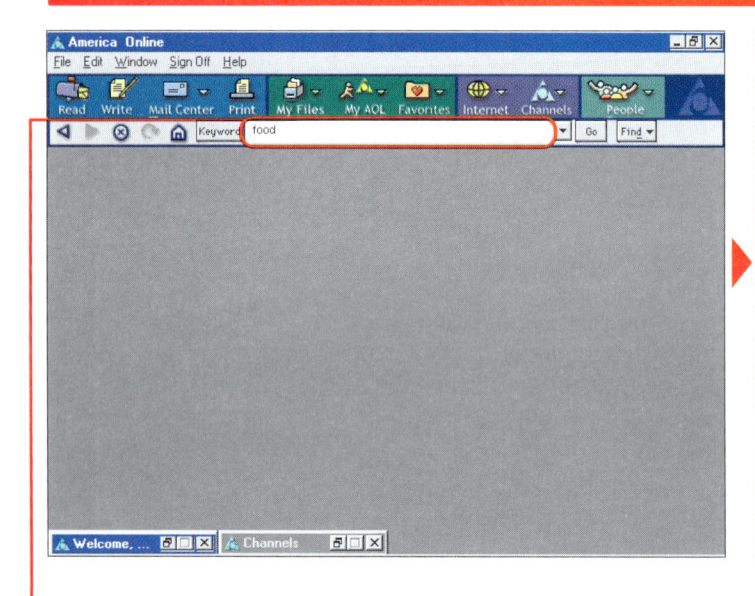

1 Click this area and then type the keyword for the AOL area you want to visit.

2 Press the Enter key.

■ The AOL area appears.

FIND INFORMATION ON AOL

When I find an area of interest on AOL, how can I find out its keyword?

If an area on AOL has a keyword, the keyword will usually be shown at the bottom of the window. While browsing through AOL, you may want to write down keywords for places you want to visit again.

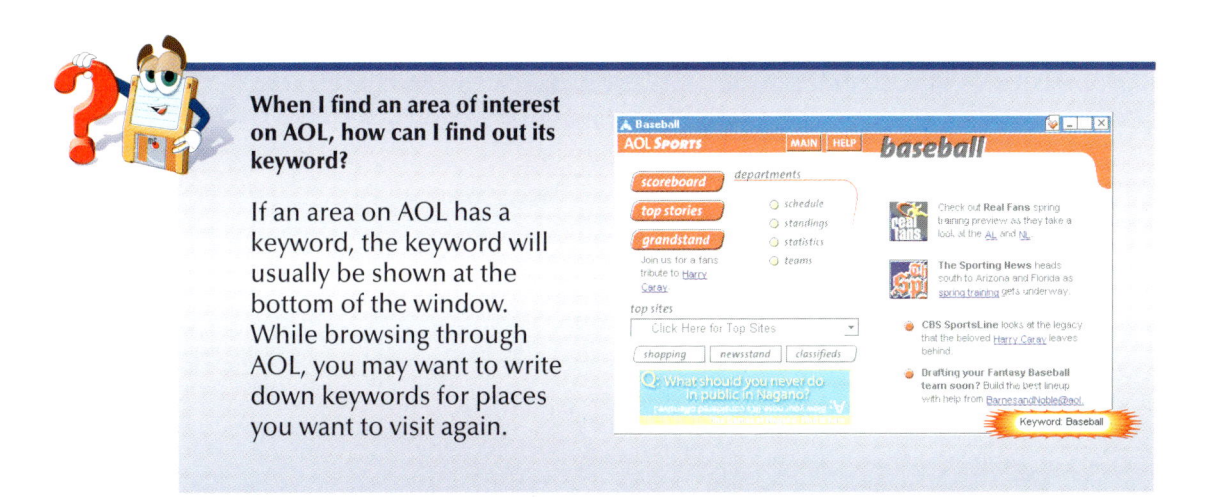

DISPLAY LIST OF KEYWORDS

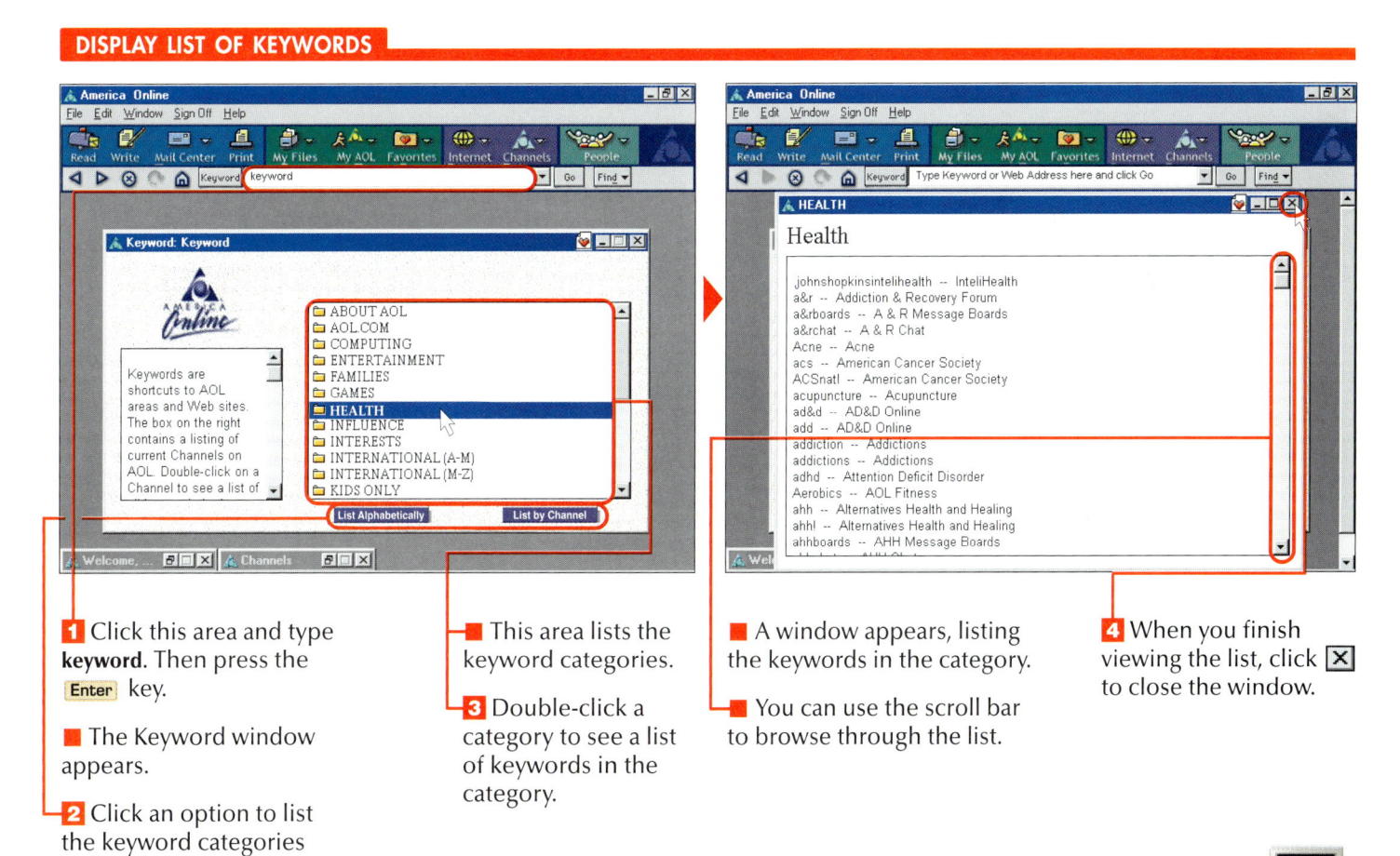

■ Click this area and type **keyword**. Then press the **Enter** key.

■ The Keyword window appears.

■ Click an option to list the keyword categories alphabetically or by channel.

■ This area lists the keyword categories.

■ Double-click a category to see a list of keywords in the category.

■ A window appears, listing the keywords in the category.

■ You can use the scroll bar to browse through the list.

■ When you finish viewing the list, click ✕ to close the window.

33

KEYWORD EXAMPLES

Here are some keywords you may want to try.

AOL

AOL Insider	New
AOL Sound	Perks
Billing	Preview
Events	Upgrade
Members' Choice	
Neighborhood Watch	

COMPUTING

AppleComputer	Help Desk
Buyer's Guide	IBM
Computing Newsstand	On the Net
Computing Tips	Online Classroom
Dell	
Download Software	

ENTERTAINMENT

Court TV	Rolling Stone
Daily Fix	SciFi Channel
Hollywood	TV
Magazine Outlet	VH1
Playbill	
Premiere	

FAMILIES

Babies	Moms Online
Family Life	Parenting
Family Ties	Roots
Family Timesavers	Teens
Family Travel Network	
Kids and Teens	

FIND INFORMATION ON AOL

GAMES

- Classic Cards
- Countdown
- Game Shows
- Games Celeb
- Games Insider
- NTN Hockey
- Online Casino
- PC Games
- Puzzle Zone
- WorldPlay Backgammon

HEALTH

- Allergies
- Alternative Medicine
- Healthy Living
- Illness
- Medical Experts
- Men's Health
- Mental Health
- Stress Management
- Wellness
- Women's Health

INFLUENCE

- Arts and Leisure
- BarnesandNoble
- CigarCafe
- CultureFinder
- ELLE
- George
- Media & Money
- NYObserver
- Smithsonian
- Worth

INTERESTS

- Auto Center
- Collecting
- Cooking Club
- Crafts Magazine
- Cycle World
- Food
- HomeMag
- HouseNet
- Pets
- Pop Photo

INTERNATIONAL

- Africa
- Asia
- Europe
- Global Meeting Place
- Intl Business
- Intl Cultures
- Middle East
- North America
- Oceania
- South America

KIDS ONLY

- Cartoon
- Kidzine
- KO Clubs
- KO News
- KO Speak
- KO Sports
- Techie Pals
- ToyBuzz
- Trivia Live
- VirtualFun

KEYWORD EXAMPLES

These keywords will instantly take you to an area on AOL.

LIFESTYLES

Ages&Stages	Religion
College Online	Romance
Communities	Self Improvement
Ethnicity	SeniorNet
Hub	
Online Psych	

LOCAL

DC Personals	Local Real Estate
Local Autos	Local Traffic
Local Chat	
Local Classifieds	
Local Movies	
Local News	

NEWS

Business News	Politics
Daily Chuckle	TechNews
Great Debate	USWorld
Industrial News	Weather
LifeNews	
Lottery	

PERSONAL FINANCE

Advice & Planning	Online Investor
Insurance	Stock Reports
Investing Basics	Tax
MoneyWhiz	
Mutual Funds	
NYSE	

2
FIND INFORMATION ON AOL

THINGS TO DO

after I have tea

SHOPPING

Avon	Fragrance Counter
Books & Music Shop	Gourmet Gifts
Cybershop	Office Shop
Department Stores	Shop Fitness
FAO Schwarz	
Flowers	

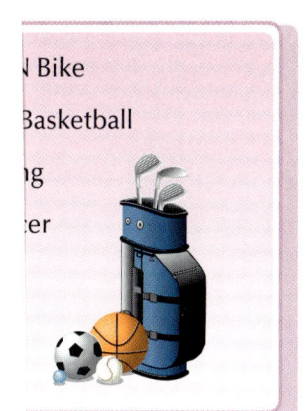

ine Campus
neBook
ding
nce

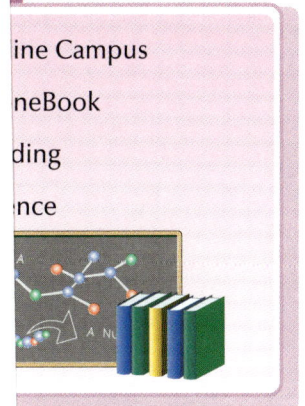

TRAVEL

Airline	Preview Travel
B&B	Travel Reservations
Bargain Box	Travel Store
Cruise Critic	
Destinations	
Hotel	
Last Minute	

Bike
Basketball
ng
er

Finance Center
Find a Job

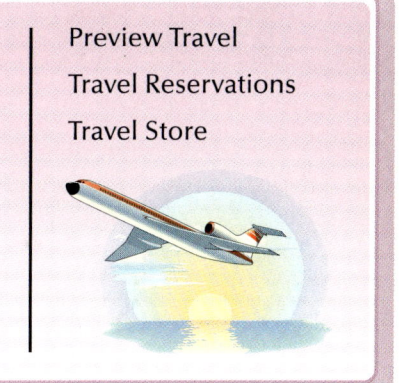

ne Business
& Marketing
Up
Business

37

FIND INFORMATION ON AOL

> You can search AOL to find information on a topic of interest to you.

FIND INFORMATION ON AOL

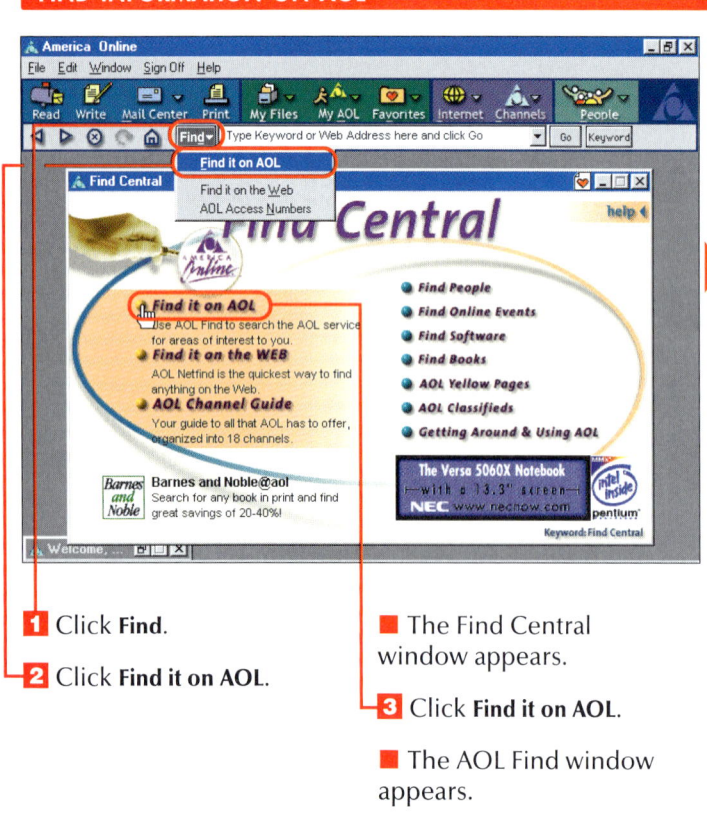

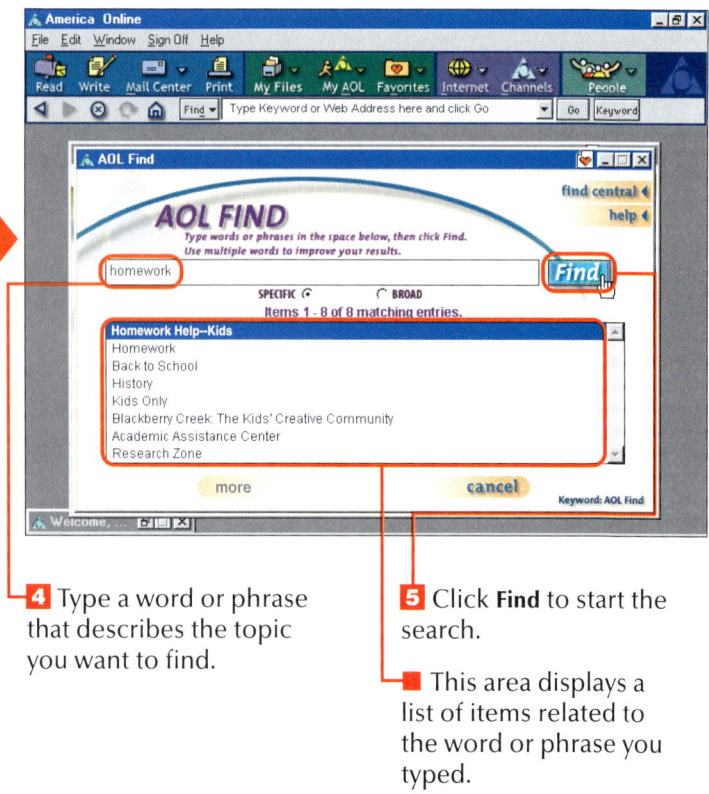

1 Click **Find**.

2 Click **Find it on AOL**.

■ The Find Central window appears.

3 Click **Find it on AOL**.

■ The AOL Find window appears.

4 Type a word or phrase that describes the topic you want to find.

5 Click **Find** to start the search.

■ This area displays a list of items related to the word or phrase you typed.

FIND INFORMATION ON AOL

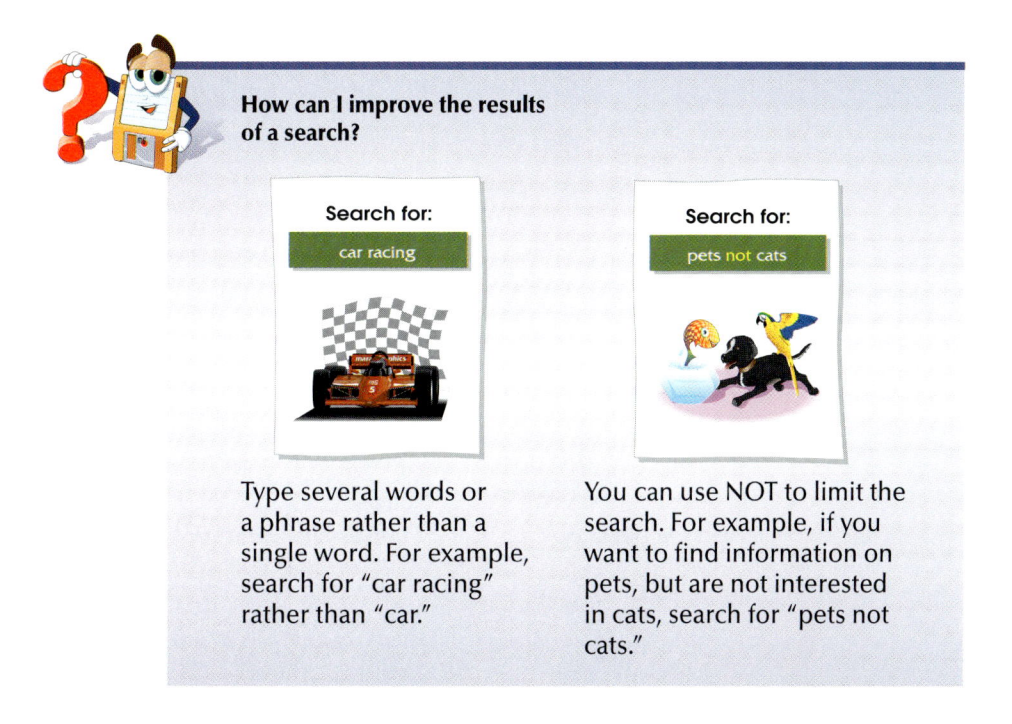

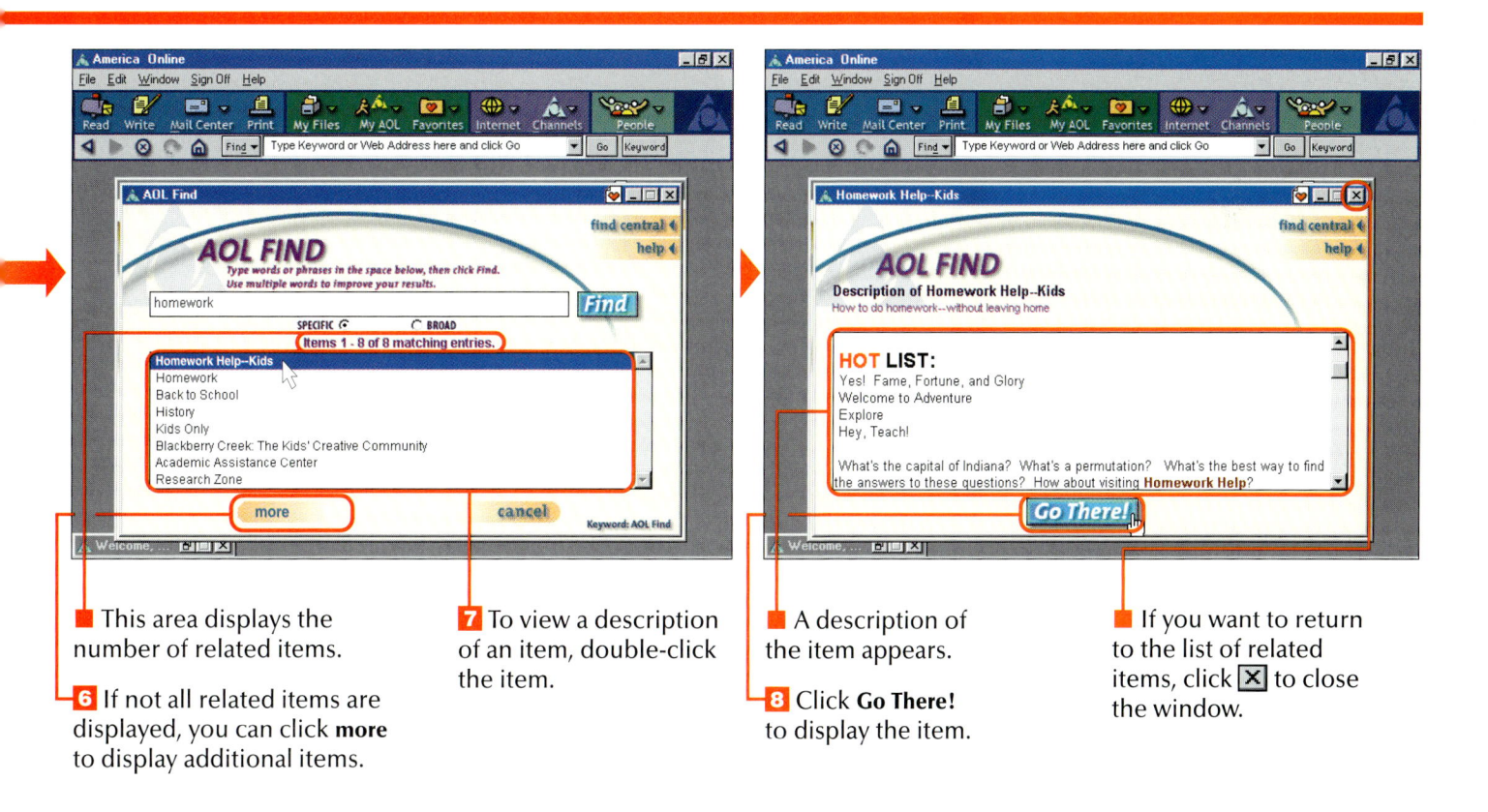

How can I improve the results of a search?

Search for: car racing

Type several words or a phrase rather than a single word. For example, search for "car racing" rather than "car."

Search for: pets not cats

You can use NOT to limit the search. For example, if you want to find information on pets, but are not interested in cats, search for "pets not cats."

■ This area displays the number of related items.

6 If not all related items are displayed, you can click **more** to display additional items.

7 To view a description of an item, double-click the item.

■ A description of the item appears.

8 Click **Go There!** to display the item.

■ If you want to return to the list of related items, click ☒ to close the window.

39

WAL-MART
America Online - [USA TODAY]
USA TODAY
News
Sports
Money
Life
Weather
2/17/98 - Updated 11:36 AM ET
Clinton to plead case on Iraq
Discovery ONLINE
Art Apart
Iditarod
Cops
America Online - [MINOLTA/English]
http://www.minolta.com/
MINOLTA
Join us
About Minolta
Corporate Information
Magical Tour
America Online - [The Smithsonian Institution Home Page]
http://www.si.edu/newstart.htm
The SMITHSONIAN
MUSEUMS ORGANIZATIONS
RESOURCES TOURS
EVENTS ACTIVITIES
MEMBERSHIPS SHOPS
What's New on the SI Web? See the Electric Guitar
America Online - [Campbell's Community]
File Edit Window Sign Off Help
Read Write Mail Center Print My Files My AOL Favorites Internet Channels People
Keyword
http://www.campbellsoup.com/
Campbell's Community
www.campbellsoup.com
Creative Kitchen
Wondering what to make for dinner tonight? Tell us what ingredients you have on hand, and the Campbell's Creative Kitchen will help
Community Center
Enter Campbell's Community Center and explore the world's favorite food company!
See what's new at Campbell's
America Online - [Yahoo!]
File Edit Window Sign Off Help
Read Write Mail Center Print My Files My AOL Favorites Internet Channels People
Keyword
http://www.yahoo.com/
Go
Find
YAHOO!
New
Cool
Today's News
More Yahoos
'98 Winter Games
Tax Center
Free listings thru 3/4
ONSALE
Win an $8000 Digital Theater
Search
options
Yahoo! Mail - get your free @yahoo.com email address
Yellow Pages - People Search - Maps - Classifieds - Personals - Chat - Free Email
My Yahoo! - News - Sports - Weather - Stock Quotes - more...

CHAPTER 3

BROWSE THE WEB

What is the Web? In this chapter you will learn how the Web works, what it has to offer and how information transfers to your computer from sites around the world.

Introduction to the Web 42

Display a Specific Web Page 44

Select a Link 46

Stop Transfer of Information 47

Move Through Web Pages 48

Refresh a Web Page .49

Find Web Pages 50

Display and Change Your Home Page 52

Cool Web Pages 54

INTRODUCTION TO THE WEB

The World Wide Web is part of the Internet, which is the largest computer system in the world. The Web consists of a huge collection of documents stored on hundreds of thousands of computers.

Web Pages

A Web page is a document on the Web. You can find Web pages on every subject imaginable. There are Web pages that offer information such as newspaper and magazine articles, movie clips, recipes, Shakespearean plays, airline schedules and more. You can also purchase items, do your banking and get programs and games on the Web.

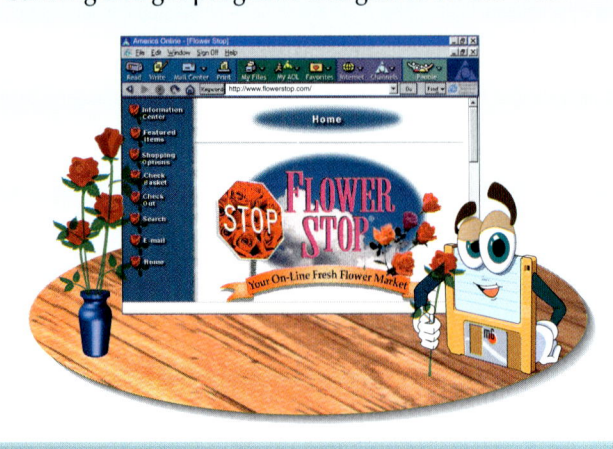

Web Sites

A Web site is a collection of Web pages maintained by a college, university, government agency, company or individual.

BROWSE THE WEB

URLs

Each Web page has a unique address, called a Uniform Resource Locator (URL). You can display any Web page if you know its URL. Most Web page URLs start with **http** (HyperText Transfer Protocol).

Links

Web pages contain highlighted text or images, called links, that connect to other pages on the Web. You can select a link on a Web page to display another page located on the same computer or on a computer across the city, country or world.

Links allow you to easily move through a vast amount of information by jumping from one Web page to another. This is known as "browsing the Web."

HTML

HyperText Markup Language (HTML) is a computer language used to create Web pages. HTML consists of plain text with codes, called tags, that define how text and graphics will appear on a Web page.

43

DISPLAY A SPECIFIC WEB PAGE

You can easily display a page on the Web that you have heard or read about.

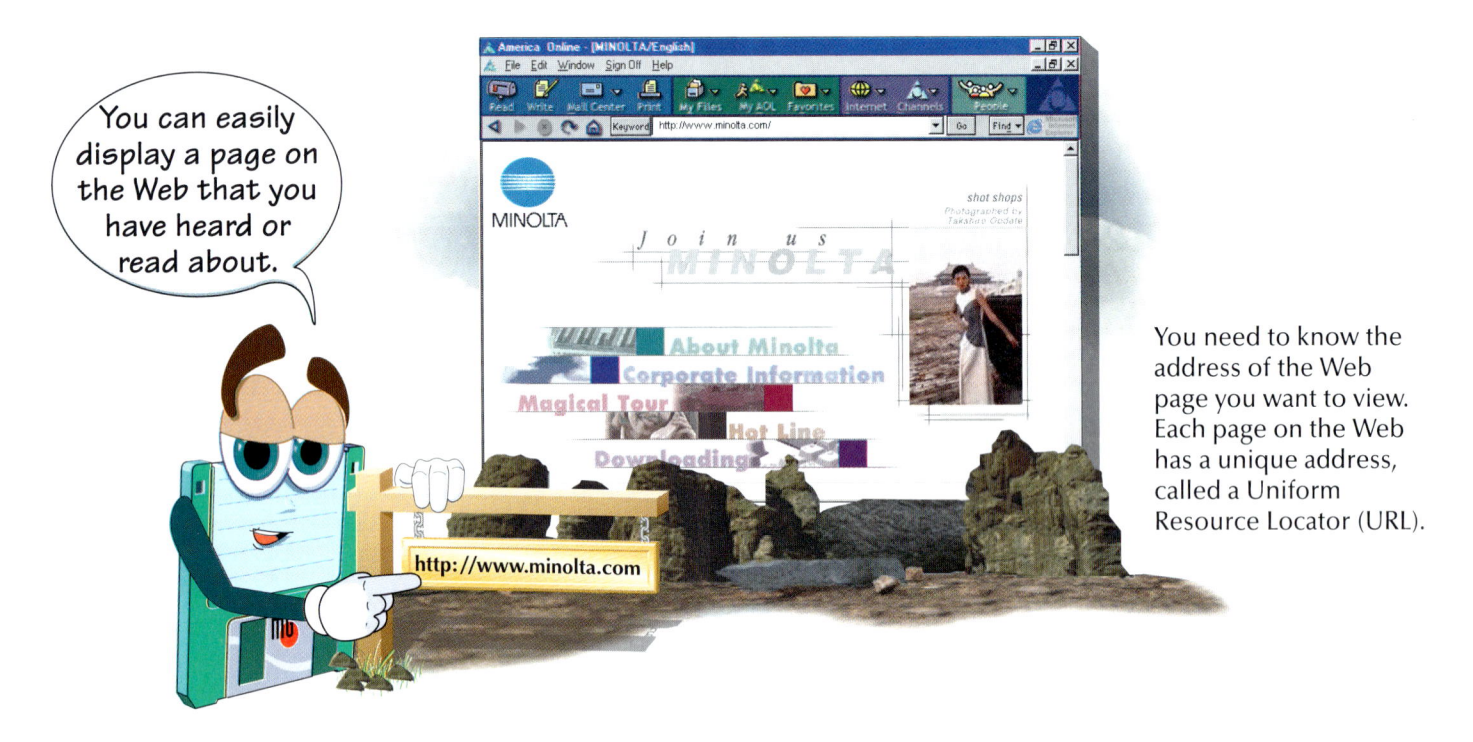

You need to know the address of the Web page you want to view. Each page on the Web has a unique address, called a Uniform Resource Locator (URL).

DISPLAY A SPECIFIC WEB PAGE

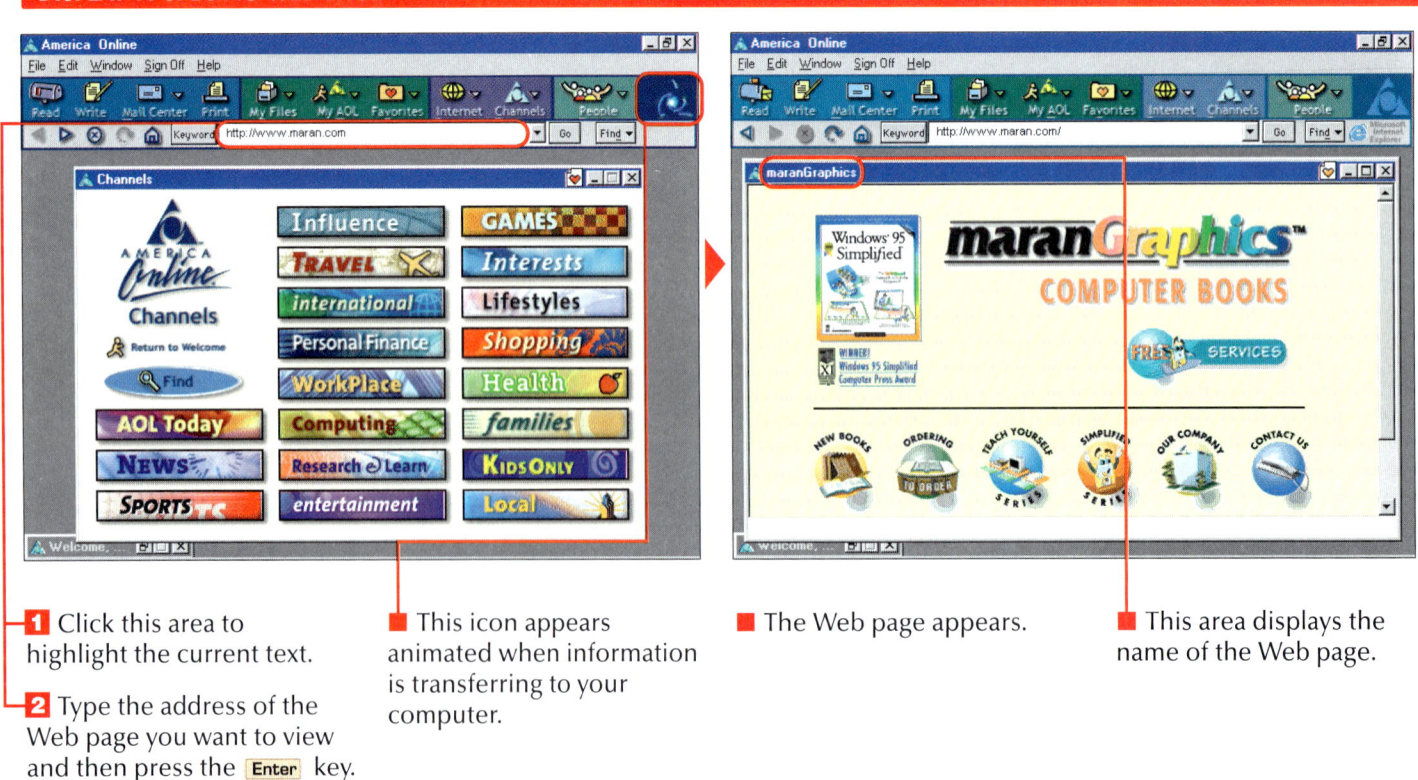

■ **1** Click this area to highlight the current text.

■ **2** Type the address of the Web page you want to view and then press the Enter key.

■ This icon appears animated when information is transferring to your computer.

■ The Web page appears.

■ This area displays the name of the Web page.

BROWSE THE WEB

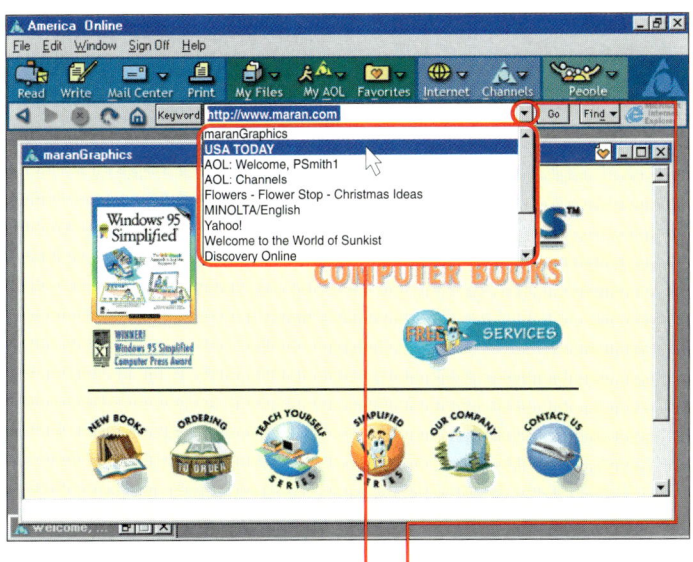

How can I save time when typing Web page addresses?

You can leave off **http://** when typing a Web page address. For example, you could type **http://www.maran.com** or **www.maran.com** to display the maranGraphics Web page.

RETURN TO A WEB PAGE

You can display a list of the Web pages you have recently visited and quickly return to one of these pages.

1 Click ▼ in this area.

2 Click the Web page you want to display.

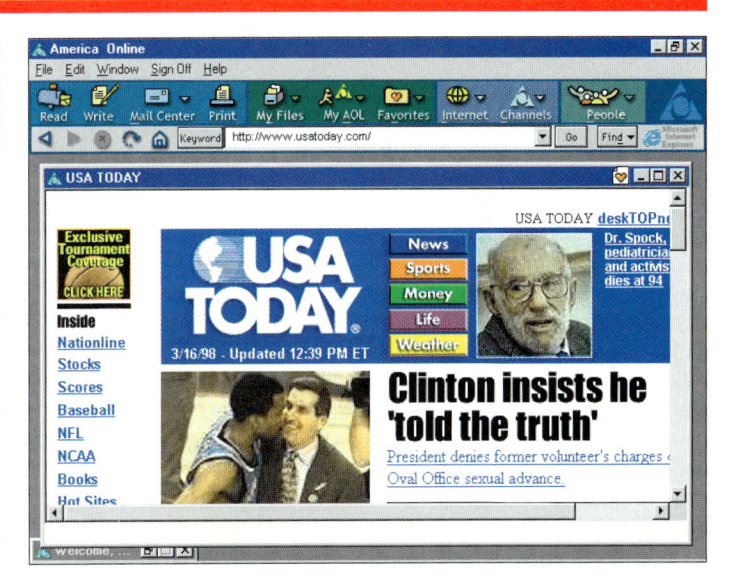

■ The Web page appears.

45

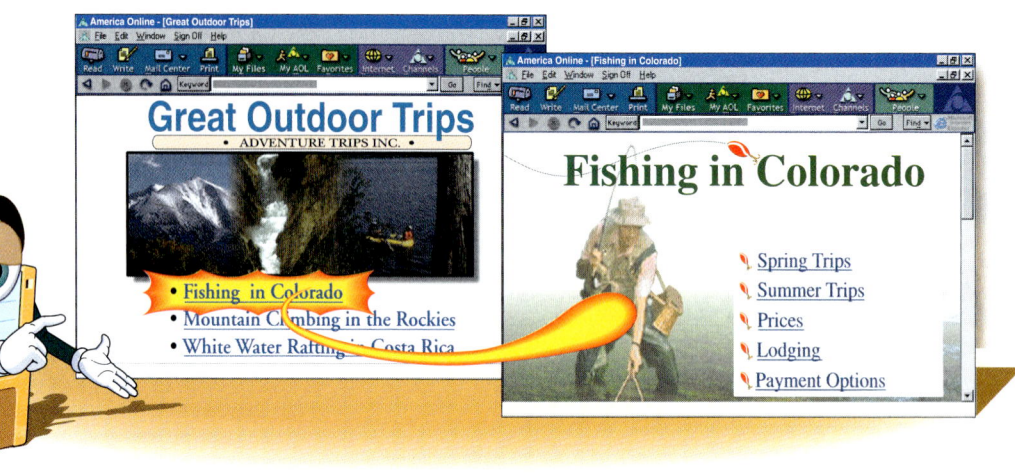

SELECT A LINK

A link connects text or a picture on one Web page to another Web page. When you select the text or picture, the other Web page appears.

Text links are usually underlined and a different color than the rest of the text on a Web page.

SELECT A LINK

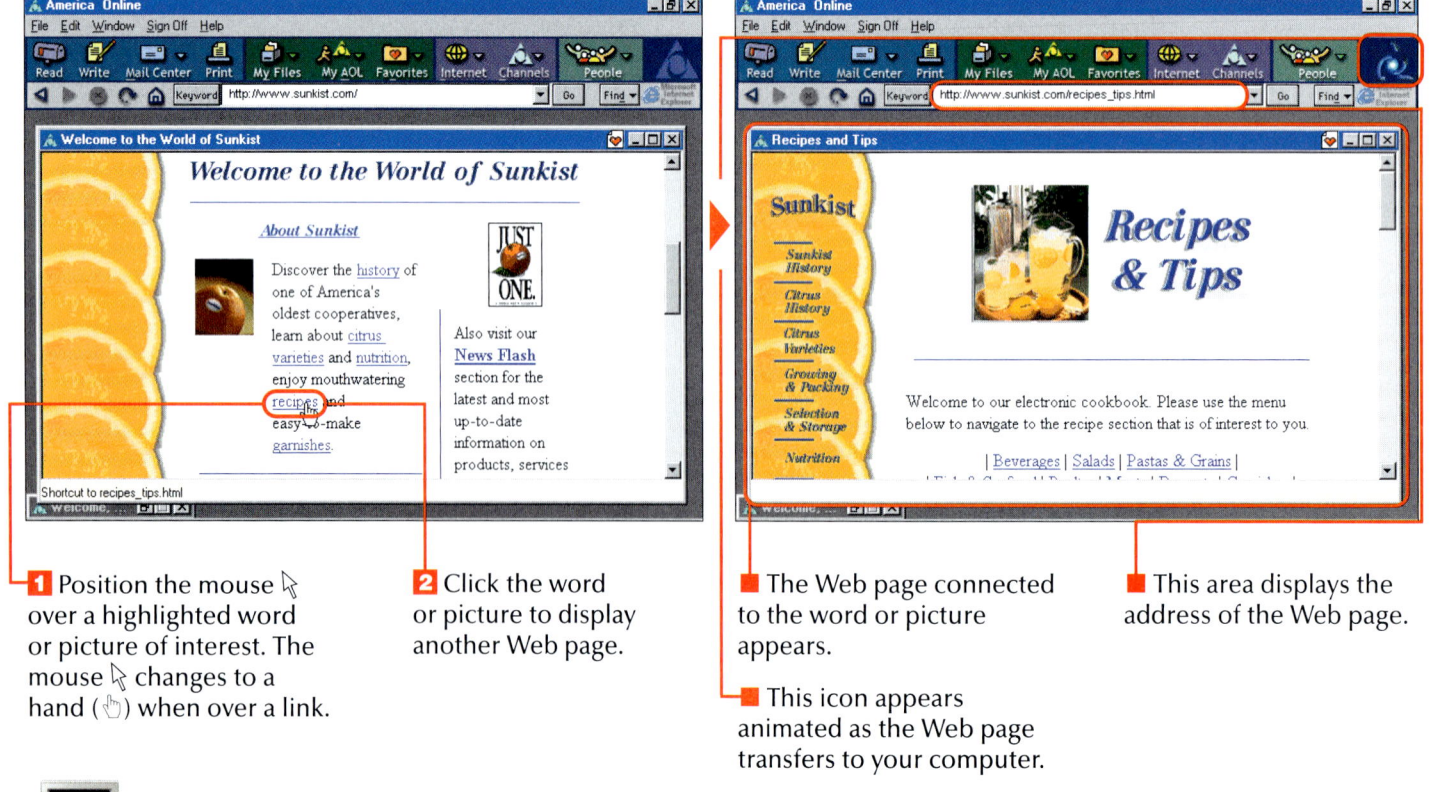

1 Position the mouse over a highlighted word or picture of interest. The mouse changes to a hand ( ) when over a link.

2 Click the word or picture to display another Web page.

■ The Web page connected to the word or picture appears.

■ This icon appears animated as the Web page transfers to your computer.

■ This area displays the address of the Web page.

46

STOP TRANSFER OF INFORMATION

BROWSE THE WEB — 3

> If a Web page is taking a long time to appear on your screen, you can stop transferring the page and try connecting again later.

The best time to try connecting to a Web site is during off-peak hours, such as nights and weekends, when fewer people are using the Internet.

STOP TRANSFER OF INFORMATION

■ This icon appears animated when information is transferring to your computer.

■ This area indicates the progress of the transfer.

1 Click ⊗ to stop the transfer of information.

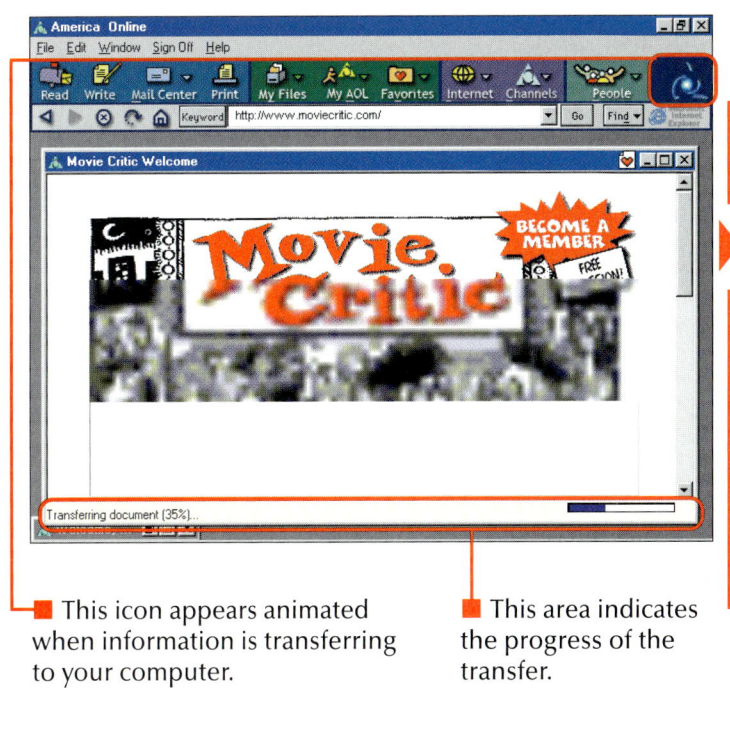

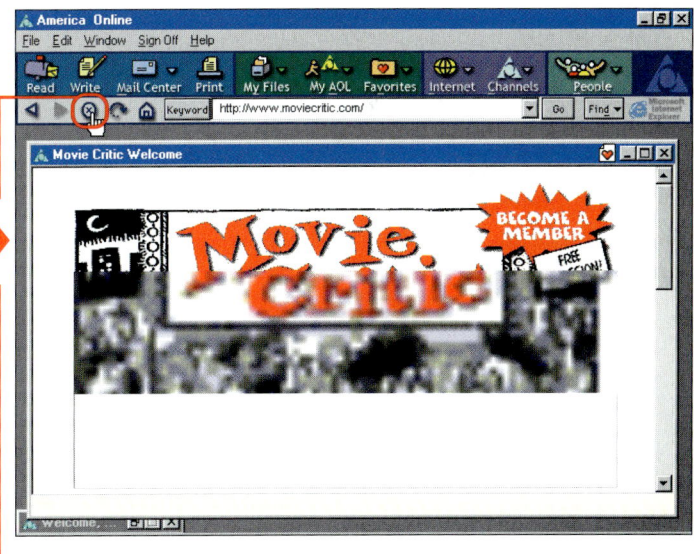

■ You may also want to stop the transfer of information if you realize a Web page is of no interest to you.

47

MOVE THROUGH WEB PAGES

You can easily move back and forth through Web pages you have viewed since you last started the AOL program.

MOVE THROUGH WEB PAGES

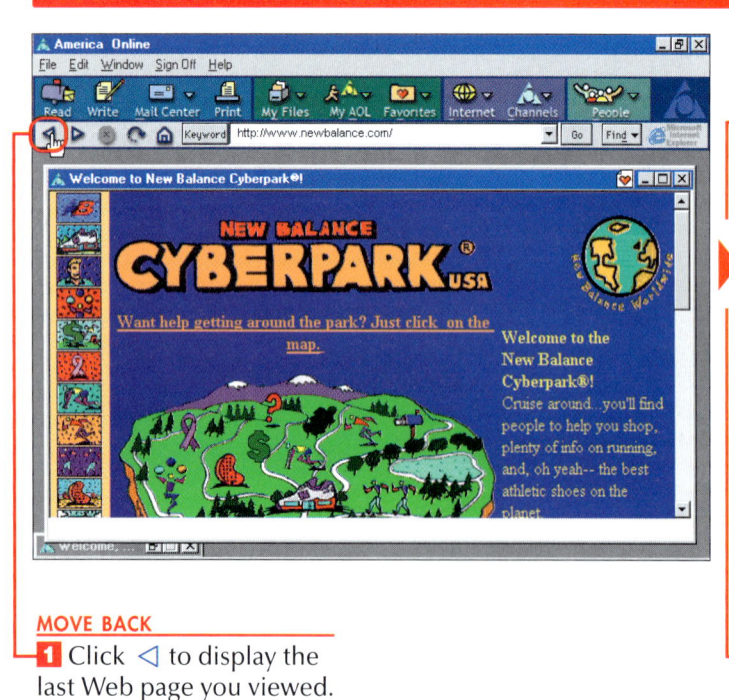

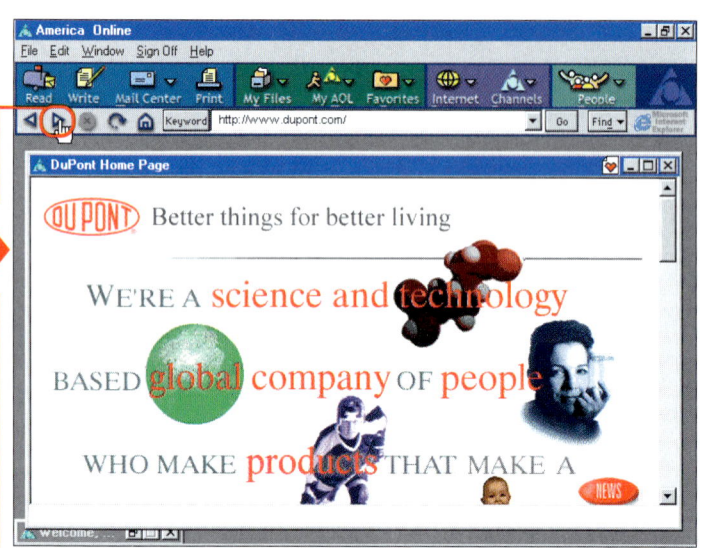

MOVE BACK

1 Click ◁ to display the last Web page you viewed.

MOVE FORWARD

1 Click ▷ to move forward through the Web pages you have viewed.

48

REFRESH A WEB PAGE

BROWSE THE WEB

> You can refresh a Web page to update the displayed information, such as the current news. A fresh copy of the Web page will transfer to your computer.

REFRESH A WEB PAGE

1 Click ↻ to transfer a fresh copy of the displayed Web page to your computer.

■ A fresh copy of the Web page appears on your screen.

49

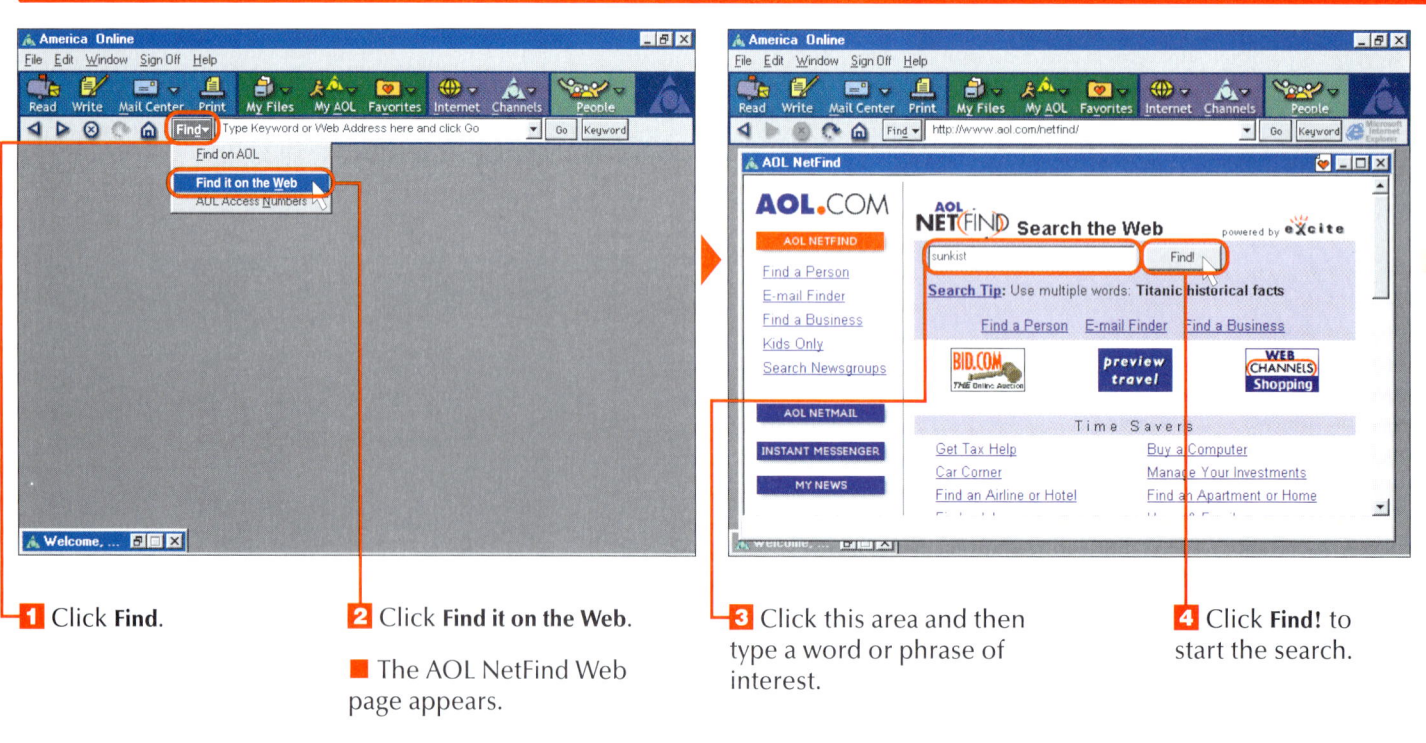

FIND WEB PAGES

You can find pages on the Web that discuss topics of interest to you.

Searching for information will not find every page on the Web that discusses a topic, but it will give you a good starting point.

FIND WEB PAGES

1 Click **Find**.

2 Click **Find it on the Web**.

■ The AOL NetFind Web page appears.

3 Click this area and then type a word or phrase of interest.

4 Click **Find!** to start the search.

BROWSE THE WEB

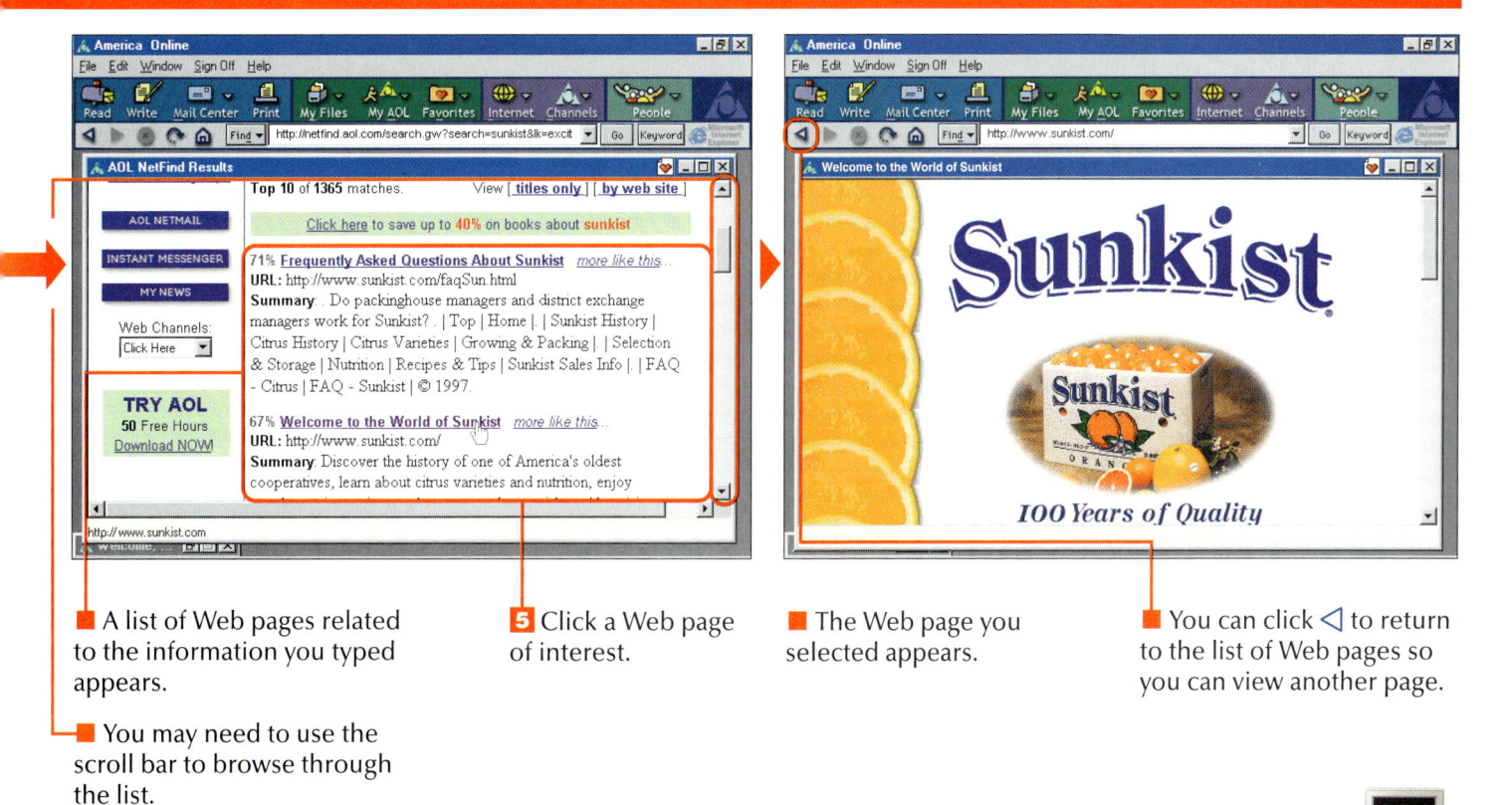

Are there other places on the Web that allow me to search for Web pages?

Here are some popular search services that allow you to find pages on the Web.

AltaVista
www.altavista.digital.com

HotBot
www.hotbot.com

Infoseek
www.infoseek.com

Yahoo!
www.yahoo.com

■ A list of Web pages related to the information you typed appears.

■ You may need to use the scroll bar to browse through the list.

5 Click a Web page of interest.

■ The Web page you selected appears.

■ You can click ◁ to return to the list of Web pages so you can view another page.

51

DISPLAY AND CHANGE YOUR HOME PAGE

You can specify which Web page you want to set as your home page.

The home page appears when you click the Home button (🏠).

DISPLAY YOUR HOME PAGE

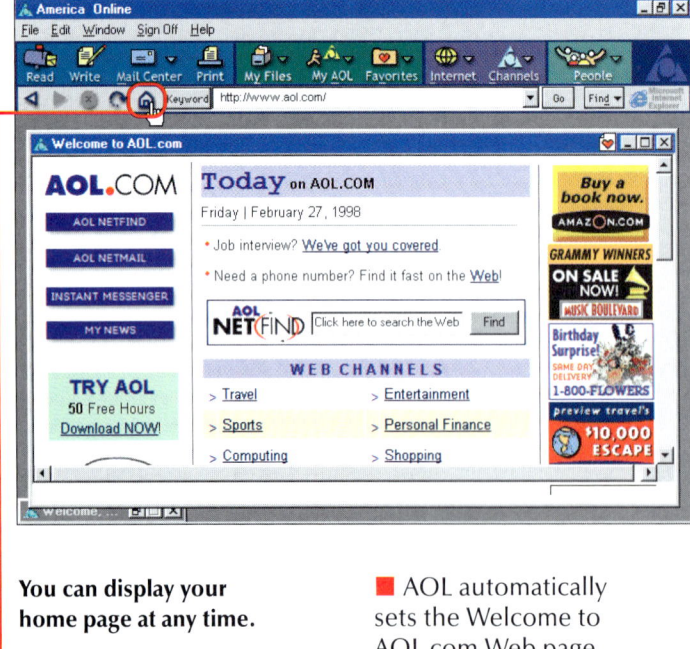

You can display your home page at any time.

1 Click 🏠 to display your home page.

■ AOL automatically sets the Welcome to AOL.com Web page as your home page.

CHANGE YOUR HOME PAGE

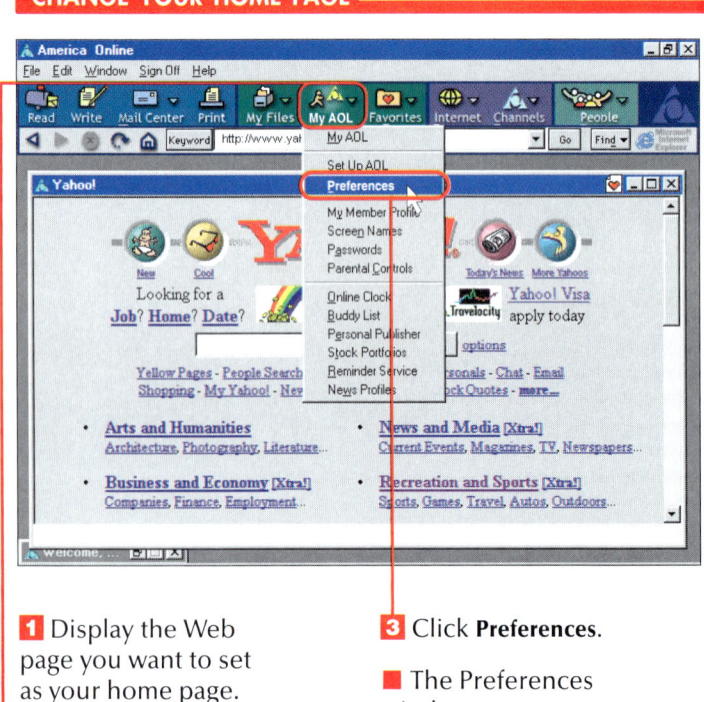

1 Display the Web page you want to set as your home page.

Note: To display a specific Web page, see page 44.

2 Click **My AOL**.

3 Click **Preferences**.

■ The Preferences window appears.

52

BROWSE THE WEB — 3

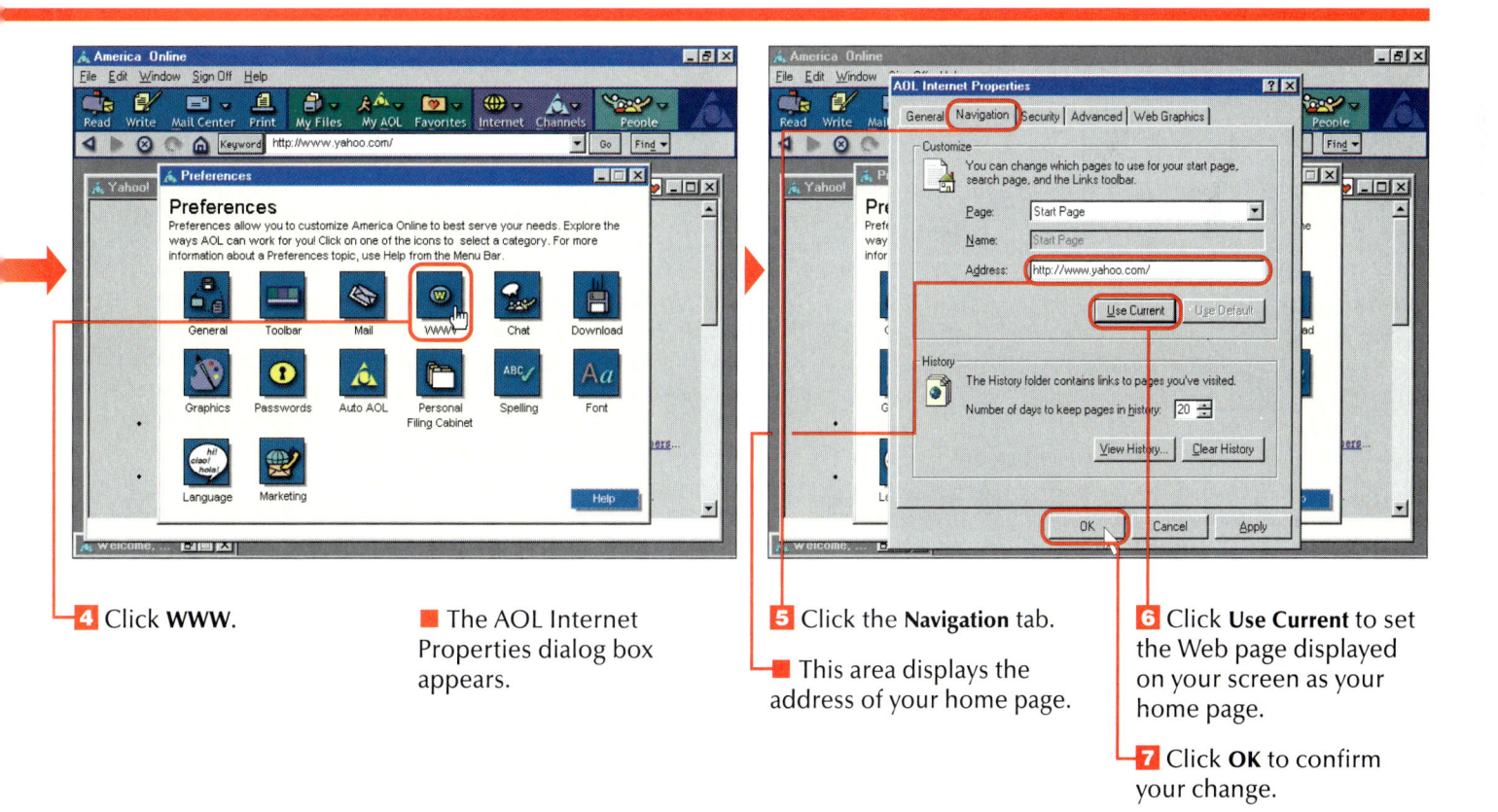

Which Web page should I set as my home page?

You can set any page on the Web as your home page. You may want to choose a home page that provides a good starting point for exploring the Web. Your home page can also be a Web page that you visit frequently.

4 Click **WWW**.

■ The AOL Internet Properties dialog box appears.

5 Click the **Navigation** tab.

■ This area displays the address of your home page.

6 Click **Use Current** to set the Web page displayed on your screen as your home page.

7 Click **OK** to confirm your change.

53

COOL WEB PAGES

Best Western
URL www.bestwestern.com

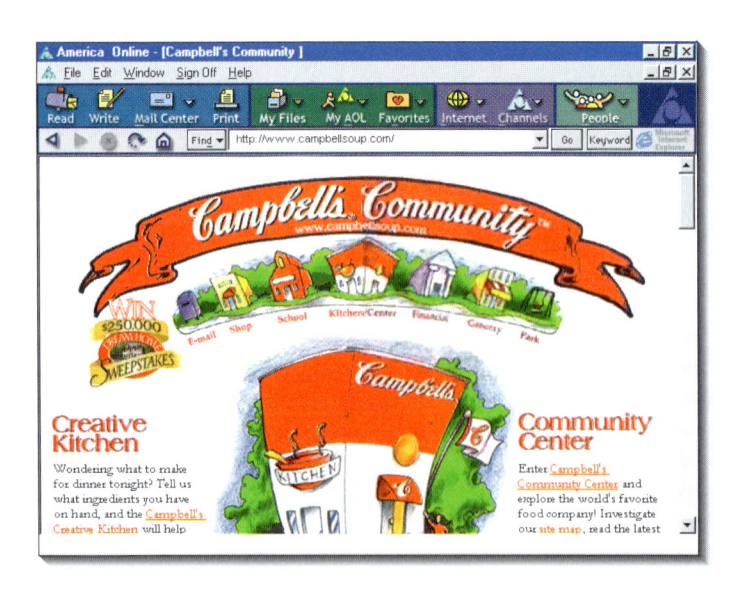

Campbell's Soup
URL www.campbellsoup.com

CBS SportsLine
URL www.sportsline.com

54

3
BROWSE THE WEB

Discovery Channel Online
URL www.discovery.com

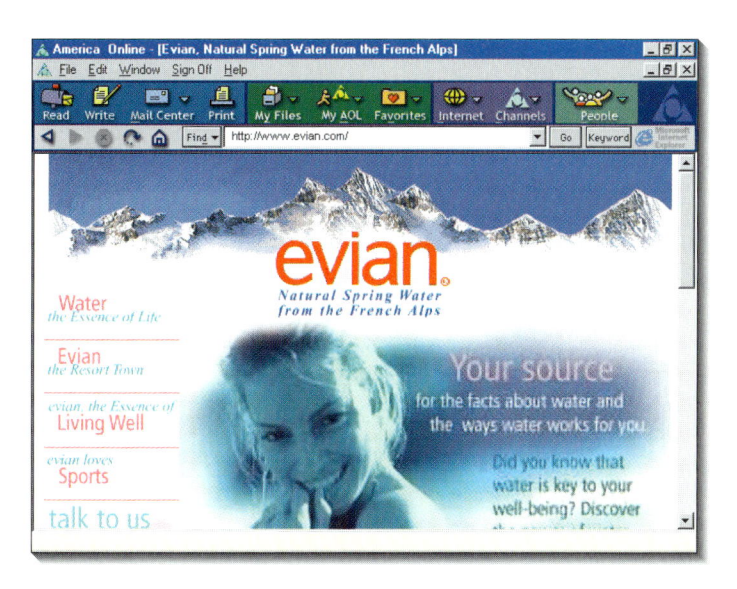

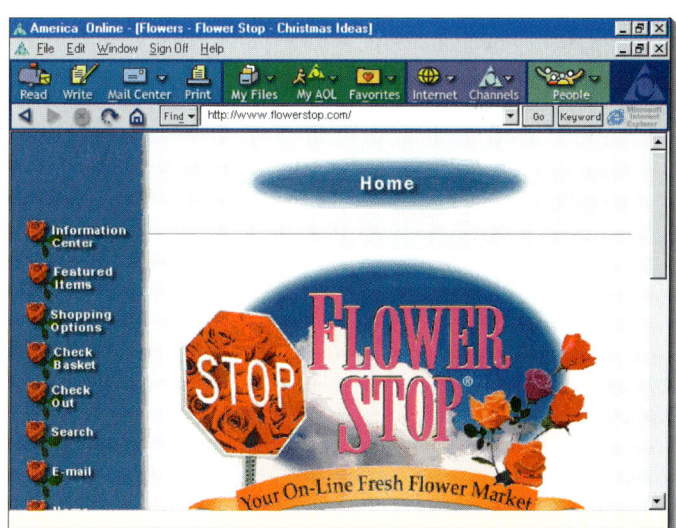

DuPont Company
URL www.dupont.com

Evian
URL www.evian.com

Flower Stop
URL www.flowerstop.com

55

COOL WEB PAGES

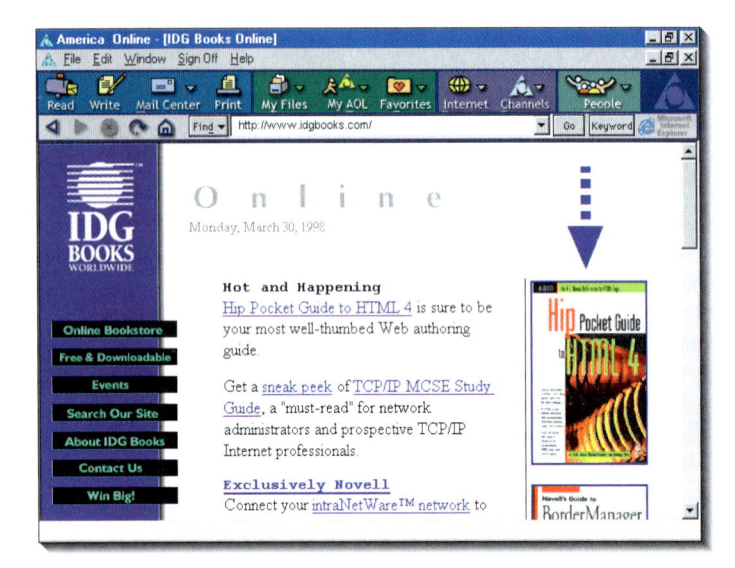

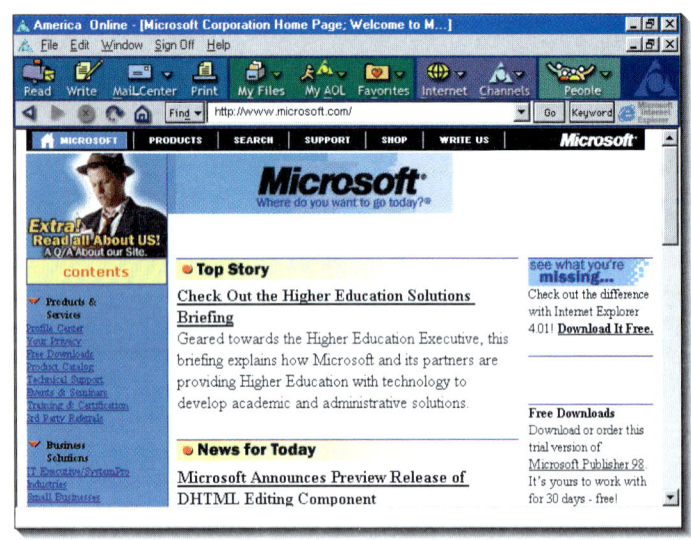

IDG Books
URL www.idgbooks.com

Microsoft
URL www.microsoft.com

Minolta
URL www.minolta.com

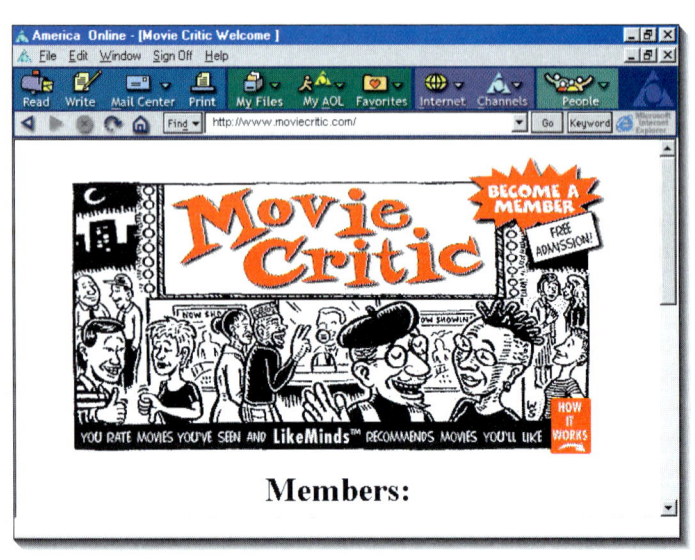

Movie Critic
URL www.moviecritic.com

56

3
BROWSE THE WEB

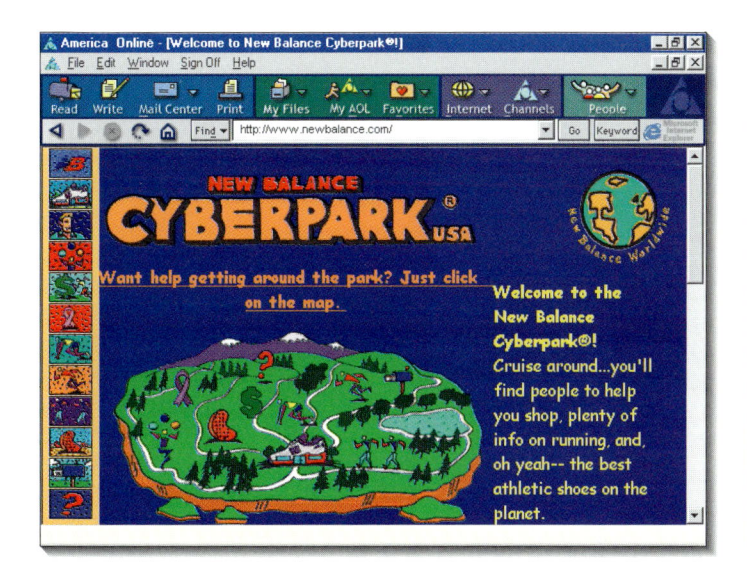

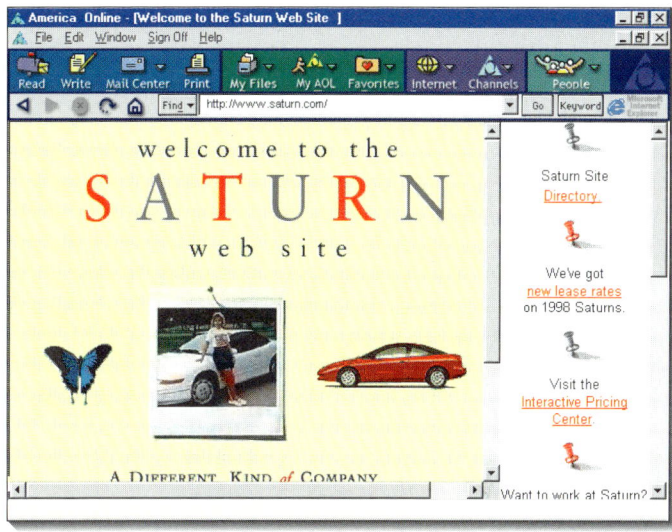

New Balance Cyberpark
URL www.newbalance.com

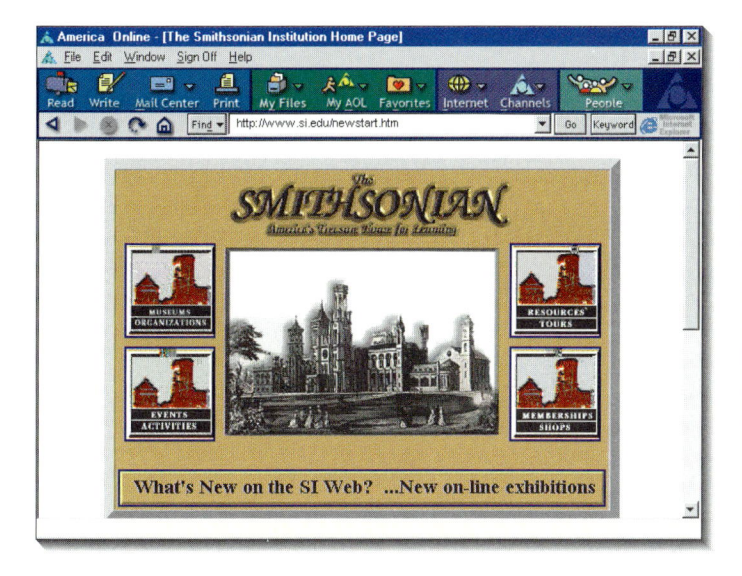

Saturn
URL www.saturn.com

Smithsonian Institution
URL www.si.edu

Spiegel
URL www.spiegel.com

57

COOL WEB PAGES

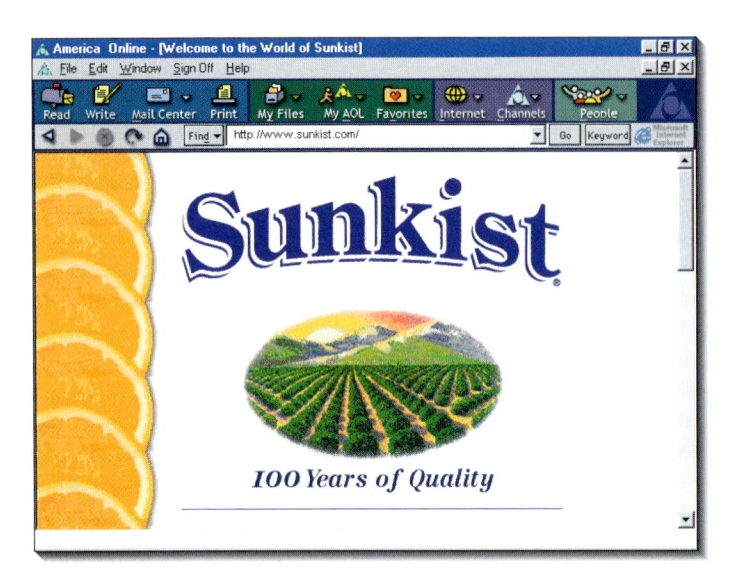

Sunkist
URL www.sunkist.com

Ticketmaster
URL www.ticketmaster.com

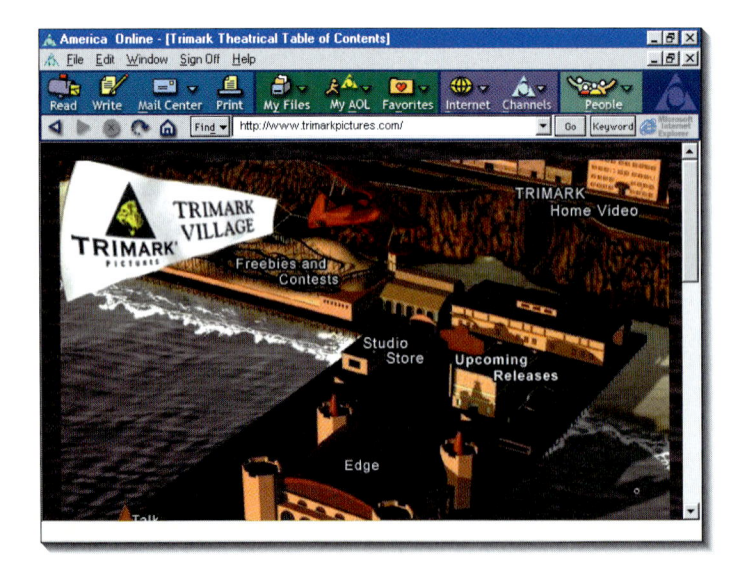

Trimark Pictures
URL www.trimarkpictures.com

USA TODAY Online
URL www.usatoday.com

BROWSE THE WEB

Wal-mart
URL www.wal-mart.com

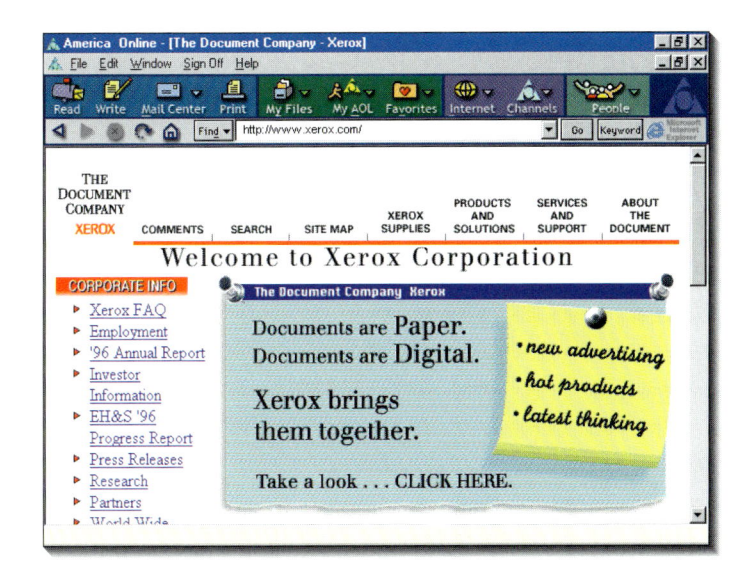

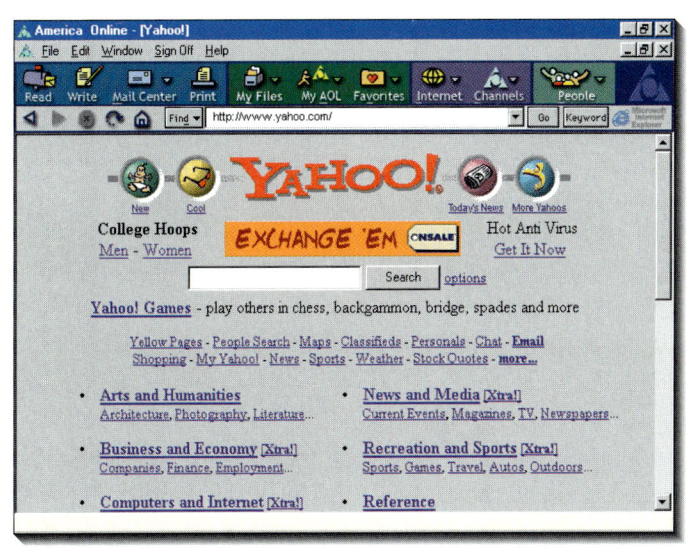

The White House
URL www.whitehouse.gov

Xerox Corporation
URL www.xerox.com

Yahoo
URL www.yahoo.com

MAIL CENTRE
AMERICA Online
E-MAIL ADDRESSES
Name
Address
Jack Thomas
jthomas@aol.com
Sue Jones
Bill Carey
E-MAIL ADDRESSES
Name
Address
Silvia Parker
Joy Smart
bcarey@aol.com

CHAPTER 4

READ AND COMPOSE E-MAIL

How do I send electronic mail using AOL? In this chapter you will learn how to send and receive e-mail messages, how to create your own e-mail address book and how to find e-mail addresses.

Introduction to E-mail 62

Read Messages 64

Send a Message 66

Reply to a Message 68

Forward a Message 70

Add a Name to the Address Book 72

Add a Group to the Address Book 74

Select a Name from the Address Book 76

Find an E-mail Address 78

INTRODUCTION TO E-MAIL

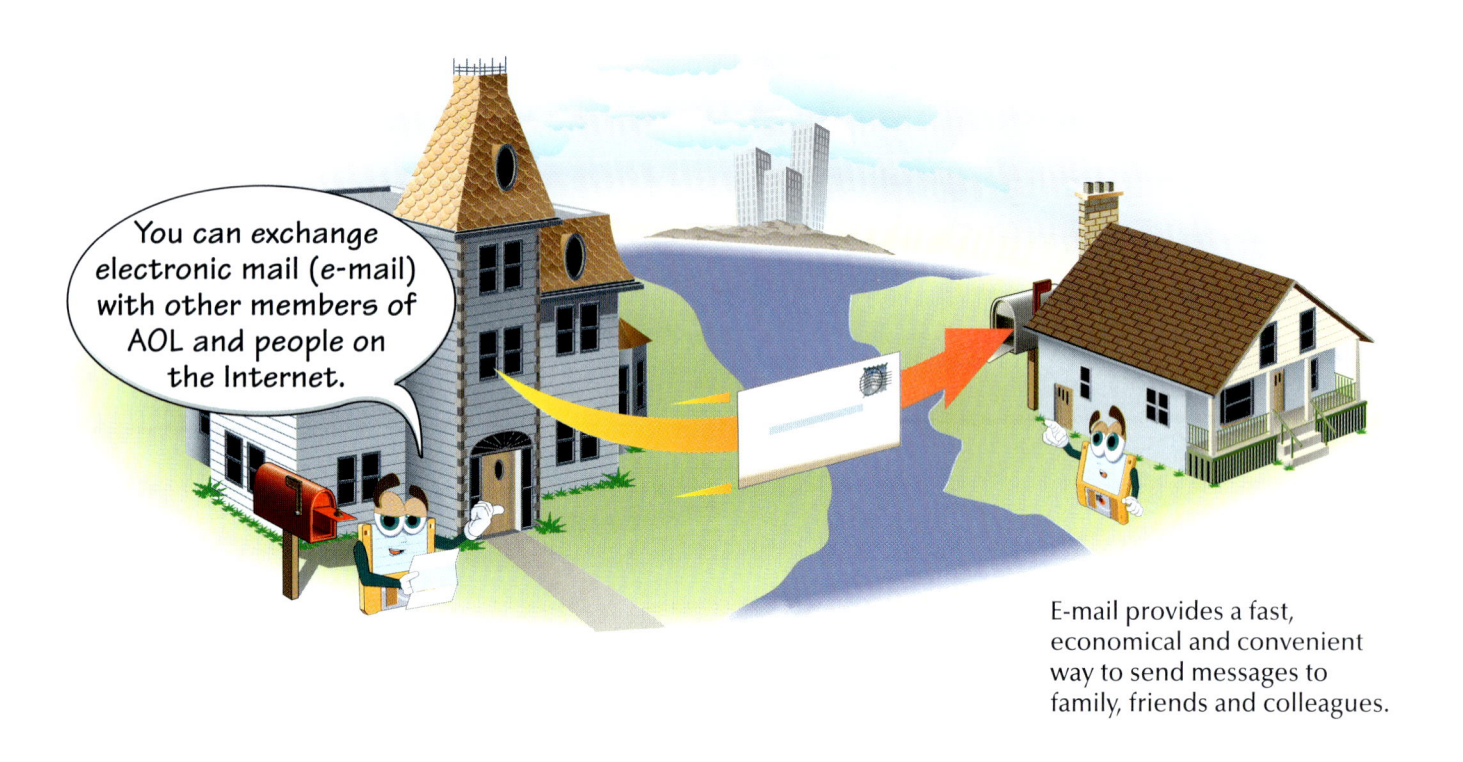

You can exchange electronic mail (e-mail) with other members of AOL and people on the Internet.

E-mail provides a fast, economical and convenient way to send messages to family, friends and colleagues.

Cost

After you join AOL, there is no charge for sending and receiving e-mail. You do not have to pay extra if you send a long message or if the message travels around the world.

Exchanging e-mail can save you money on long-distance calls. The next time you are about to pick up the telephone, consider sending an e-mail message instead.

Convenience

You can create and send e-mail messages at any time. Unlike telephone calls, the person receiving the message does not have to be at their computer when you send a message. E-mail makes communicating with people in different time zones very convenient.

READ AND COMPOSE E-MAIL

E-Mail Addresses

You can send a message to anyone around the world if you know the person's e-mail address. An e-mail address defines the location of an individual's mailbox.

Exchange Messages with AOL Members

When you want to send a message to another AOL member, use the person's screen name as the address. Each person chooses a screen name when they join AOL. A screen name can be a real name or a nickname.

Exchange Messages over the Internet

When you want to send a message to a person on the Internet, use the person's Internet address. This address consists of two parts separated by the @ ("at") symbol.

When a person on the Internet wants to send you a message, the person should use your screen name, followed by @**aol.com**.

■ The **user name** is the name of the person's account. This can be a real name or a nickname.

■ The **domain name** is the location of the person's account on the Internet. Periods (.) separate the various parts of the domain name.

63

READ MESSAGES

You can easily open a message to read its contents.

America Online will keep messages you have read for 3 days and messages you have not read for about 27 days. Messages are deleted to keep the AOL computer system from overflowing with messages.

READ MESSAGES

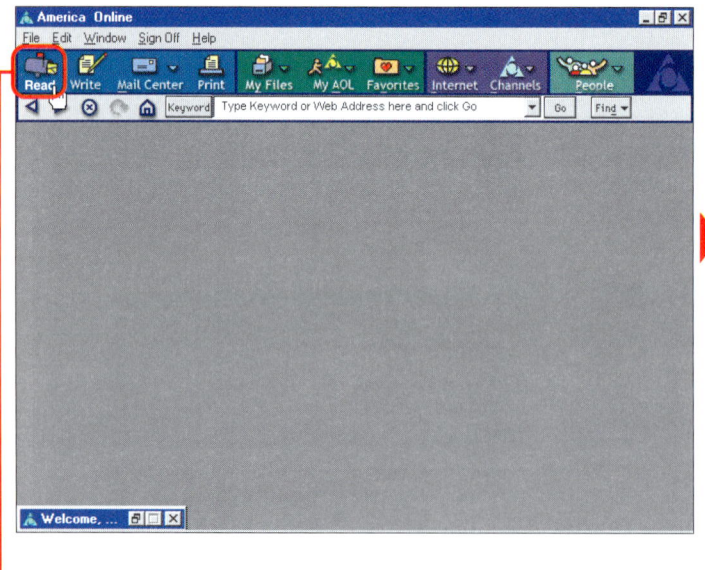

1 Click **Read** to read your messages.

■ When you have new messages, the flag on the mailbox will be up.

■ The Online Mailbox window appears.

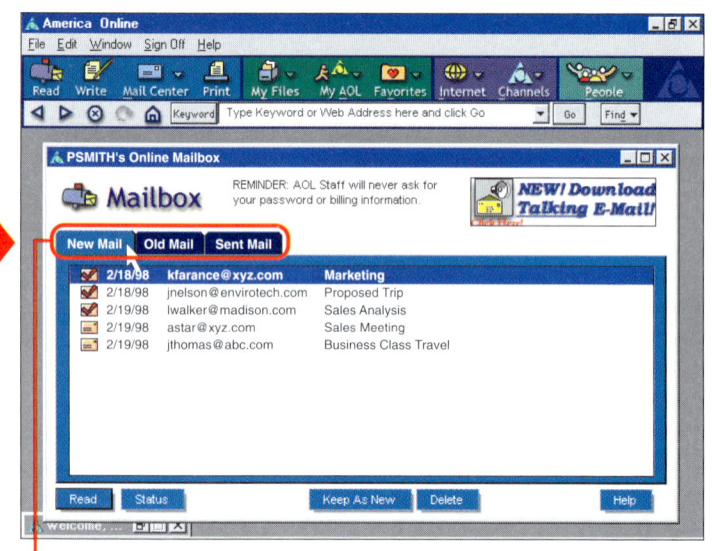

2 Click the tab that displays the messages you want to read.

New Mail
New messages.

Old Mail
Messages you have previously read.

Sent Mail
Messages you have sent.

READ AND COMPOSE E-MAIL

Why do some of my messages display extra information?

When you receive a message over the Internet, extra information appears in the message showing how the message was sent over the Internet. Messages you receive from other AOL members do not contain extra information since the messages do not transfer over the Internet.

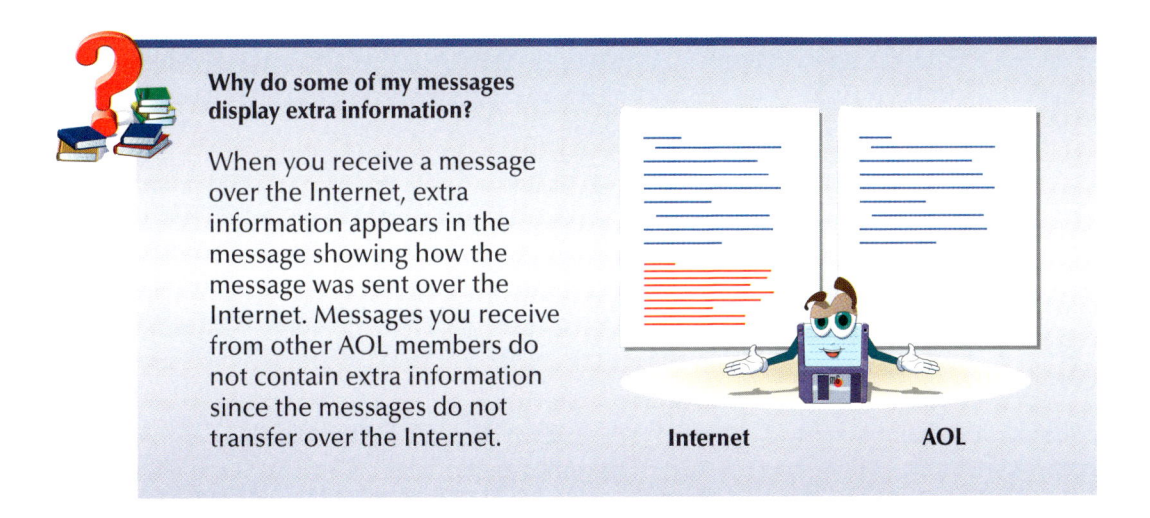

Internet **AOL**

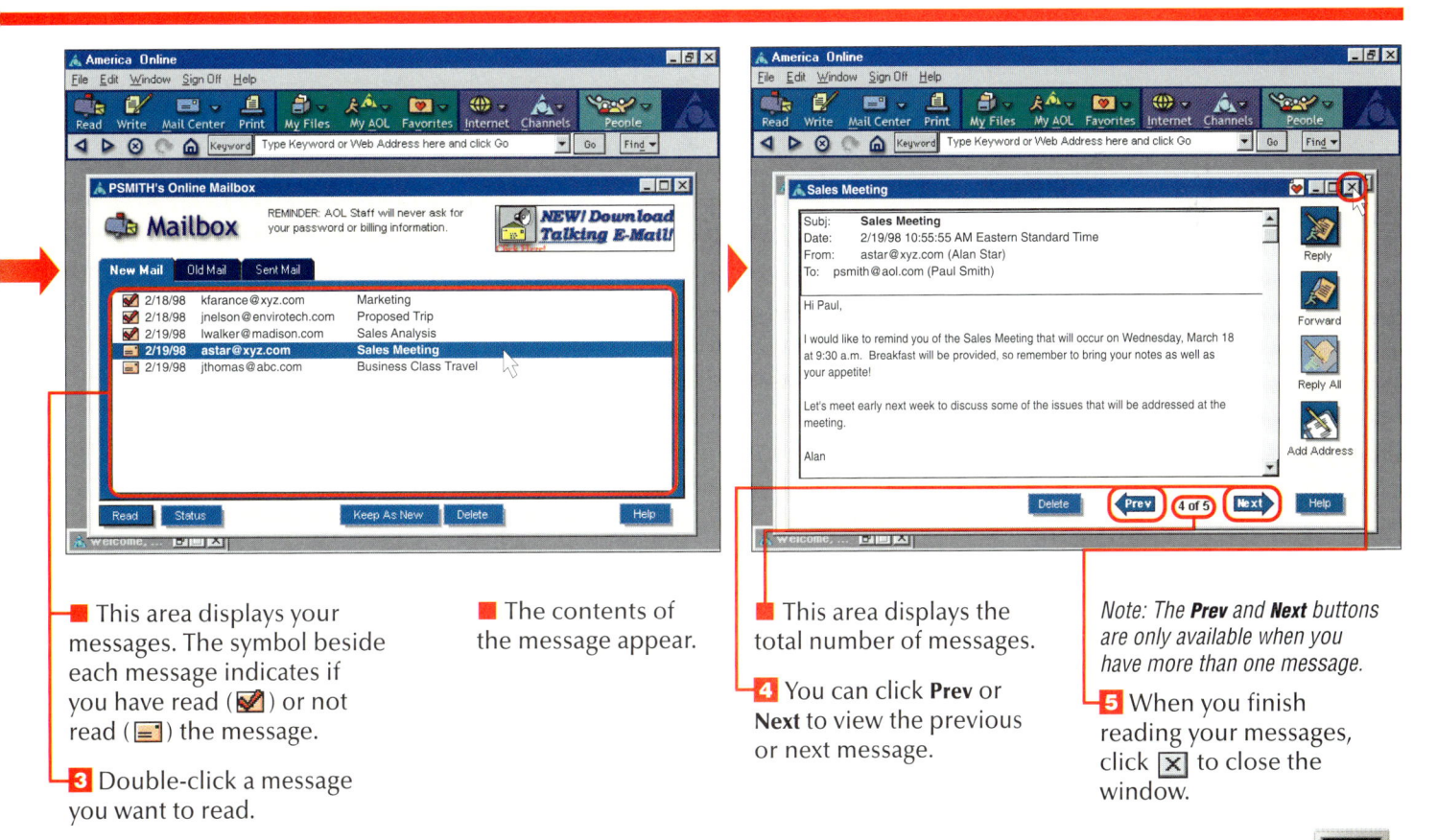

- This area displays your messages. The symbol beside each message indicates if you have read (☑) or not read (✉) the message.

3 Double-click a message you want to read.

- The contents of the message appear.

- This area displays the total number of messages.

4 You can click **Prev** or **Next** to view the previous or next message.

*Note: The **Prev** and **Next** buttons are only available when you have more than one message.*

5 When you finish reading your messages, click ☒ to close the window.

SEND A MESSAGE

You can send a message to exchange ideas or request information.

SEND A MESSAGE

1 Click **Write** to send a new message.

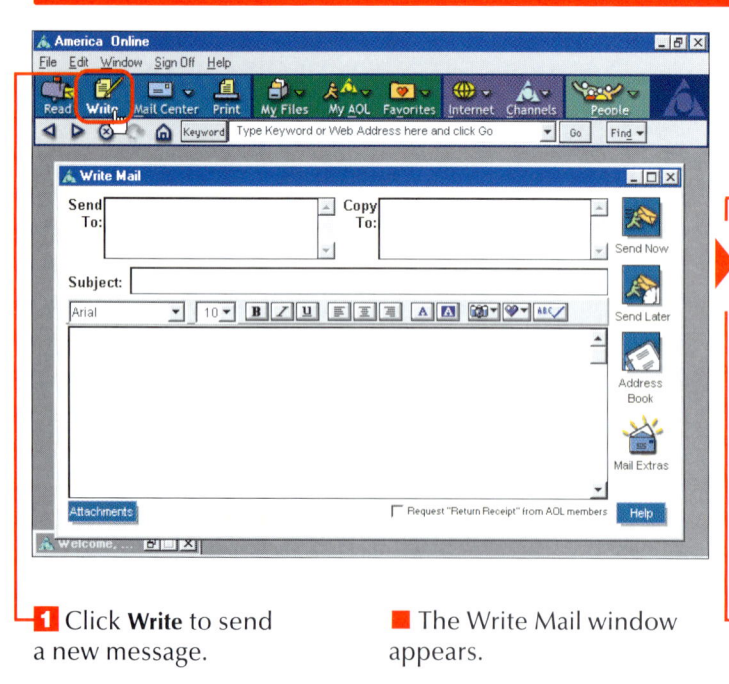

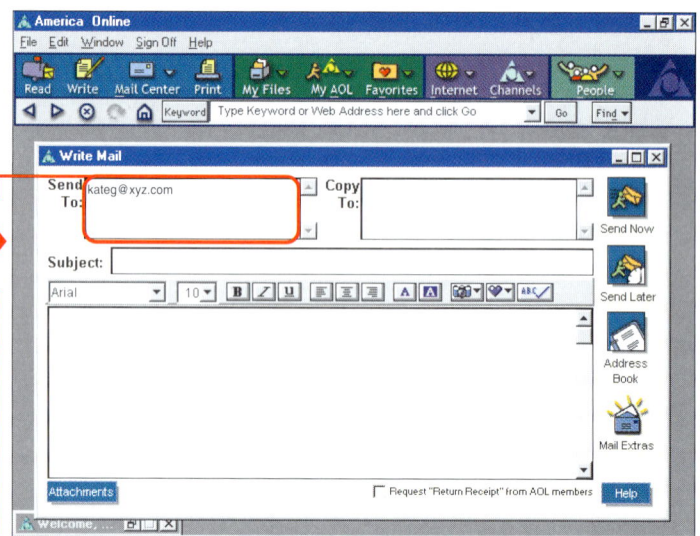

■ The Write Mail window appears.

2 Type the e-mail address of the person you want to receive the message.

■ To send the message to more than one person, separate each e-mail address with a comma (,).

Note: To select a name from the address book, see page 76. Then skip to step 4.

66

READ AND COMPOSE E-MAIL

How can I address a message I want to send?

Send To

Send the message to the person you specify.

Copy To

Send an exact copy of the message to a person who is not directly involved, but would be interested in the message.

Blind Copy

Send an exact copy of the message to a person without anyone else knowing that the person received the message.

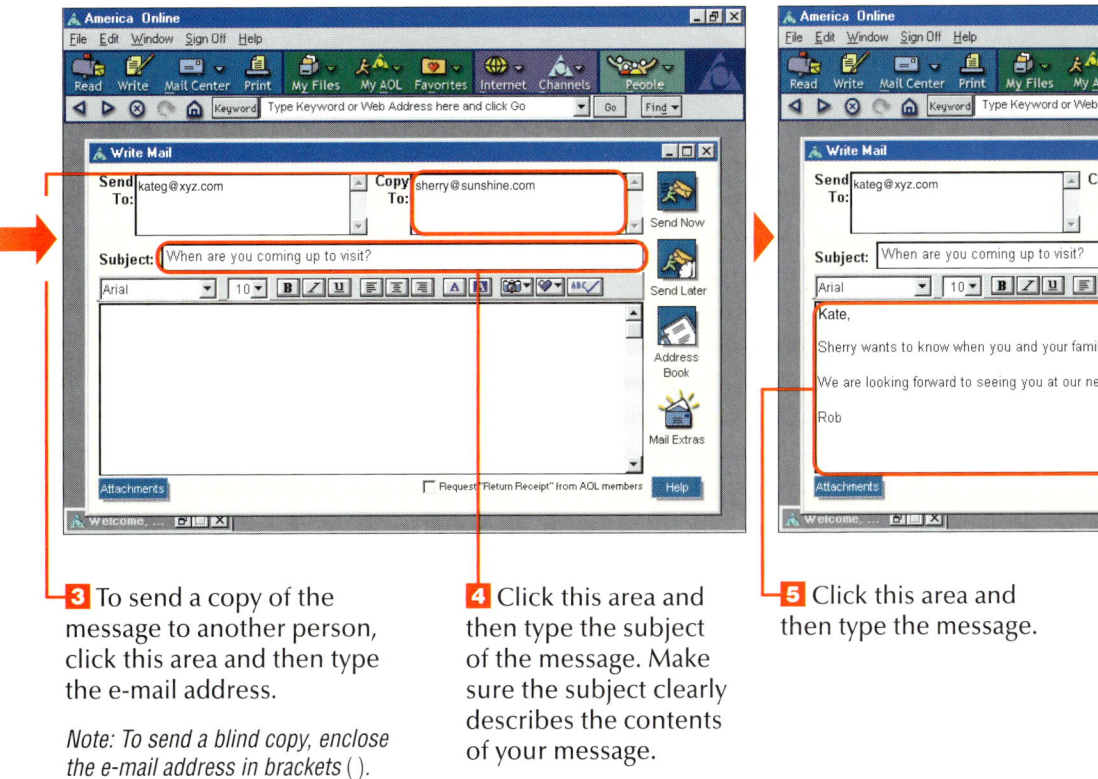

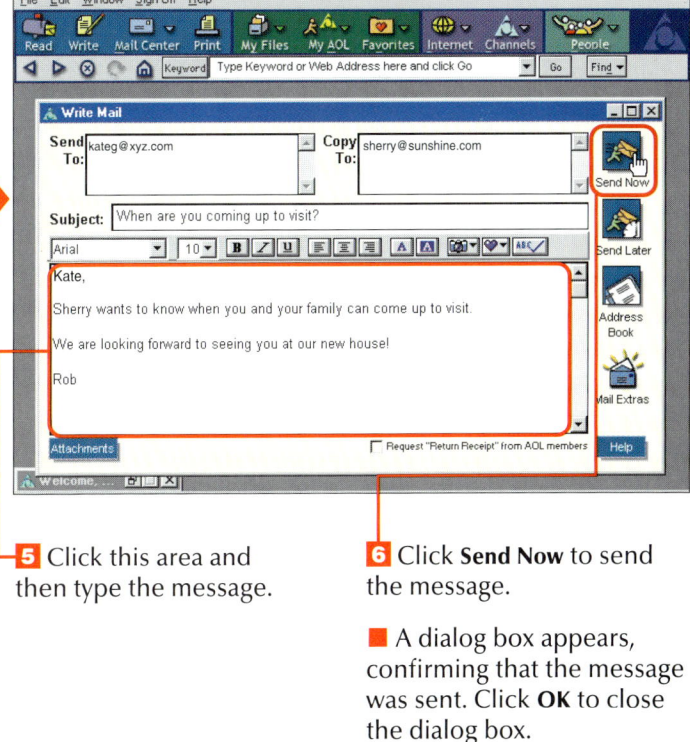

---

3 To send a copy of the message to another person, click this area and then type the e-mail address.

Note: To send a blind copy, enclose the e-mail address in brackets ( ).

4 Click this area and then type the subject of the message. Make sure the subject clearly describes the contents of your message.

5 Click this area and then type the message.

6 Click **Send Now** to send the message.

■ A dialog box appears, confirming that the message was sent. Click **OK** to close the dialog box.

67

REPLY TO A MESSAGE

> You can reply to a message to answer a question or comment on the message.

You can include all or part of the original message in your reply to help the reader identify which message you are replying to. This is called quoting.

REPLY TO A MESSAGE

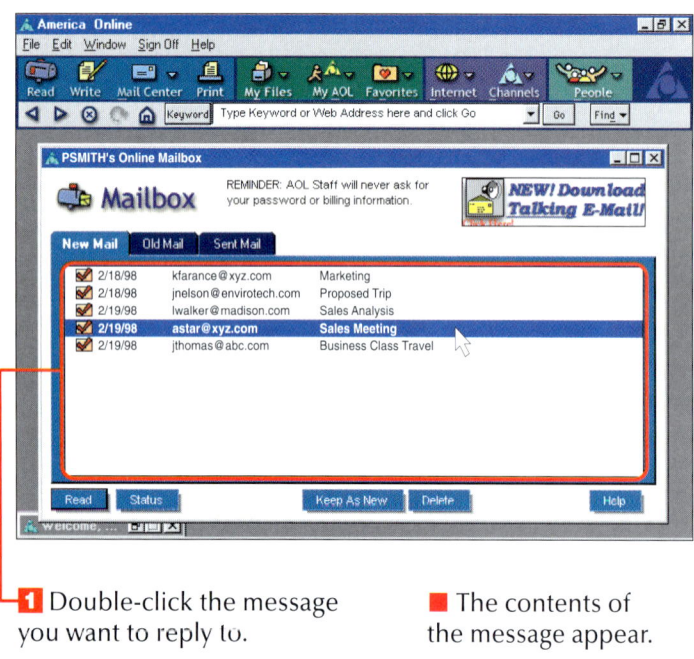

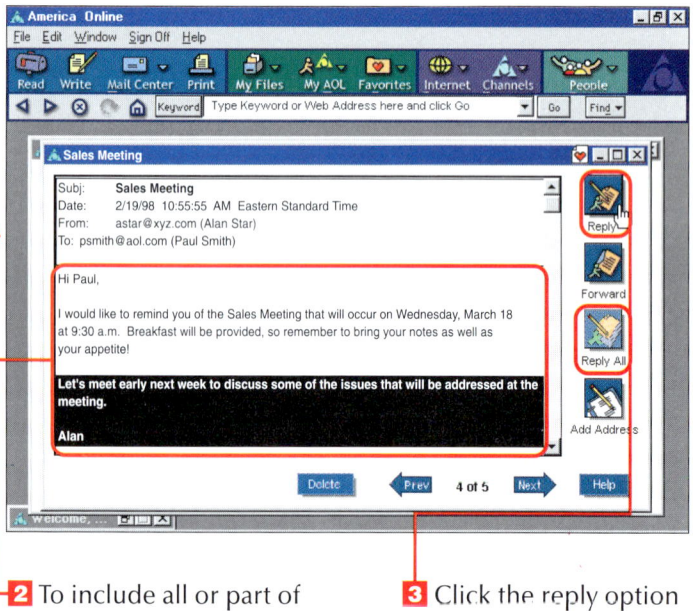

1 Double-click the message you want to reply to.

■ The contents of the message appear.

Note: For information on reading messages, see page 64.

2 To include all or part of the original message in your reply, drag the mouse over the text you want to include.

3 Click the reply option you want to use.

Note: For information on the reply options, see the top of page 69.

READ AND COMPOSE E-MAIL

How can I reply to a message?

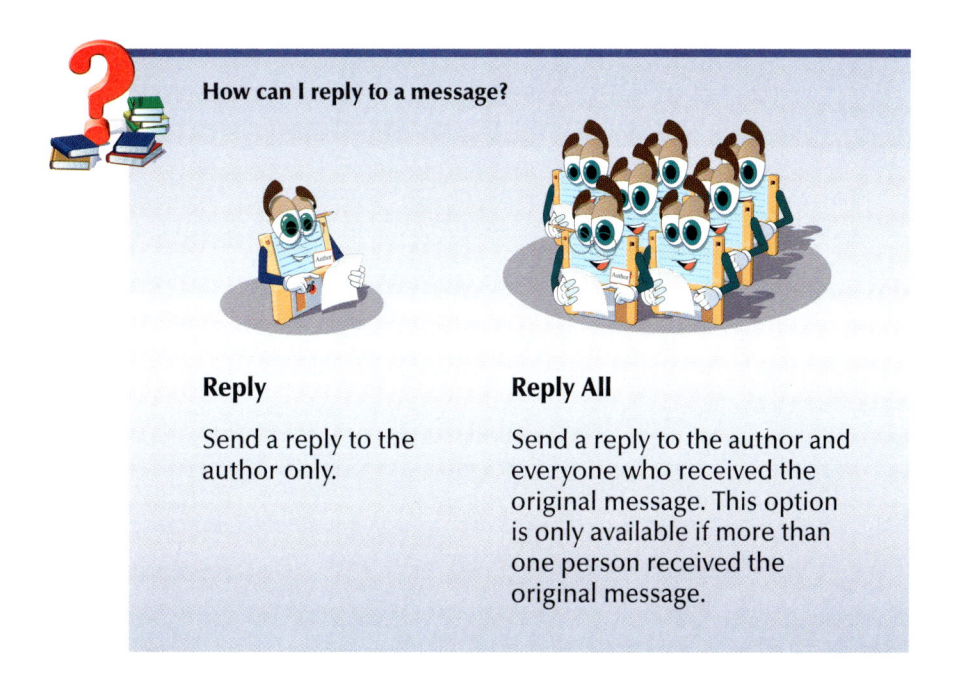

Reply

Send a reply to the author only.

Reply All

Send a reply to the author and everyone who received the original message. This option is only available if more than one person received the original message.

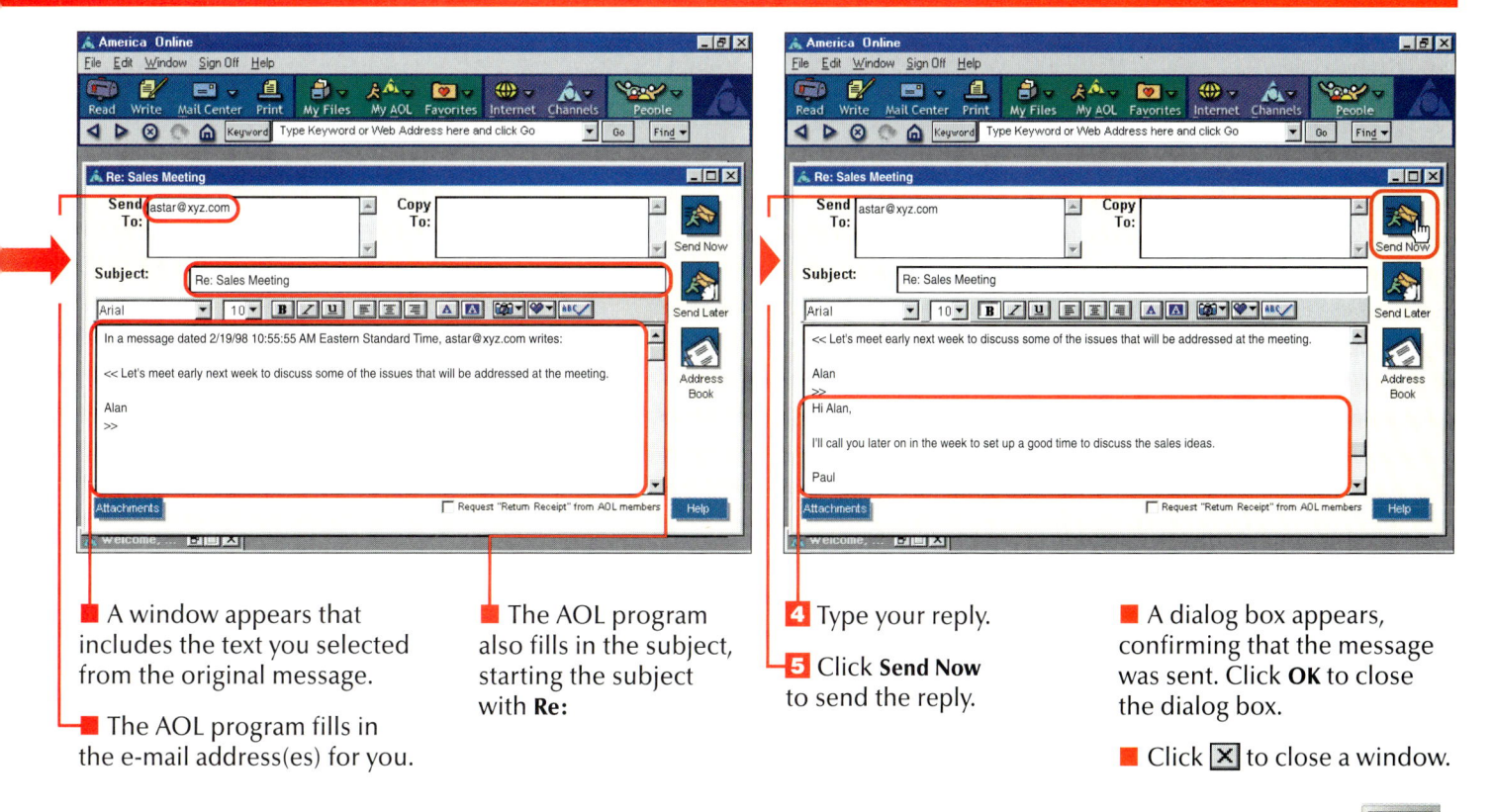

■ A window appears that includes the text you selected from the original message.

■ The AOL program fills in the e-mail address(es) for you.

■ The AOL program also fills in the subject, starting the subject with **Re:**.

4 Type your reply.

5 Click **Send Now** to send the reply.

■ A dialog box appears, confirming that the message was sent. Click **OK** to close the dialog box.

■ Click ☒ to close a window.

69

FORWARD A MESSAGE

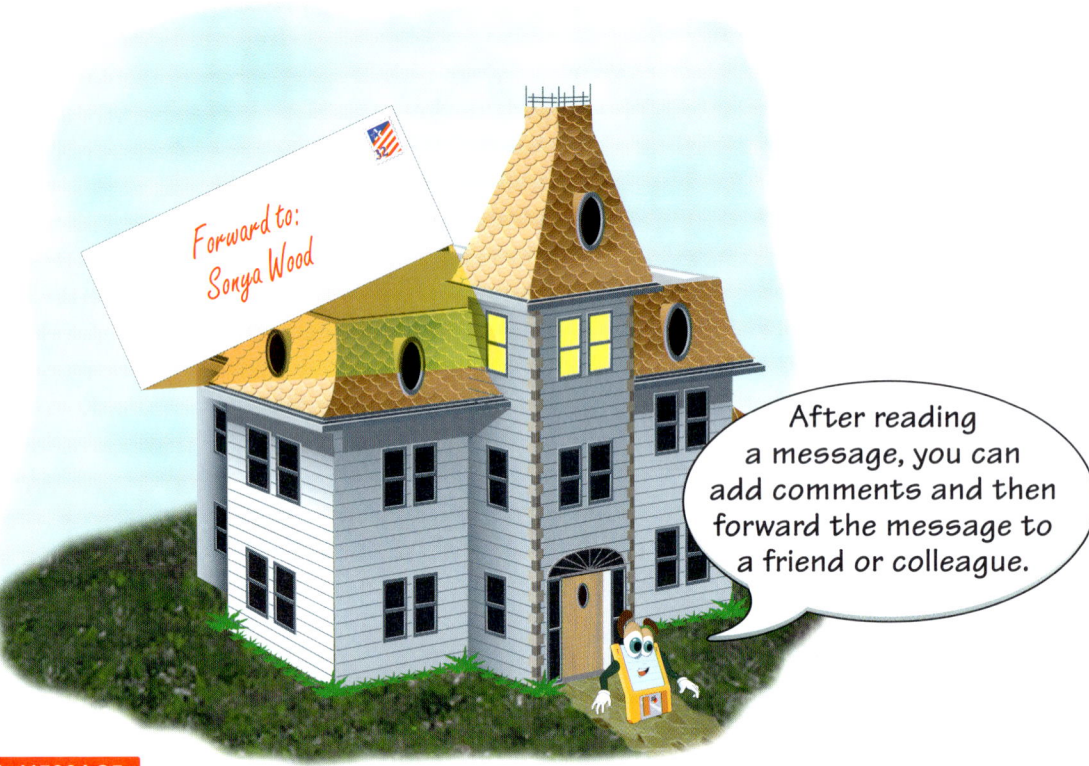

After reading a message, you can add comments and then forward the message to a friend or colleague.

FORWARD A MESSAGE

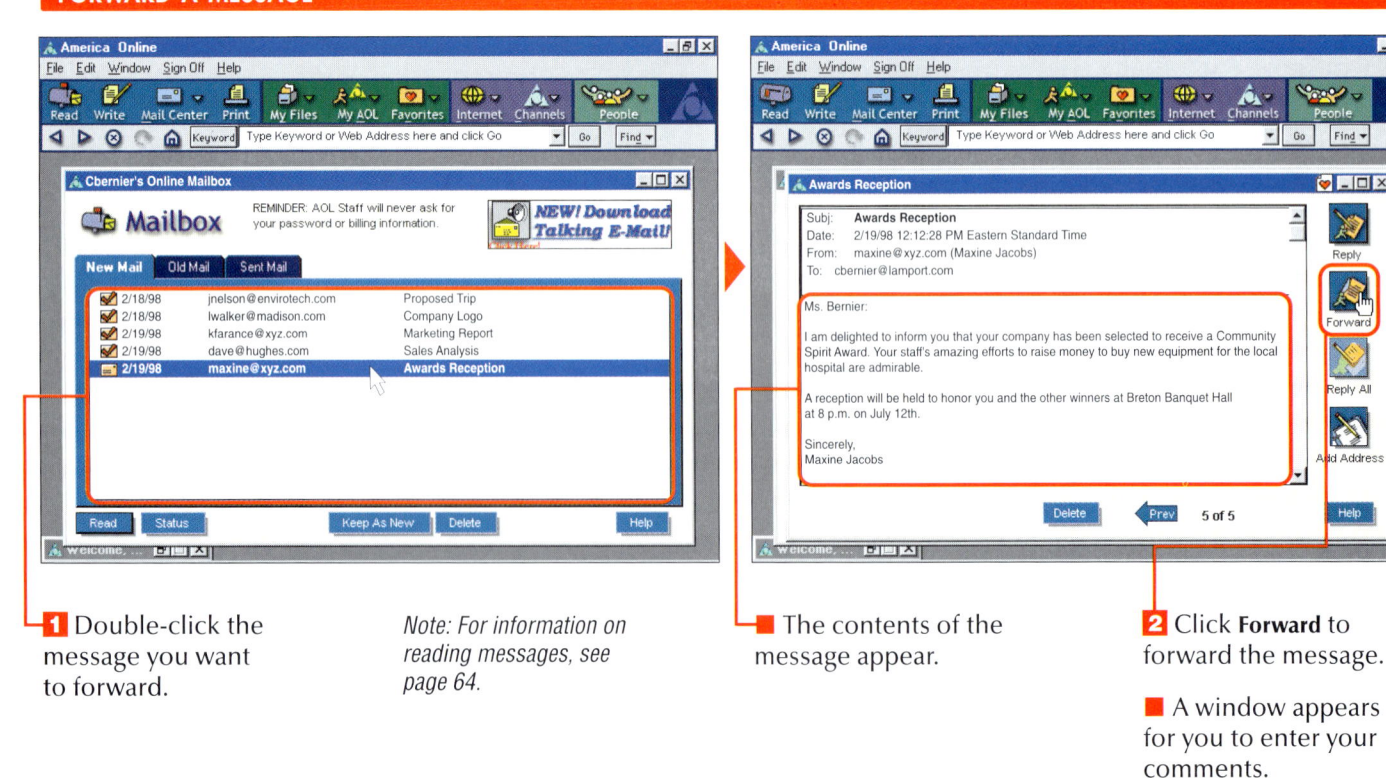

1 Double-click the message you want to forward.

Note: For information on reading messages, see page 64.

■ The contents of the message appear.

2 Click **Forward** to forward the message.

■ A window appears for you to enter your comments.

READ AND COMPOSE E-MAIL

What will a forwarded message look like?

The person receiving the message will see the comments you typed, followed by the forwarded message.

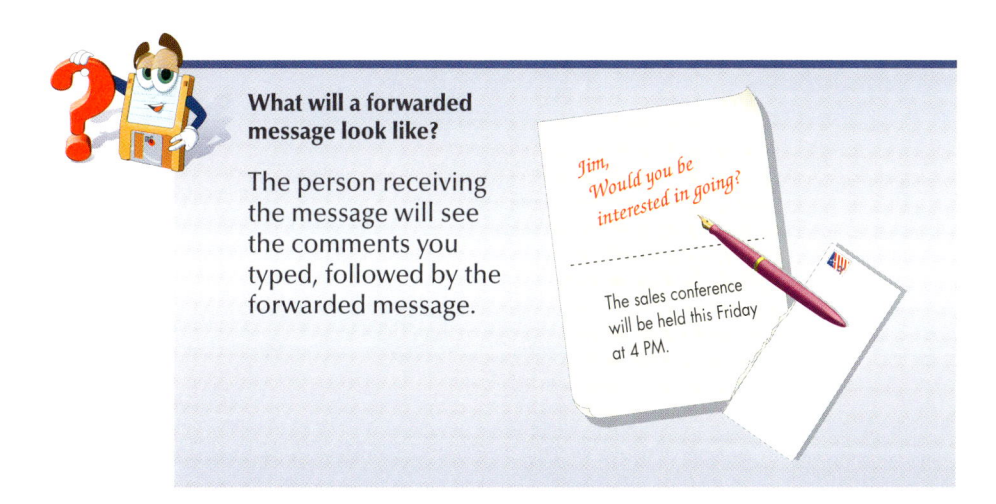

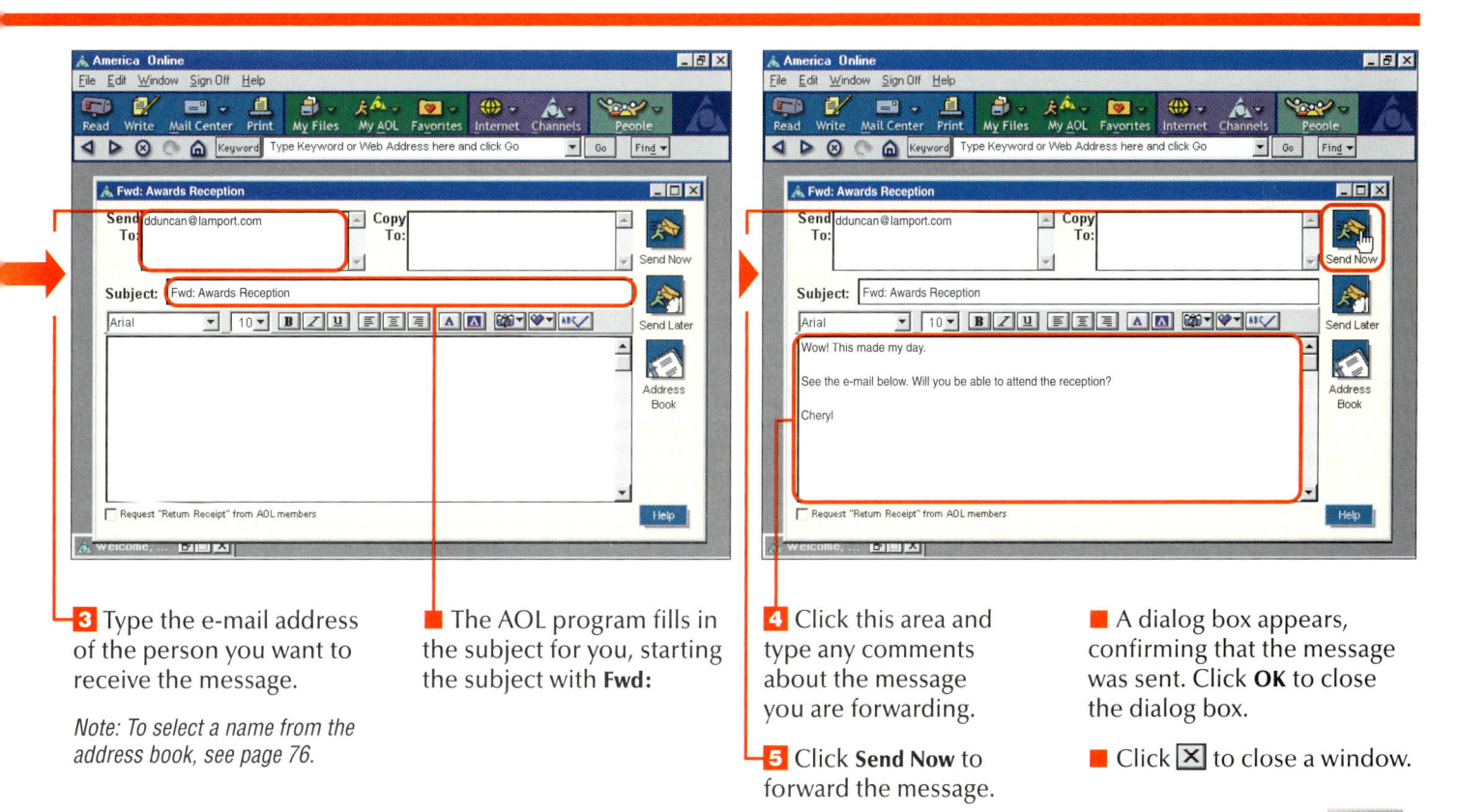

---

3 Type the e-mail address of the person you want to receive the message.

Note: To select a name from the address book, see page 76.

■ The AOL program fills in the subject for you, starting the subject with **Fwd:**

4 Click this area and type any comments about the message you are forwarding.

5 Click **Send Now** to forward the message.

■ A dialog box appears, confirming that the message was sent. Click **OK** to close the dialog box.

■ Click ✕ to close a window.

71

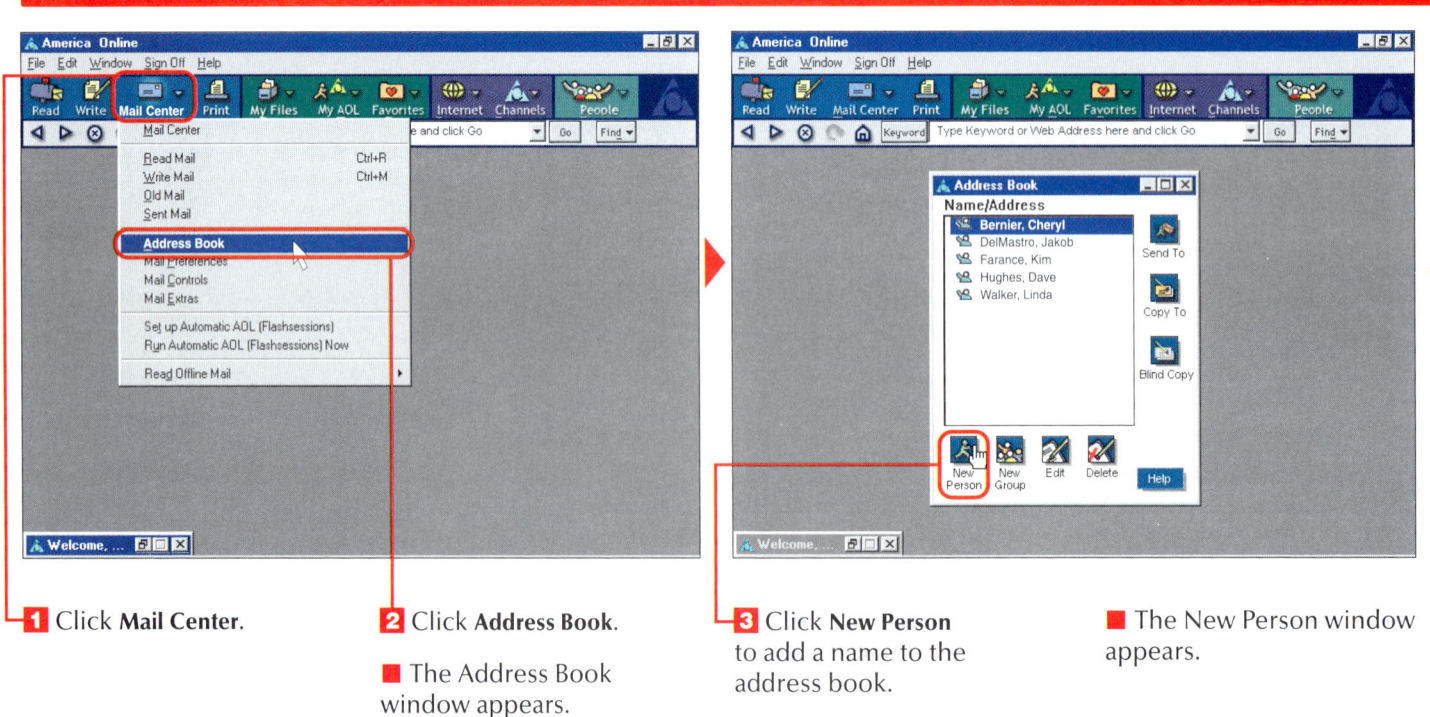

ADD A NAME TO THE ADDRESS BOOK

You can use the address book to store the e-mail addresses of people you frequently send messages to.

ADD A NAME TO THE ADDRESS BOOK

1 Click **Mail Center**.

2 Click **Address Book**.

■ The Address Book window appears.

3 Click **New Person** to add a name to the address book.

■ The New Person window appears.

72

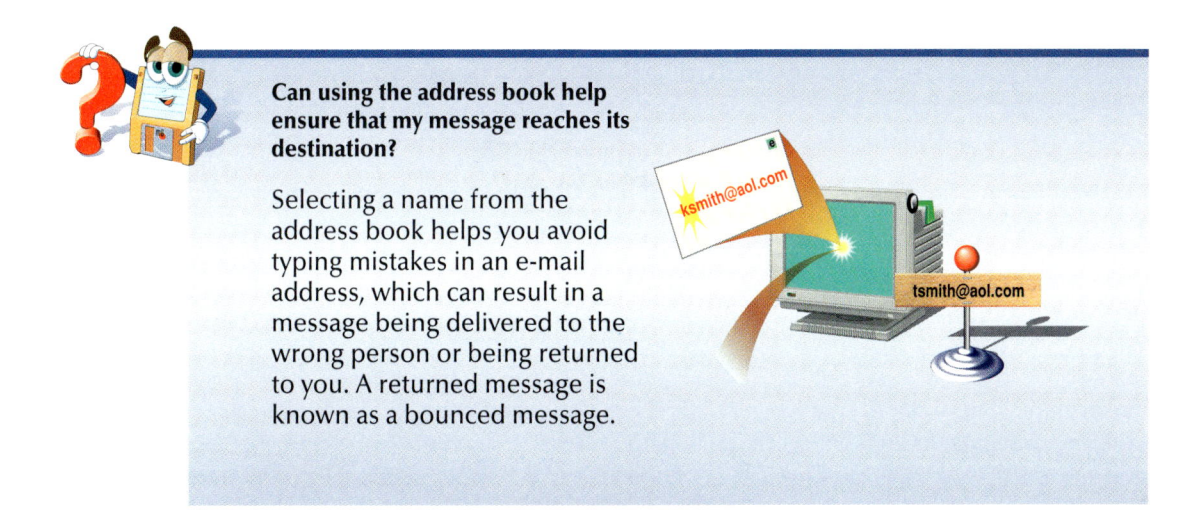

READ AND COMPOSE E-MAIL

Can using the address book help ensure that my message reaches its destination?

Selecting a name from the address book helps you avoid typing mistakes in an e-mail address, which can result in a message being delivered to the wrong person or being returned to you. A returned message is known as a bounced message.

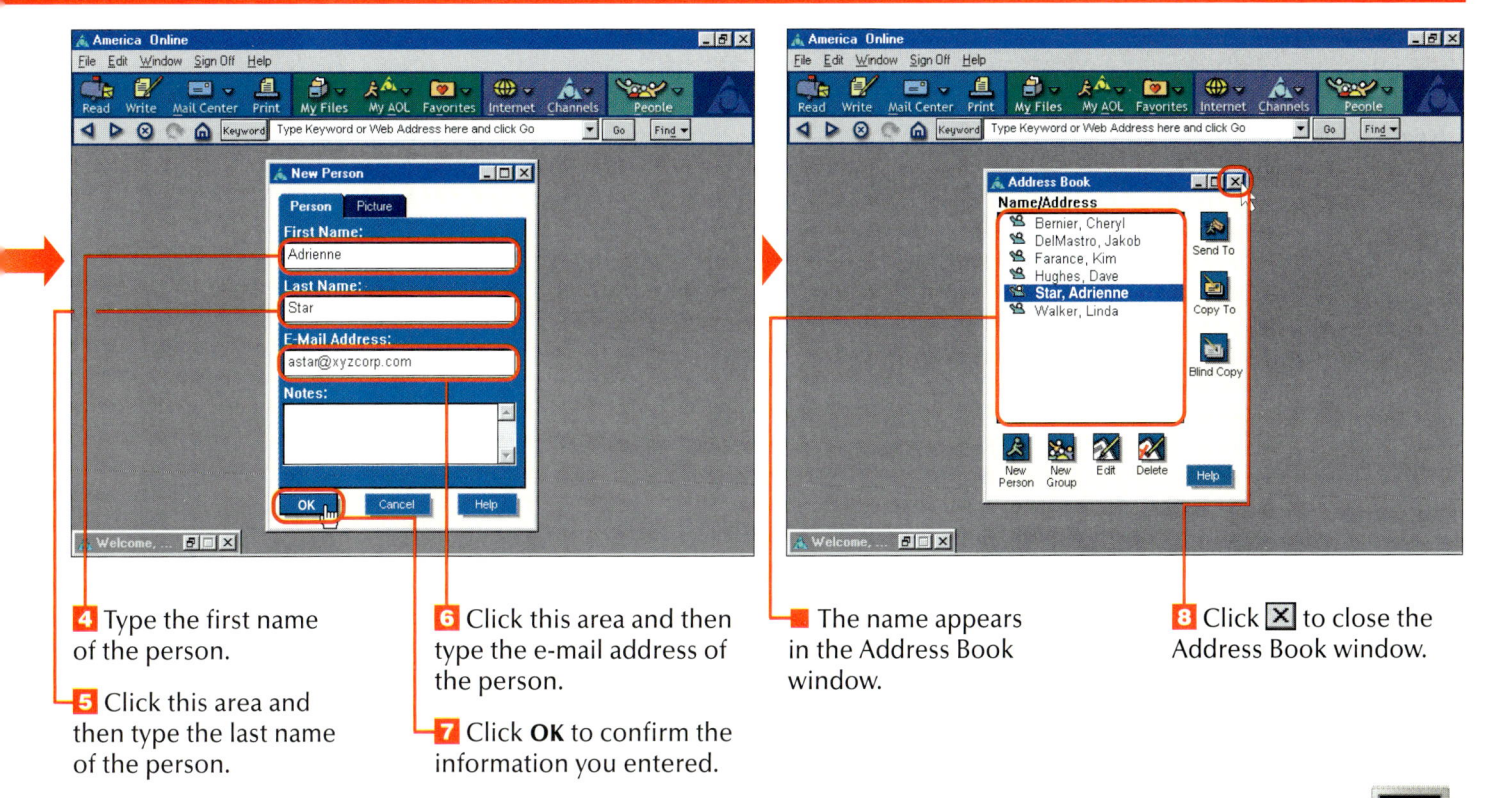

4 Type the first name of the person.

5 Click this area and then type the last name of the person.

6 Click this area and then type the e-mail address of the person.

7 Click **OK** to confirm the information you entered.

■ The name appears in the Address Book window.

8 Click ✕ to close the Address Book window.

73

ADD A GROUP TO THE ADDRESS BOOK

You can send a message to many people at once by creating a group in your address book.

You can create groups for colleagues, friends and family members. When sending a message, you can select the group name to have AOL send the message to every person in the group.

ADD A GROUP TO THE ADDRESS BOOK

1 Click **Mail Center**.

2 Click **Address Book**.

■ The Address Book window appears.

3 Click **New Group**.

■ The New Group window appears.

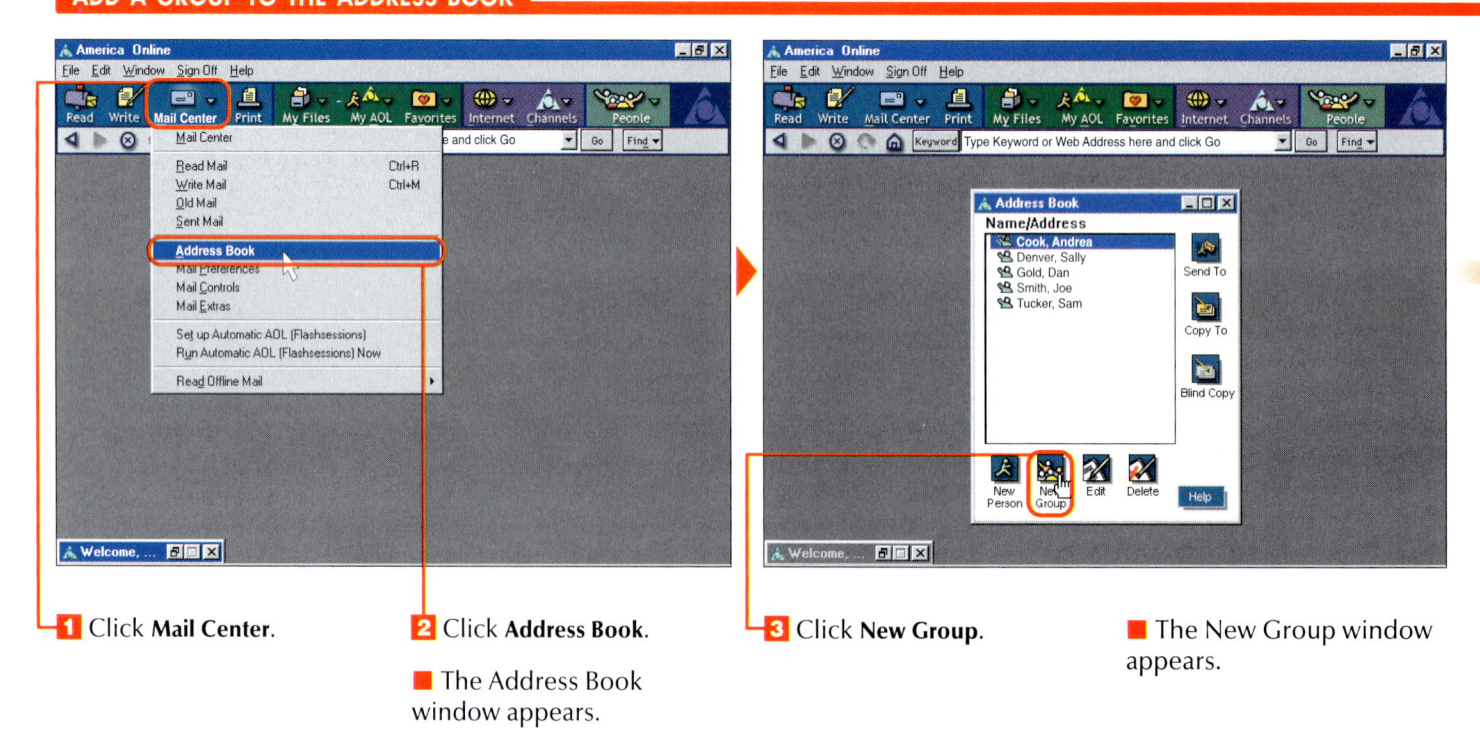

74

READ AND COMPOSE E-MAIL

Do I have to create a group to send a message to more than one person?

No. You can simply type the screen name or e-mail address of each person you want to receive the message, separated by commas, in the Write Mail window. See page 66.

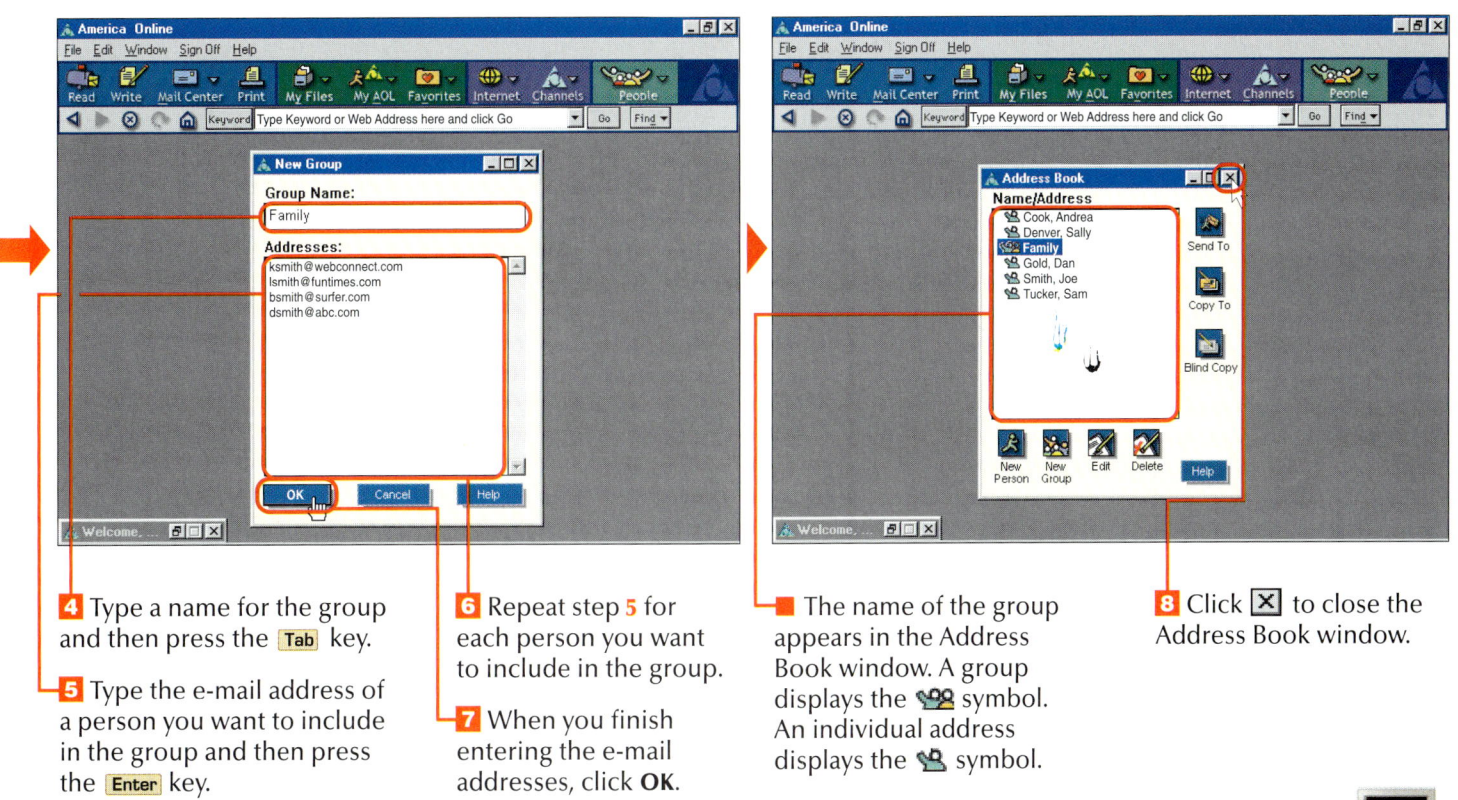

jsmith, kjohnson, mroney

---

4 Type a name for the group and then press the `Tab` key.

5 Type the e-mail address of a person you want to include in the group and then press the `Enter` key.

6 Repeat step **5** for each person you want to include in the group.

7 When you finish entering the e-mail addresses, click **OK**.

■ The name of the group appears in the Address Book window. A group displays the 👥 symbol. An individual address displays the 👤 symbol.

8 Click ❌ to close the Address Book window.

75

SELECT A NAME FROM THE ADDRESS BOOK

When sending a message, you can select the name of the person you want to receive the message from the address book.

Selecting names from the address book saves you from having to remember e-mail addresses you often use.

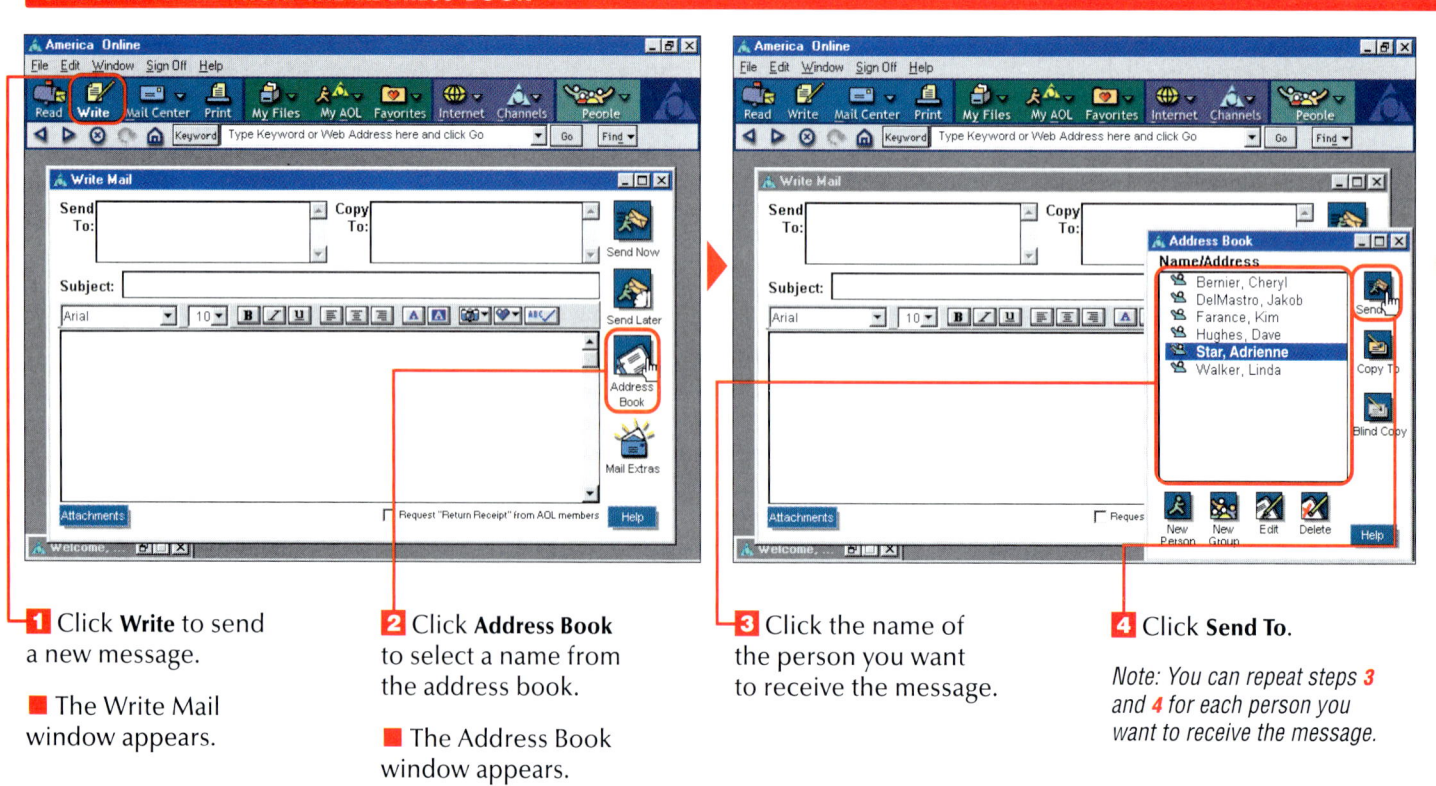

SELECT A NAME FROM THE ADDRESS BOOK

1 Click **Write** to send a new message.

■ The Write Mail window appears.

2 Click **Address Book** to select a name from the address book.

■ The Address Book window appears.

3 Click the name of the person you want to receive the message.

4 Click **Send To**.

Note: You can repeat steps 3 and 4 for each person you want to receive the message.

76

4

READ AND COMPOSE E-MAIL

How can I address a message I want to send?

Send To

Send the message to the person you specify.

Copy To

Send an exact copy of the message to a person who is not directly involved, but would be interested in the message.

Blind Copy

Send an exact copy of the message to a person without anyone else knowing that the person received the message.

5 To send a copy of the message to another person, click the person's name.

6 Click the way you want to send the copy.

Note: You can repeat steps 5 and 6 for each person you want to receive a copy of the message.

7 Click ⊠ to close the Address Book window.

■ This area displays the name of each person you selected from the address book.

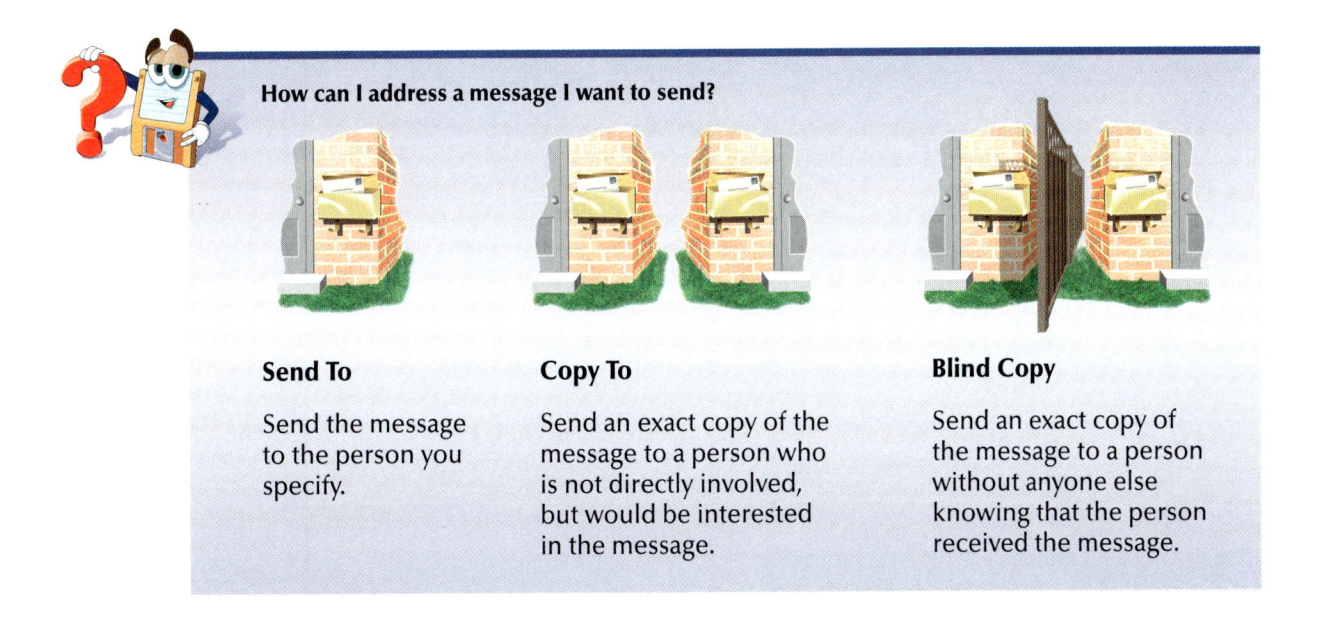

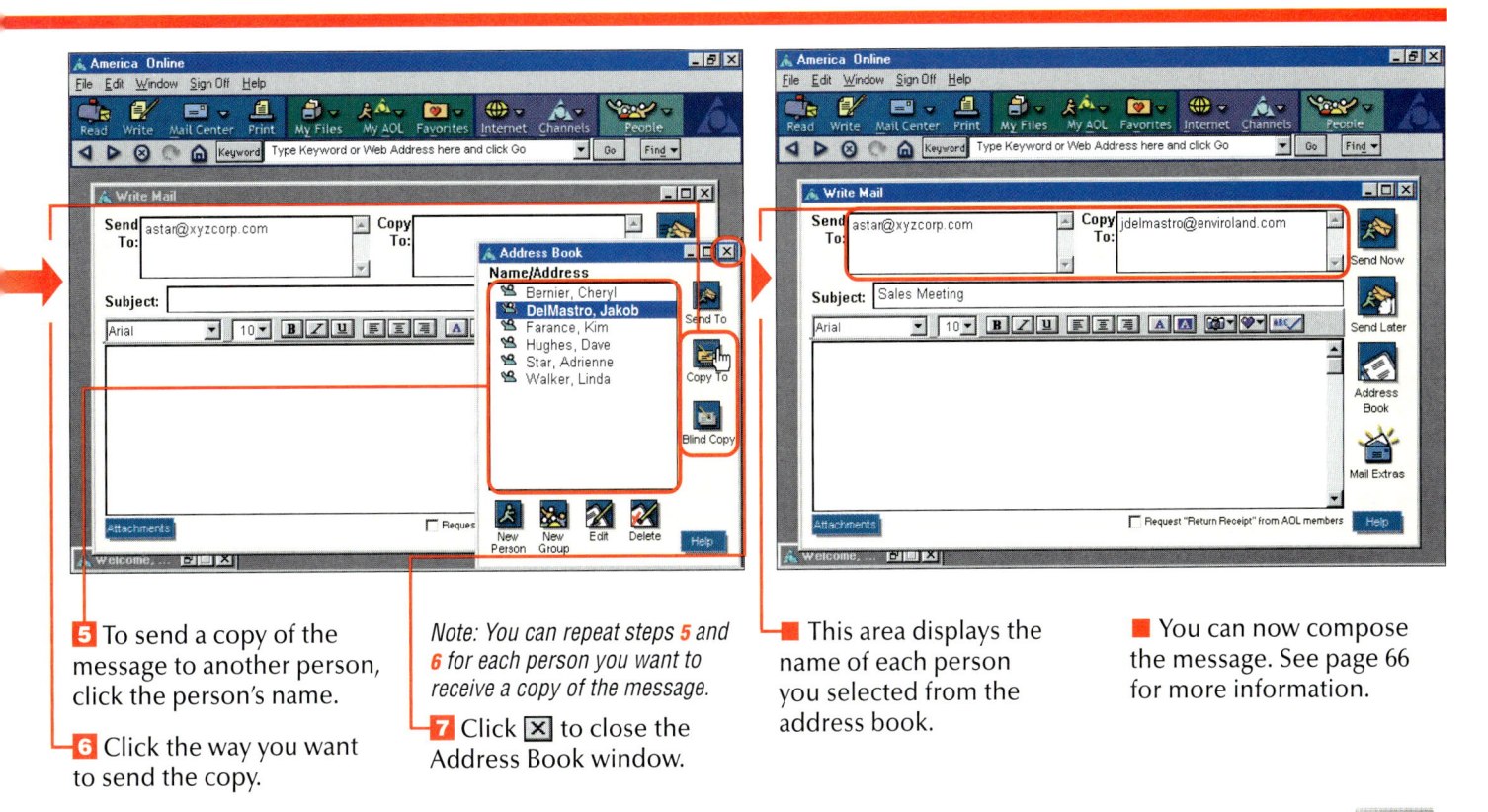

■ You can now compose the message. See page 66 for more information.

77

FIND AN E-MAIL ADDRESS

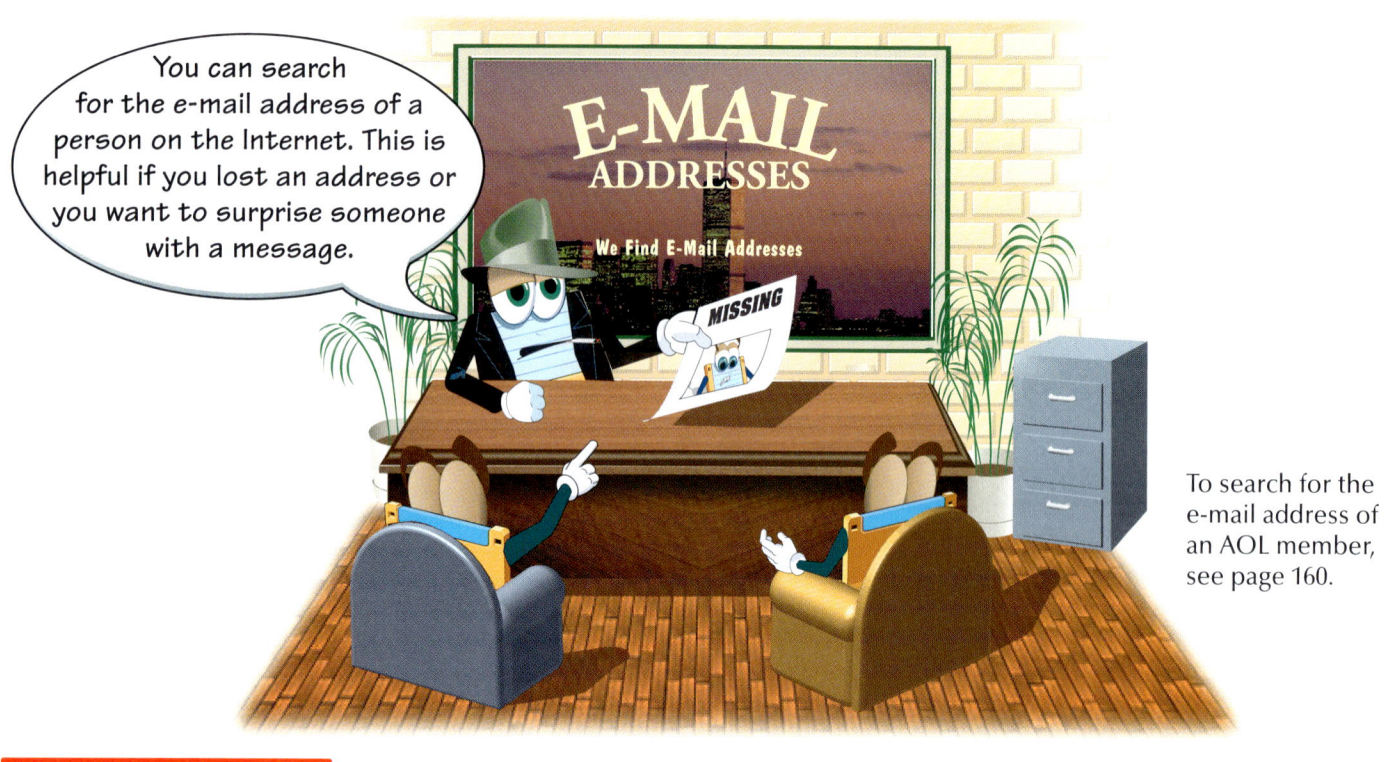

You can search for the e-mail address of a person on the Internet. This is helpful if you lost an address or you want to surprise someone with a message.

To search for the e-mail address of an AOL member, see page 160.

FIND AN E-MAIL ADDRESS

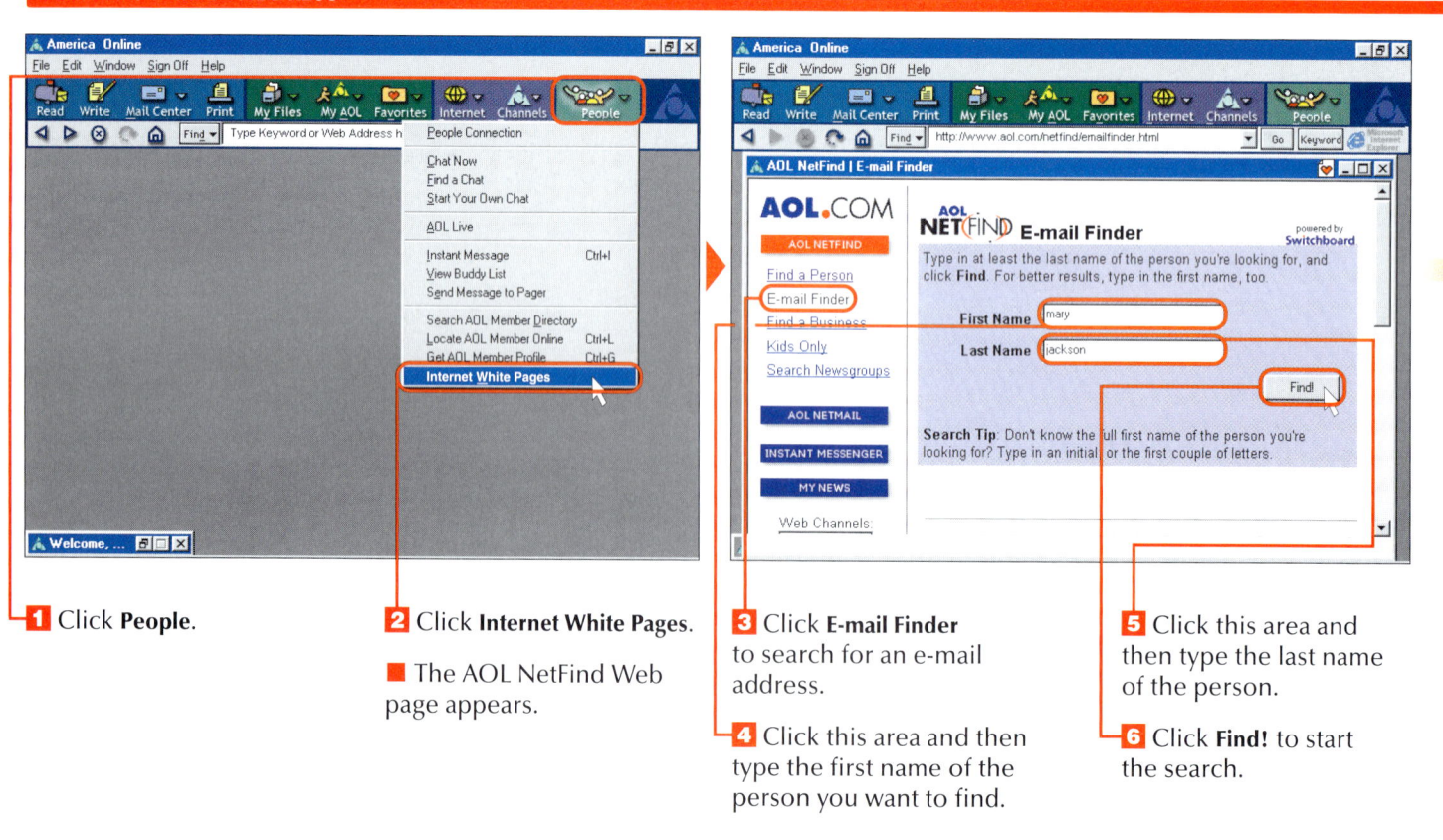

1 Click **People**.

2 Click **Internet White Pages**.

■ The AOL NetFind Web page appears.

3 Click **E-mail Finder** to search for an e-mail address.

4 Click this area and then type the first name of the person you want to find.

5 Click this area and then type the last name of the person.

6 Click **Find!** to start the search.

78

READ AND COMPOSE E-MAIL

Why can't I find an e-mail address?

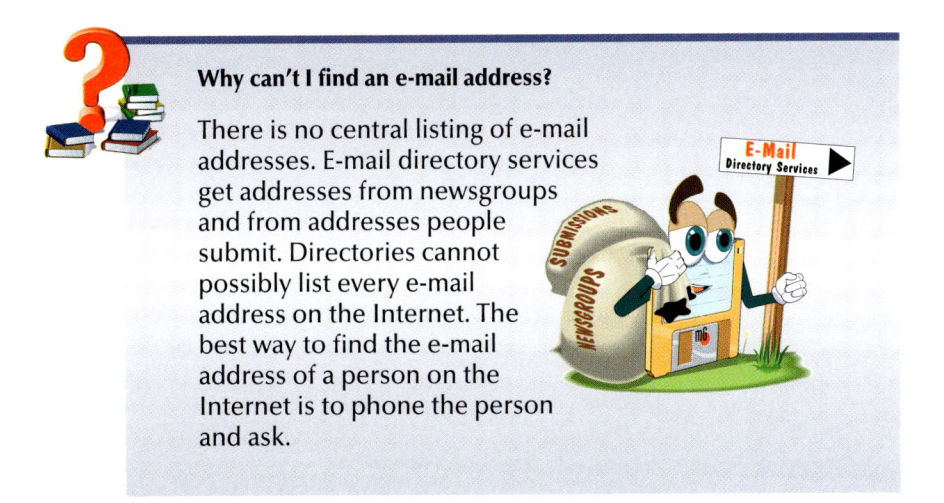

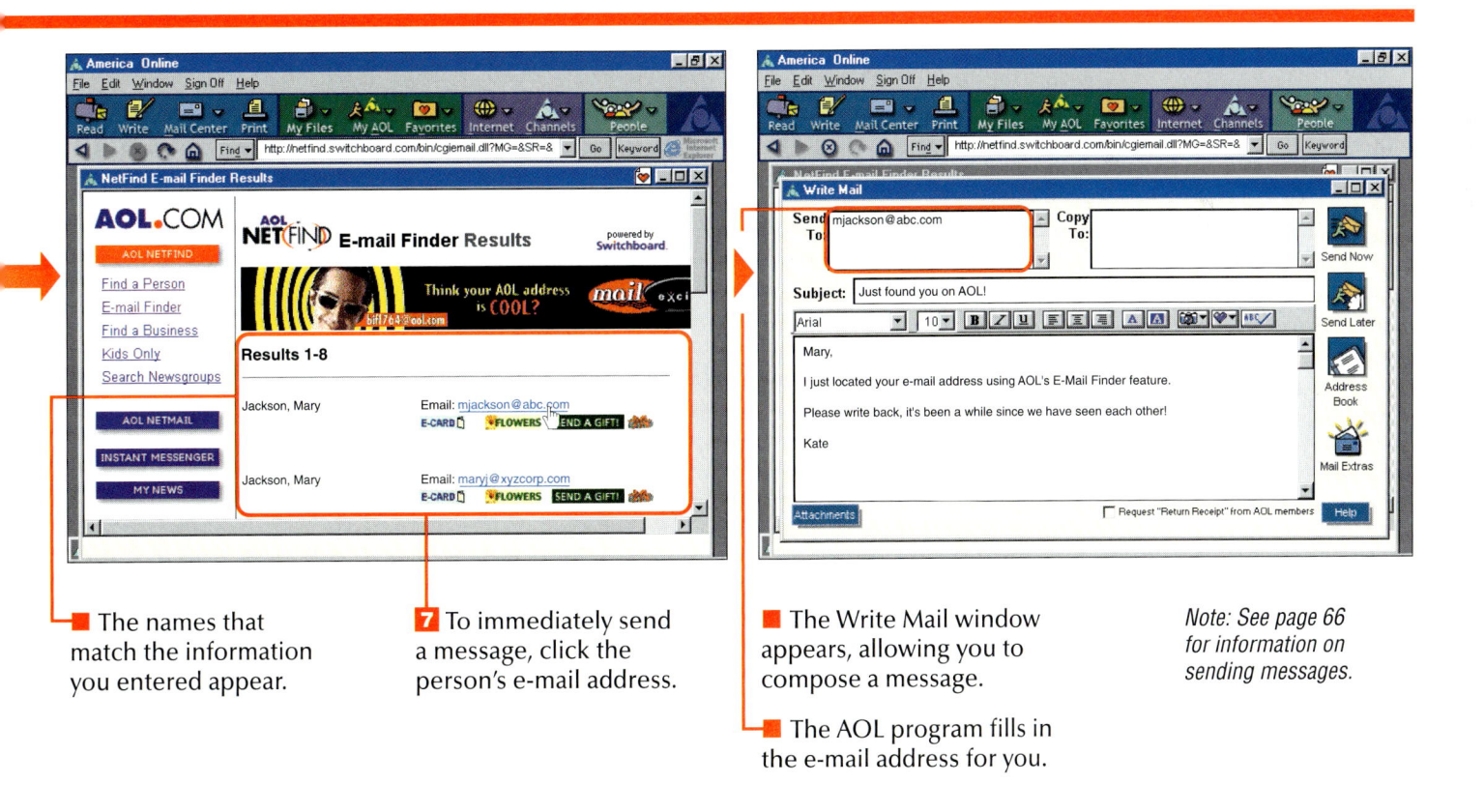

There is no central listing of e-mail addresses. E-mail directory services get addresses from newsgroups and from addresses people submit. Directories cannot possibly list every e-mail address on the Internet. The best way to find the e-mail address of a person on the Internet is to phone the person and ask.

- The names that match the information you entered appear.

7 To immediately send a message, click the person's e-mail address.

- The Write Mail window appears, allowing you to compose a message.

- The AOL program fills in the e-mail address for you.

Note: See page 66 for information on sending messages.

79

Jim,
I had a great time fishing this weekend. Thanks for inviting me. I've attached a picture of your catch. It's surely one for the record books!
Roger
Dictionary

CHAPTER 5

WORK WITH E-MAIL

What are the advantages of e-mail? In this chapter you will learn how to work with your messages to increase their effectiveness, as well as how to change your send and receive options.

Print a Message 82

Save a Message 83

Delete a Message 84

Mark Read Message as New 85

Attach a File to a Message 86

Download an Attached File 88

Spell Check a Message 90

Change Font and Font Size 92

Bold, Italic and Underline 94

Change Text Alignment 95

Change Text Color 96

Change Background Color 97

Request Return Receipt 98

Add Favorite Place to Message 99

Send a Message Later 100

Unsend a Message 102

Change How Long AOL Keeps
    Read Messages 103

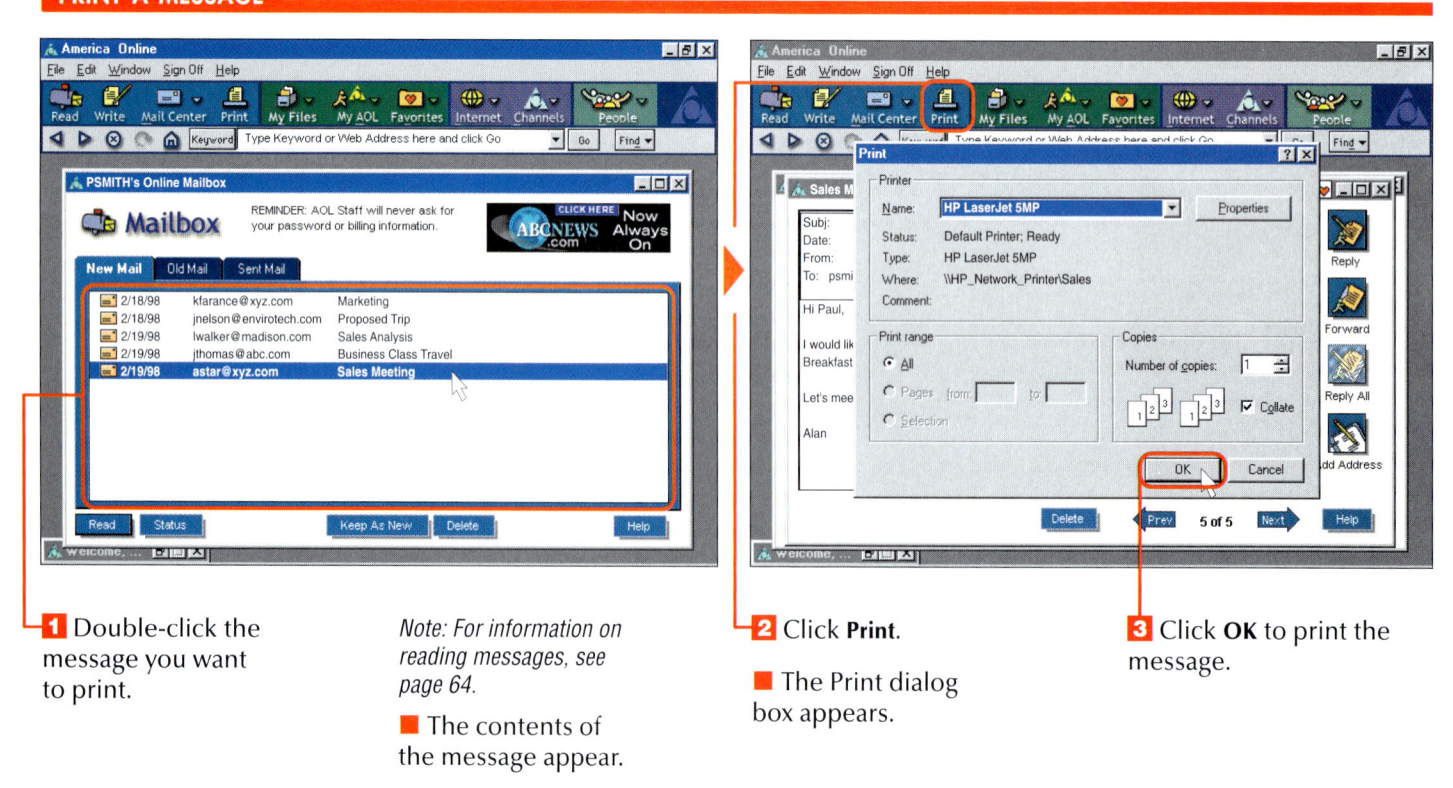

PRINT A MESSAGE

You can produce a paper copy of a message.

A printed message includes the date, your screen name and the page number at the bottom of the page.

PRINT A MESSAGE

1 Double-click the message you want to print.

Note: For information on reading messages, see page 64.

■ The contents of the message appear.

2 Click **Print**.

■ The Print dialog box appears.

3 Click **OK** to print the message.

SAVE A MESSAGE

WORK WITH E-MAIL — 5

When you receive an important message, you may want to save the message.

AOL will keep a message you have read for 3 days and a message you have not read for about 27 days. If you want to keep a message for a longer time period, you must save the message.

SAVE A MESSAGE

■ **1** To display the contents of the message you want to save, perform steps **1** to **3** on page 64.

■ **2** Click **File**.

■ **3** Click **Save to Personal Filing Cabinet**.

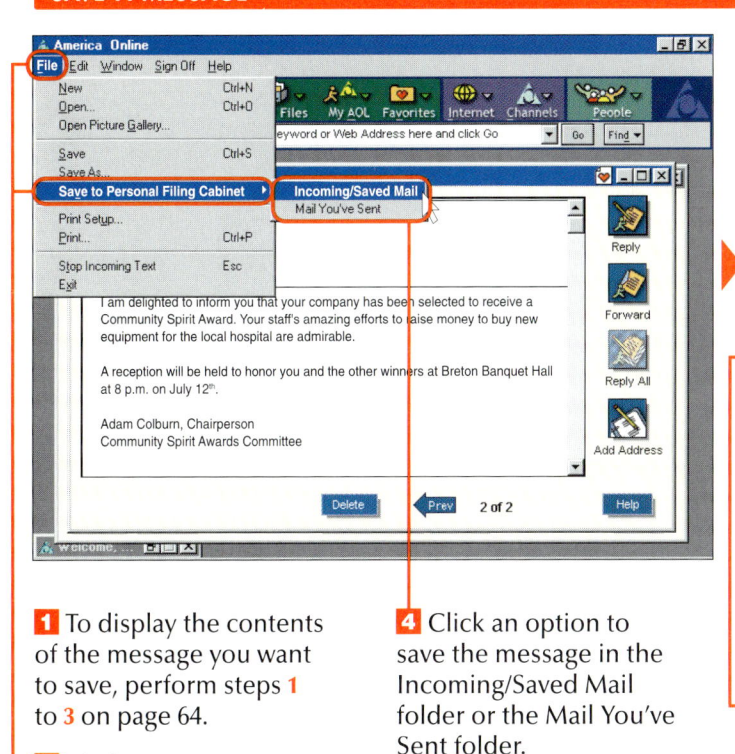

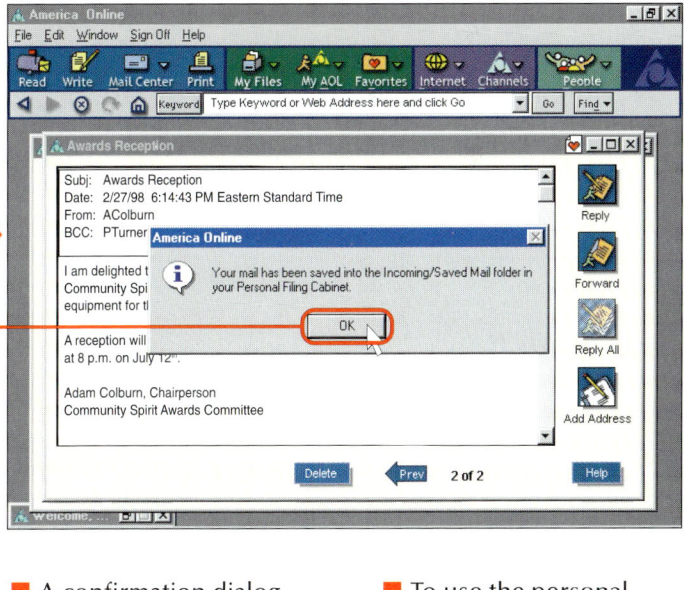

■ **4** Click an option to save the message in the Incoming/Saved Mail folder or the Mail You've Sent folder.

■ A confirmation dialog box appears.

■ **5** Click **OK** to close the dialog box.

■ To use the personal filing cabinet to view the message, see page 202.

83

DELETE A MESSAGE

> You can delete a message you no longer need. This prevents your mailbox from becoming cluttered with messages.

Messages are automatically deleted on a regular basis to keep the AOL computer system from overflowing with messages.

DELETE A MESSAGE

1 Click the message you want to delete.

2 Click **Delete**.

■ The message is deleted.

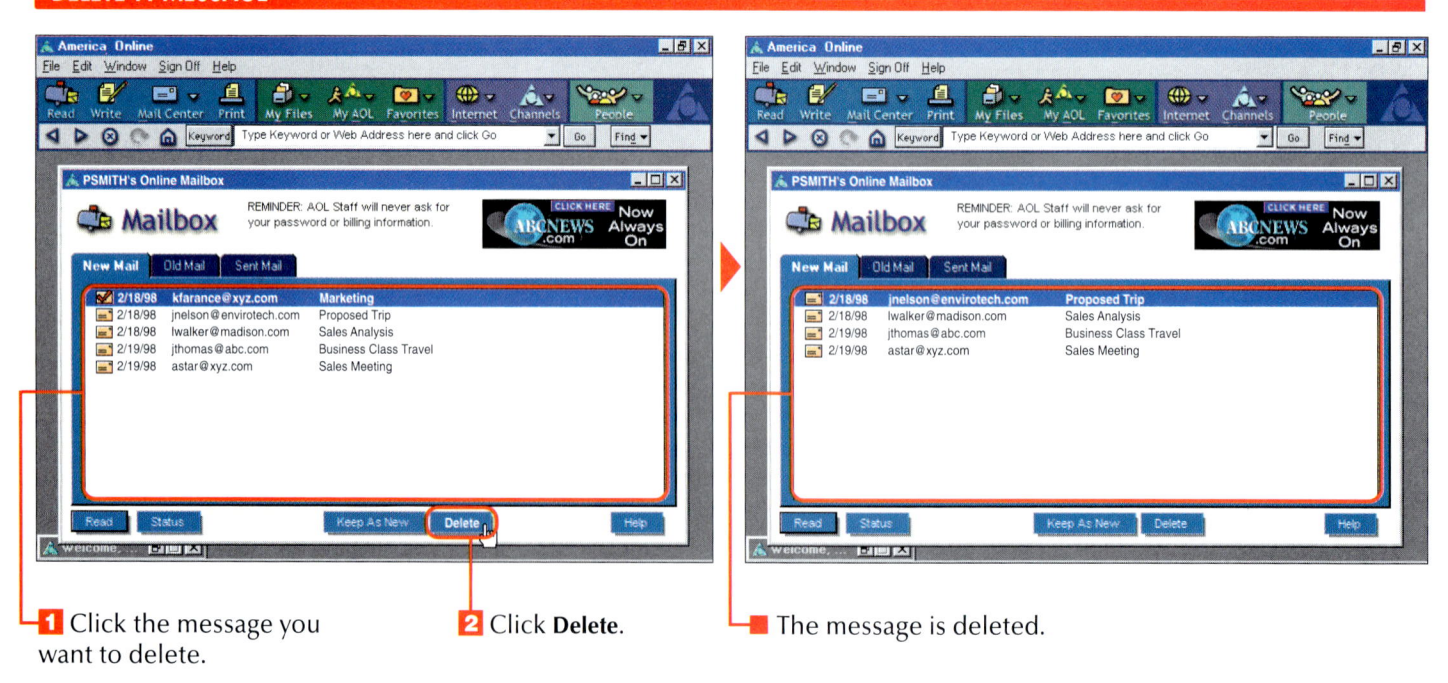

Note: For information on reading messages, see page 64.

MARK READ MESSAGE AS NEW

WORK WITH E-MAIL — 5

> You can mark a message you have read as a new message. This allows you to keep the message for a longer time period and can remind you to later review the message.

AOL will keep messages you have read for 3 days and messages you have not read for about 27 days.

MARK READ MESSAGE AS NEW

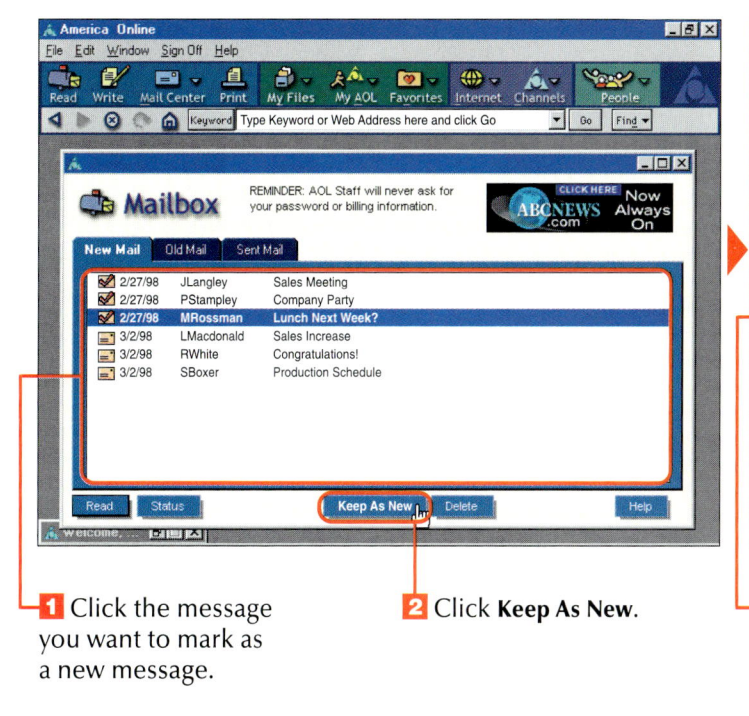

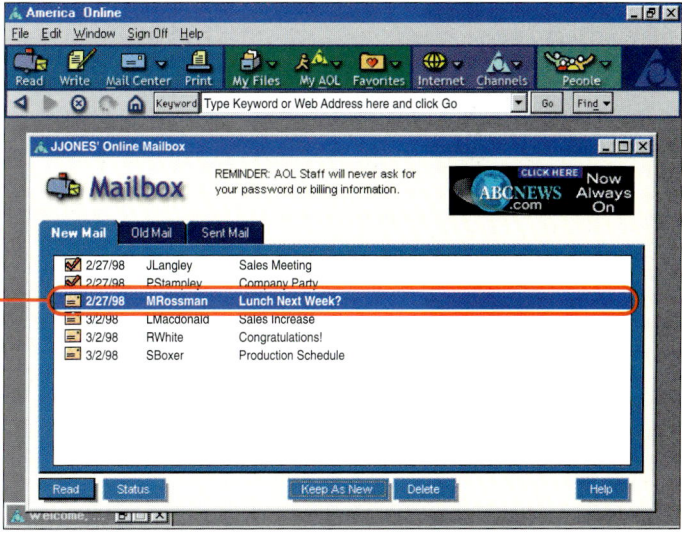

1 Click the message you want to mark as a new message.

2 Click **Keep As New**.

■ The symbol beside the message changes from ☑ to 📩 to indicate that the message is new.

85

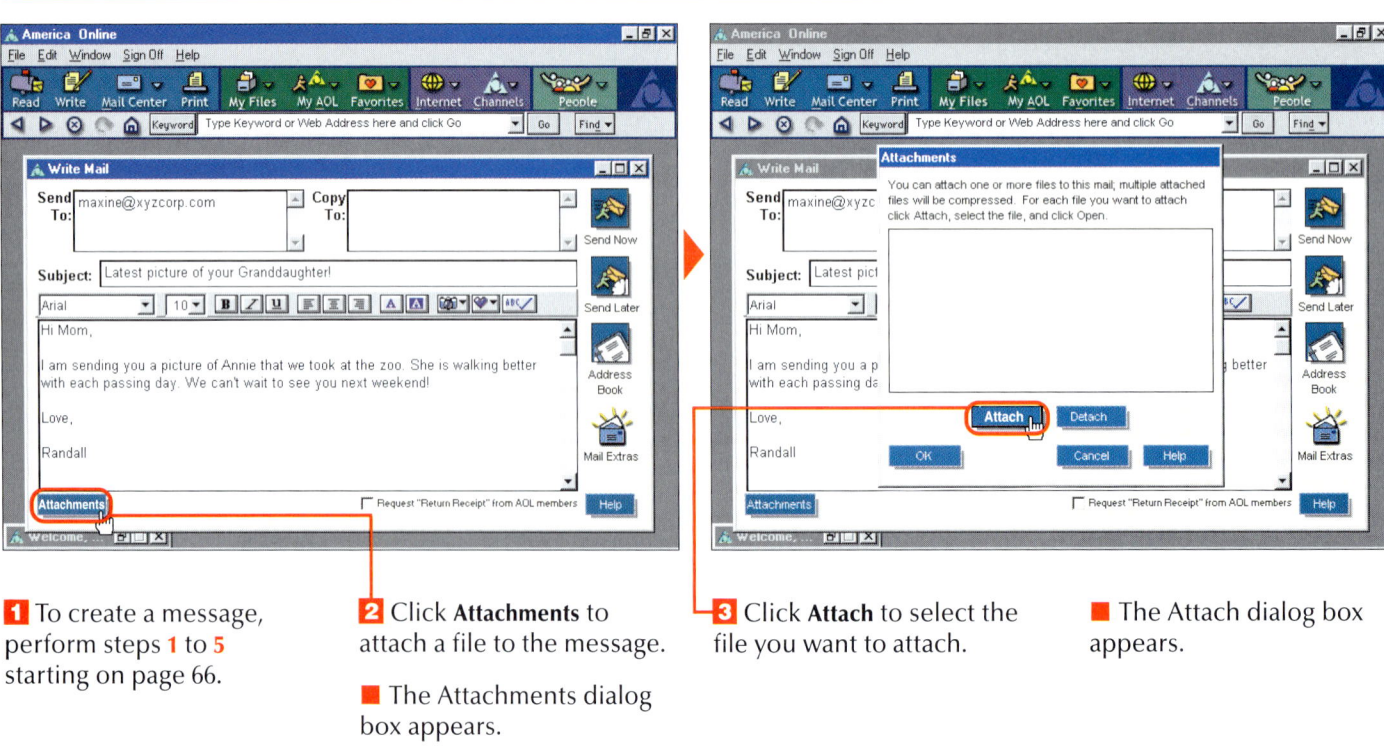

ATTACH A FILE TO A MESSAGE

You can attach a file to a message you are sending. Attaching a file is useful when you want to include additional information with a message.

ATTACH A FILE TO A MESSAGE

1 To create a message, perform steps **1** to **5** starting on page 66.

2 Click **Attachments** to attach a file to the message.

■ The Attachments dialog box appears.

3 Click **Attach** to select the file you want to attach.

■ The Attach dialog box appears.

86

WORK WITH E-MAIL

What types of files can I attach to a message?

You can attach files such as documents, pictures, programs, sounds and videos to a message. The computer receiving the message must have the necessary hardware and software to display or play the file.

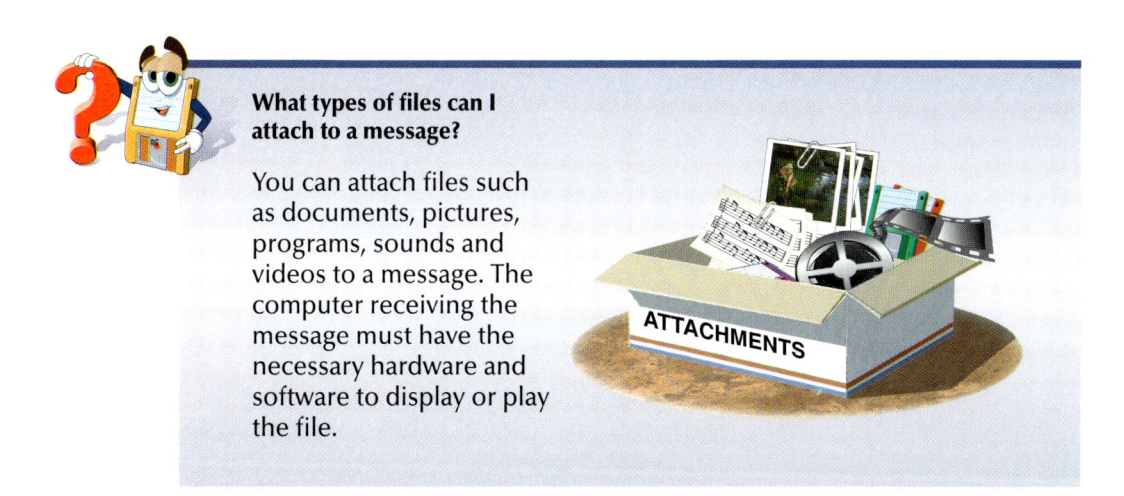

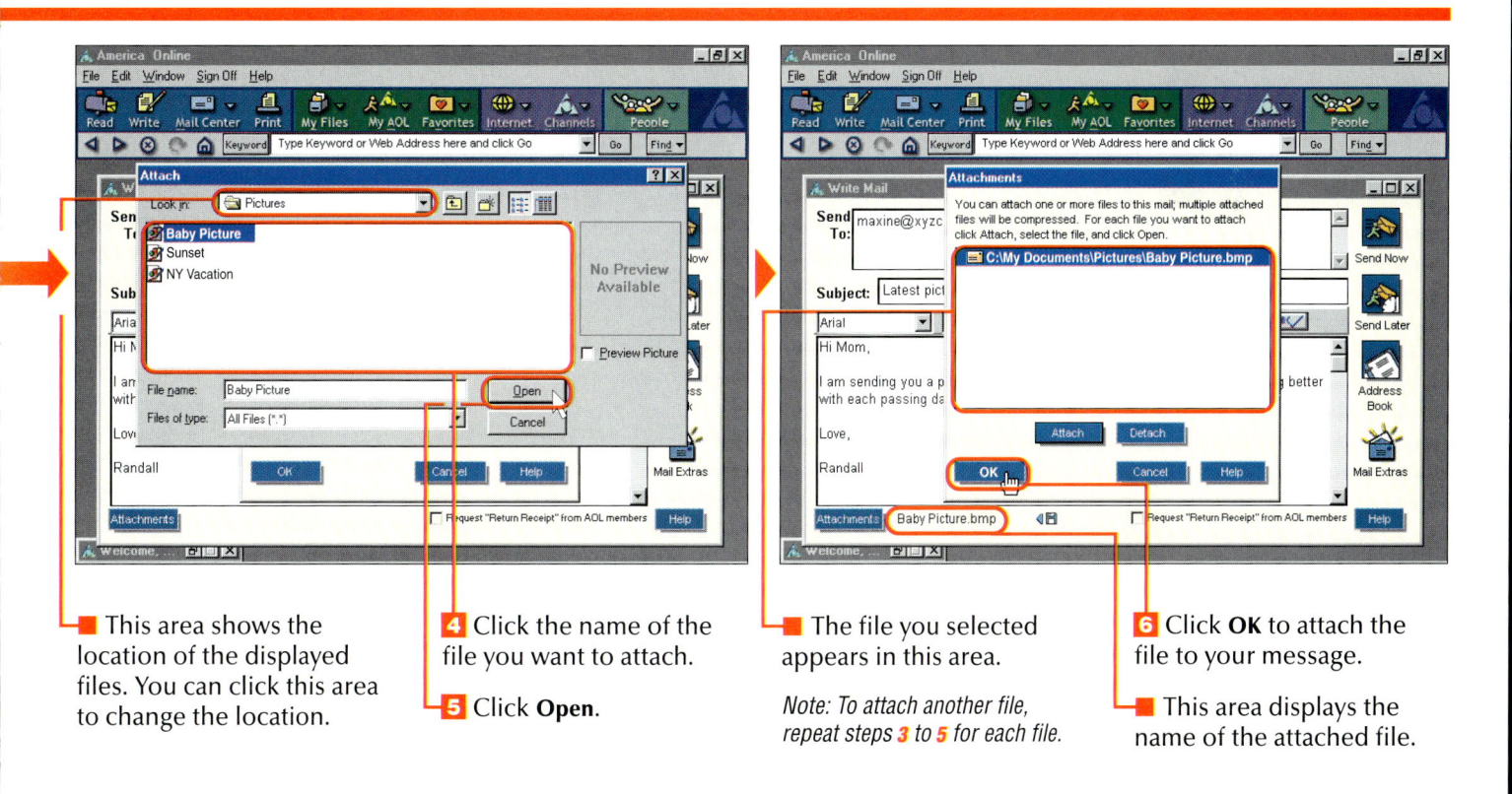

■ This area shows the location of the displayed files. You can click this area to change the location.

◪ Click the name of the file you want to attach.

◪ Click **Open**.

■ The file you selected appears in this area.

Note: To attach another file, repeat steps 3 to 5 for each file.

◪ Click **OK** to attach the file to your message.

■ This area displays the name of the attached file.

87

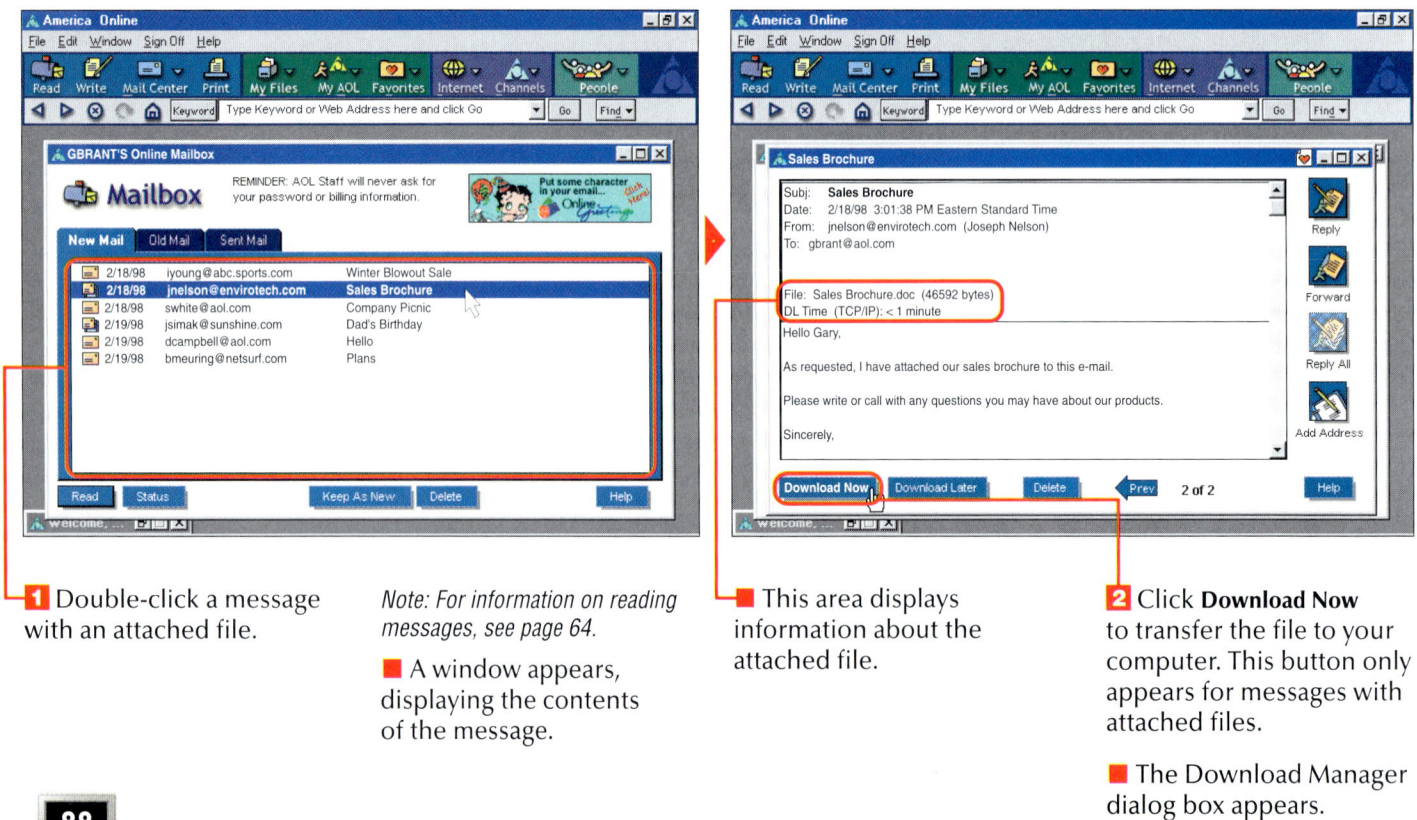

DOWNLOAD AN ATTACHED FILE

When you receive a message with an attached file, you can transfer the file to your computer to view the contents of the file.

Attached files can contain text, images, sounds, videos or programs. Your computer must have the necessary software and hardware to display or play the files you receive.

DOWNLOAD AN ATTACHED FILE

1 Double-click a message with an attached file.

Note: For information on reading messages, see page 64.

■ A window appears, displaying the contents of the message.

■ This area displays information about the attached file.

2 Click **Download Now** to transfer the file to your computer. This button only appears for messages with attached files.

■ The Download Manager dialog box appears.

88

WORK WITH E-MAIL

Is it safe to download attached files?

You should only download files sent by people you trust. A file containing a virus could damage the contents of your computer. You can get anti-virus programs, such as Norton AntiVirus, that can help protect your computer from viruses.

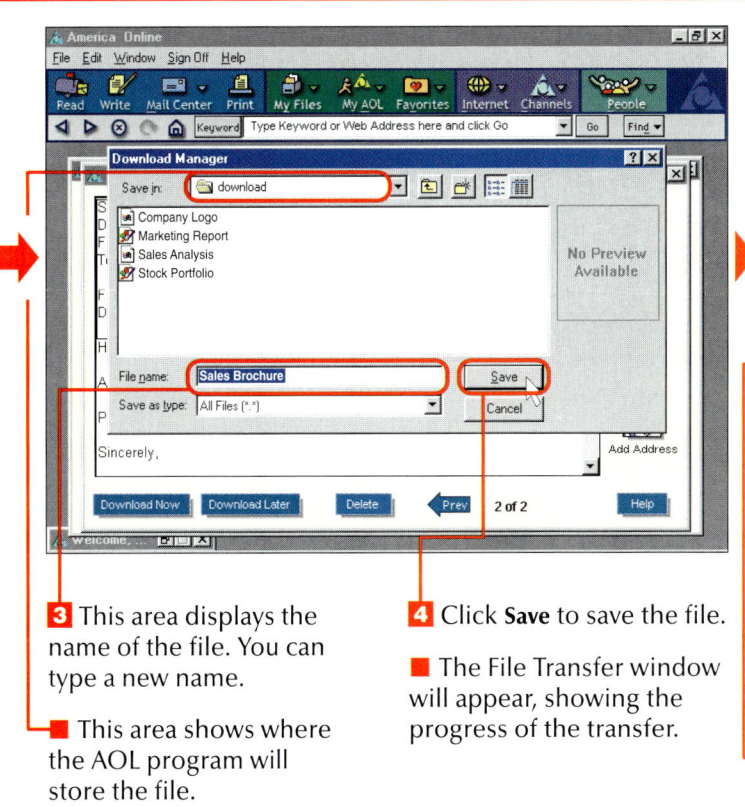

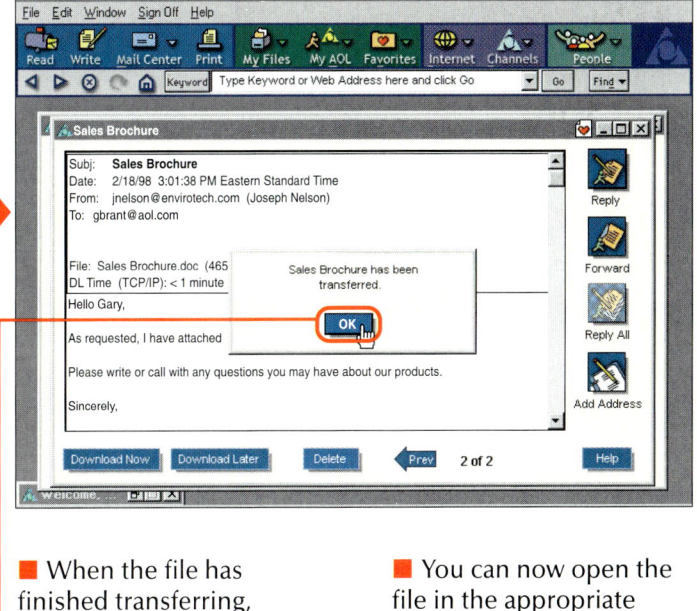

3 This area displays the name of the file. You can type a new name.

■ This area shows where the AOL program will store the file.

4 Click **Save** to save the file.

■ The File Transfer window will appear, showing the progress of the transfer.

■ When the file has finished transferring, a confirmation dialog box may appear.

5 Click **OK** to close the dialog box.

■ You can now open the file in the appropriate program.

Note: The contents of some files may automatically appear on your screen.

89

SPELL CHECK A MESSAGE

You can quickly find and correct all the spelling errors in a message you are about to send.

SPELL CHECK A MESSAGE

■ **1** To create a message, perform steps **1** to **5** starting on page 66.

■ **2** To start the spell check at the beginning of your message, click to the left of the first character in the message.

■ **3** Click [ABC] to start the spell check.

■ The Check Spelling dialog box appears if your message contains a spelling error.

■ This area displays a misspelled word.

■ Suggestions to correct the word appear in this area.

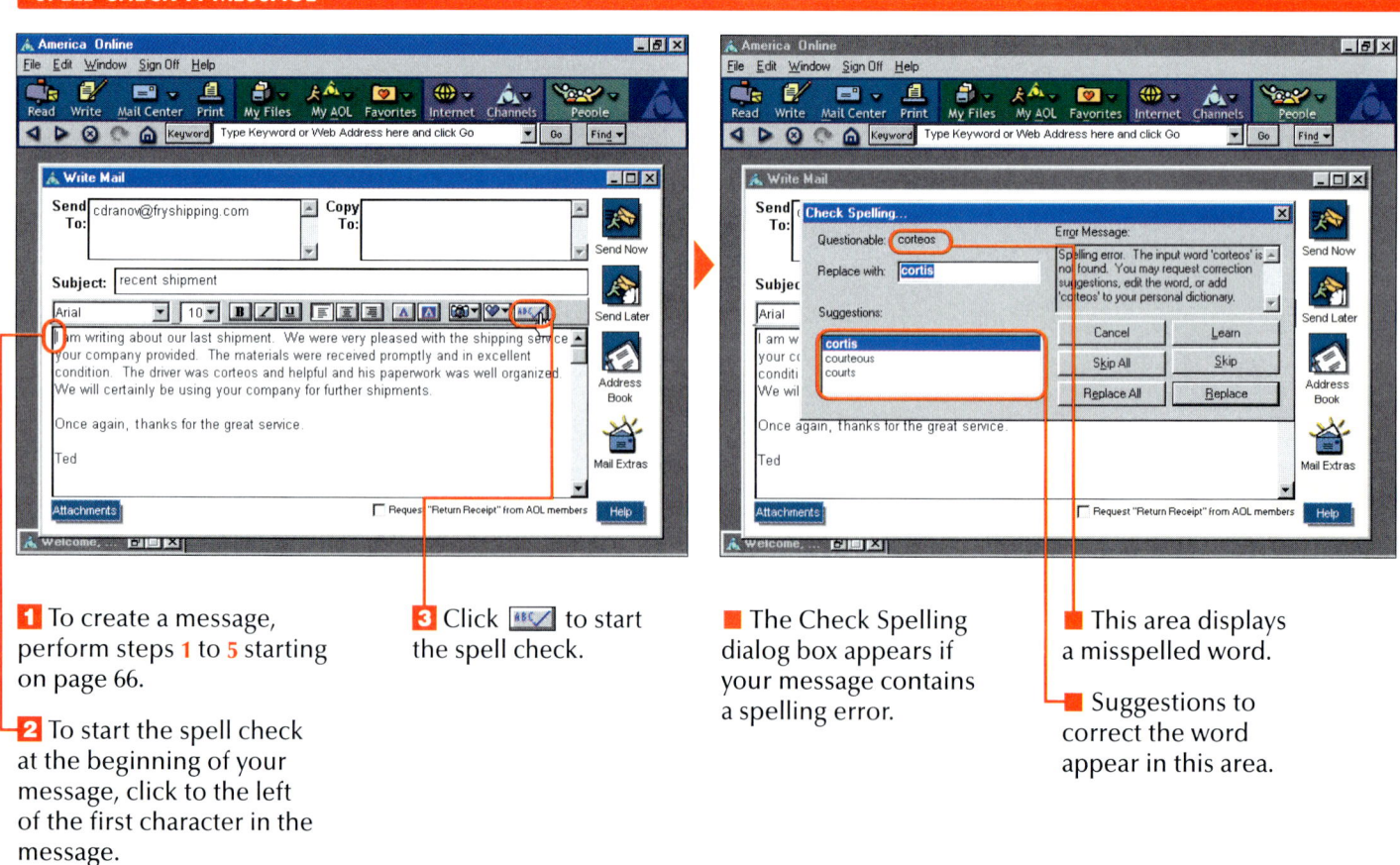

90

WORK WITH E-MAIL

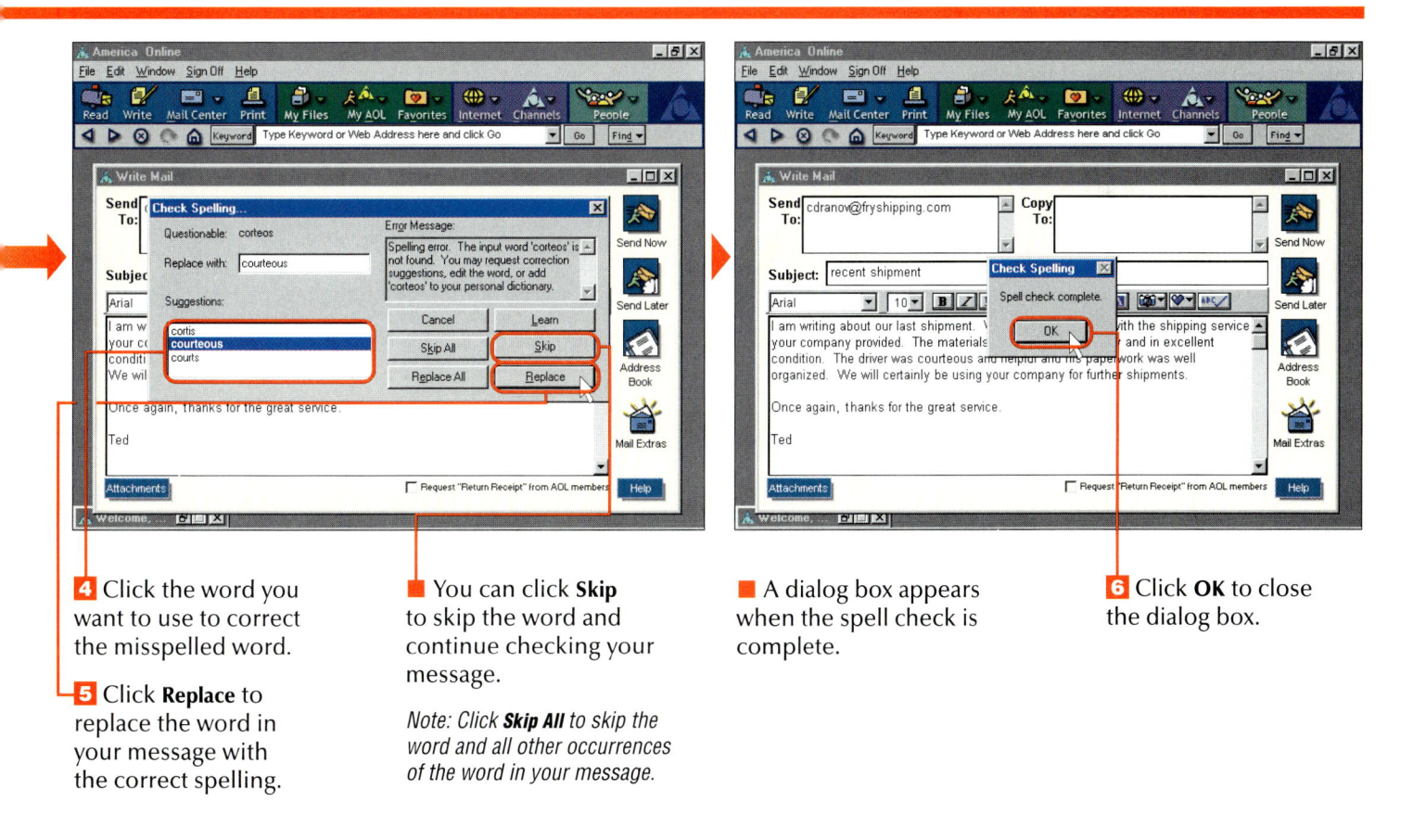

Will the AOL program find all the spelling errors in my message?

The AOL program compares every word in your message to words in its own dictionary. If a word does not exist in the dictionary, the program considers the word misspelled.

The AOL program will not find a correctly spelled word used in the wrong context such as "The girl is **sit** years old." You should carefully reread your message to find this type of error.

■ **4** Click the word you want to use to correct the misspelled word.

■ **5** Click **Replace** to replace the word in your message with the correct spelling.

■ You can click **Skip** to skip the word and continue checking your message.

*Note: Click **Skip All** to skip the word and all other occurrences of the word in your message.*

■ A dialog box appears when the spell check is complete.

■ **6** Click **OK** to close the dialog box.

91

CHANGE FONT AND FONT SIZE

You can change the design and size of text in a message.

Changing the design and size of text allows you to emphasize text and make your message more interesting and attractive.

CHANGE FONT

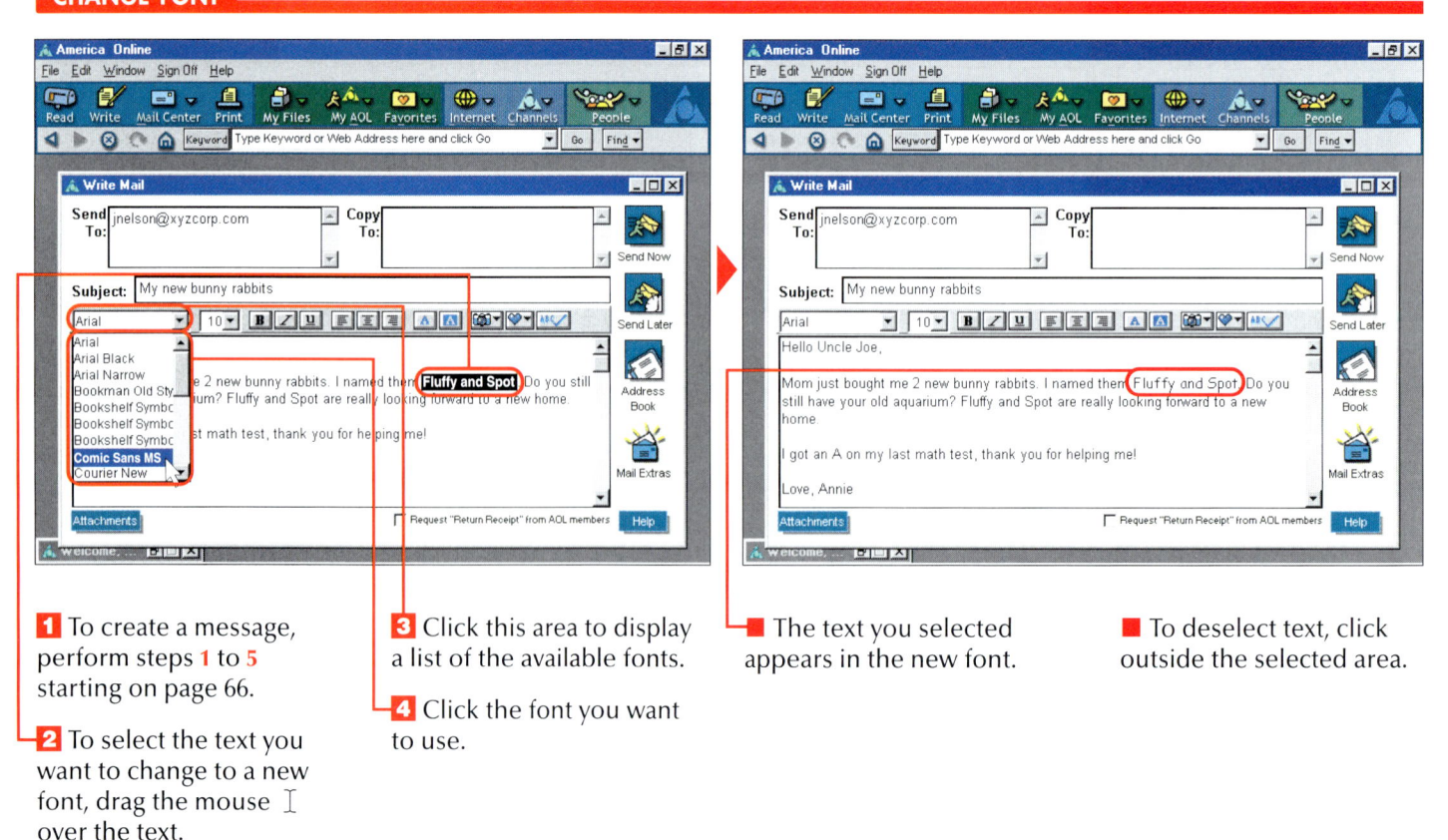

1 To create a message, perform steps **1** to **5** starting on page 66.

2 To select the text you want to change to a new font, drag the mouse I over the text.

3 Click this area to display a list of the available fonts.

4 Click the font you want to use.

■ The text you selected appears in the new font.

■ To deselect text, click outside the selected area.

92

WORK WITH E-MAIL

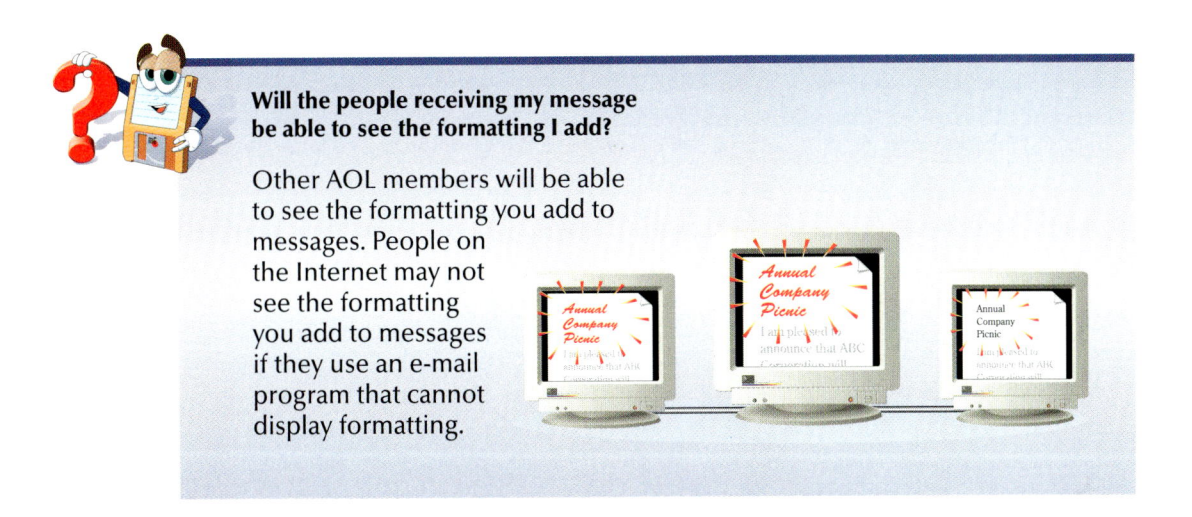

Will the people receiving my message be able to see the formatting I add?

Other AOL members will be able to see the formatting you add to messages. People on the Internet may not see the formatting you add to messages if they use an e-mail program that cannot display formatting.

CHANGE FONT SIZE

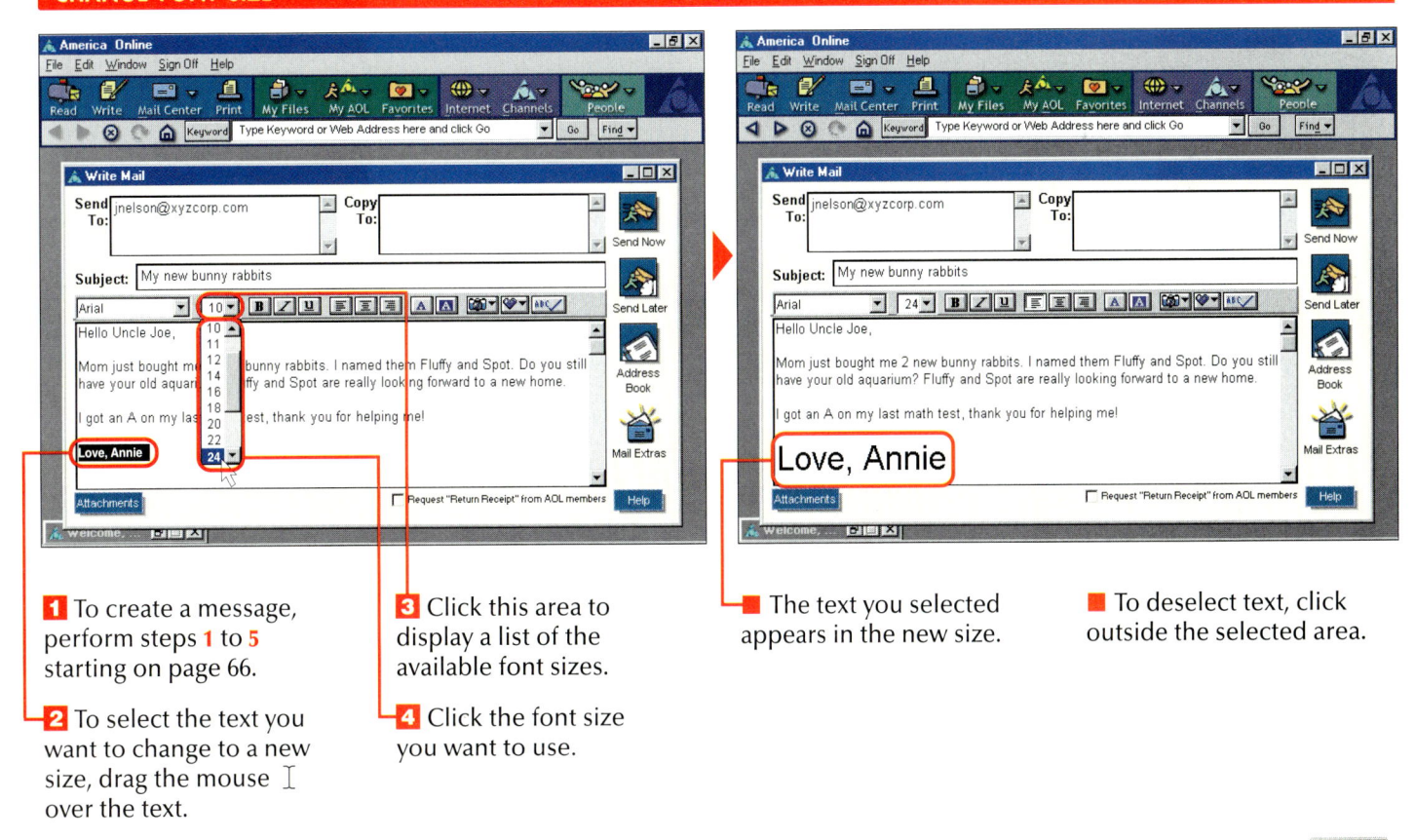

■ **1** To create a message, perform steps **1** to **5** starting on page 66.

■ **2** To select the text you want to change to a new size, drag the mouse I over the text.

■ **3** Click this area to display a list of the available font sizes.

■ **4** Click the font size you want to use.

■ The text you selected appears in the new size.

■ To deselect text, click outside the selected area.

93

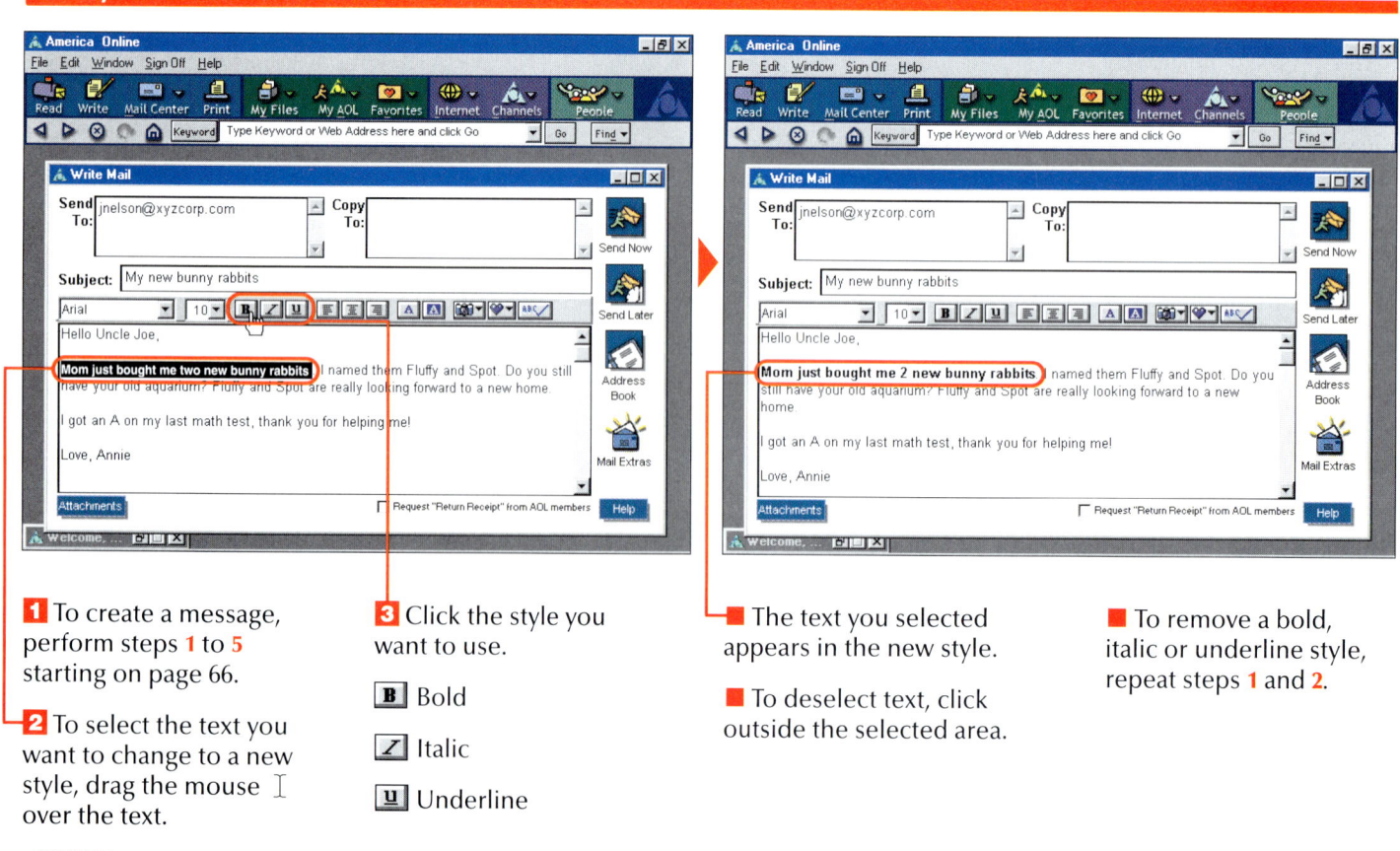

BOLD, ITALIC AND UNDERLINE

You can use the bold, italic and underline styles to emphasize information in a message.

BOLD, ITALIC AND UNDERLINE

1 To create a message, perform steps **1** to **5** starting on page 66.

2 To select the text you want to change to a new style, drag the mouse over the text.

3 Click the style you want to use.

- **B** Bold
- *I* Italic
- U Underline

■ The text you selected appears in the new style.

■ To deselect text, click outside the selected area.

■ To remove a bold, italic or underline style, repeat steps **1** and **2**.

94

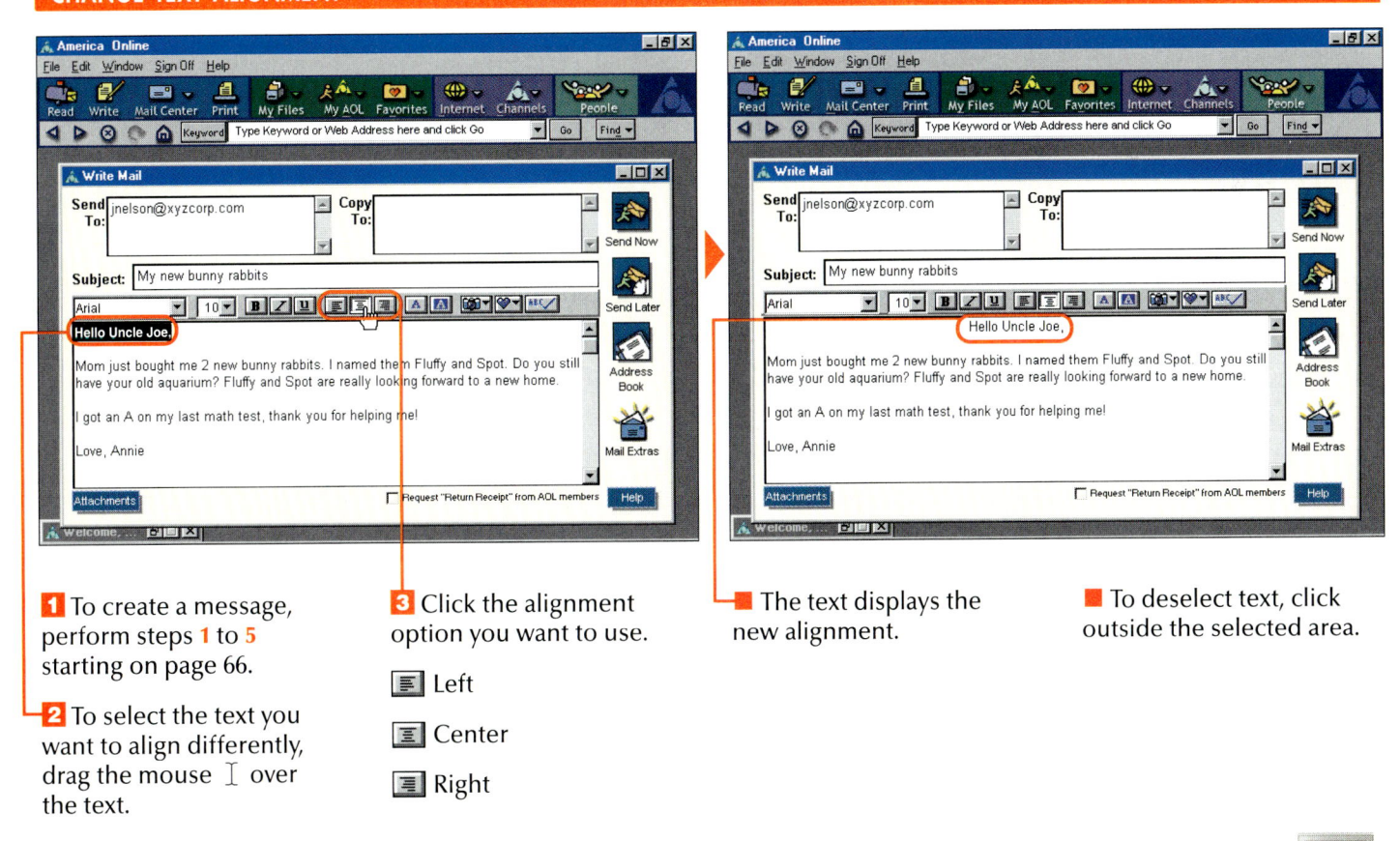

CHANGE TEXT ALIGNMENT

WORK WITH E-MAIL

You can align text in three different ways.

April 16, 1998 → Right

← Ball Season's Back! → Center

Ken:

I have two tickets to the White Sox game on Saturday afternoon. Are you interested in coming along?

It should be a good game. I expect it to be an excellent season for the Sox.

Let me know as soon as possible.

Rob

← Left

CHANGE TEXT ALIGNMENT

1 To create a message, perform steps **1** to **5** starting on page 66.

2 To select the text you want to align differently, drag the mouse I over the text.

3 Click the alignment option you want to use.

▤ Left
▤ Center
▤ Right

■ The text displays the new alignment.

■ To deselect text, click outside the selected area.

95

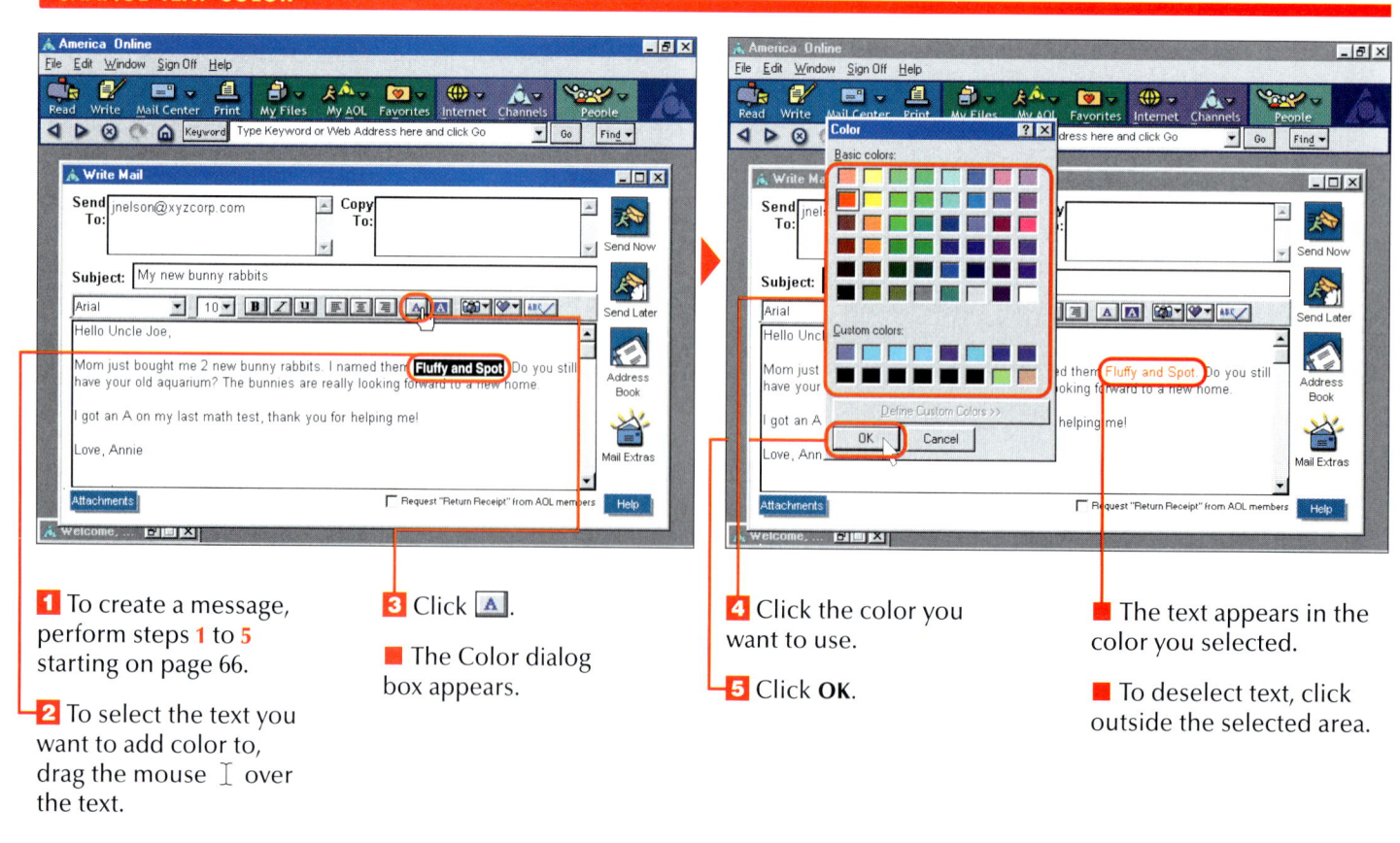

CHANGE TEXT COLOR

You can change the color of text in your message to draw attention to important information.

CHANGE TEXT COLOR

1 To create a message, perform steps **1** to **5** starting on page 66.

2 To select the text you want to add color to, drag the mouse I over the text.

3 Click A.

■ The Color dialog box appears.

4 Click the color you want to use.

5 Click **OK**.

■ The text appears in the color you selected.

■ To deselect text, click outside the selected area.

96

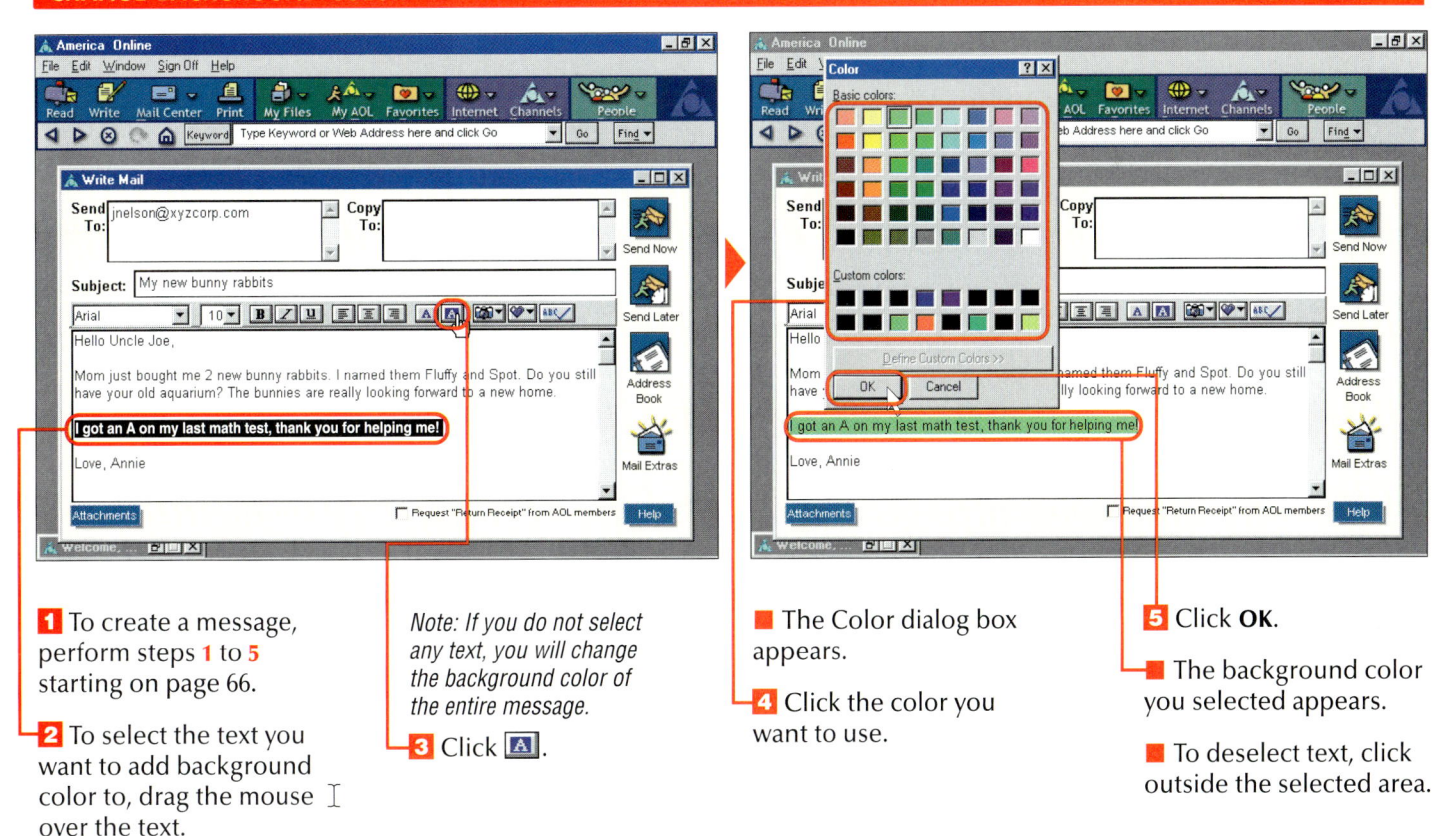

CHANGE BACKGROUND COLOR

WORK WITH E-MAIL 5

> You can change the background color of text you select or the entire message.

CHANGE BACKGROUND COLOR

1 To create a message, perform steps **1** to **5** starting on page 66.

2 To select the text you want to add background color to, drag the mouse over the text.

Note: If you do not select any text, you will change the background color of the entire message.

3 Click 🅰.

■ The Color dialog box appears.

4 Click the color you want to use.

5 Click **OK**.

■ The background color you selected appears.

■ To deselect text, click outside the selected area.

97

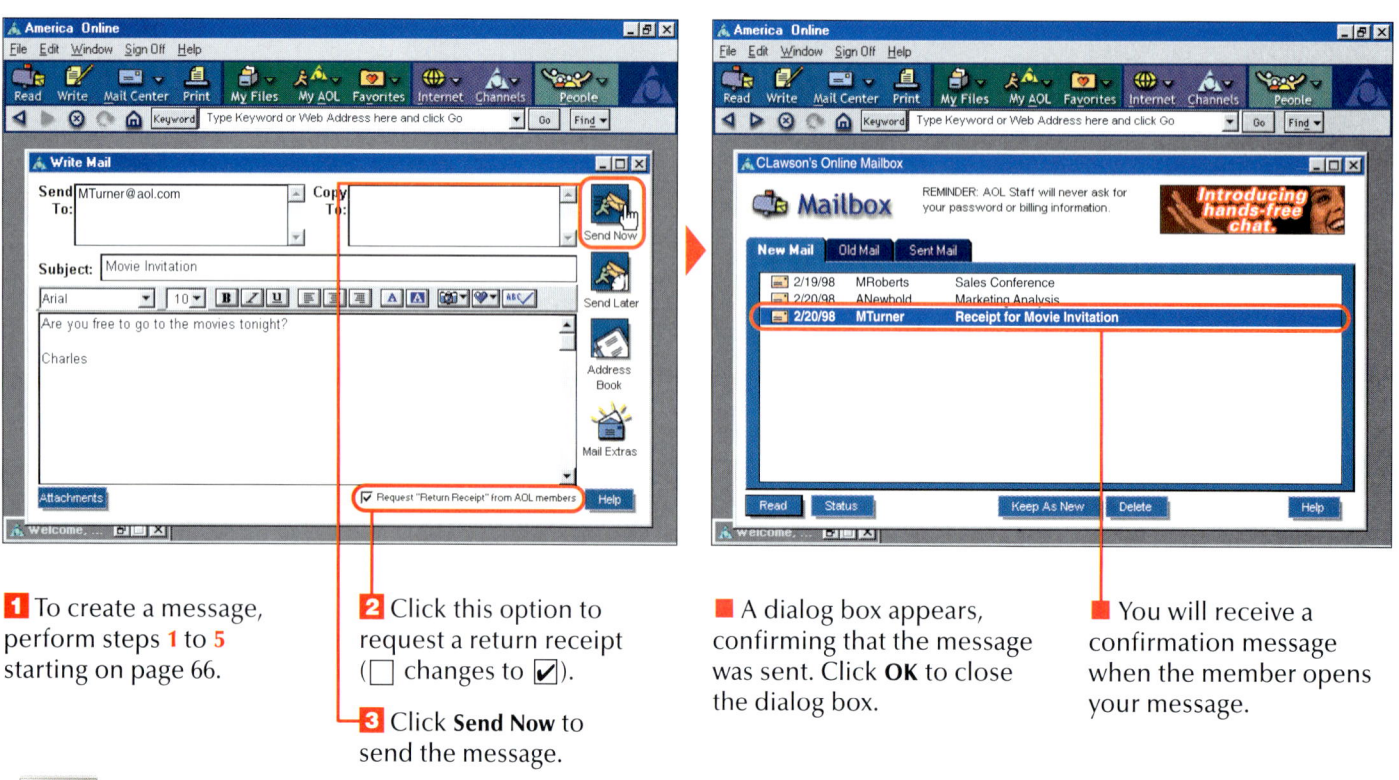

REQUEST RETURN RECEIPT

You can receive a confirmation message when an AOL member opens a message you sent.

You cannot receive a confirmation message for a message you send over the Internet.

REQUEST RETURN RECEIPT

1 To create a message, perform steps **1** to **5** starting on page 66.

2 Click this option to request a return receipt (☐ changes to ☑).

3 Click **Send Now** to send the message.

■ A dialog box appears, confirming that the message was sent. Click **OK** to close the dialog box.

■ You will receive a confirmation message when the member opens your message.

98

ADD FAVORITE PLACE TO MESSAGE

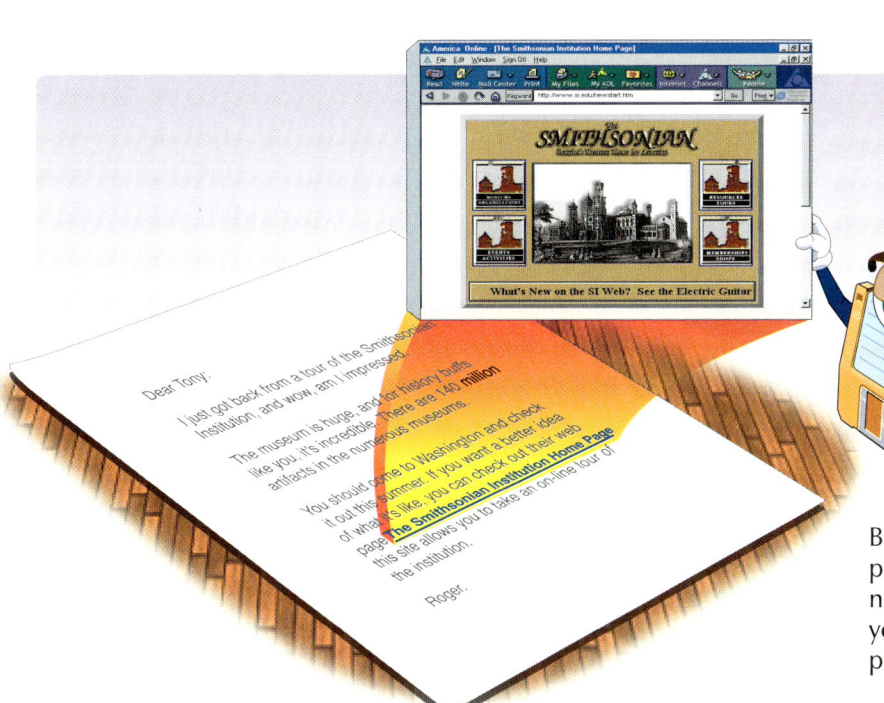

WORK WITH E-MAIL — 5

You can share your favorite places with friends and family members. Including a favorite place in a message allows the person receiving the message to immediately display the place.

Before adding a favorite place to a message, you need to add the place to your list of favorites. See page 184 for information.

ADD FAVORITE PLACE TO MESSAGE

1 Click the location where you want to add the favorite place.

2 Click 💙 to display a list of your favorite places.

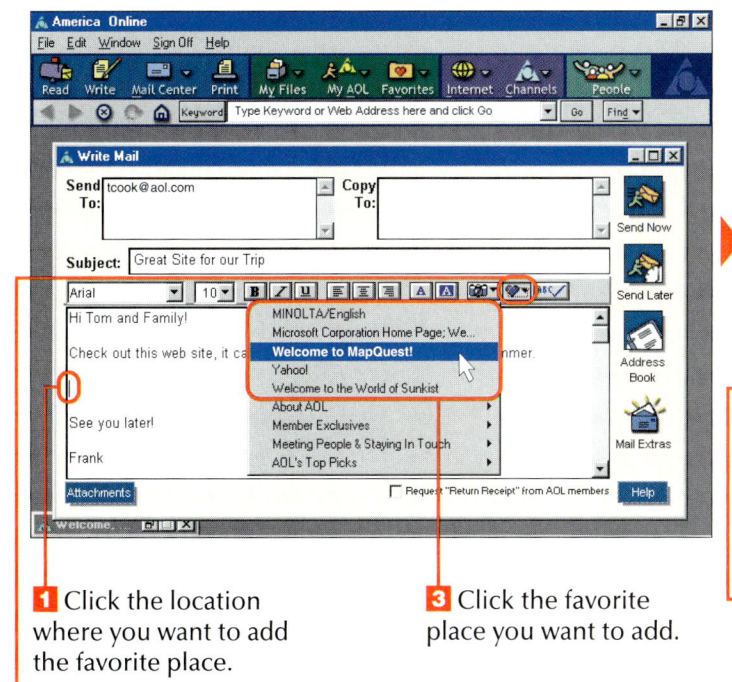

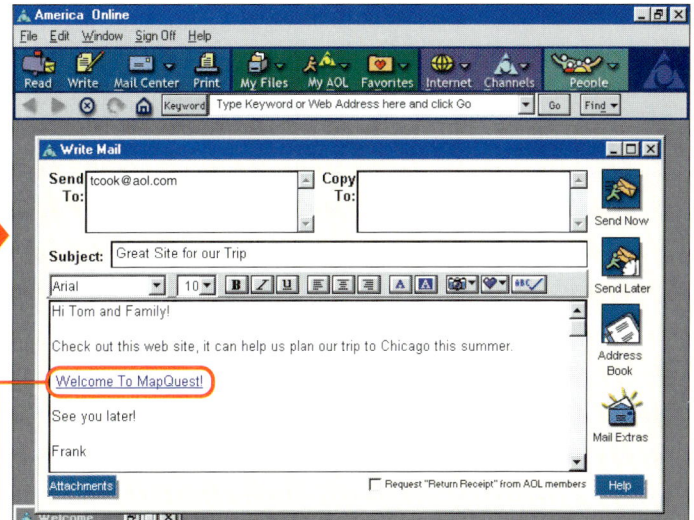

3 Click the favorite place you want to add.

■ A link to the favorite place appears in the message as blue text with an underline.

■ The person receiving the message will be able to click the link to immediately display the favorite place.

Note: If the person receiving the message is not an AOL member, they may not be able to display the favorite place.

99

SEND A MESSAGE LATER

After you create a message, you do not have to immediately send the message. You can send the message at a later time so you can once again review the message and make any necessary changes.

You can also create a message offline and then send the message later when you connect to AOL. This allows you to keep your telephone line free while you create messages.

SEND A MESSAGE LATER

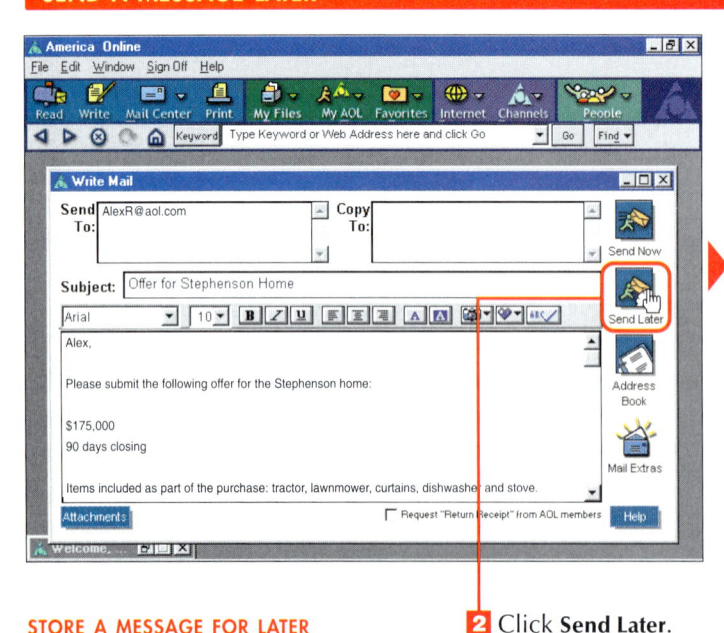

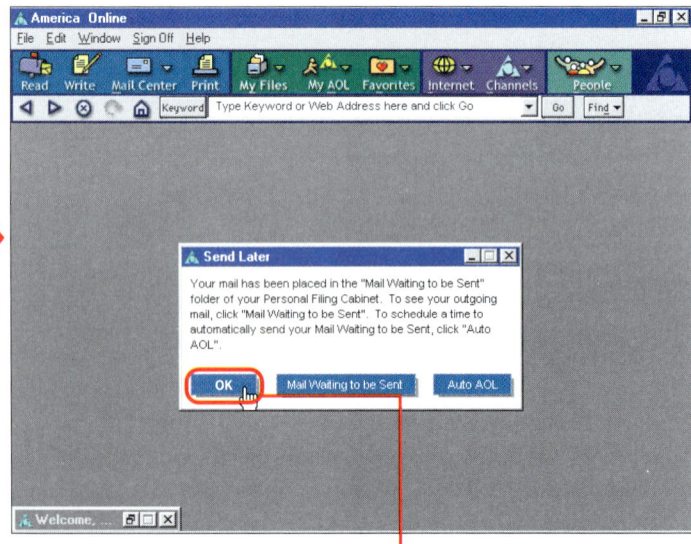

STORE A MESSAGE FOR LATER

■ 1 To create a message, perform steps 1 to 5 starting on page 66.

■ 2 Click **Send Later**.

■ A window appears, stating that your message was placed in the Mail Waiting to be Sent folder.

■ 3 Click **OK** to close the window.

100

WORK WITH E-MAIL

Why does this dialog box appear when I connect to AOL?

Mail Waiting To Be Sent

You have mail waiting to be sent. To send all mail in your Mail Waiting to be Sent Folder, click Send Now. To see your outgoing mail, click Mail Folders. To send the mail later, click Send Later.

☐ Do not ask me again

[Send Now] [Mail Folders] [Send Later]

You have messages waiting to be sent. Click one of the following options.

Send Now
Send all messages now.

Mail Folders
See the messages waiting to be sent.

Send Later
Send the messages later.

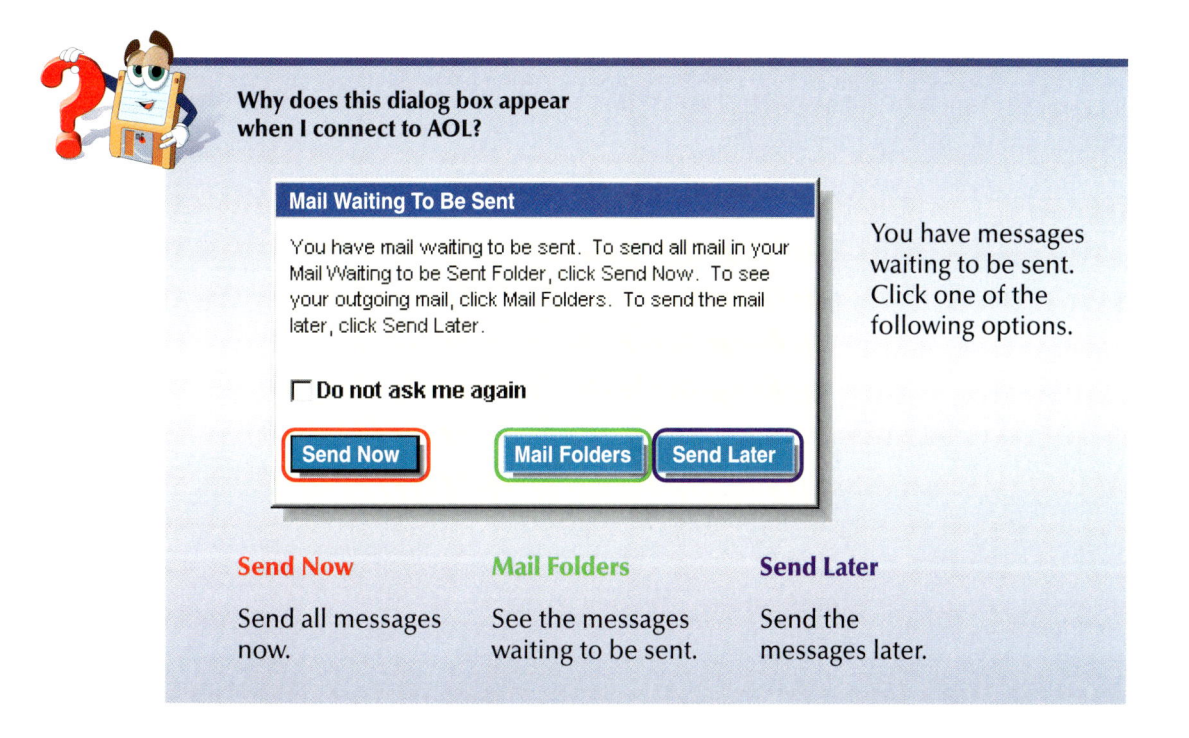

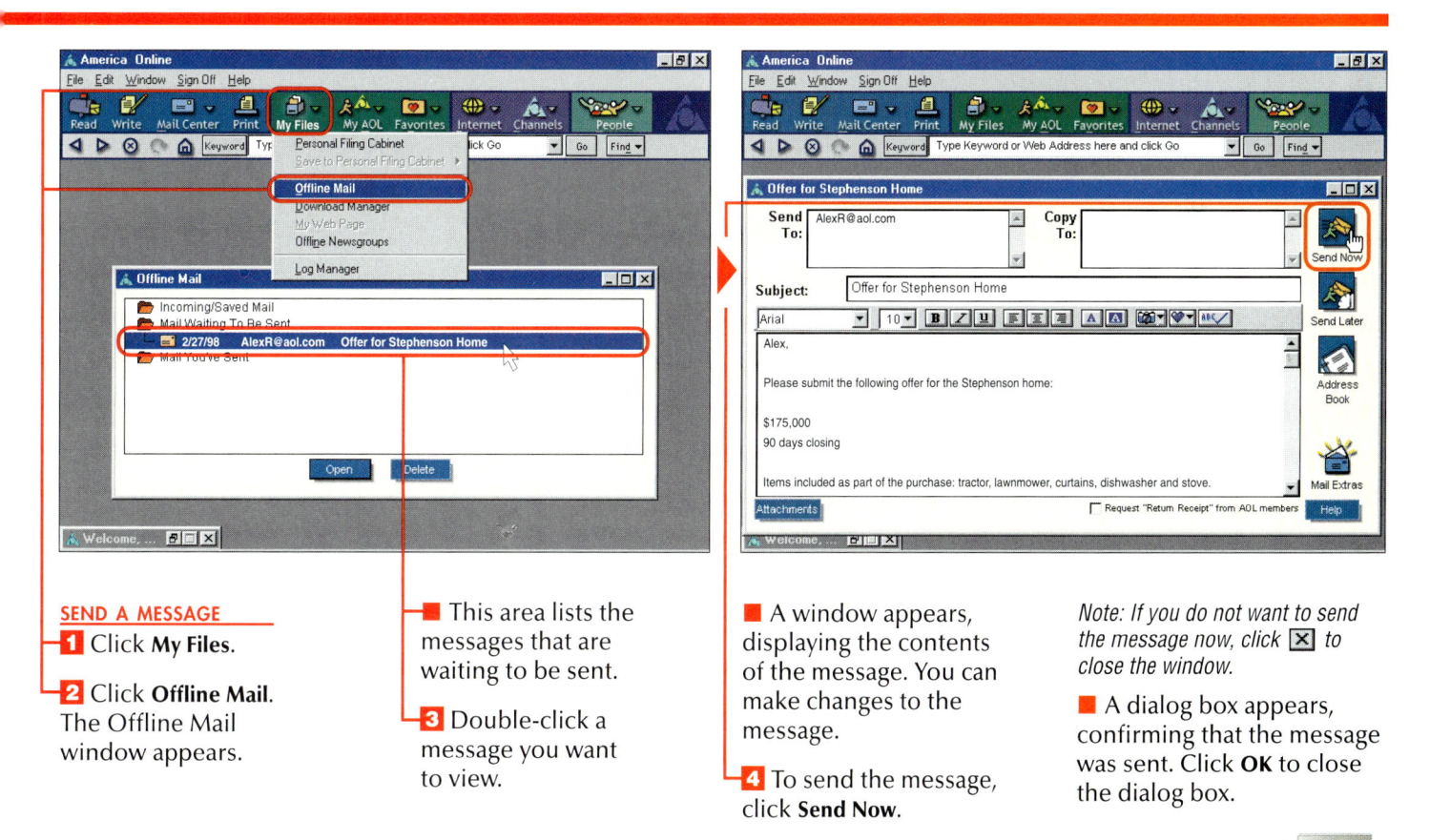

SEND A MESSAGE

1 Click **My Files**.

2 Click **Offline Mail**. The Offline Mail window appears.

■ This area lists the messages that are waiting to be sent.

3 Double-click a message you want to view.

■ A window appears, displaying the contents of the message. You can make changes to the message.

4 To send the message, click **Send Now**.

Note: If you do not want to send the message now, click ☒ to close the window.

■ A dialog box appears, confirming that the message was sent. Click **OK** to close the dialog box.

101

UNSEND A MESSAGE

If you realize you have sent a message to the wrong person or have second thoughts about a message, you can unsend the message.

You can only unsend messages you have sent to other AOL members that have not yet been read.

UNSEND A MESSAGE

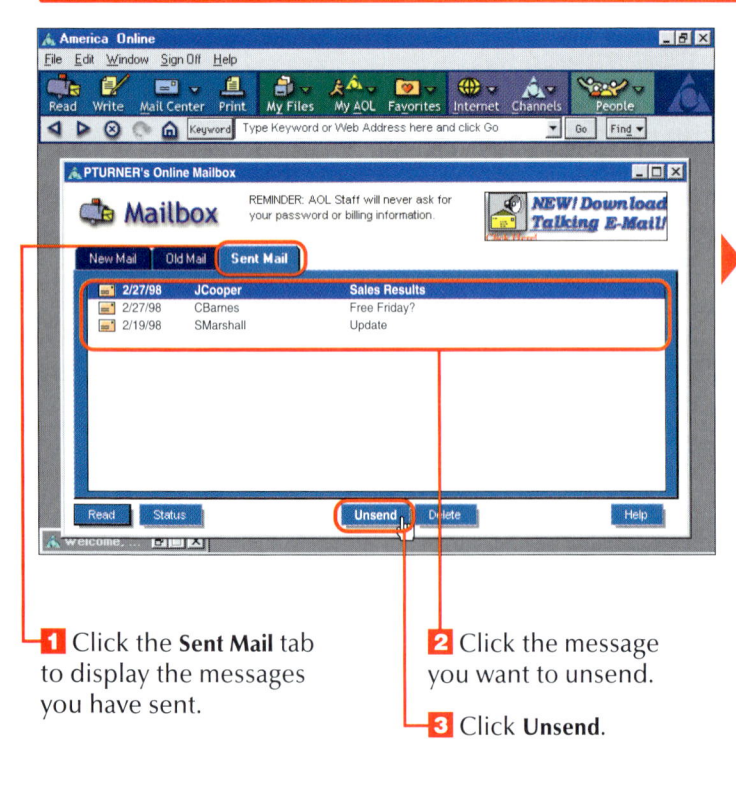

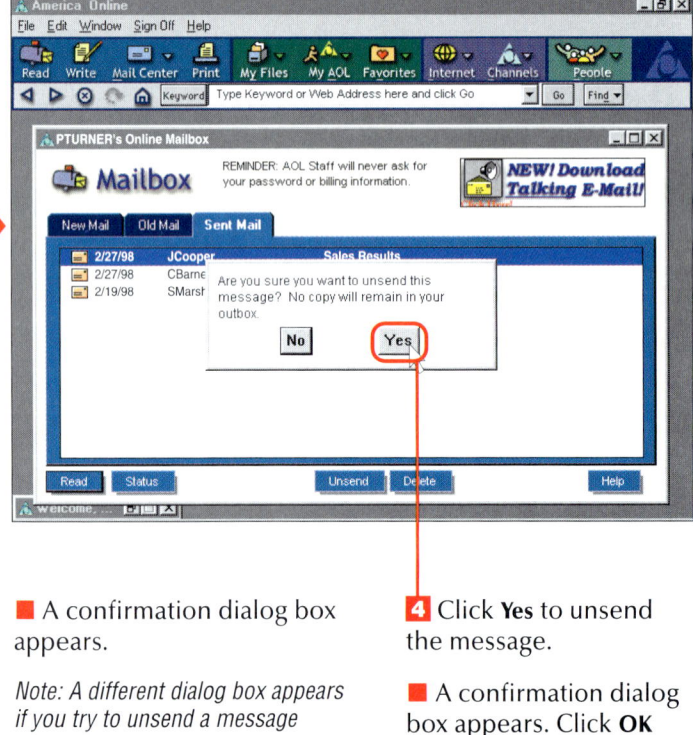

■ Click the **Sent Mail** tab to display the messages you have sent.

■ Click the message you want to unsend.

■ Click **Unsend**.

■ A confirmation dialog box appears.

Note: A different dialog box appears if you try to unsend a message someone has already read.

■ Click **Yes** to unsend the message.

■ A confirmation dialog box appears. Click **OK** to close the dialog box.

102

CHANGE HOW LONG AOL KEEPS READ MESSAGES

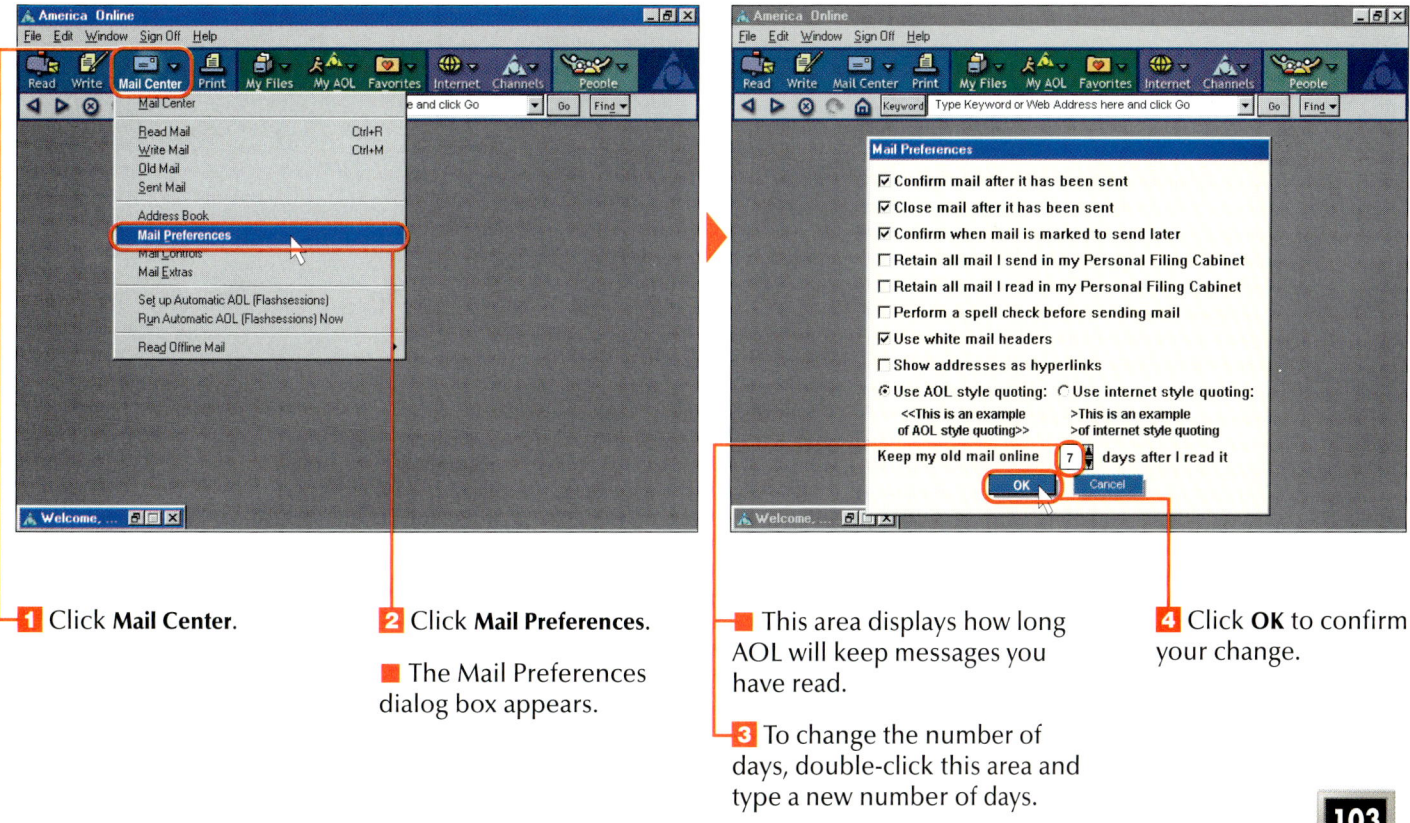

WORK WITH E-MAIL

You can change how long AOL will keep messages you have read.

AOL initially stores your read messages for 3 days. You can set AOL to store your read messages for a maximum of 7 days. Unread messages are stored for about 27 days.

CHANGE HOW LONG AOL KEEPS READ MESSAGES

1 Click **Mail Center**.

2 Click **Mail Preferences**.

■ The Mail Preferences dialog box appears.

■ This area displays how long AOL will keep messages you have read.

3 To change the number of days, double-click this area and type a new number of days.

4 Click **OK** to confirm your change.

103

WE BUY AND SELL USED CARS!

READ

USED CARS!

New Movies

Family Travel

WE BUY AND SELL USED CARS!

CHAPTER 6

USING MESSAGE BOARDS

What is a message board? In this chapter you will learn about message boards and how they enable AOL members to exchange opinions about topics of common interest.

Introduction to Message Boards 106

Read Messages 108

Print a Message 110

Mark Message Board as Read 111

Reply to a Message 112

Add a Message 114

INTRODUCTION TO MESSAGE BOARDS

You can use message boards to exchange information with other AOL members who share your interests.

Like Internet newsgroups, message boards allow people to exchange information about topics of interest. However, AOL message boards are limited to AOL members and provide fewer topics.

Message Board Topics
Each message board discusses information on a specific topic. Message board topics include animals, books, budgeting, the changing workplace, games, hardware, health care issues, parenting, travel destinations and more.

Check Content
Check your messages for spelling, grammar and clarity. Also make sure a message will not be misinterpreted. For example, a reader may not realize a statement is meant to be sarcastic.

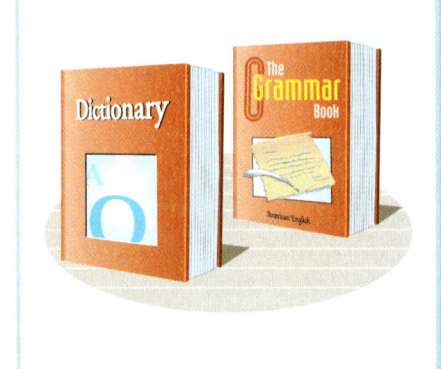

Avoid Offensive Language
Avoid using insulting, obscene or disruptive language in your messages. People of all ages and backgrounds can read messages you send.

My @#!#? car broke down again. Does anyone know a good mechanic in the NY area?

USING MESSAGE BOARDS

Avoid Chain Letters or Advertisements
Do not send chain letters or advertisements to message boards. There are a few message boards designed specifically for advertisements.

Avoid Shouting
DO NOT TYPE MESSAGES IN ALL CAPITAL LETTERS. This is called shouting and will annoy and distract other members reading the message board.

Avoid Spamming
Do not send a single message to several message boards. This is called spamming. Send one message to the most appropriate message board to ensure the people most interested in your comments will see your message.

Read Messages
Read the messages on a message board before sending a message. This is a great way to learn how people on the message board communicate and prevents you from sending information others have already read.

Avoid Including Private Information
Do not include private information about yourself, such as your phone number or address. You can always send this information to individual members by e-mail, if needed.

Copyright
You can discuss information you have read, but you should avoid sending information from another source without consent from the author. For example, do not send recipes you did not create without permission from the author.

READ MESSAGES

You can read messages on a message board of interest to learn the opinions and ideas of other AOL members.

You will find message boards all over AOL. Most AOL areas have message boards that discuss information related to the area.

READ MESSAGES

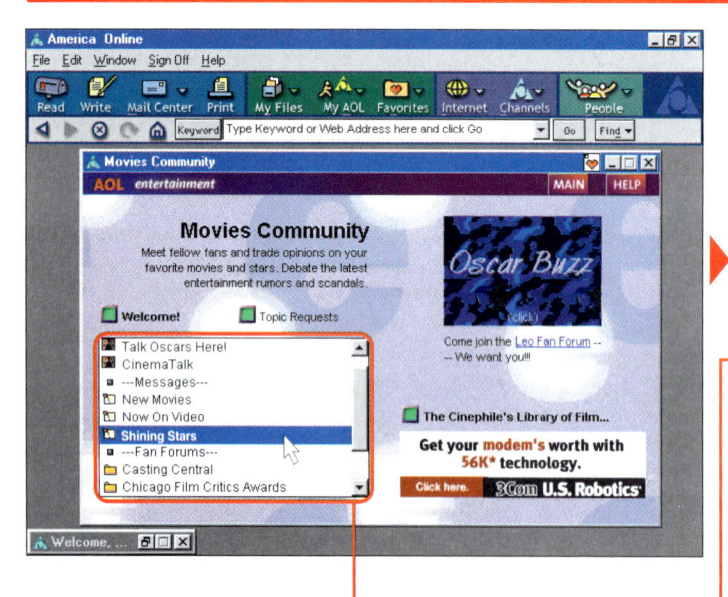

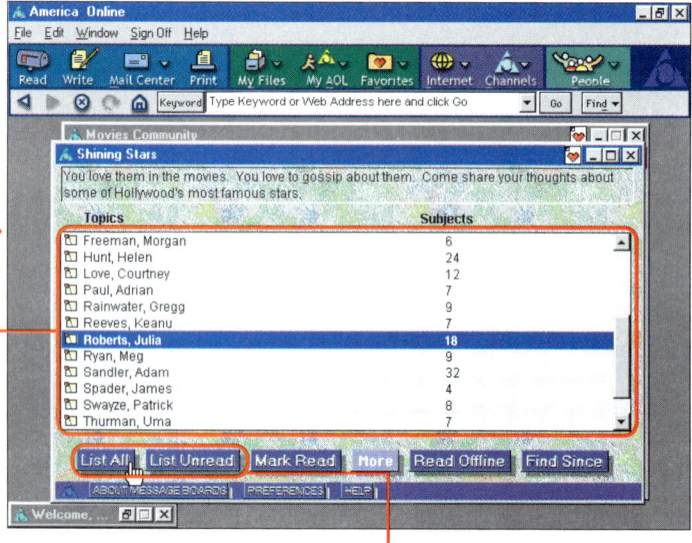

1 Locate a message board of interest. Message boards display the bulletin board symbol ( ).

*Note: In this example, we used the keyword **movies community** to display the Movies Community window. See page 32 for information on using keywords.*

2 Double-click the message board of interest.

■ A window appears, listing the message boards and the number of subjects on each board.

3 Click a message board of interest.

4 Click **List All** or **List Unread** to list all the subjects on the message board or just the subjects you have not read.

108

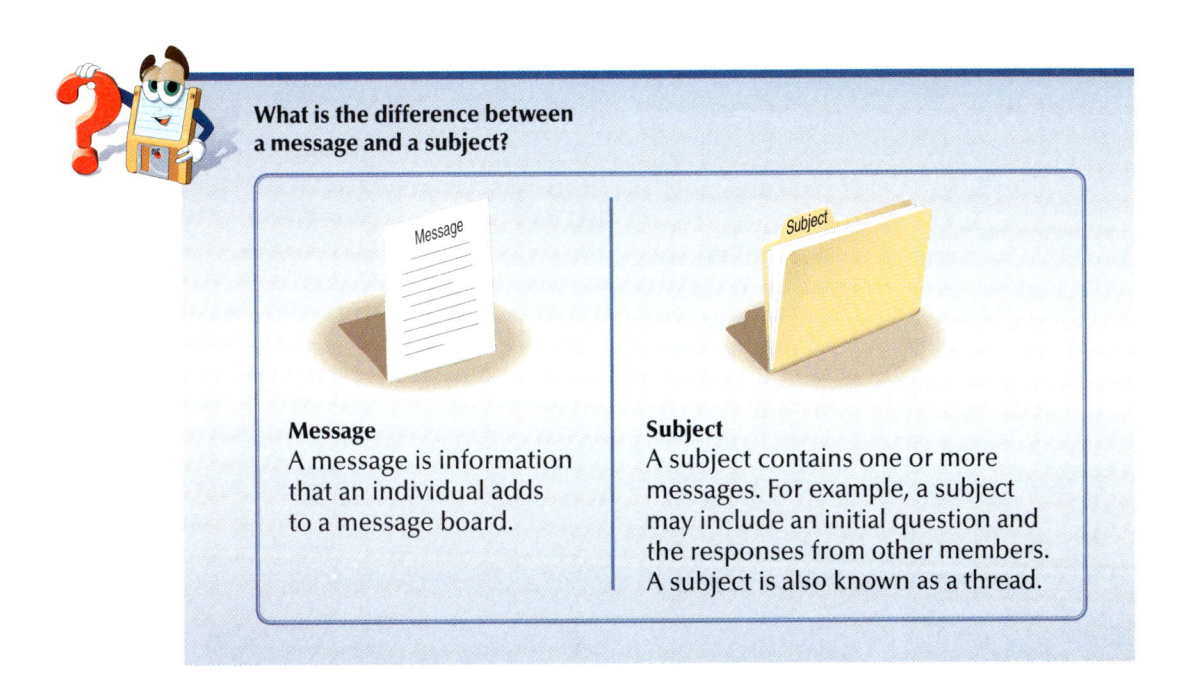

USING MESSAGE BOARDS

What is the difference between a message and a subject?

Message
A message is information that an individual adds to a message board.

Subject
A subject contains one or more messages. For example, a subject may include an initial question and the responses from other members. A subject is also known as a thread.

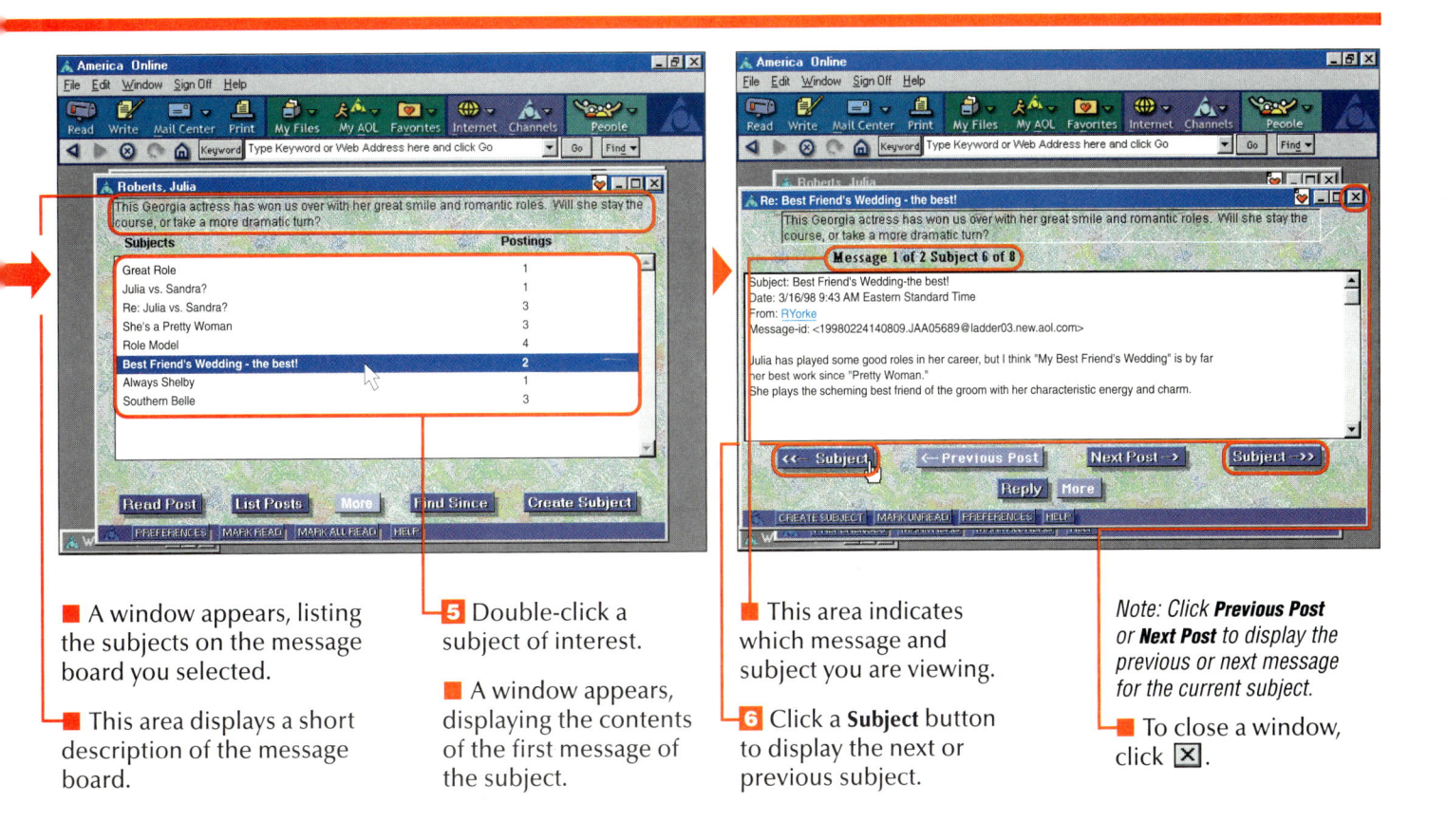

■ A window appears, listing the subjects on the message board you selected.

■ This area displays a short description of the message board.

5 Double-click a subject of interest.

■ A window appears, displaying the contents of the first message of the subject.

■ This area indicates which message and subject you are viewing.

6 Click a **Subject** button to display the next or previous subject.

*Note: Click **Previous Post** or **Next Post** to display the previous or next message for the current subject.*

■ To close a window, click ⊠.

109

PRINT A MESSAGE

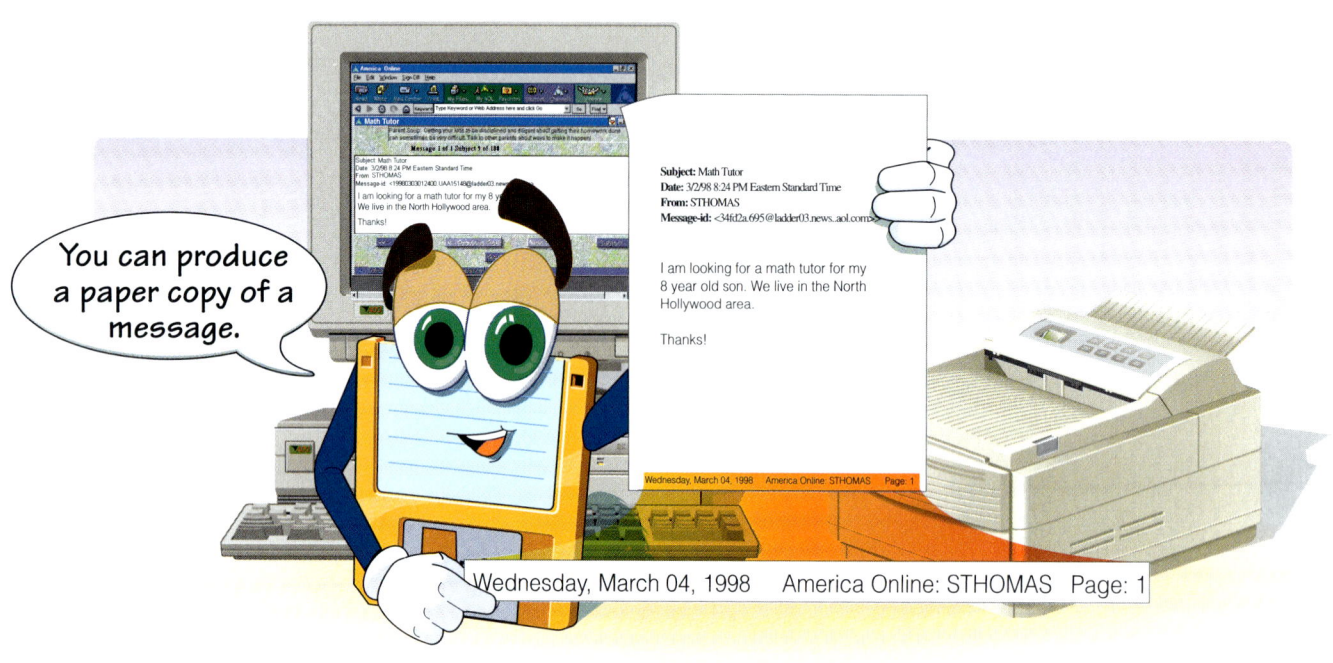

You can produce a paper copy of a message.

A printed message displays the date, your screen name and the page number at the bottom of the page.

PRINT A MESSAGE

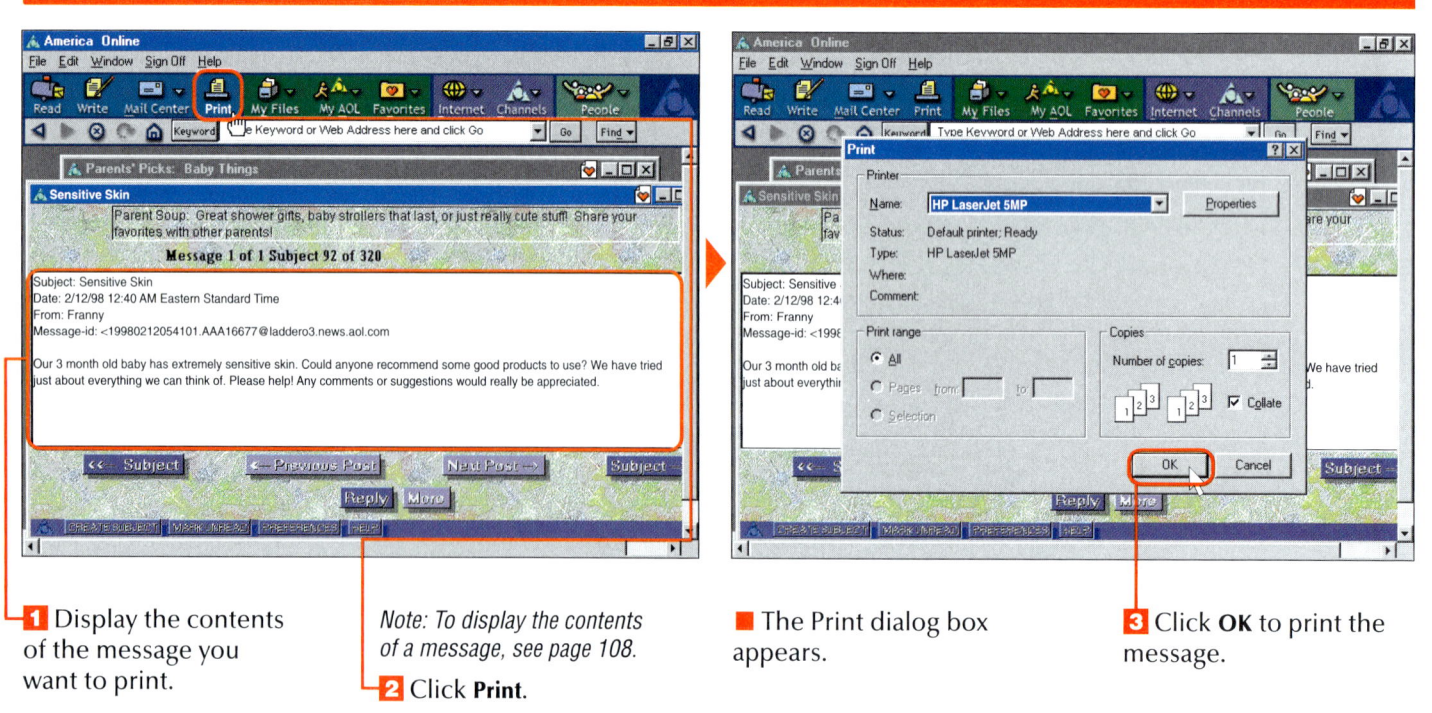

1 Display the contents of the message you want to print.

Note: To display the contents of a message, see page 108.

2 Click **Print**.

■ The Print dialog box appears.

3 Click **OK** to print the message.

MARK MESSAGE BOARD AS READ

USING MESSAGE BOARDS

When you finish reading all the messages of interest in a message board, you can mark the message board as read.

The next time you visit a message board you marked as read, you can instantly see which messages were added since you last visited the message board.

MARK MESSAGE BOARD AS READ

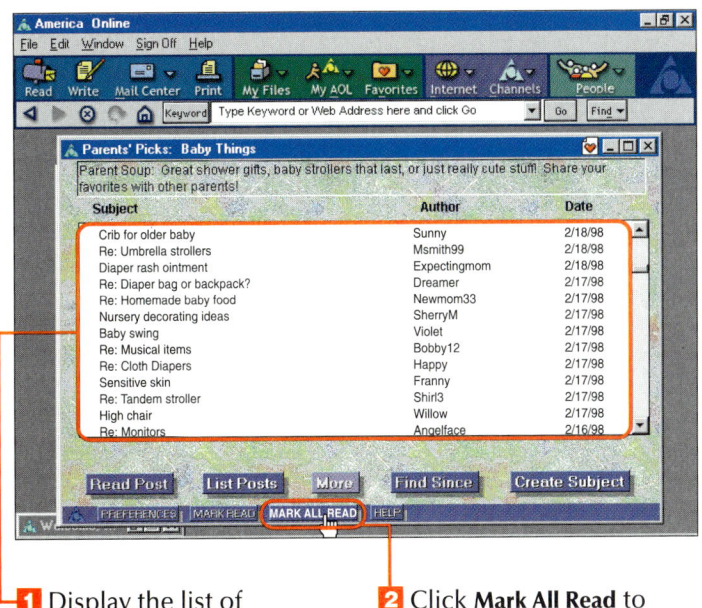

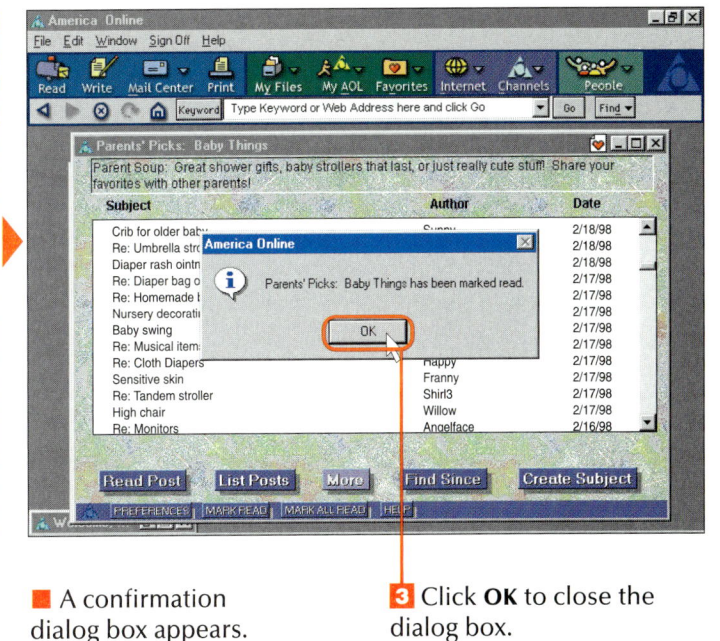

1 Display the list of subjects in the message board you want to mark as read.

2 Click **Mark All Read** to mark all the messages in the message board as read.

■ A confirmation dialog box appears.

3 Click **OK** to close the dialog box.

Note: To display a list of subjects in a message board, see page 108.

111

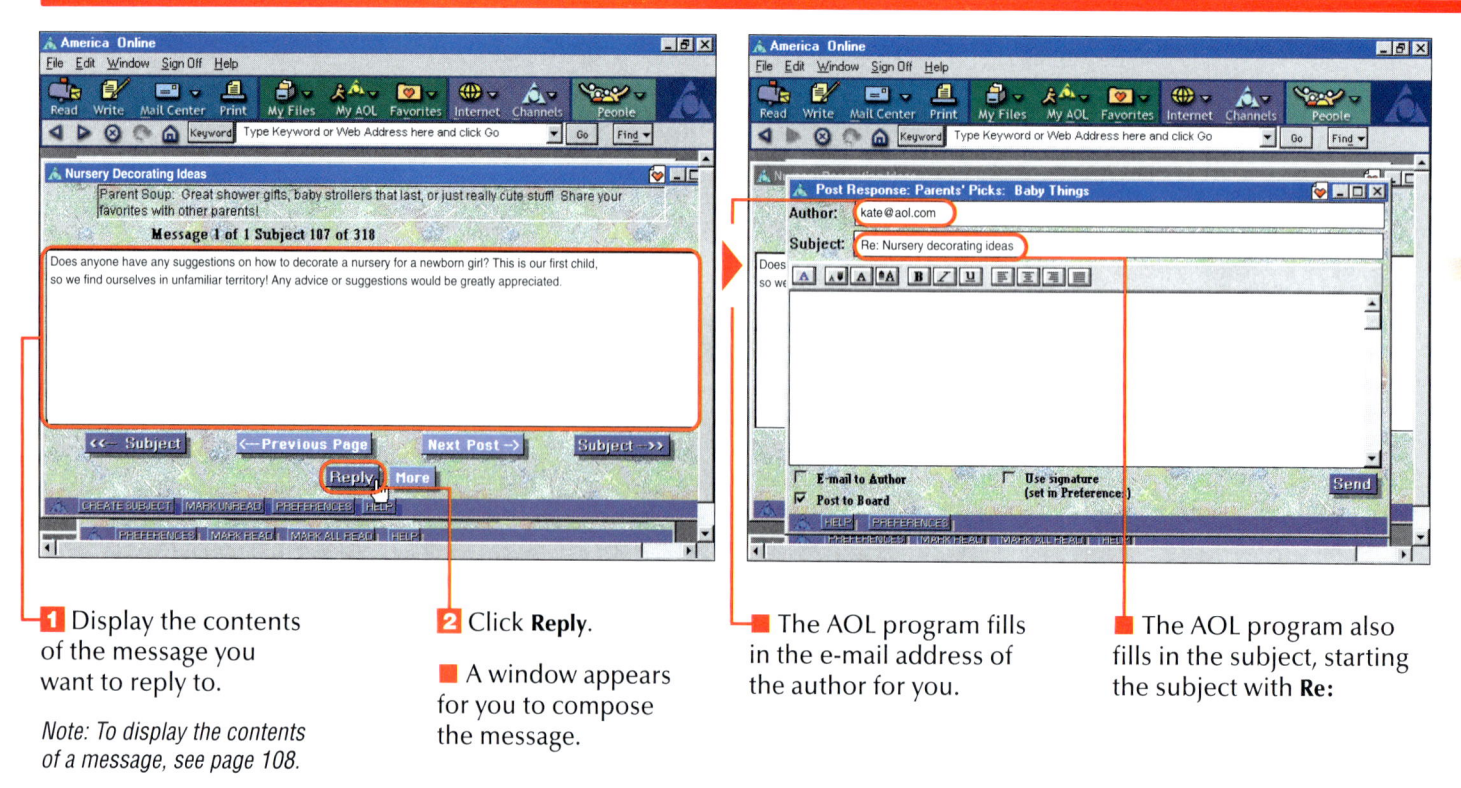

REPLY TO A MESSAGE

You can reply to a message to answer a question, express an opinion or offer additional information.

Reply to a message only when you have something important to say. A reply such as "Me too" or "I agree" is not very informative.

REPLY TO A MESSAGE

1 Display the contents of the message you want to reply to.

Note: To display the contents of a message, see page 108.

2 Click **Reply**.

■ A window appears for you to compose the message.

■ The AOL program fills in the e-mail address of the author for you.

■ The AOL program also fills in the subject, starting the subject with **Re:**

USING MESSAGE BOARDS

How can I reply to a message?

You can send a reply to just the author of the message, post a reply to the message board, or both. Send a reply to just the author when your reply would not be of interest to others reading the message board or if you want to send a private response.

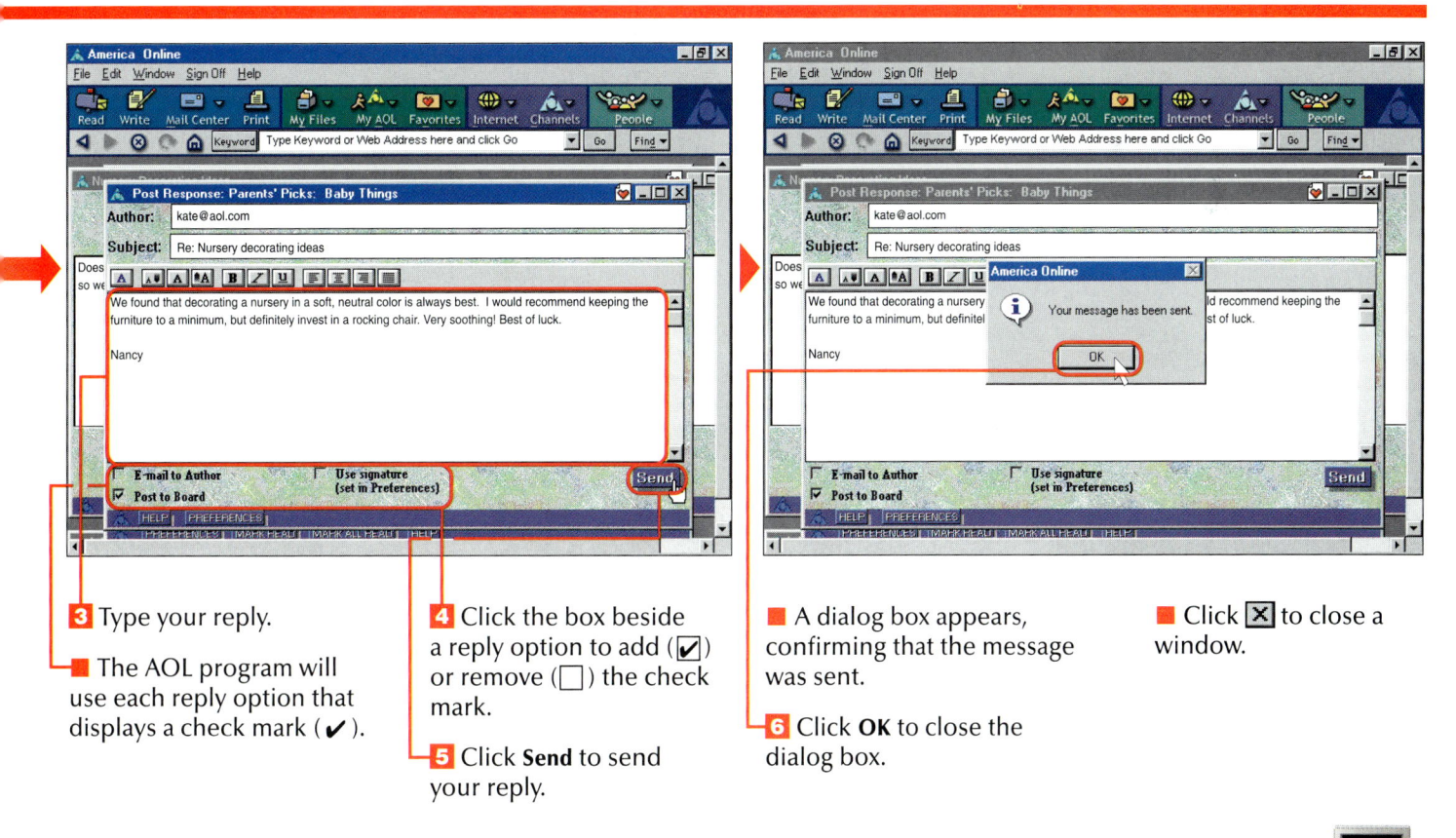

3 Type your reply.

■ The AOL program will use each reply option that displays a check mark (✔).

4 Click the box beside a reply option to add (✔) or remove (☐) the check mark.

5 Click **Send** to send your reply.

■ A dialog box appears, confirming that the message was sent.

6 Click **OK** to close the dialog box.

■ Click ✖ to close a window.

113

ADD A MESSAGE

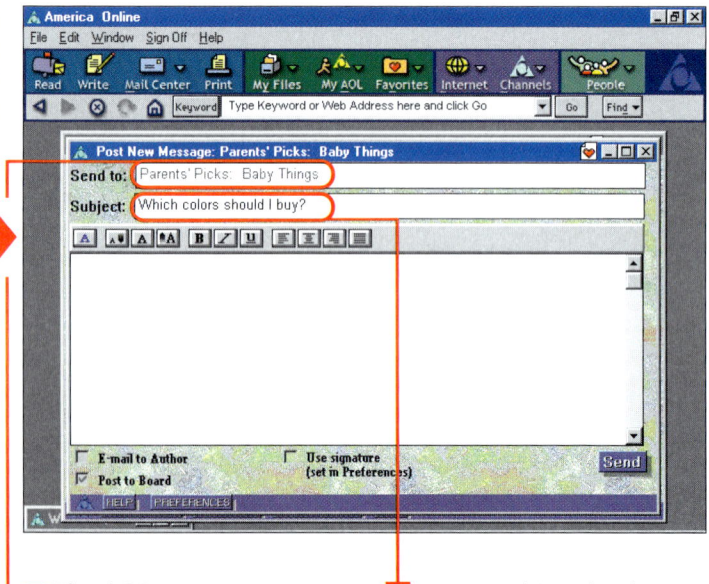

You can add a message to a message board to ask a question, express an opinion and make new friends.

ADD A MESSAGE

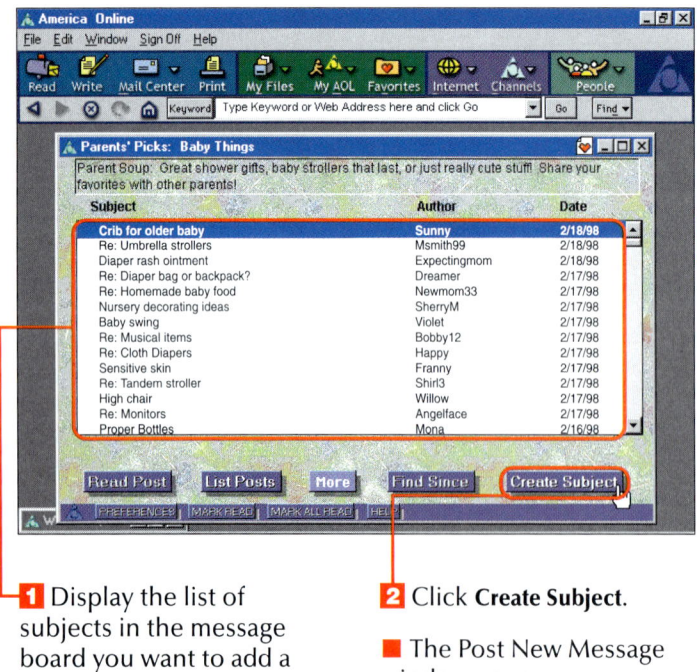

1 Display the list of subjects in the message board you want to add a message to.

Note: To display the list of subjects in a message board, see page 108.

2 Click **Create Subject**.

■ The Post New Message window appears.

■ The AOL program fills in the name of the message board for you.

3 Type a subject for the message. Make sure the subject clearly identifies the contents of your message.

114

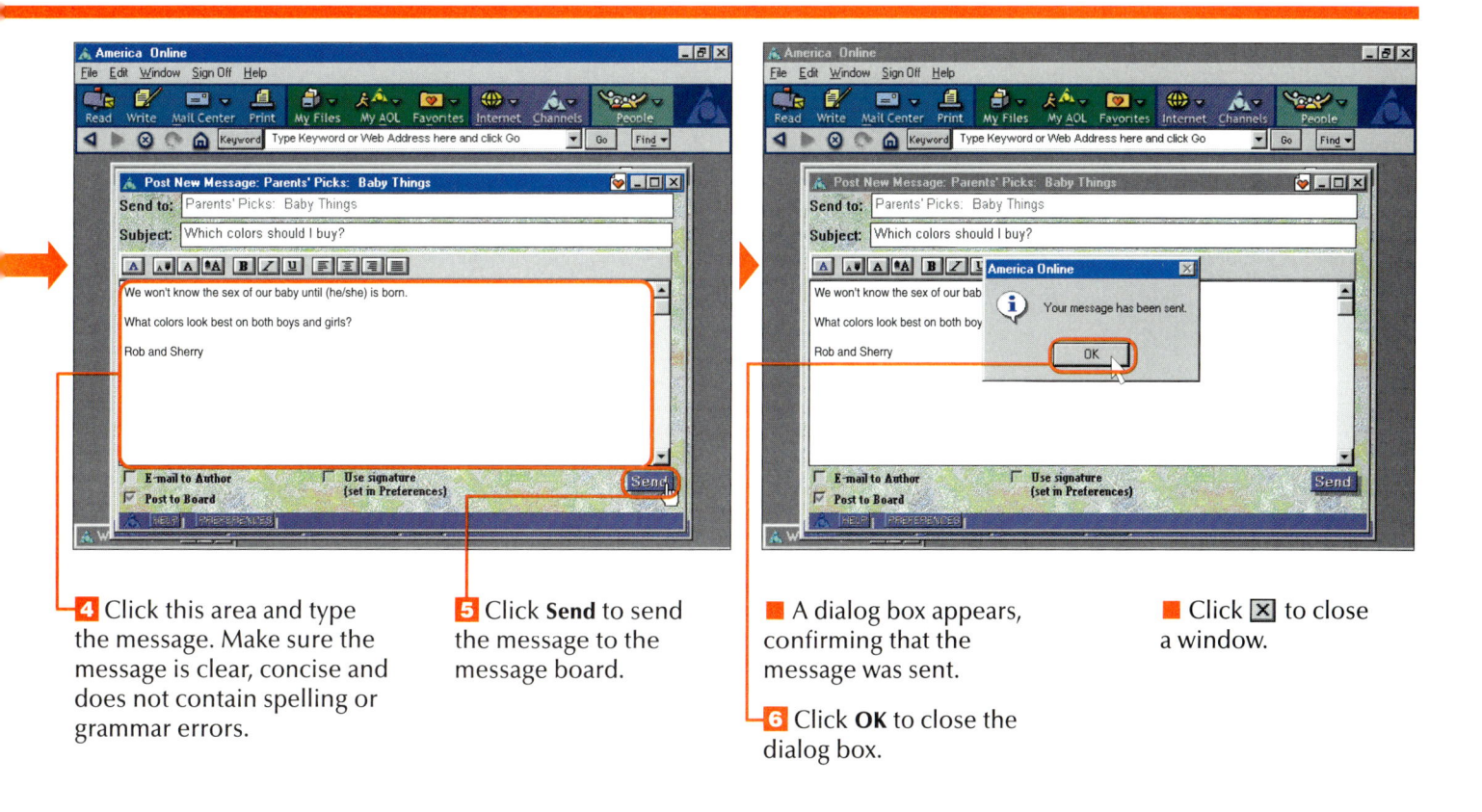

USING MESSAGE BOARDS

Can I add a message to any message board?

Each message board discusses a specific subject. Make sure you add a message to the appropriate message board. Adding an unrelated message to a message board will annoy other members.

■ **4** Click this area and type the message. Make sure the message is clear, concise and does not contain spelling or grammar errors.

■ **5** Click **Send** to send the message to the message board.

■ A dialog box appears, confirming that the message was sent.

■ **6** Click **OK** to close the dialog box.

■ Click ☒ to close a window.

115

soc.history

rec.biking

rec.

CHAPTER 7

USING NEWSGROUPS

How can I communicate with people on the Internet who share my interests? In this chapter you will learn how to subscribe to newsgroups, compose messages and much more.

Introduction to Newsgroups 118

Search for Newsgroups 120

Subscribe to a Newsgroup Quickly 124

Unsubscribe from a Newsgroup 125

Read Messages 126

Print a Message 128

Mark Newsgroup as Read 129

Reply to a Message 130

Send a New Message 132

INTRODUCTION TO NEWSGROUPS

A newsgroup is a discussion group on the Internet that allows people with common interests to communicate with each other.

The Newsgroups window provides a starting point for exploring thousands of newsgroups on every subject imaginable. Each newsgroup discusses a particular topic, such as golf or classical music.

OPEN THE NEWSGROUPS WINDOW

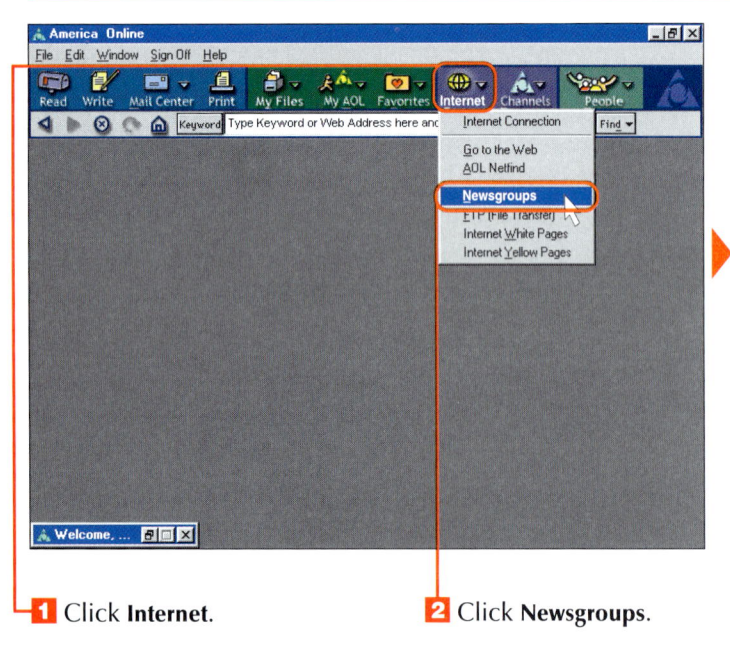

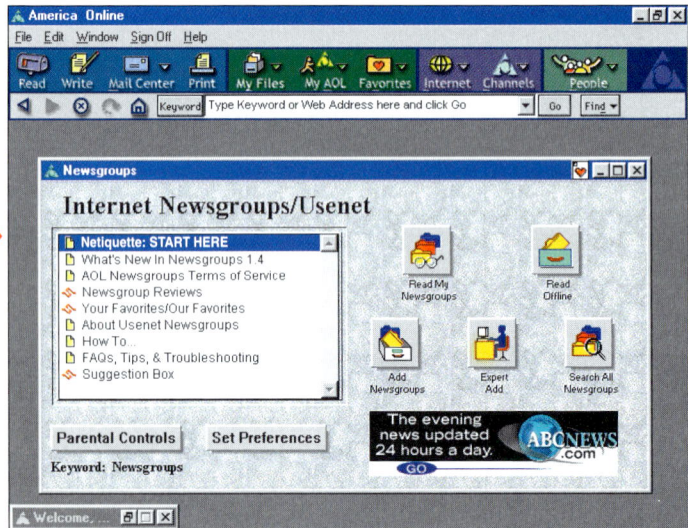

1 Click **Internet**.

2 Click **Newsgroups**.

■ The Newsgroups window appears. You can use this window to find newsgroups of interest and read newsgroup messages.

USING NEWSGROUPS

Newsgroup Names

The name of a newsgroup describes the type of information discussed in the newsgroup. A newsgroup name consists of two or more words, separated by dots (.).

The first word describes the main topic (example: rec for recreation). Each of the following words narrows the topic.

FAQs

Many newsgroups include a FAQ (Frequently Asked Questions), which is a message containing a list of questions and answers that regularly appear in a newsgroup. The FAQ is designed to prevent new readers from asking questions that have already been answered. The news.answers newsgroup provides FAQs for a wide variety of newsgroups.

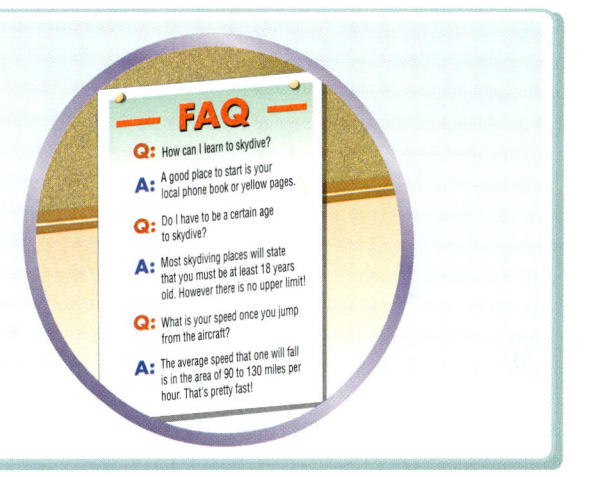

News Servers

A news server is a computer that stores newsgroup messages. When you send a message to a newsgroup, the news server keeps a copy of the message and then distributes the message to other news servers around the world.

After a few days or weeks, newsgroup messages are removed to make room for new messages.

SEARCH FOR NEWSGROUPS

You can search for newsgroups in specific categories, such as computers, news, recreation and science.

When you find a newsgroup of interest, you can subscribe to the newsgroup so you can easily read the newsgroup on a regular basis.

SEARCH FOR NEWSGROUPS BY CATEGORY

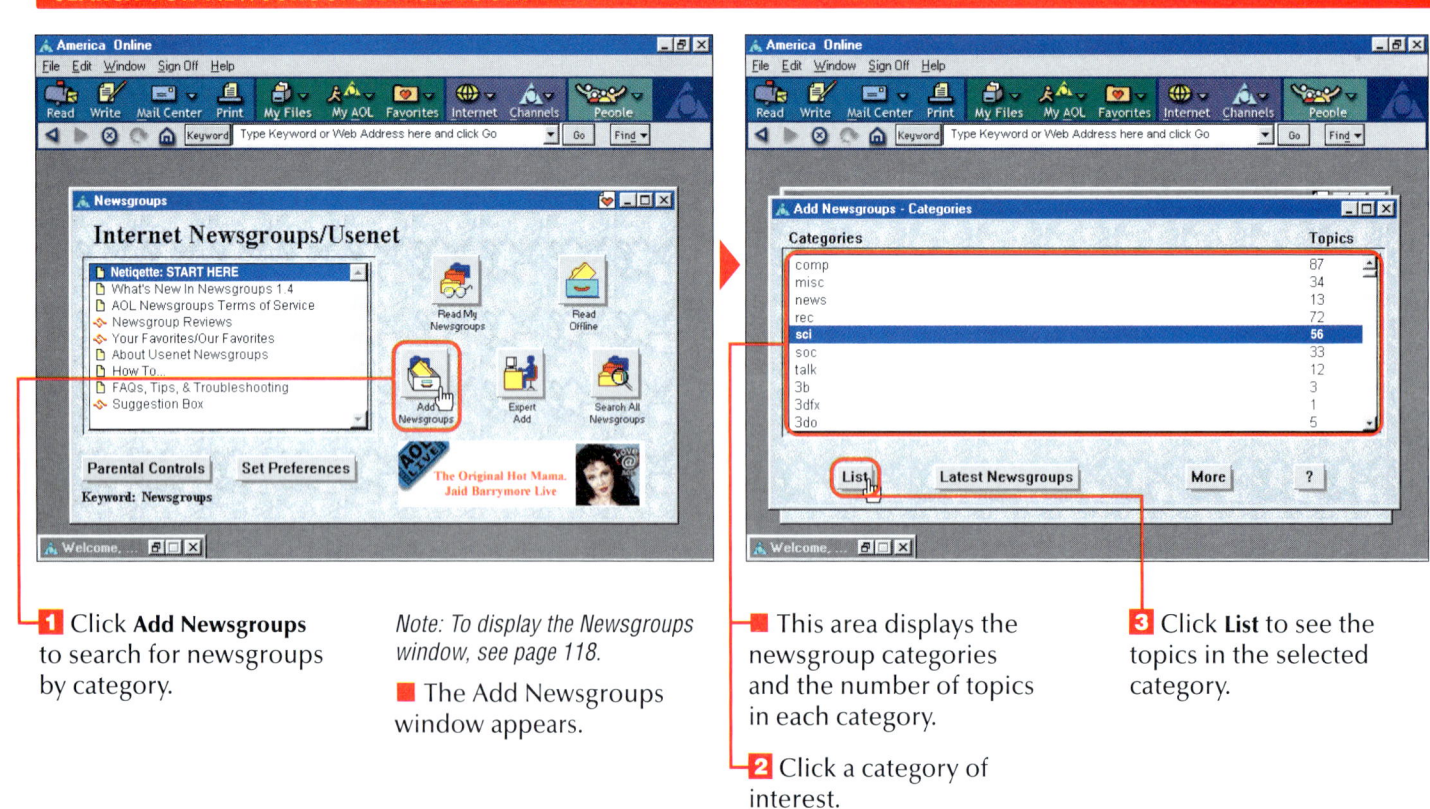

1 Click **Add Newsgroups** to search for newsgroups by category.

Note: To display the Newsgroups window, see page 118.

■ The Add Newsgroups window appears.

■ This area displays the newsgroup categories and the number of topics in each category.

2 Click a category of interest.

3 Click **List** to see the topics in the selected category.

120

USING NEWSGROUPS

What are the main newsgroup categories?

- alt (alternative)
- aol (America Online)
- bit (bitnet)
- biz (business)
- comp (computers)
- misc (miscellaneous)
- news
- rec (recreation)
- sci (science)
- soc (social)
- talk

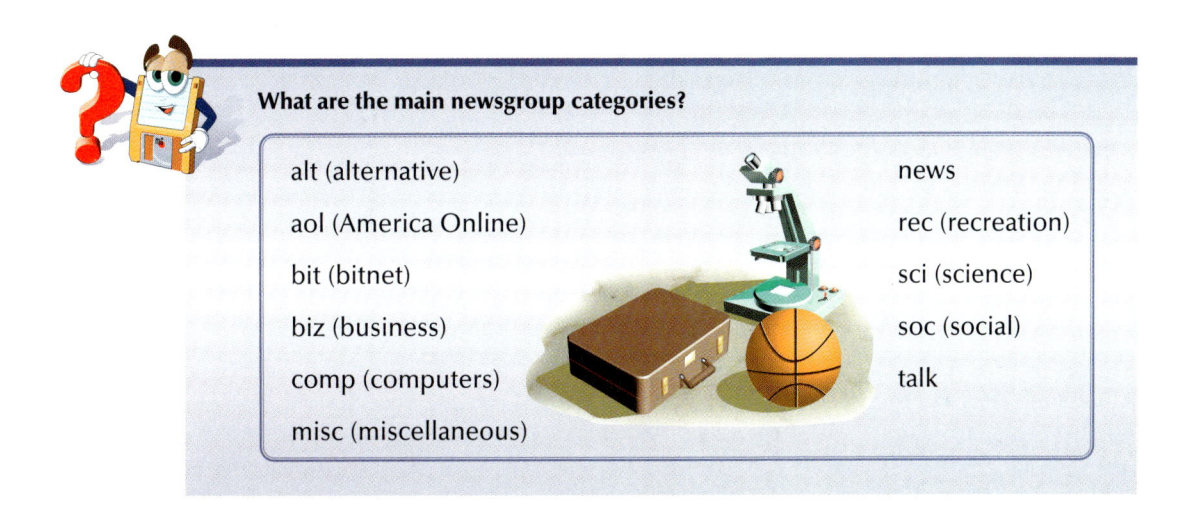

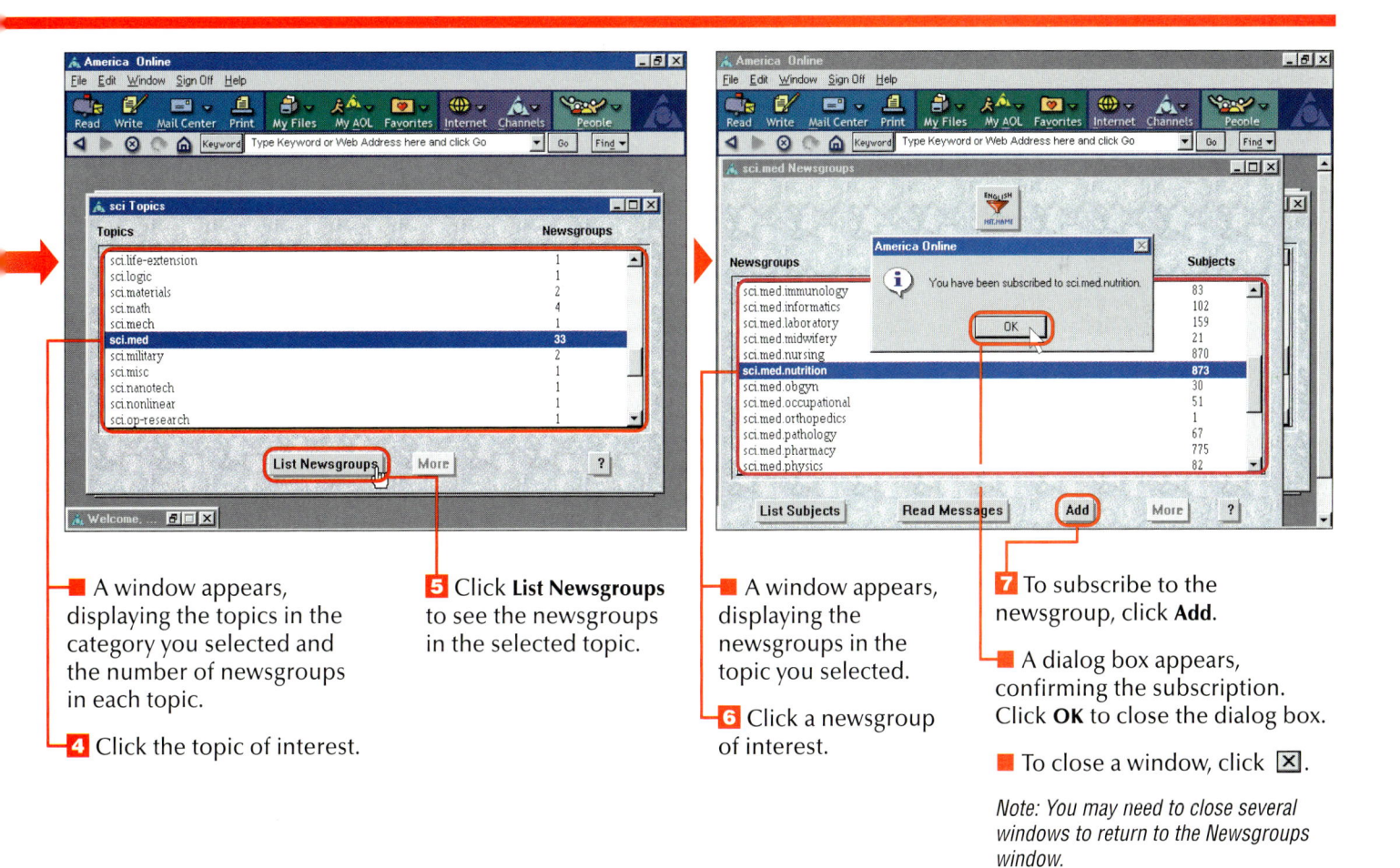

■ A window appears, displaying the topics in the category you selected and the number of newsgroups in each topic.

4 Click the topic of interest.

5 Click **List Newsgroups** to see the newsgroups in the selected topic.

■ A window appears, displaying the newsgroups in the topic you selected.

6 Click a newsgroup of interest.

7 To subscribe to the newsgroup, click **Add**.

■ A dialog box appears, confirming the subscription. Click **OK** to close the dialog box.

■ To close a window, click ⊠.

Note: You may need to close several windows to return to the Newsgroups window.

121

SEARCH FOR NEWSGROUPS

You can search for newsgroups that deal with topics of interest to you.

When you find a newsgroup of interest, you can subscribe to the newsgroup so you can easily read the newsgroup on a regular basis.

SEARCH FOR NEWSGROUPS BY NAME

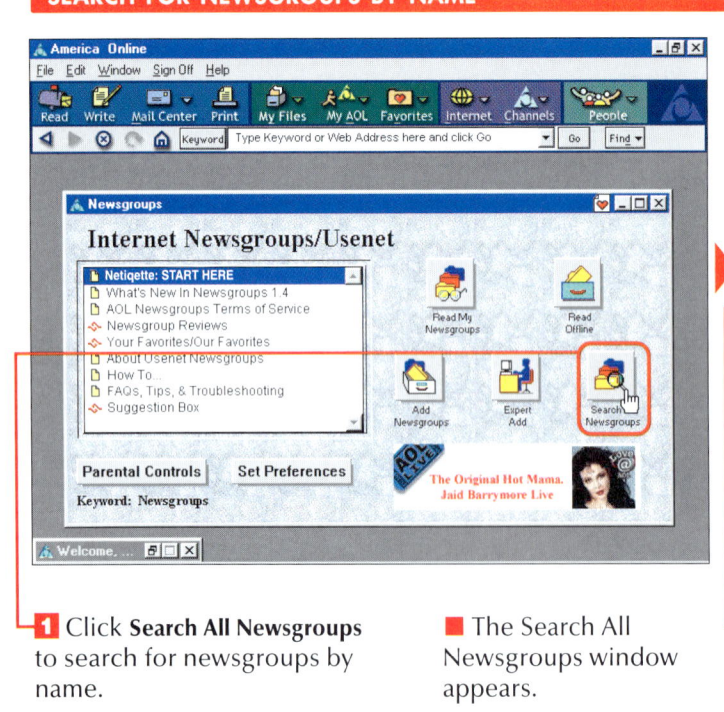

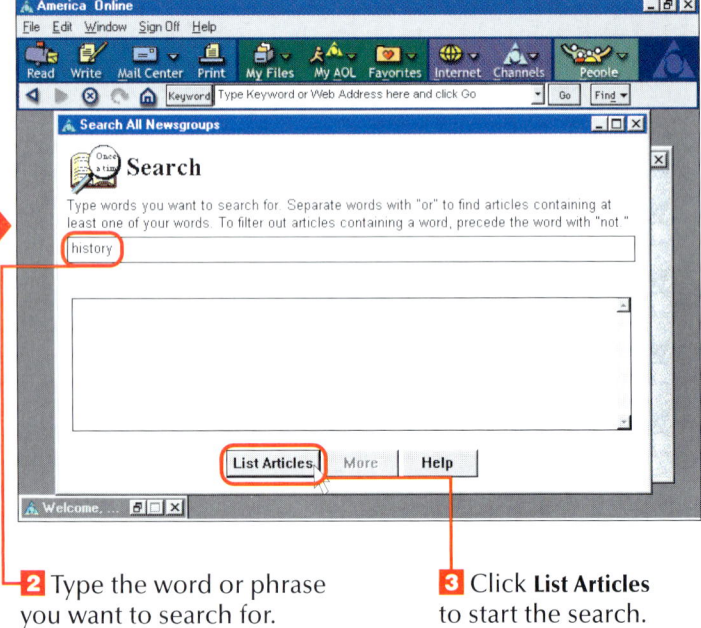

1 Click **Search All Newsgroups** to search for newsgroups by name.

Note: To display the Newsgroups window, see page 118.

■ The Search All Newsgroups window appears.

2 Type the word or phrase you want to search for.

3 Click **List Articles** to start the search.

122

USING NEWSGROUPS

Why can't I find a newsgroup of interest?

You may need to perform several searches before you find a newsgroup of interest. For example, if you want to find a newsgroup on cars, you can first try searching for **car** and then try searching for **auto** or **vehicle**.

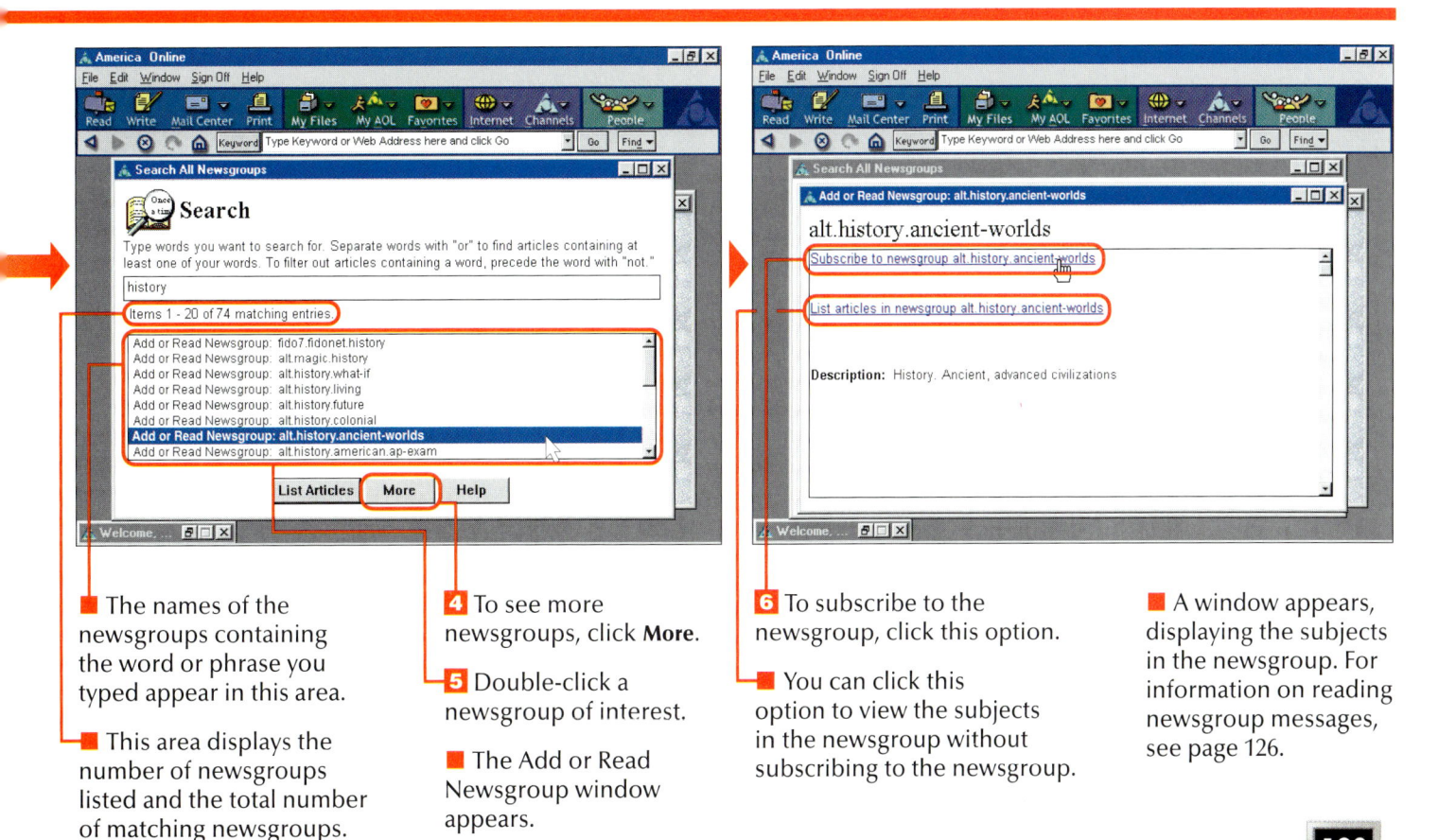

■ The names of the newsgroups containing the word or phrase you typed appear in this area.

■ This area displays the number of newsgroups listed and the total number of matching newsgroups.

4 To see more newsgroups, click **More**.

5 Double-click a newsgroup of interest.

■ The Add or Read Newsgroup window appears.

6 To subscribe to the newsgroup, click this option.

■ You can click this option to view the subjects in the newsgroup without subscribing to the newsgroup.

■ A window appears, displaying the subjects in the newsgroup. For information on reading newsgroup messages, see page 126.

123

SUBSCRIBE TO A NEWSGROUP QUICKLY

> If you know the exact name of a newsgroup you want to join, you can quickly subscribe to the newsgroup. Subscribing allows you to easily read the newsgroup on a regular basis.

SUBSCRIBE TO A NEWSGROUP QUICKLY

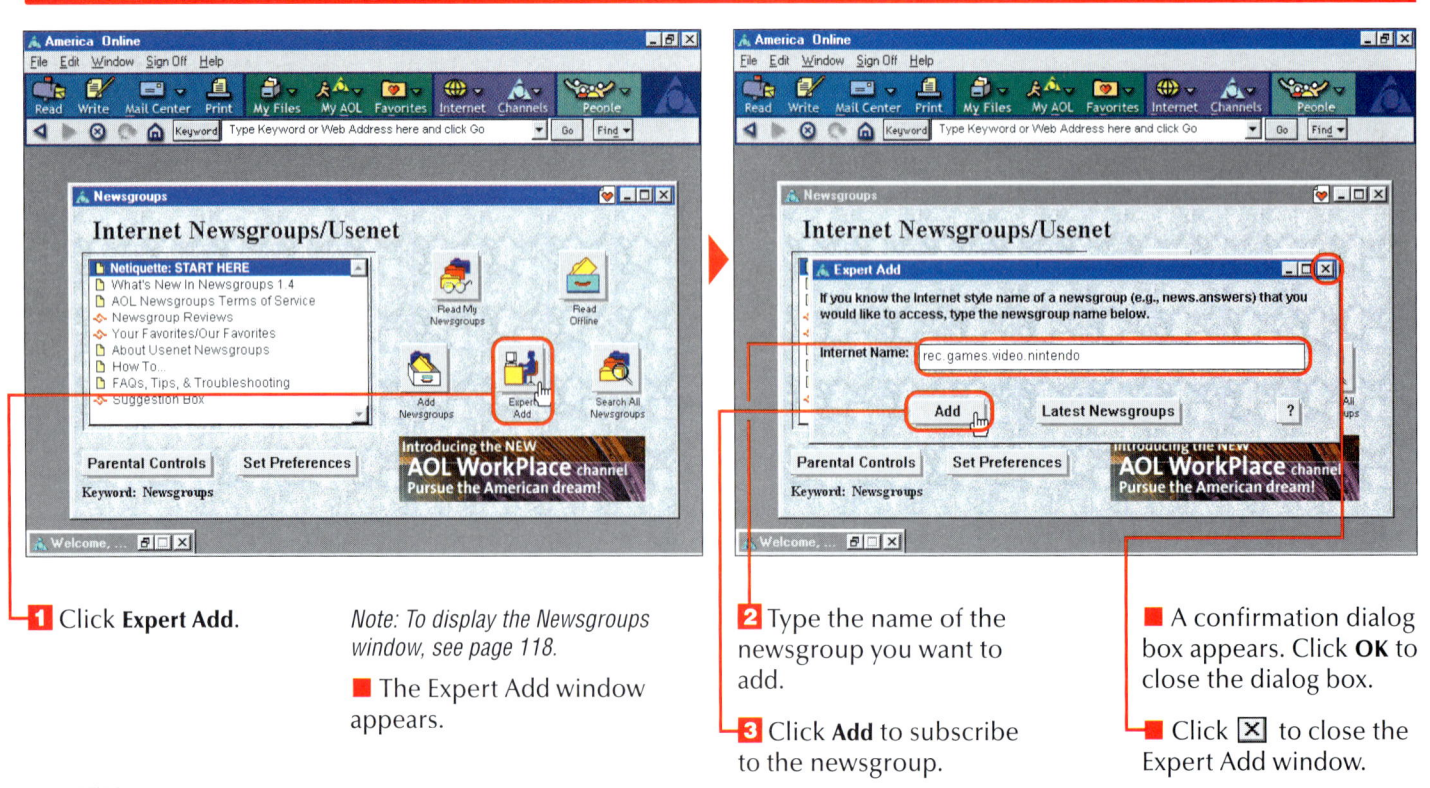

1 Click **Expert Add**.

Note: To display the Newsgroups window, see page 118.

■ The Expert Add window appears.

2 Type the name of the newsgroup you want to add.

3 Click **Add** to subscribe to the newsgroup.

■ A confirmation dialog box appears. Click **OK** to close the dialog box.

■ Click ☒ to close the Expert Add window.

124

UNSUBSCRIBE FROM A NEWSGROUP

USING NEWSGROUPS

You can unsubscribe from a newsgroup at any time if the subject material no longer interests you.

UNSUBSCRIBE FROM A NEWSGROUP

1 Click the newsgroup you want to unsubscribe from.

Note: To display a list of your subscribed newsgroups, perform step 1 on page 126.

2 Click **Remove**.

■ A confirmation dialog box appears.

3 Click **OK** to close the dialog box.

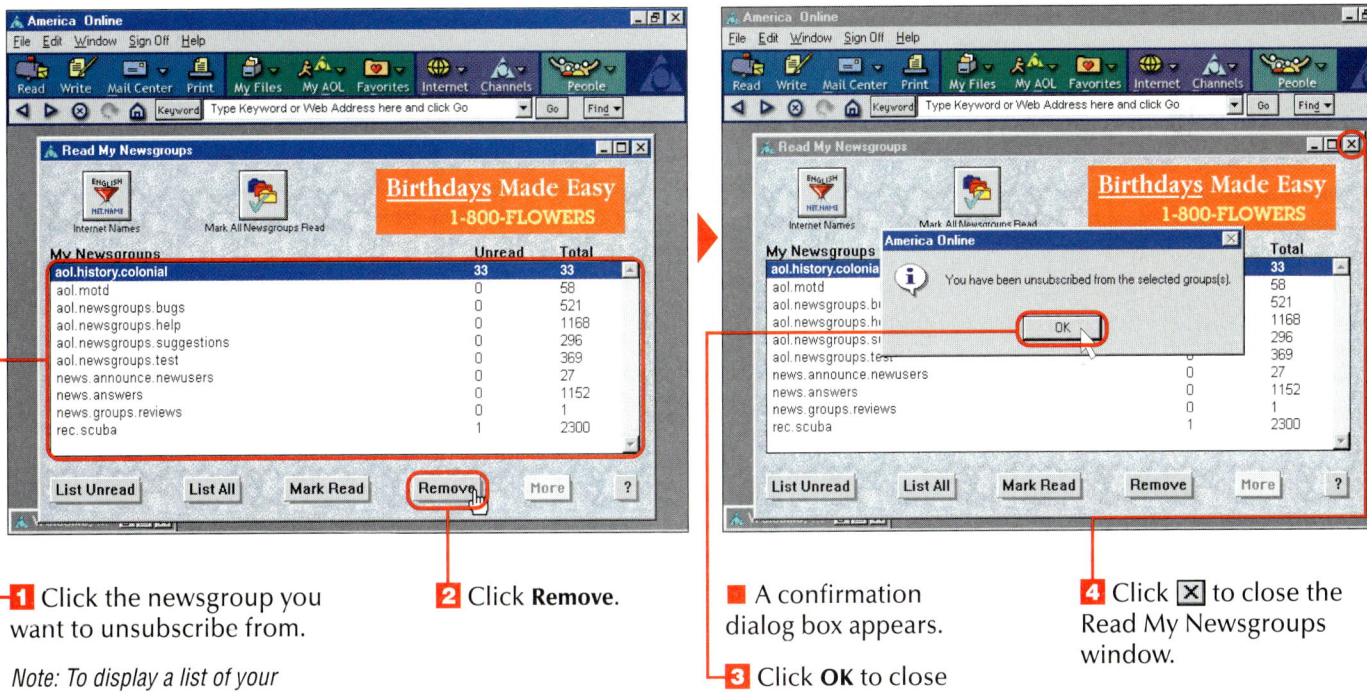

4 Click ⊠ to close the Read My Newsgroups window.

125

READ MESSAGES

NEWSGROUP MESSAGES

You can read the messages in a newsgroup to learn the opinions and ideas of thousands of people around the world.

AOL automatically subscribes you to several newsgroups, such as aol.newsgroups.help and news.answers, to help you get started.

READ MESSAGES

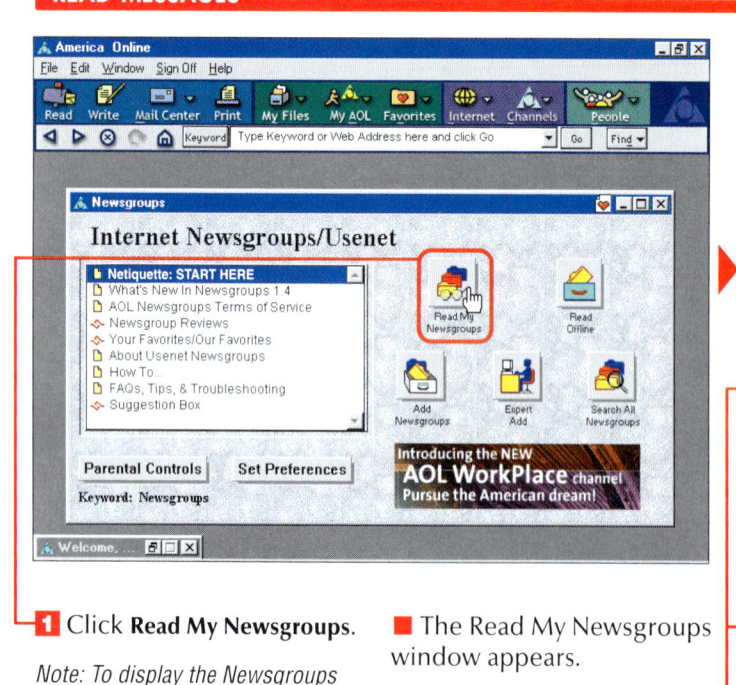

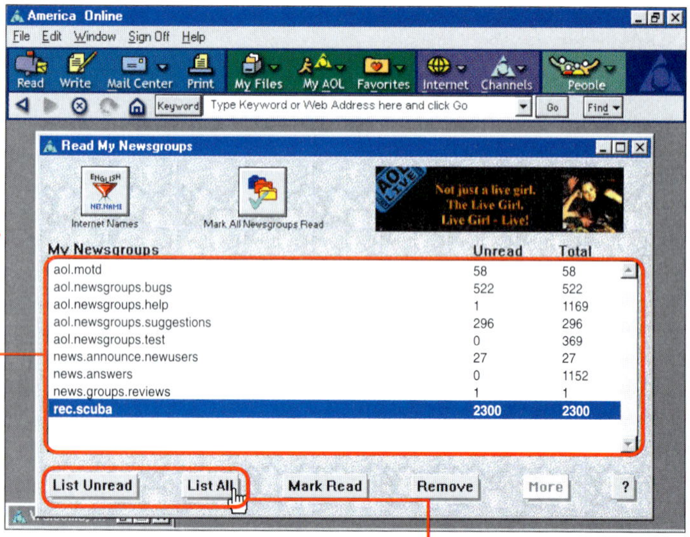

1 Click **Read My Newsgroups**.

Note: To display the Newsgroups window, see page 118.

■ The Read My Newsgroups window appears.

■ This area lists the newsgroups you are subscribed to and the number of unread and total number of messages in each newsgroup.

2 Click a newsgroup of interest.

3 Click an option to list just the unread subjects or all the subjects in the selected newsgroup.

126

7
USING NEWSGROUPS

What is the difference between a message and a subject?

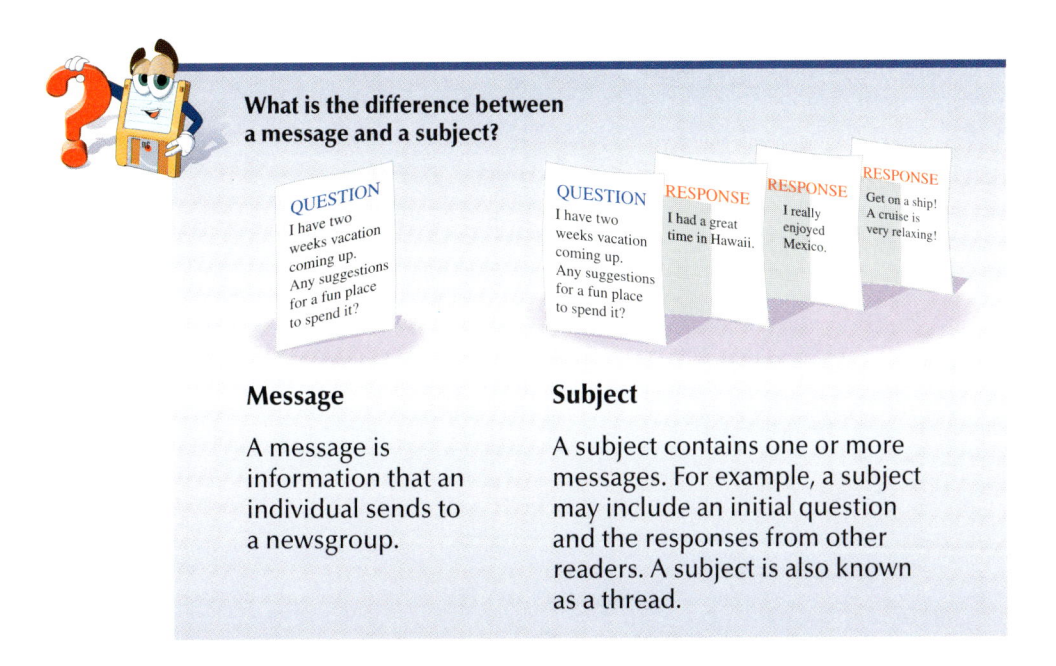

Message

A message is information that an individual sends to a newsgroup.

Subject

A subject contains one or more messages. For example, a subject may include an initial question and the responses from other readers. A subject is also known as a thread.

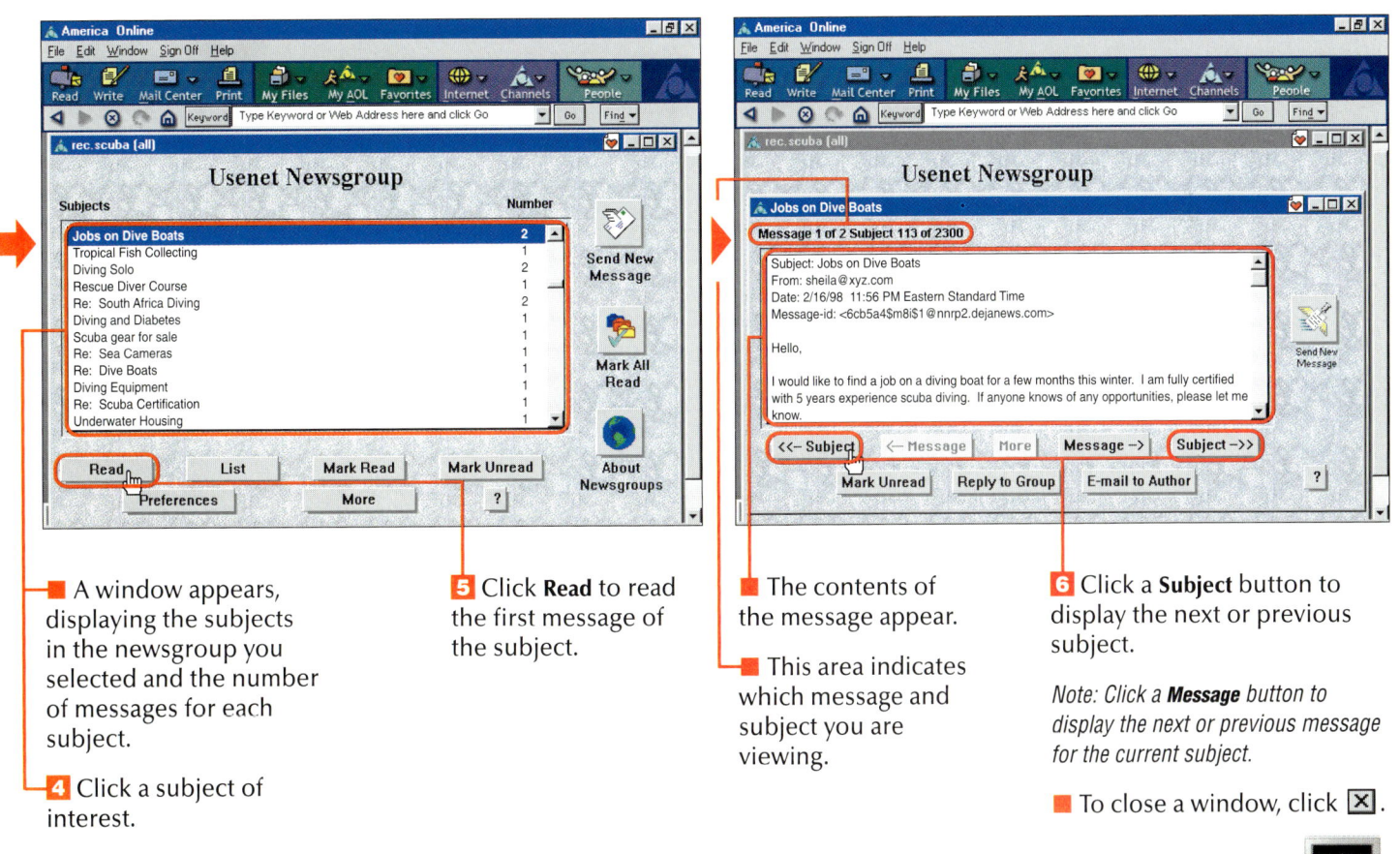

■ A window appears, displaying the subjects in the newsgroup you selected and the number of messages for each subject.

4 Click a subject of interest.

5 Click **Read** to read the first message of the subject.

■ The contents of the message appear.

■ This area indicates which message and subject you are viewing.

6 Click a **Subject** button to display the next or previous subject.

*Note: Click a **Message** button to display the next or previous message for the current subject.*

■ To close a window, click ⊠.

127

PRINT A MESSAGE

You can produce a paper copy of a newsgroup message.

A printed newsgroup message includes the date, your screen name and the page number at the bottom of the page.

PRINT A MESSAGE

1 Display the contents of the message you want to print.

Note: To display the contents of a message, perform steps 1 to 5 on page 126.

2 Click **Print** to print the message.

■ The Print dialog box appears.

3 Click **OK** to print the message.

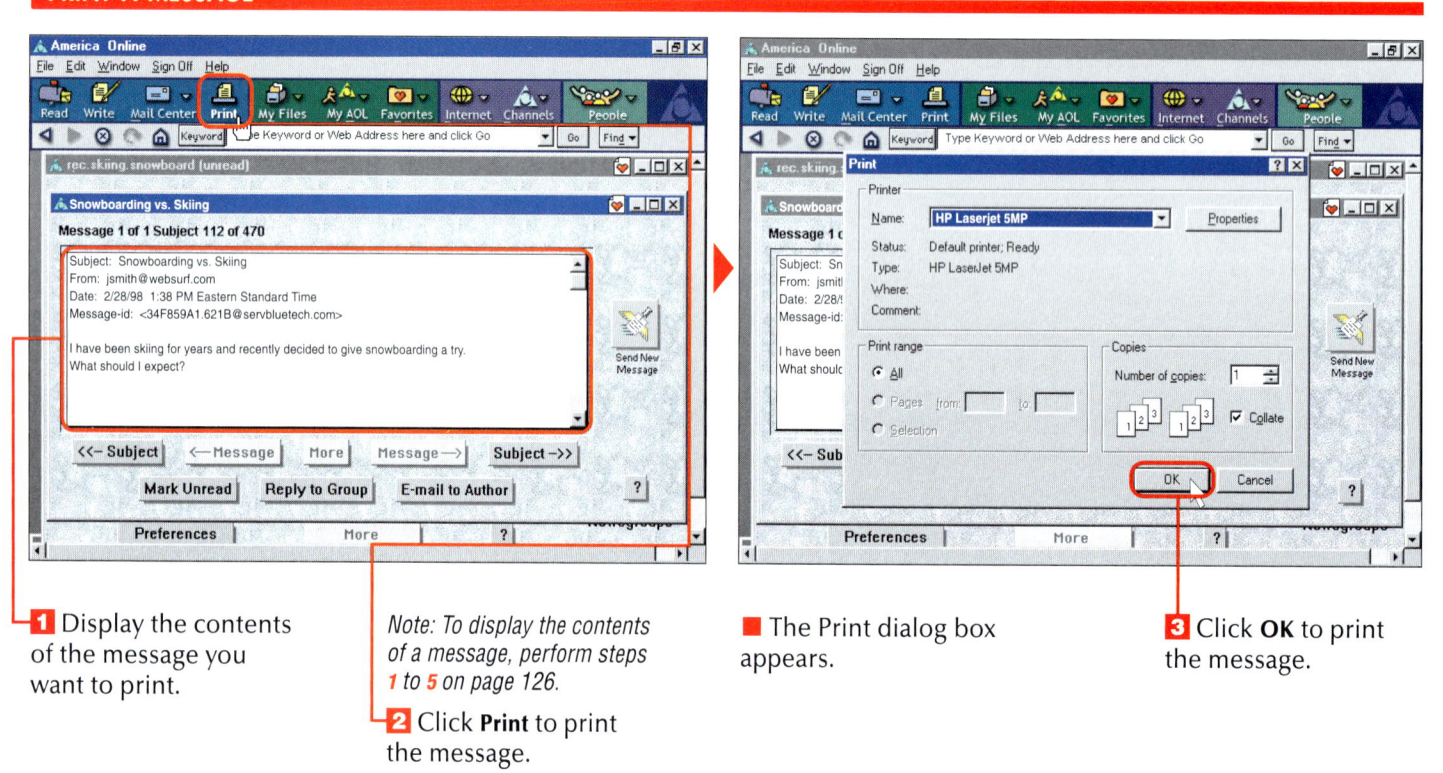

128

MARK NEWSGROUP AS READ

USING NEWSGROUPS

When you finish reading all the messages of interest in a newsgroup, you can mark the newsgroup as read.

The next time you visit a newsgroup you marked as read, you can instantly see which messages were posted since you last visited the newsgroup.

MARK NEWSGROUP AS READ

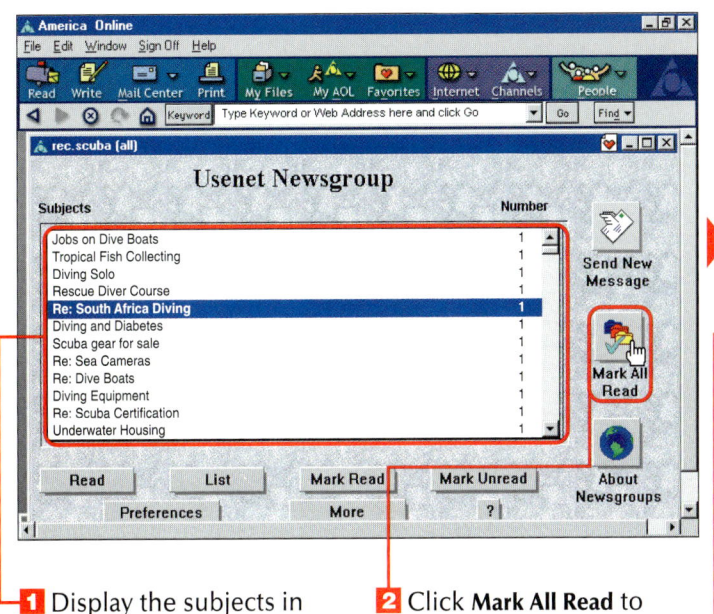

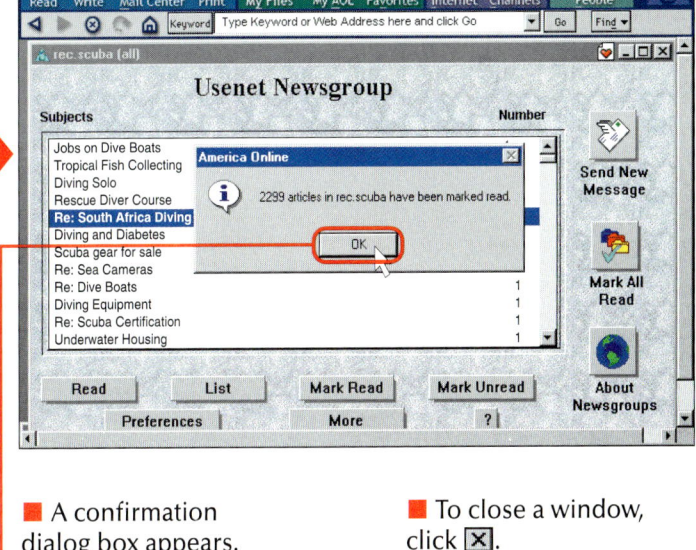

1 Display the subjects in the newsgroup you want to mark as read.

Note: To display the subjects in a newsgroup, perform steps 1 to 3 on page 126.

2 Click **Mark All Read** to mark all the messages in the newsgroup as read.

■ A confirmation dialog box appears.

3 Click **OK** to close the dialog box.

■ To close a window, click ⊠.

129

REPLY TO A MESSAGE

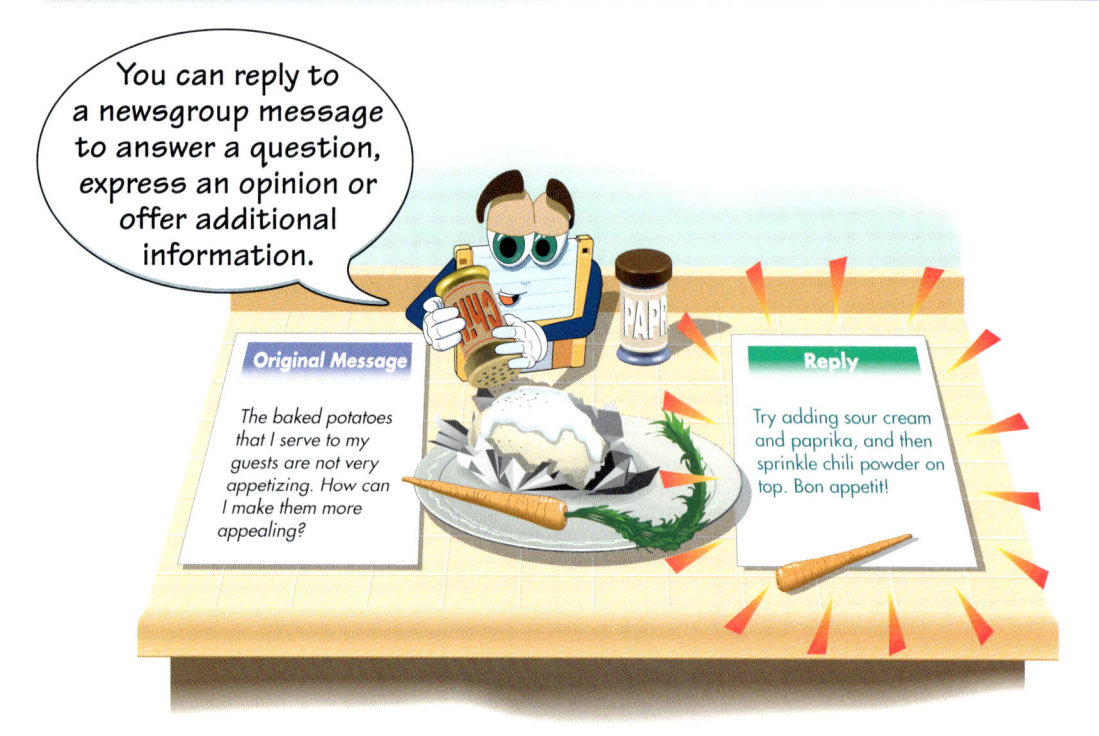

You can reply to a newsgroup message to answer a question, express an opinion or offer additional information.

Reply to a message only when you have something important to say. A reply such as "Me too" or "I agree" is not very informative.

You can include all or part of the original message in your reply to help the reader identify which message you are replying to. This is called quoting.

REPLY TO A MESSAGE

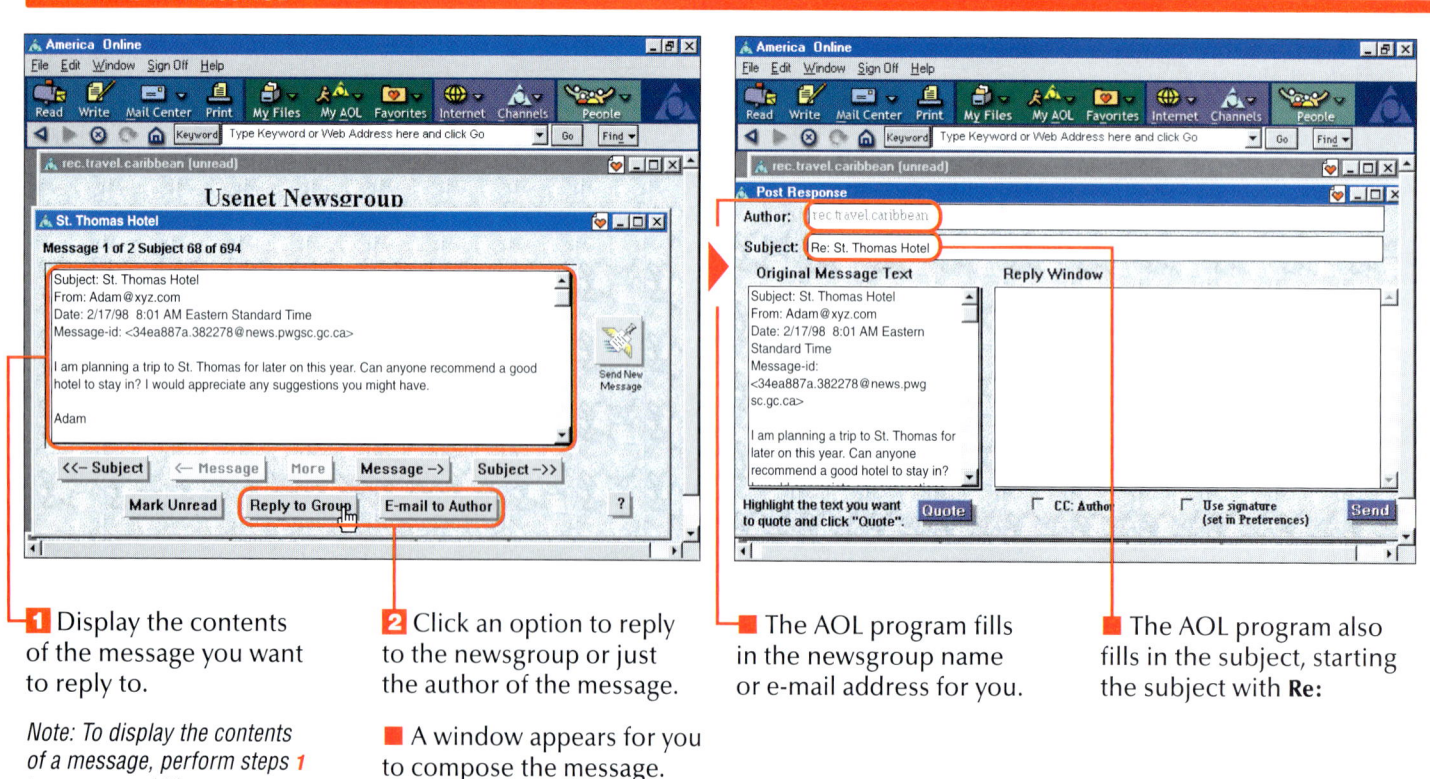

1 Display the contents of the message you want to reply to.

Note: To display the contents of a message, perform steps *1* to *5* on page 126.

2 Click an option to reply to the newsgroup or just the author of the message.

■ A window appears for you to compose the message.

■ The AOL program fills in the newsgroup name or e-mail address for you.

■ The AOL program also fills in the subject, starting the subject with **Re:**

130

USING NEWSGROUPS

How can I reply to a message?

You can send a reply to the newsgroup or just the author of the message. Send a message to just the author when your reply would not be of interest to others in a newsgroup or if you want to send a private response.

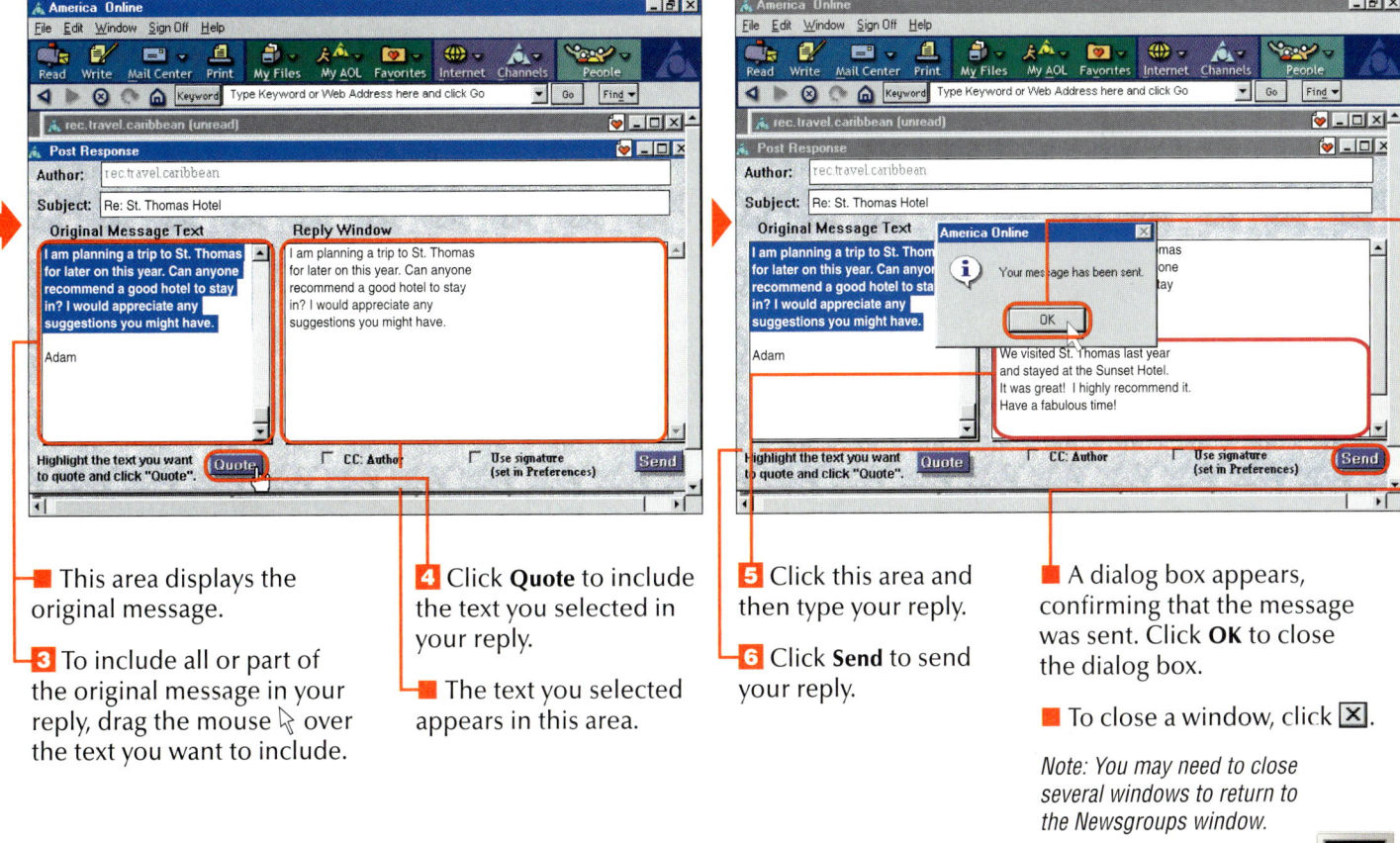

■ This area displays the original message.

3 To include all or part of the original message in your reply, drag the mouse over the text you want to include.

4 Click **Quote** to include the text you selected in your reply.

■ The text you selected appears in this area.

5 Click this area and then type your reply.

6 Click **Send** to send your reply.

■ A dialog box appears, confirming that the message was sent. Click **OK** to close the dialog box.

■ To close a window, click ⊠.

Note: You may need to close several windows to return to the Newsgroups window.

131

SEND A NEW MESSAGE

You can send a new message to a newsgroup to ask a question or express an opinion.

When sending a new message to a newsgroup, keep in mind that thousands of people around the world may read the message.

If you want to practice sending a message, send a message to the aol.newsgroups.test newsgroup. Do not send practice messages to other newsgroups.

SEND A NEW MESSAGE

1 Display the subjects in the newsgroup you want to send a new message to.

Note: To display the subjects in a newsgroup, perform steps 1 to 3 on page 126.

2 Click **Send New Message**.

■ The Post New Message window appears.

■ The AOL program fills in the name of the newsgroup for you.

3 Type a subject for the message. Make sure the subject clearly identifies the contents of your message.

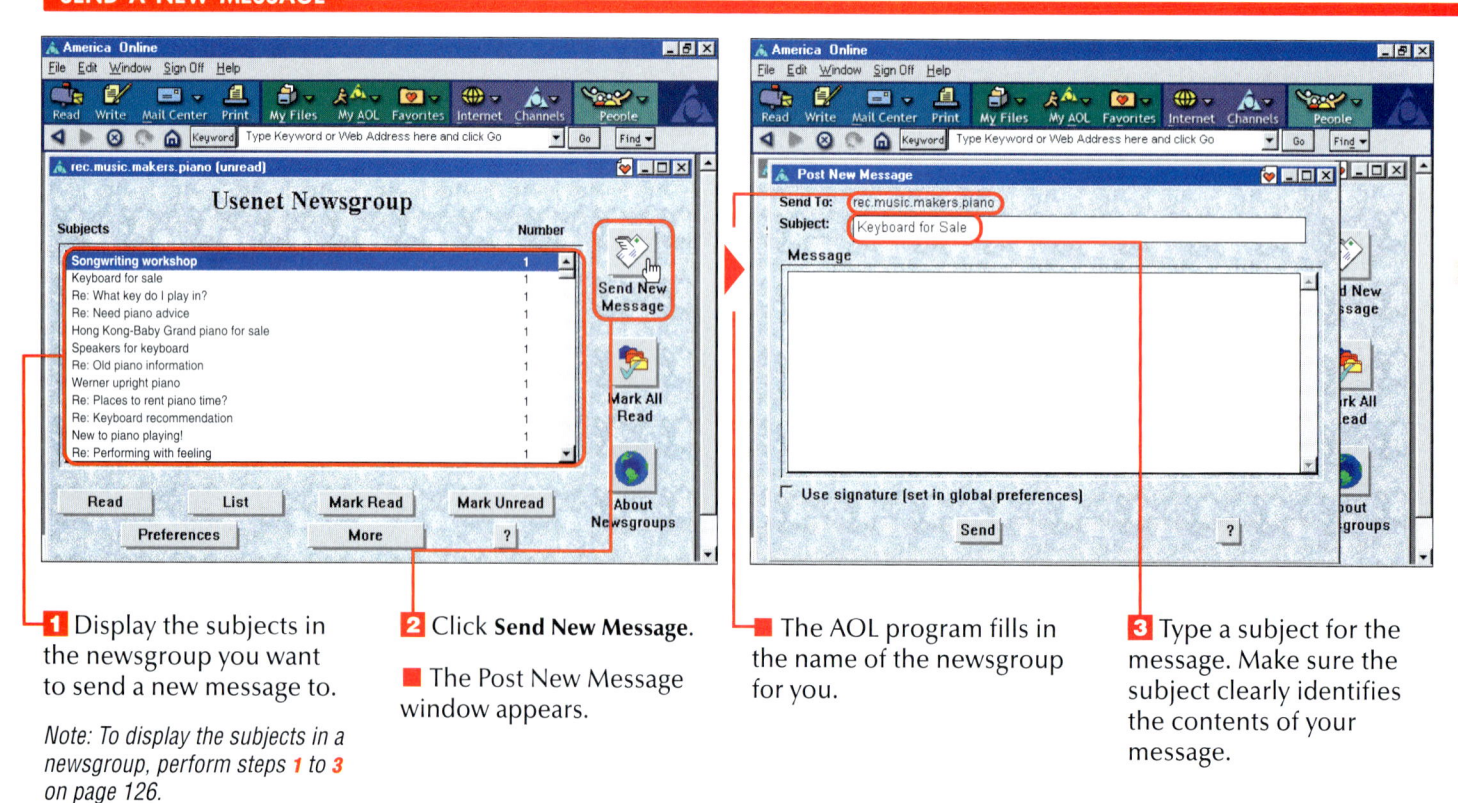

132

USING NEWSGROUPS

Should I read the messages in a newsgroup before sending a new message?

Reading the messages in a newsgroup without participating is known as lurking. Lurking helps you avoid sending information others have already read and is a great way to learn how people in a newsgroup communicate. You should lurk in a newsgroup for at least one week before sending a new message.

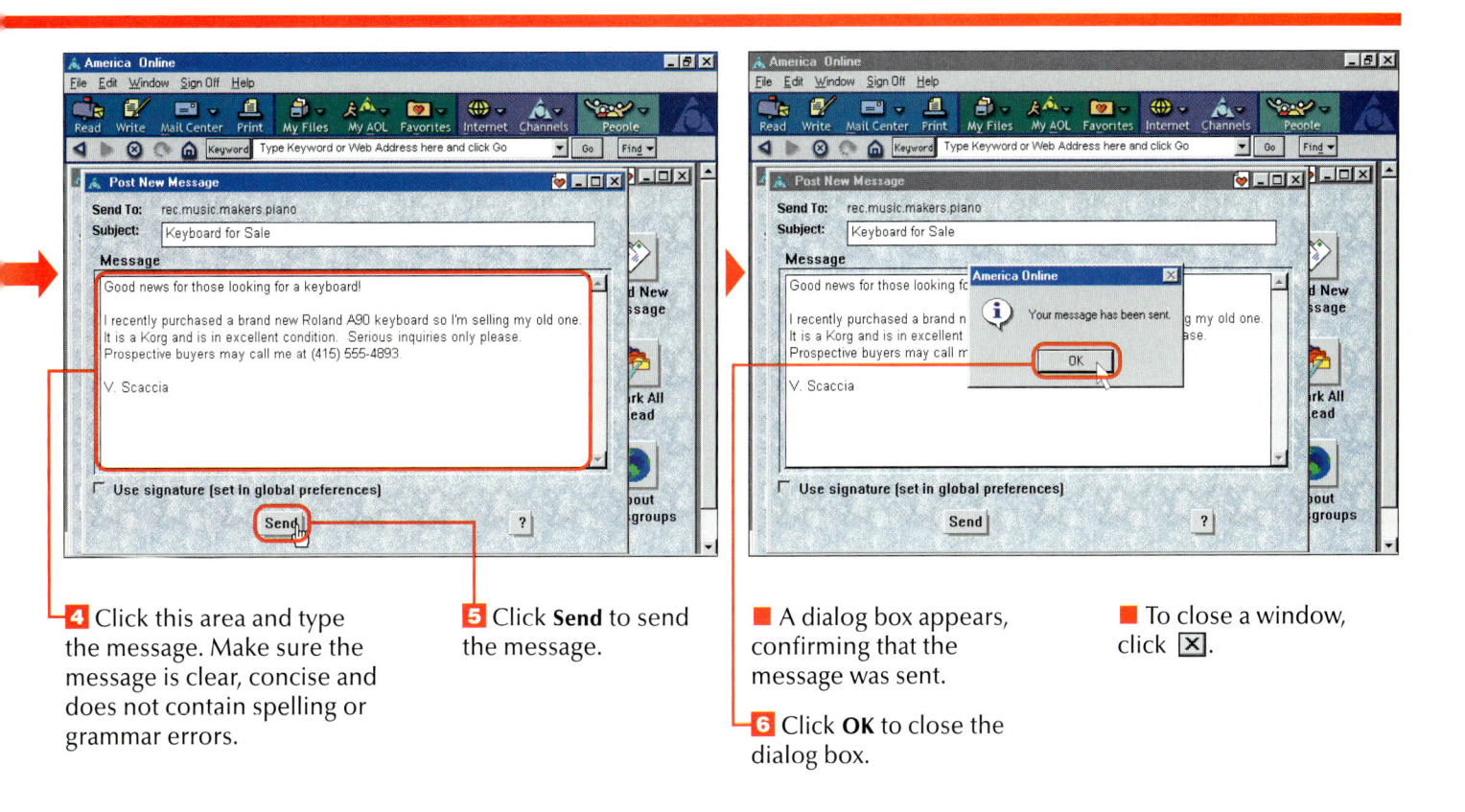

■ **4** Click this area and type the message. Make sure the message is clear, concise and does not contain spelling or grammar errors.

■ **5** Click **Send** to send the message.

■ A dialog box appears, confirming that the message was sent.

■ **6** Click **OK** to close the dialog box.

■ To close a window, click ⊠.

133

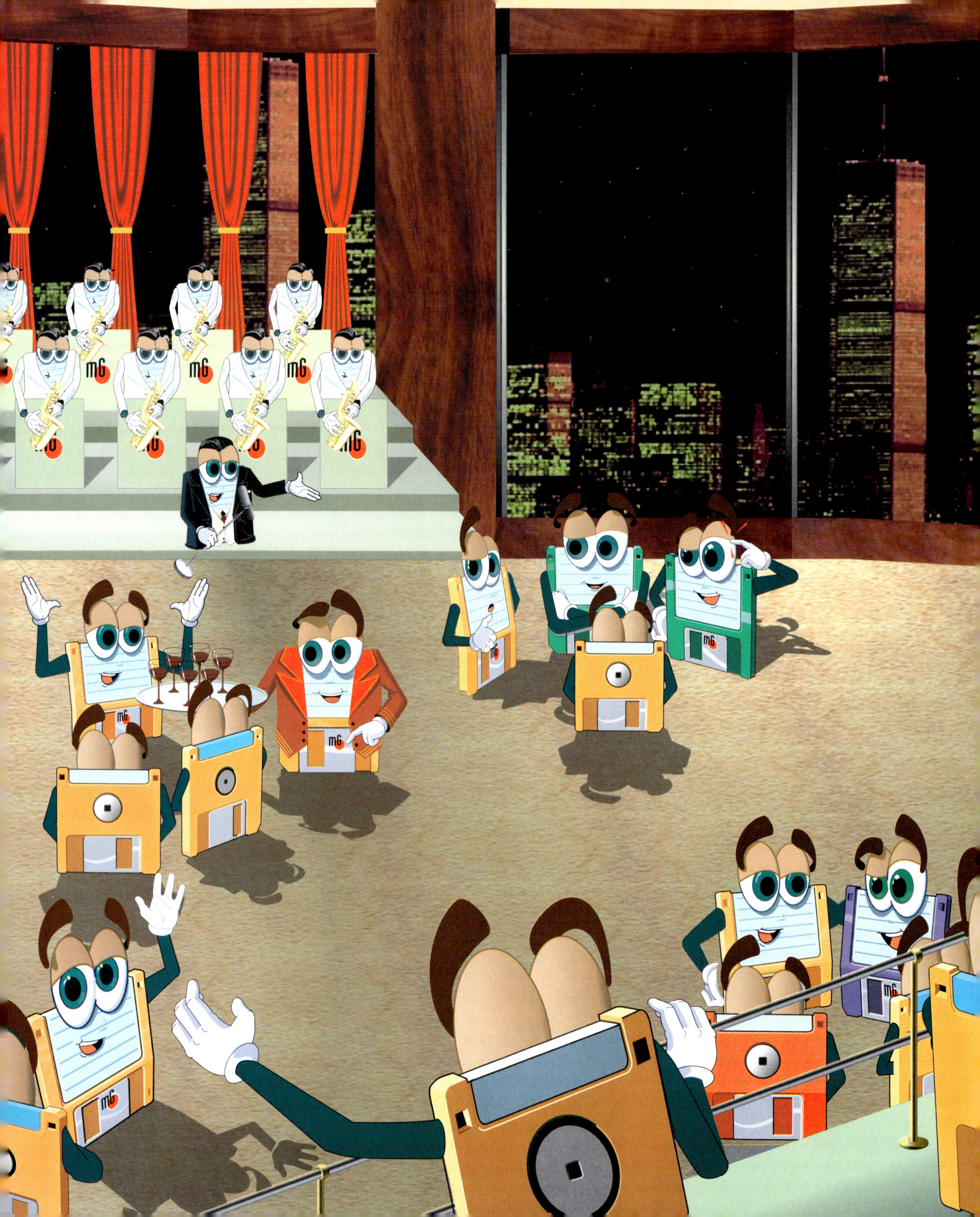

CHAPTER 8
CHAT WITH OTHER AOL MEMBERS

Do you want to talk with other AOL members? This chapter introduces you to chat rooms and the special chat features offered by AOL, which make communication easy and fun.

Introduction to Chat 136

Find a Chat Room 138

Send a Comment 140

Play Sounds in a Chat Room 141

View Member Profile Information 142

Ignore a Chat Member 143

Create a Private Chat Room 144

Send an Instant Message 146

Reply to an Instant Message 149

INTRODUCTION TO CHAT

You can instantly exchange text messages with other members of AOL. This is known as chatting. Chatting is a great way to meet other AOL members.

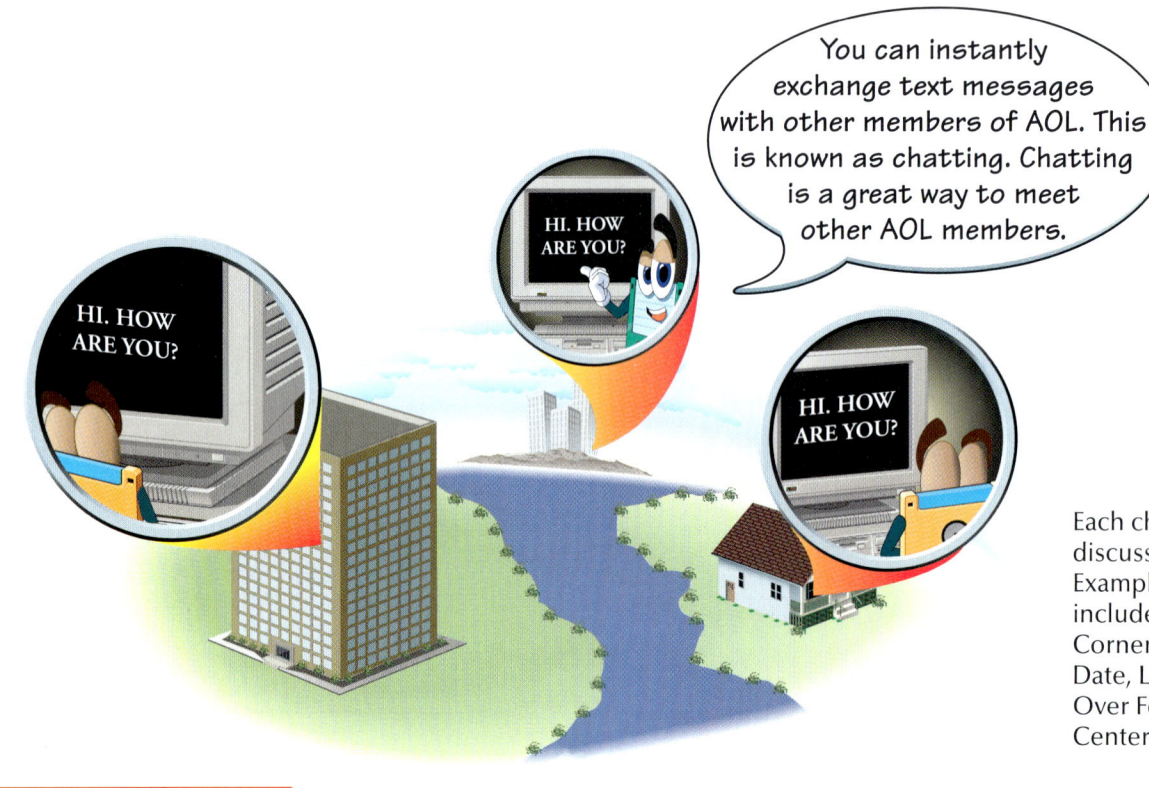

Each chat room on AOL discusses a certain subject. Examples of chat rooms include Car Chat, College Corner, Entrepreneur, First Date, Los Angeles, Music, Over Forty and Sports Center.

TYPES OF CHAT ROOMS

Featured Chat Rooms
Featured chat rooms are rooms created by AOL that all members can join. Several featured chat rooms are hosted by volunteers who greet members and make sure the conversation flows smoothly.

Member Chat Rooms
Member chat rooms are created by AOL members. All members can create and join a member chat room.

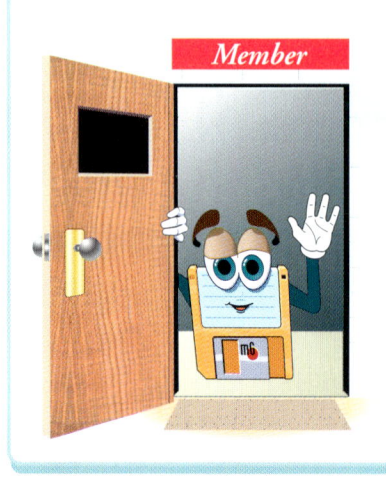

Private Chat Rooms
Private chat rooms are created by AOL members. Only members who know the name of the chat room can join. Private chat rooms allow AOL members to have business or personal conversations in private.

CHAT WITH OTHER AOL MEMBERS

AOL CHAT ETIQUETTE

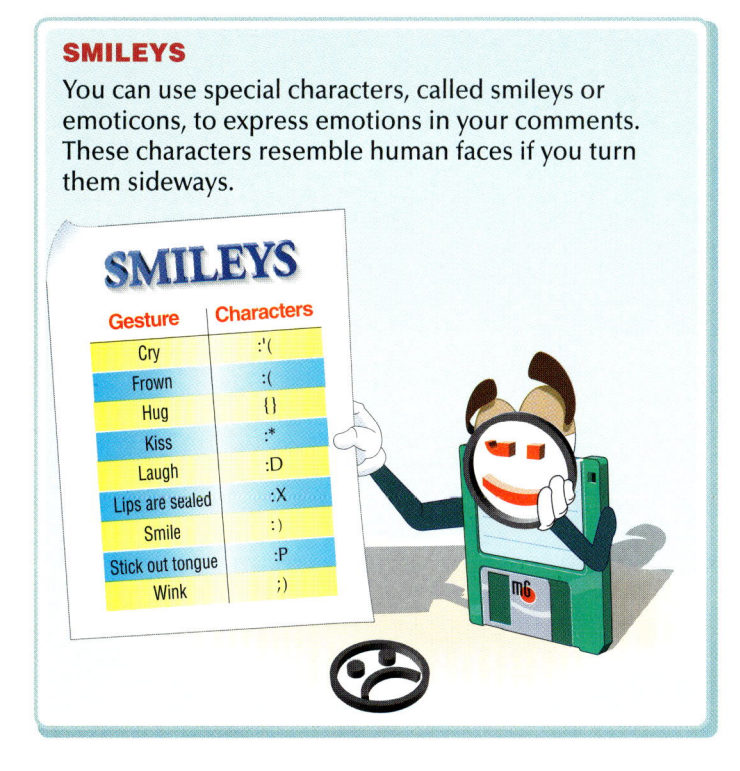

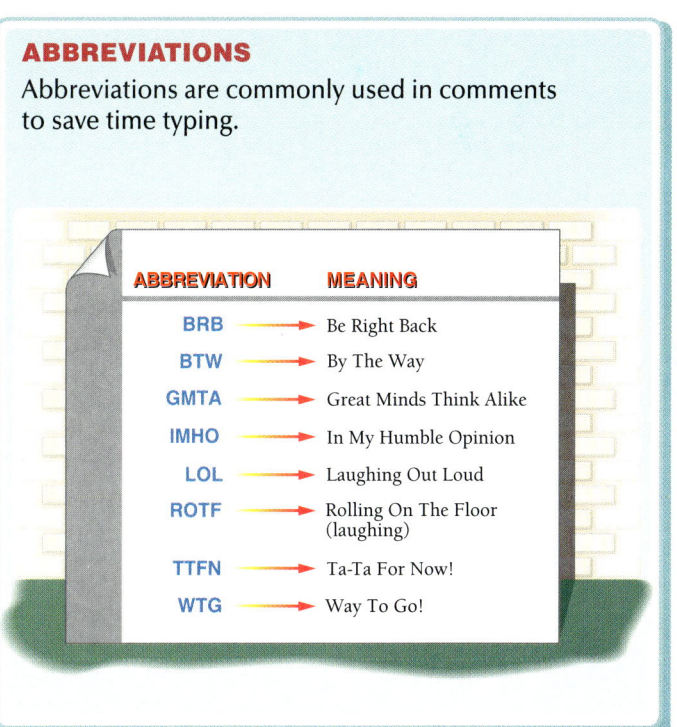

When sending comments to a chat room, you should follow some basic rules.

SPELLING & GRAMMAR

I am thinking of joining a gym. Is there specail footwear I should buy befor I get started? I'm concerned that my old shoes wont quite cut it.

Check your comments for spelling, grammar and clarity.

SHOUTING

I HAVE SOME VACATION TIME COMING UP. ARE THERE ANY CHEAP PLACES TO GO AT THIS TIME OF THE YEAR?

DO NOT TYPE COMMENTS IN ALL CAPITAL LETTERS. This is called shouting and will annoy and distract other members in the chat room.

OFFENSIVE LANGUAGE

My @#!#? car broke down again. This is the third time this week. Can anyone recommend a good mechanic in the NY area?

Do not use offensive language. People of all ages and backgrounds can join chat rooms.

SMILEYS

You can use special characters, called smileys or emoticons, to express emotions in your comments. These characters resemble human faces if you turn them sideways.

SMILEYS

Gesture	Characters
Cry	:'(
Frown	:(
Hug	{}
Kiss	:*
Laugh	:D
Lips are sealed	:X
Smile	:)
Stick out tongue	:P
Wink	;)

ABBREVIATIONS

Abbreviations are commonly used in comments to save time typing.

ABBREVIATION	MEANING
BRB	Be Right Back
BTW	By The Way
GMTA	Great Minds Think Alike
IMHO	In My Humble Opinion
LOL	Laughing Out Loud
ROTF	Rolling On The Floor (laughing)
TTFN	Ta-Ta For Now!
WTG	Way To Go!

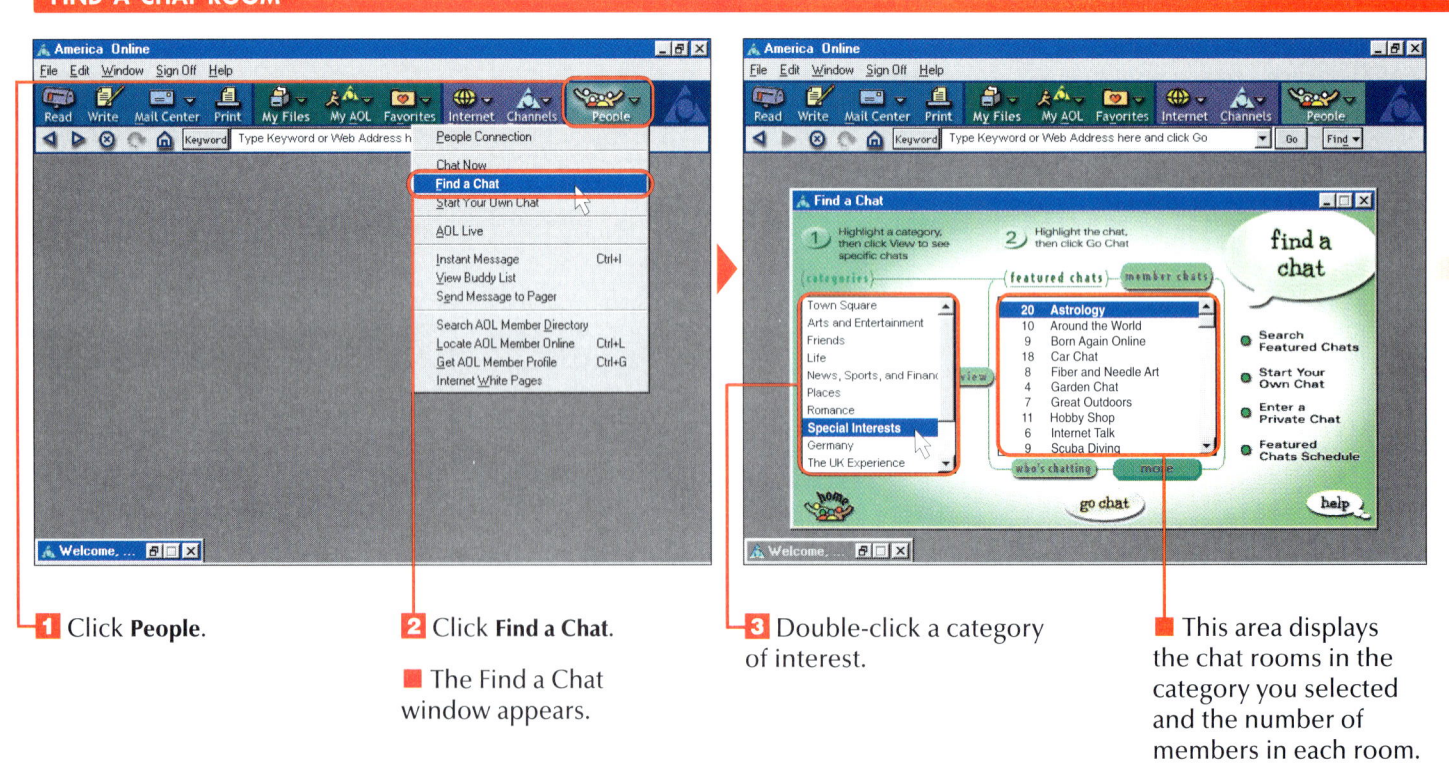

FIND A CHAT ROOM

> You can find a chat room of interest to you. AOL organizes chat rooms into various categories, such as arts and entertainment, places and romance.

FIND A CHAT ROOM

1 Click **People**.

2 Click **Find a Chat**.

■ The Find a Chat window appears.

3 Double-click a category of interest.

■ This area displays the chat rooms in the category you selected and the number of members in each room.

138

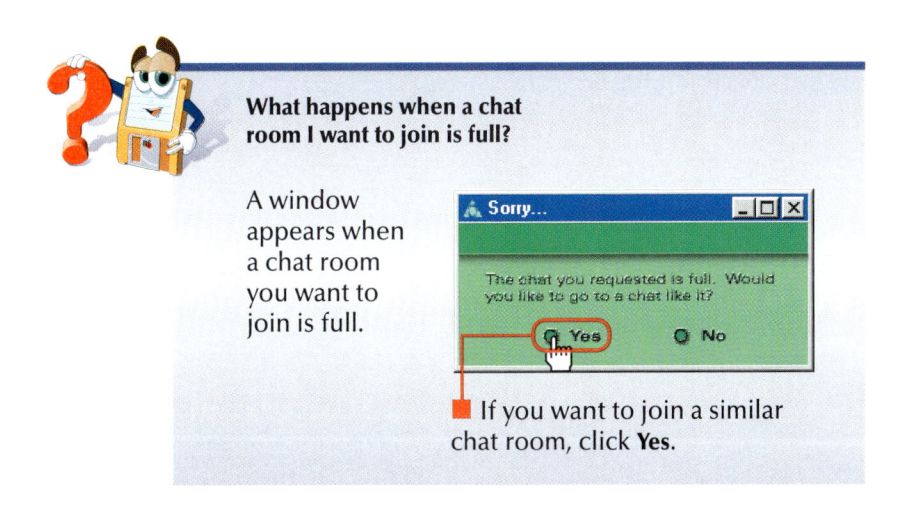

CHAT WITH OTHER AOL MEMBERS

What happens when a chat room I want to join is full?

A window appears when a chat room you want to join is full.

■ If you want to join a similar chat room, click **Yes**.

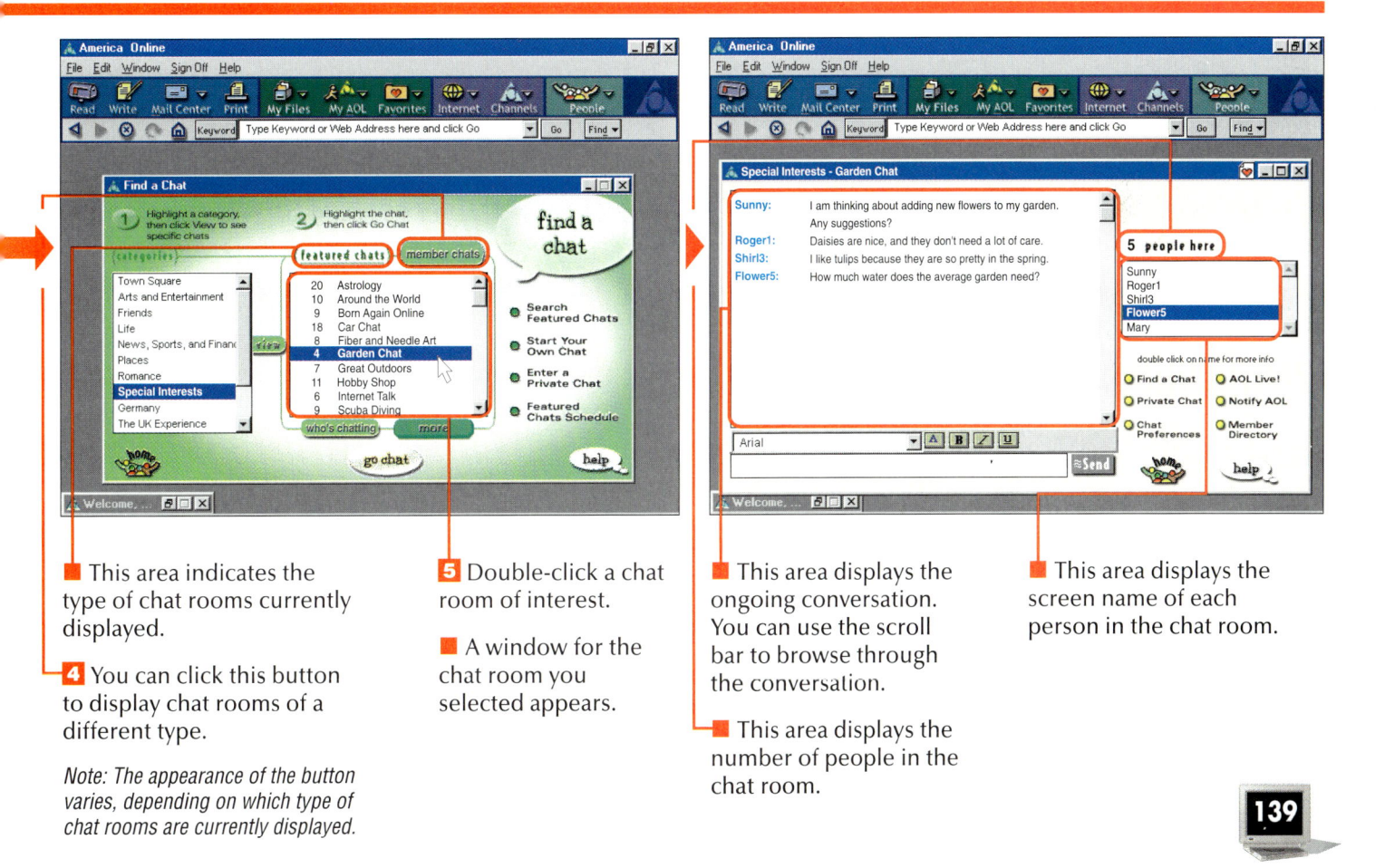

■ This area indicates the type of chat rooms currently displayed.

4 You can click this button to display chat rooms of a different type.

Note: The appearance of the button varies, depending on which type of chat rooms are currently displayed.

5 Double-click a chat room of interest.

■ A window for the chat room you selected appears.

■ This area displays the ongoing conversation. You can use the scroll bar to browse through the conversation.

■ This area displays the number of people in the chat room.

■ This area displays the screen name of each person in the chat room.

139

SEND A COMMENT

You can send a comment to a chat room to greet other chat members, ask questions or join the conversation.

SEND A COMMENT

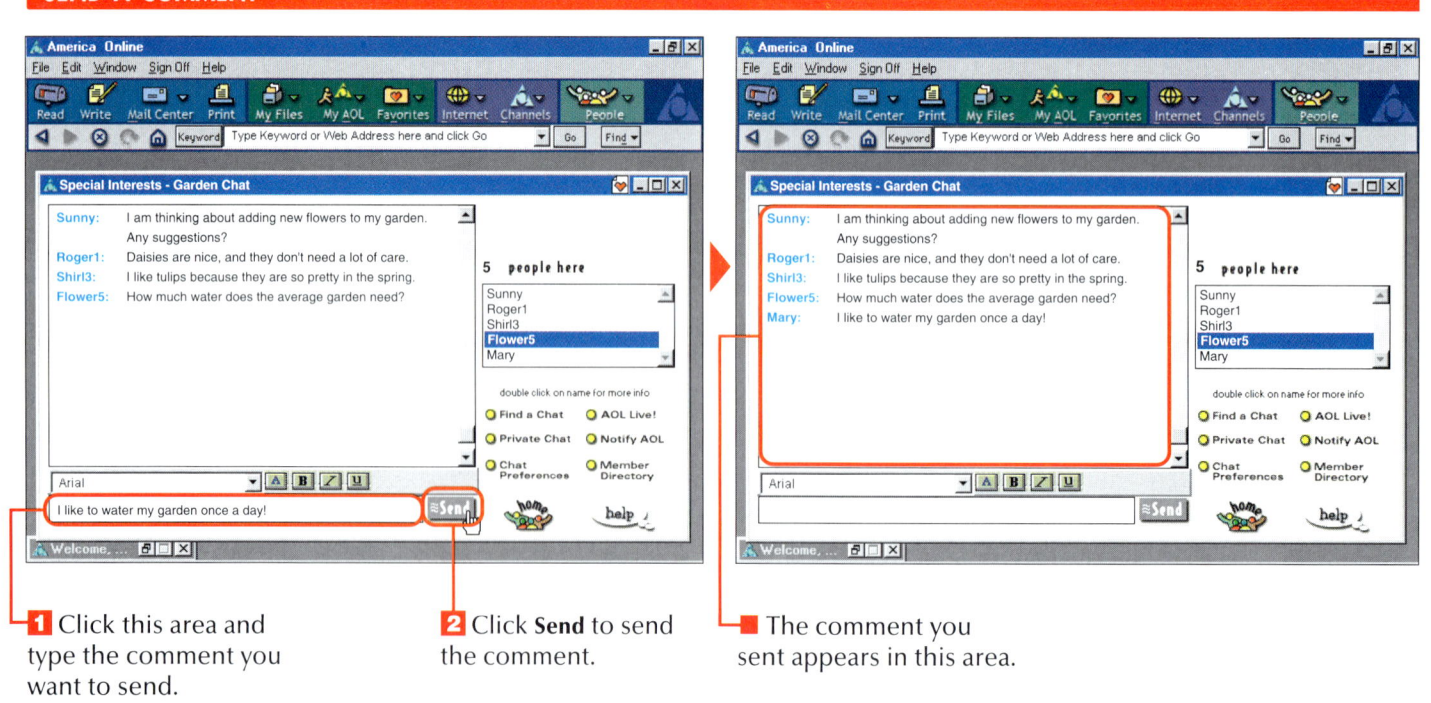

1 Click this area and type the comment you want to send.

Note: Comments are limited to 92 characters.

2 Click **Send** to send the comment.

■ The comment you sent appears in this area.

PLAY SOUNDS IN A CHAT ROOM

CHAT WITH OTHER AOL MEMBERS — 8

> You can play a sound that everyone in a chat room will hear.

SOUNDS
buddyin
buddyout
drop
filedone
goodbye
gotmail
im
welcome

These sound files come with AOL and are stored in the America Online folder on your computer.

Playing too many sounds in a chat room can annoy other members.

PLAY SOUNDS IN A CHAT ROOM

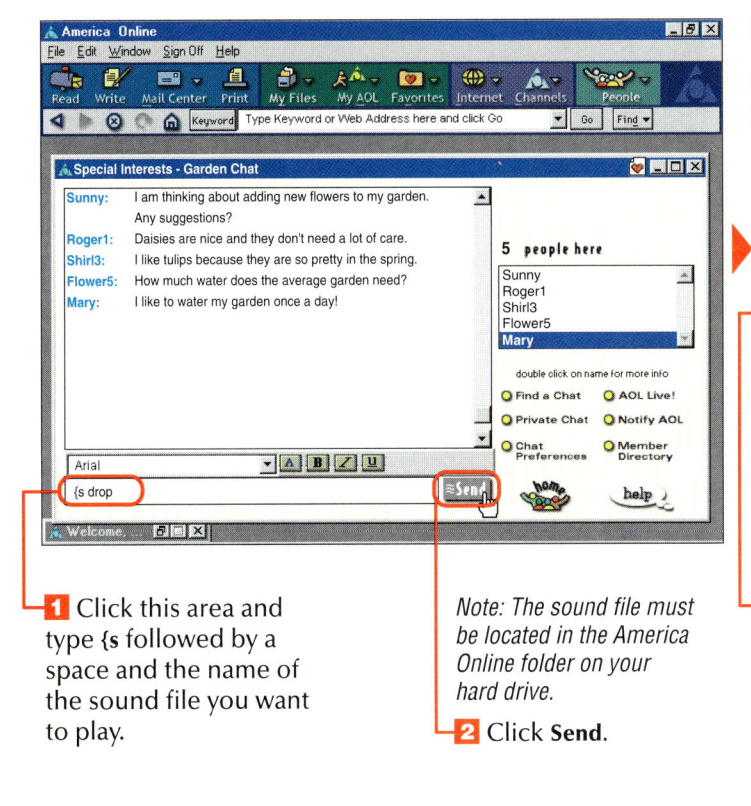

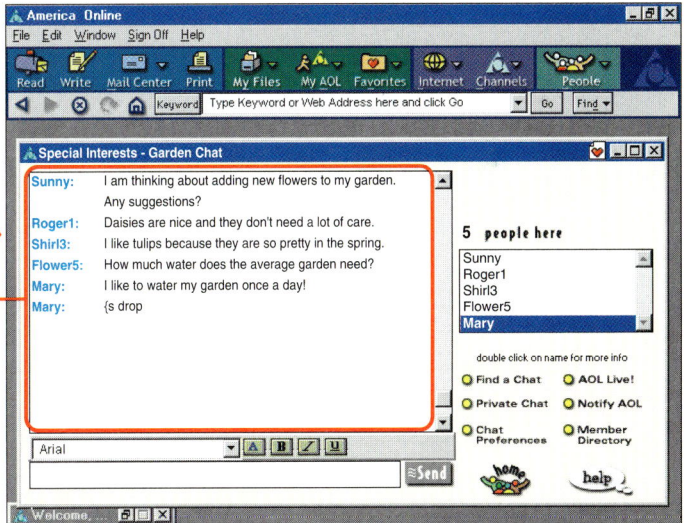

■ **1** Click this area and type **{s** followed by a space and the name of the sound file you want to play.

Note: The sound file must be located in the America Online folder on your hard drive.

■ **2** Click **Send**.

■ The text you typed appears in this area.

■ The sound plays on your computer and on the computers of the other members in the chat room.

Note: Other members will only hear the sound if their computer can play sound and the sound file exists on their computer.

141

VIEW MEMBER PROFILE INFORMATION

You can view information about another member in a chat room, such as their name, location, hobbies and occupation.

Member Name: Paul Simak
Location: New York, NY
Hobbies: Weightlifting
Biking
Swimming
Occupation: Student

To enter your own profile information, see page 162.

VIEW MEMBER PROFILE INFORMATION

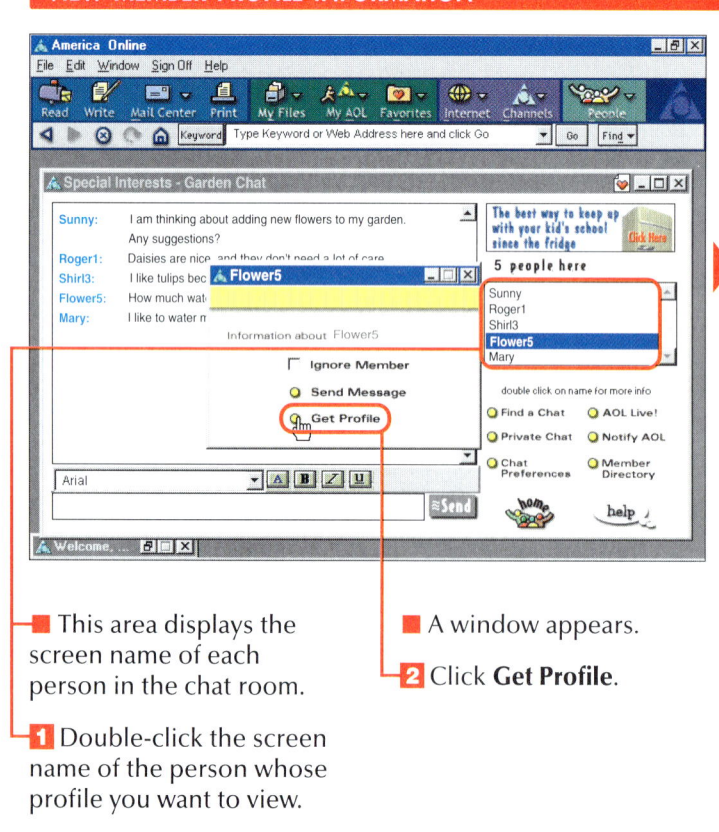

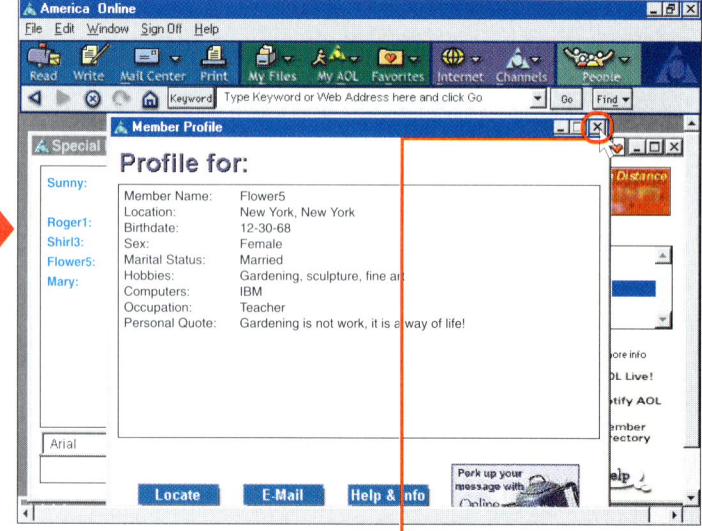

■ This area displays the screen name of each person in the chat room.

1 Double-click the screen name of the person whose profile you want to view.

■ A window appears.

2 Click **Get Profile**.

■ The Member Profile window appears, displaying information about the member.

*Note: A dialog box appears if no profile exists for the member. Click **OK** to close the dialog box.*

3 When you finish viewing the information, click ✕ to close the window.

142

IGNORE A CHAT MEMBER

CHAT WITH OTHER AOL MEMBERS — 8

> You can ignore a chat member so their comments do not appear on your screen. This is a good way to remove conversation of no interest to you.

IGNORE A CHAT MEMBER

1 Double-click the screen name of a person whose comments you no longer want to see.

■ A window appears.

2 Click the box beside **Ignore Member** (☐ changes to ☑).

3 Click ☒ to close the window.

■ If you no longer want to ignore a member, perform steps **1** to **3** (☑ changes to ☐ in step **2**).

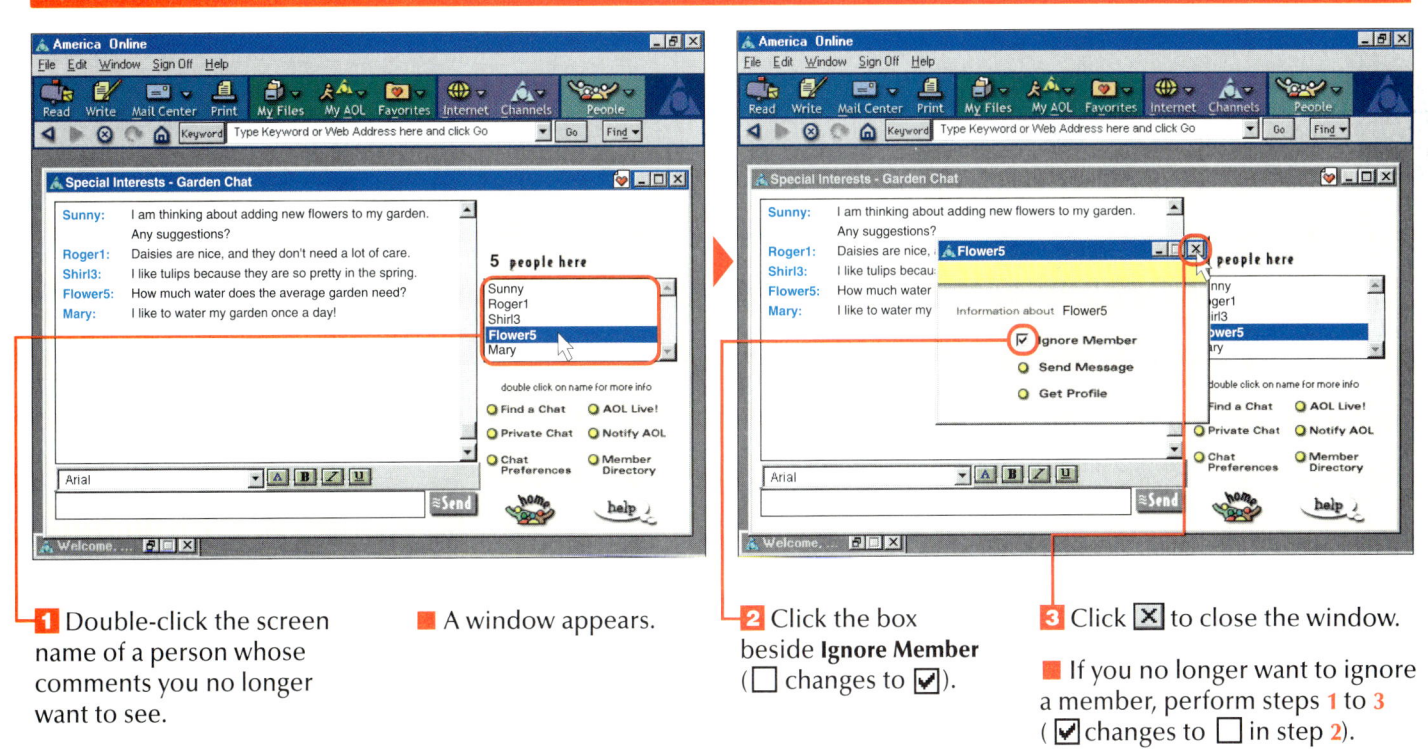

143

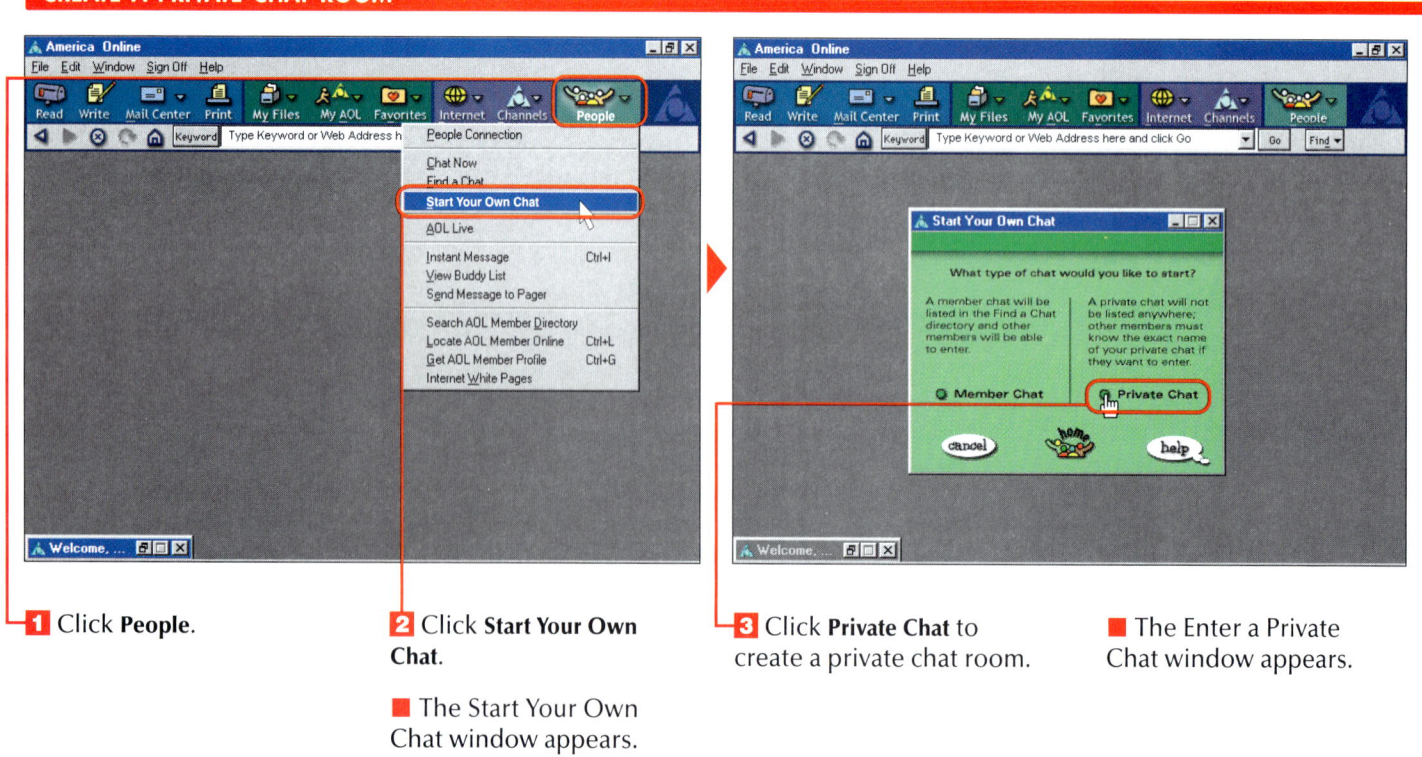

CREATE A PRIVATE CHAT ROOM

You can create your own private chat room. This is ideal for having private, long-distance discussions with colleagues or family members.

CREATE A PRIVATE CHAT ROOM

1 Click **People**.

2 Click **Start Your Own Chat**.

■ The Start Your Own Chat window appears.

3 Click **Private Chat** to create a private chat room.

■ The Enter a Private Chat window appears.

144

CHAT WITH OTHER AOL MEMBERS

Where can I find a list of private chat rooms?

There is no list of private chat rooms on AOL. You need to know the name of a private chat room to join the room.

■ Type the name of the private chat room you want to create.

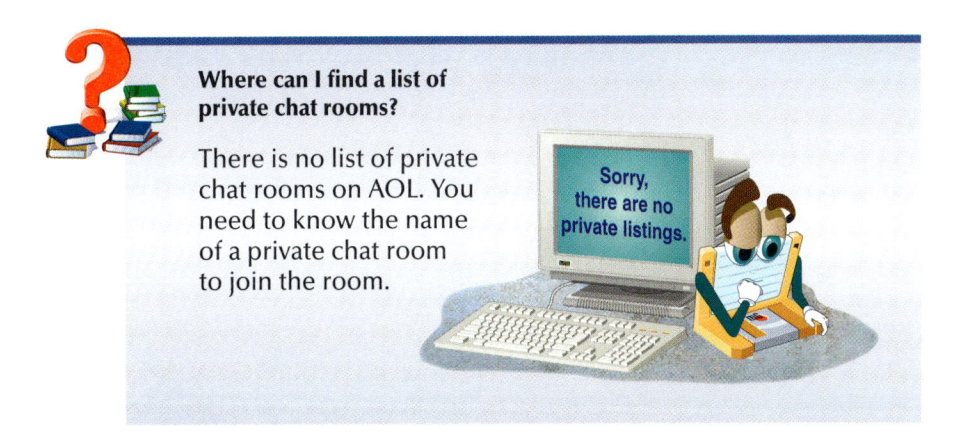

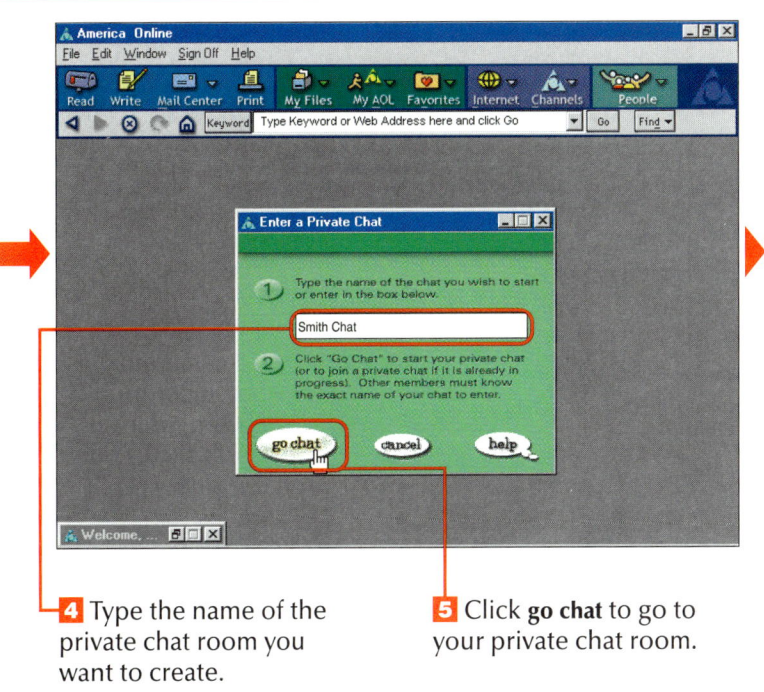

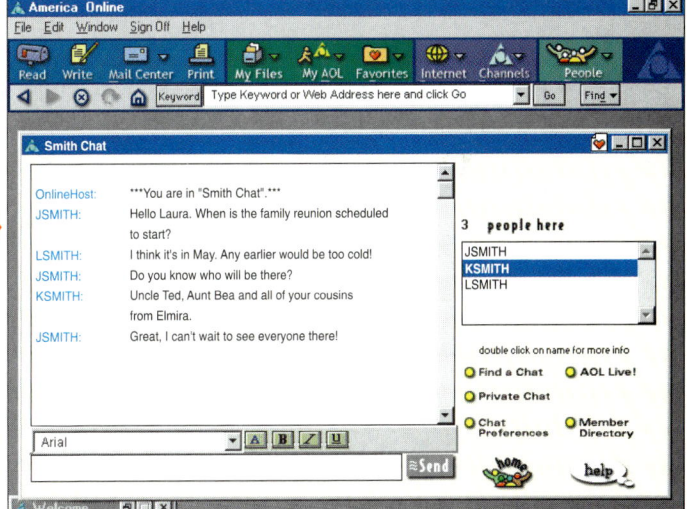

■ Click **go chat** to go to your private chat room.

■ The chat window appears. You can send and view comments as you would in any other chat room.

JOIN A PRIVATE CHAT ROOM

■ Perform steps 1 to 5, typing the name of the private chat room you want to join in step 4.

145

SEND AN INSTANT MESSAGE

While chatting, you can exchange private messages with another member. Messages you send immediately appear on the other person's screen.

Have you ever visited Hawaii before?

Send Message

Only the person you send the message to will see the message.

SEND AN INSTANT MESSAGE (WHILE CHATTING)

■ This area displays the screen name of each person in the chat room.

1 Double-click the screen name of the person you want to send an instant message to.

■ A window appears.

2 Click **Send Message** to send the person an instant message.

■ The Send Instant Message window appears.

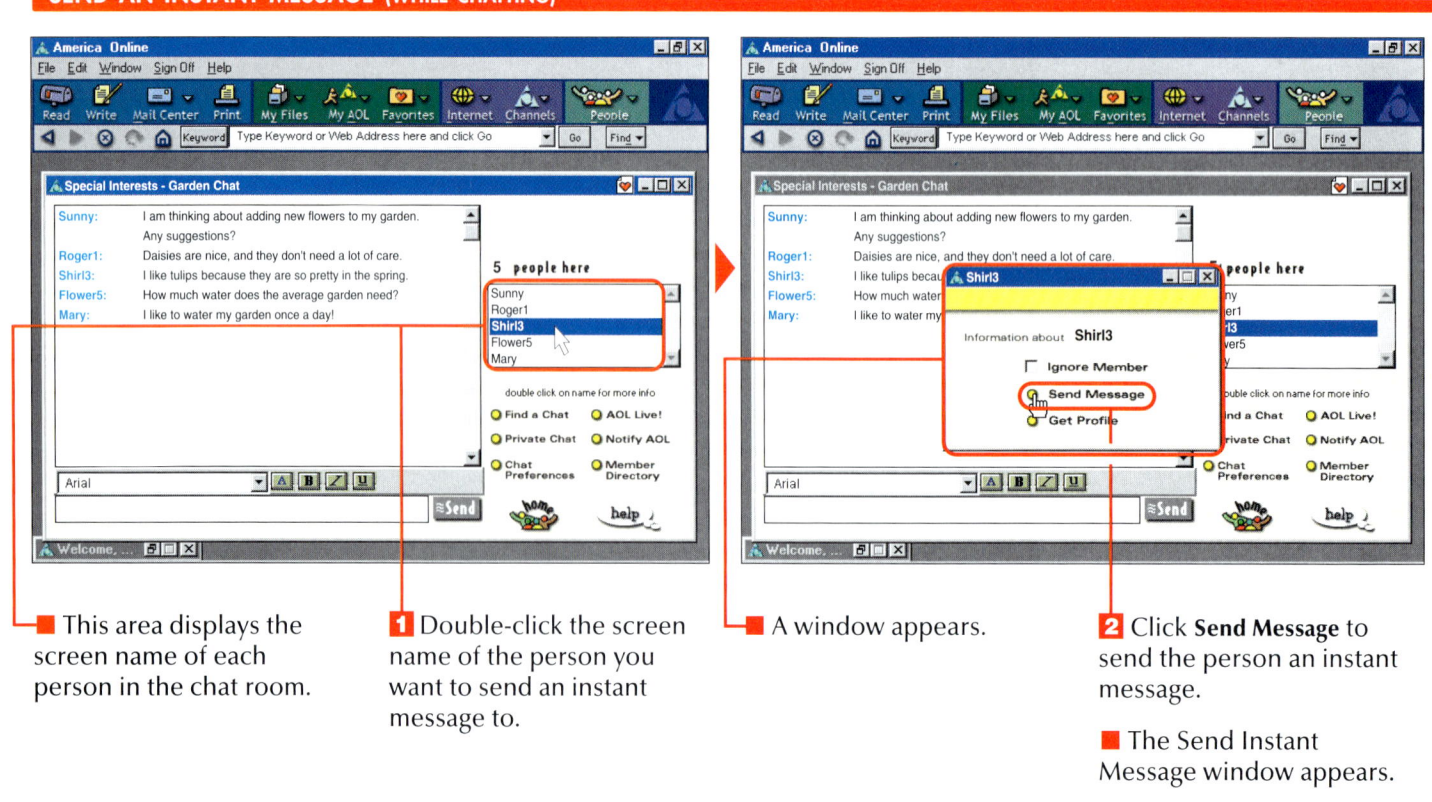

146

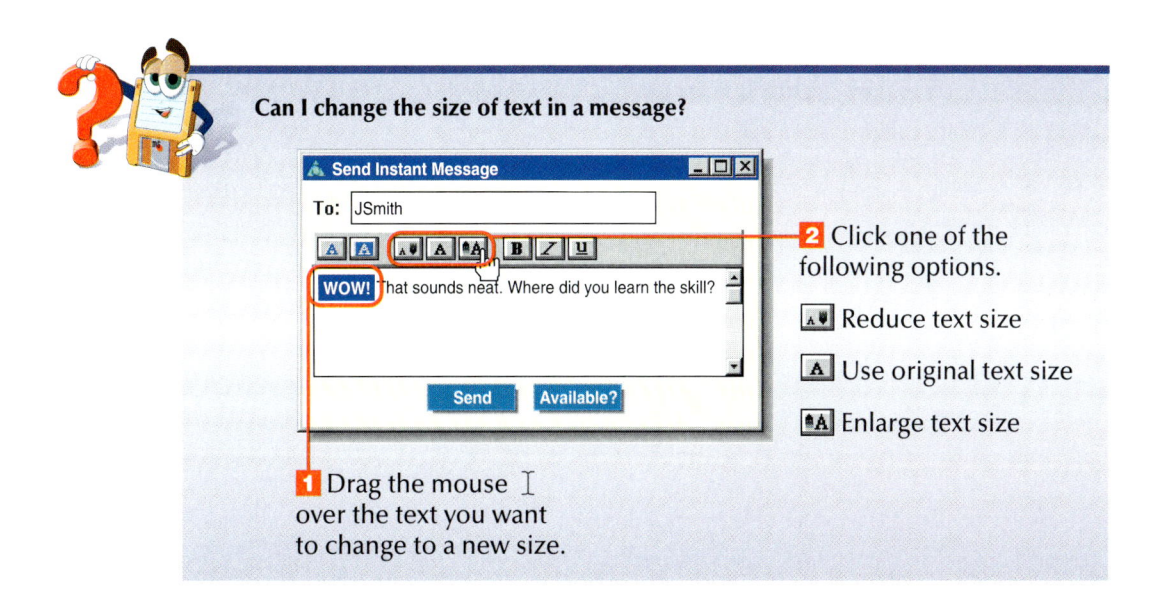

CHAT WITH OTHER AOL MEMBERS

Can I change the size of text in a message?

1 Drag the mouse over the text you want to change to a new size.

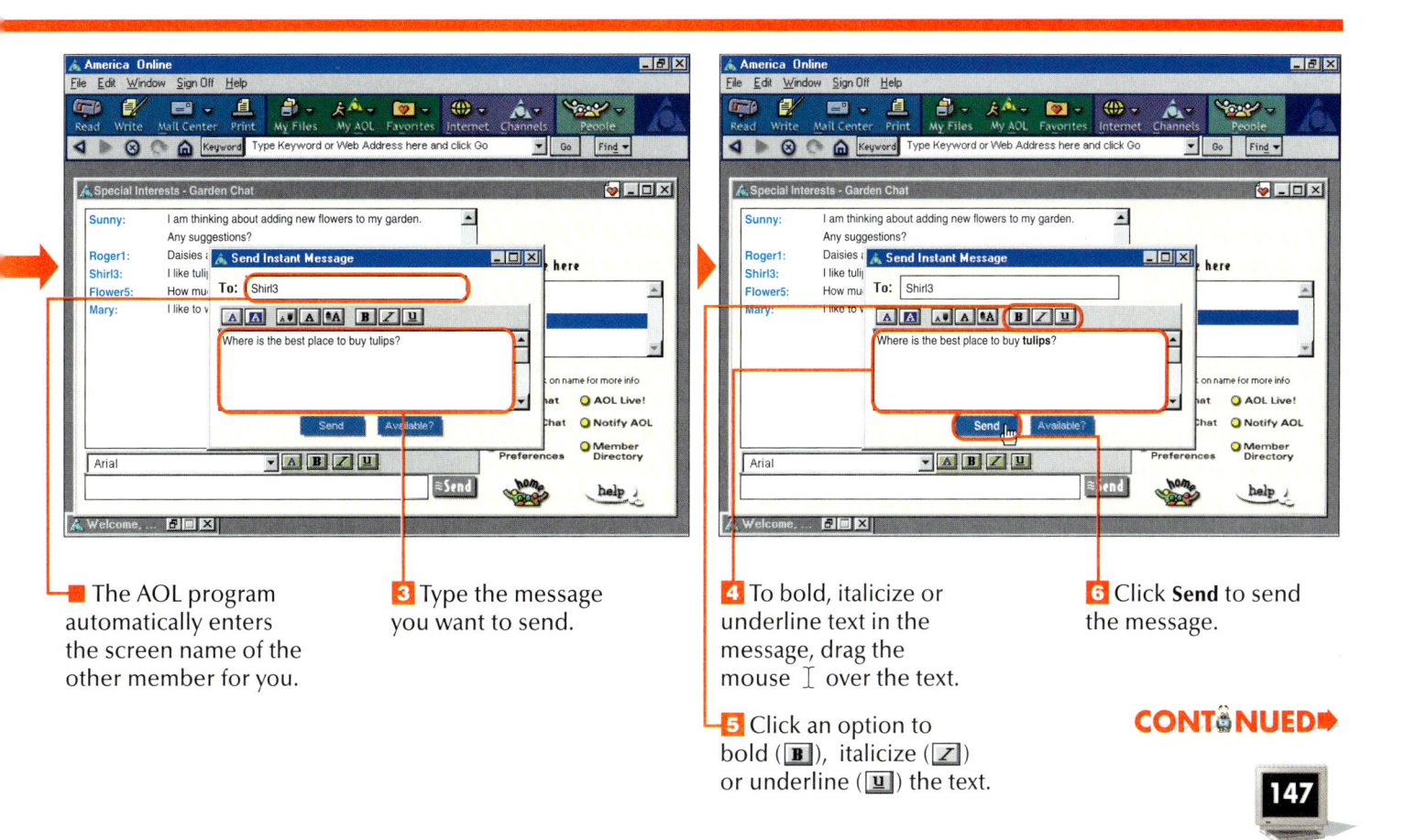

2 Click one of the following options.

- Reduce text size
- Use original text size
- Enlarge text size

■ The AOL program automatically enters the screen name of the other member for you.

3 Type the message you want to send.

4 To bold, italicize or underline text in the message, drag the mouse over the text.

5 Click an option to bold (**B**), italicize (*I*) or underline (U) the text.

6 Click **Send** to send the message.

CONTINUED

147

SEND AN INSTANT MESSAGE

You can send an instant message to start a private conversation with another AOL member at any time. The message will immediately appear on the person's screen.

Sending instant messages is a great way to communicate with family, friends or colleagues without paying long-distance charges.

The person you want to send a message to must currently be using AOL.

SEND AN INSTANT MESSAGE (AT ANY TIME)

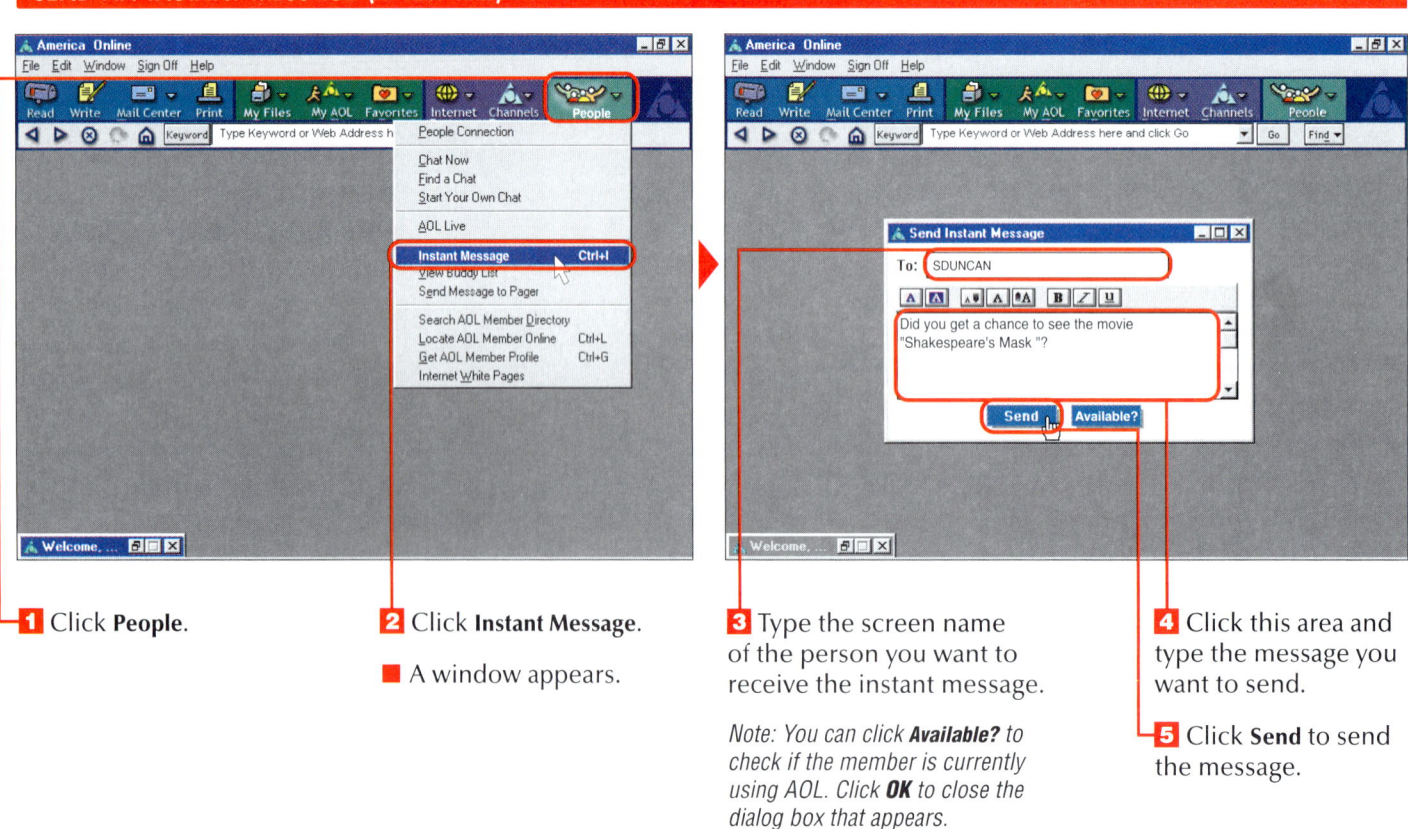

1 Click **People**.

2 Click **Instant Message**.

■ A window appears.

3 Type the screen name of the person you want to receive the instant message.

*Note: You can click **Available?** to check if the member is currently using AOL. Click **OK** to close the dialog box that appears.*

4 Click this area and type the message you want to send.

5 Click **Send** to send the message.

148

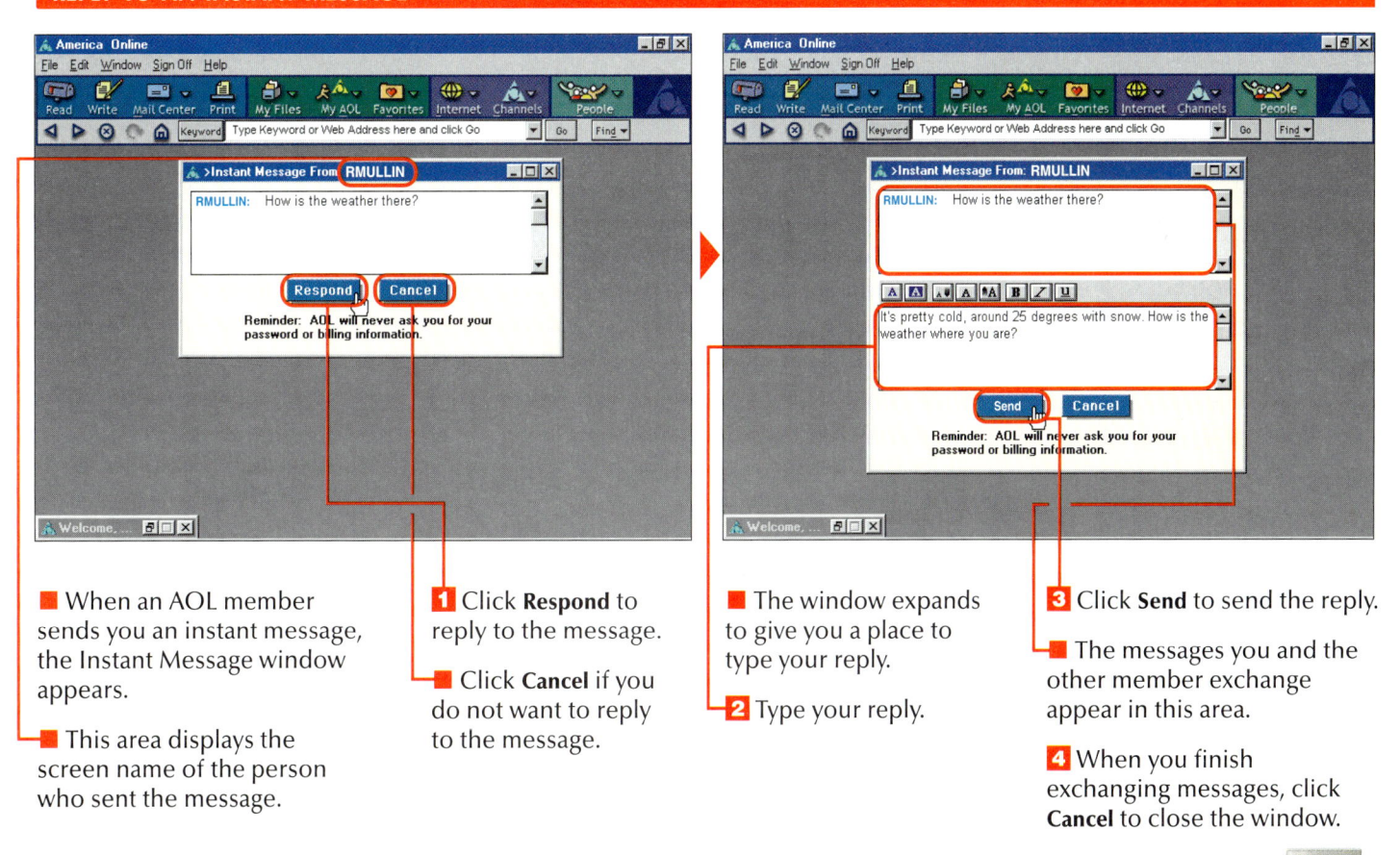

REPLY TO AN INSTANT MESSAGE

CHAT WITH OTHER AOL MEMBERS

When an AOL member sends you an instant message, the message will immediately appear on your screen. You can respond to the message.

REPLY TO AN INSTANT MESSAGE

- When an AOL member sends you an instant message, the Instant Message window appears.

- This area displays the screen name of the person who sent the message.

1 Click **Respond** to reply to the message.

- Click **Cancel** if you do not want to reply to the message.

- The window expands to give you a place to type your reply.

2 Type your reply.

3 Click **Send** to send the reply.

- The messages you and the other member exchange appear in this area.

4 When you finish exchanging messages, click **Cancel** to close the window.

149

AOL LIVE EVENTS

March 1   "Melting" Author Steve White
March 1   Football Legend Kevin Cooper

March 2   Soccer Ace Todd Webb
March 2   Comedian Bart Meuring

March 3   Romance Author Deb Campbell
March 3   Harvey Carroll

CHAPTER 9

ATTEND LIVE EVENTS

What is an AOL Live Event? In this chapter you will learn about AOL Live Events and how to view upcoming events. You will also learn how to enter an auditorium to interact with the special guest and other attending members.

View AOL Live Events 152

Enter an Auditorium 154

Turn Chat Off 155

Send Messages 156

VIEW AOL LIVE EVENTS

> AOL offers many live, interactive events where you can exchange comments and questions with special guests, including athletes, movie stars, musicians, politicians and writers.

AOL LIVE EVENTS
- March 1 "Melting" Author Steve White
- March 1 Football Legend Kevin Cooper
- March 2 Soccer Ace Todd Webb
- March 2 Comedian Bart Meuring
- March 3 Romance Author Deb Campbell
- March 3 Harvey Carroll

You can view a list of upcoming events on AOL so you can plan ahead to meet your favorite celebrities.

VIEW AOL LIVE EVENTS

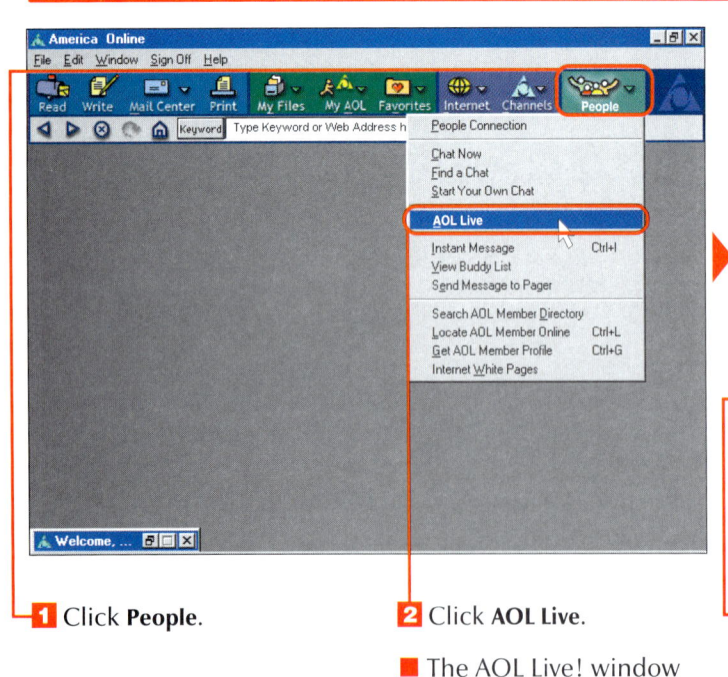

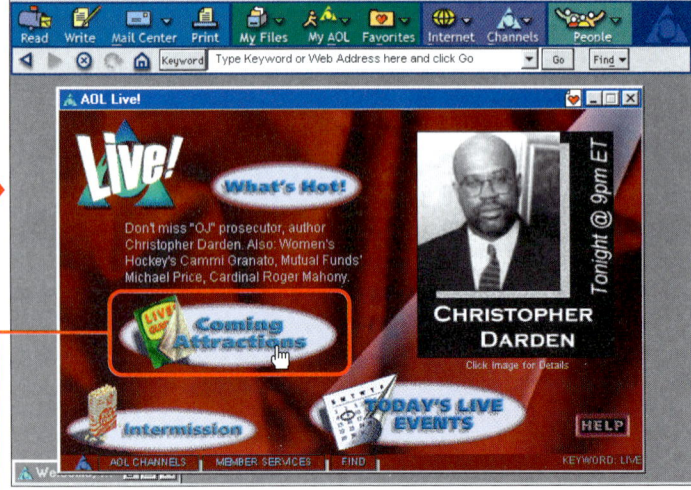

1 Click **People**.

2 Click **AOL Live**.

■ The AOL Live! window appears.

3 Click **Coming Attractions** to see a list of upcoming events.

■ The Upcoming Events window appears.

152

9

ATTEND LIVE EVENTS

Can I see a list of today's live events?

In the AOL Live! window, click **Today's Live Events**.

■ This area lists the date and name of each event.

4 Double-click an event of interest.

■ A window appears, displaying a description of the event you selected.

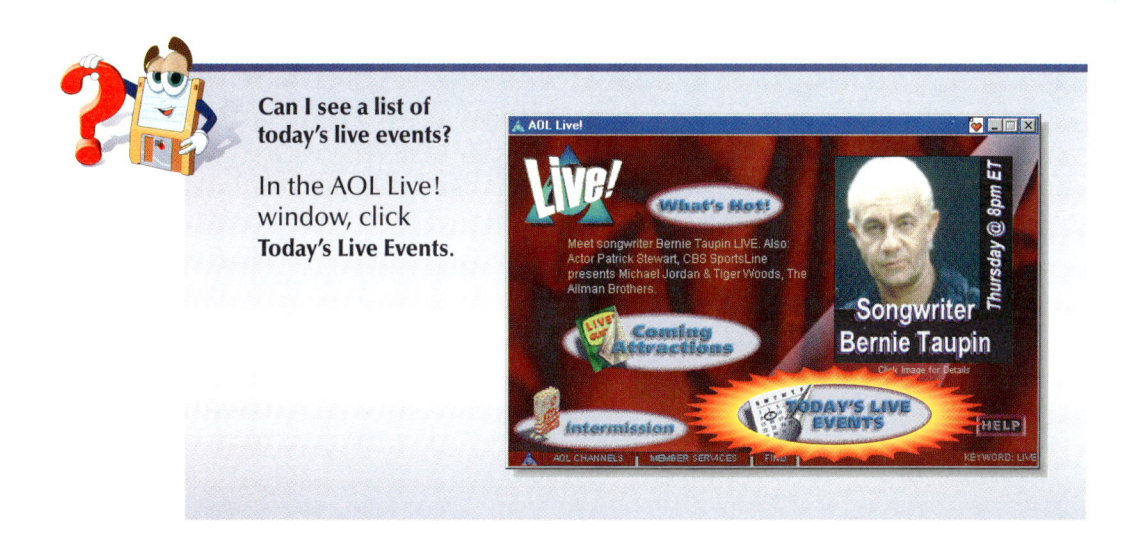

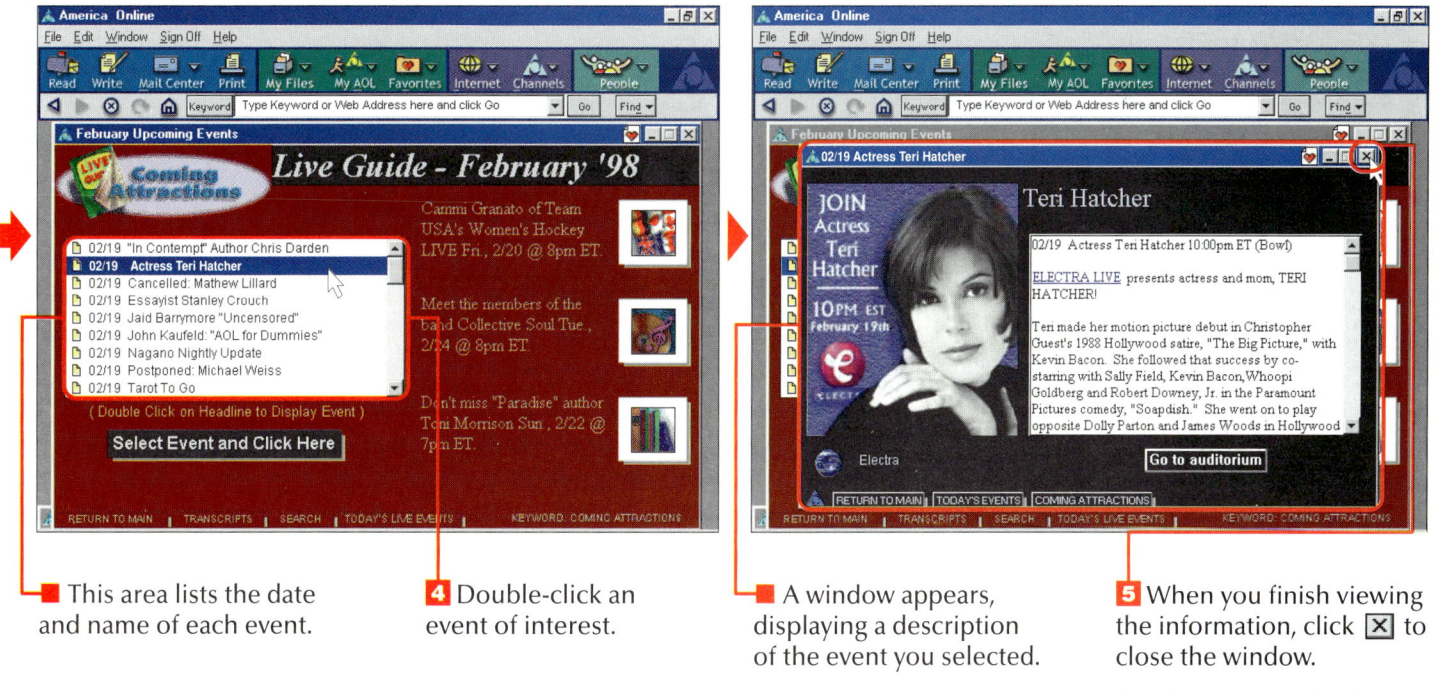

5 When you finish viewing the information, click ⊠ to close the window.

Note: To go to the auditorium and attend the event, see page 154.

153

ENTER AN AUDITORIUM

You can enter an auditorium to attend a live event. An auditorium can hold thousands of people.

The audience is organized into rows, which hold a maximum of 16 members each. When you enter an auditorium, AOL automatically places you in a row.

ENTER AN AUDITORIUM

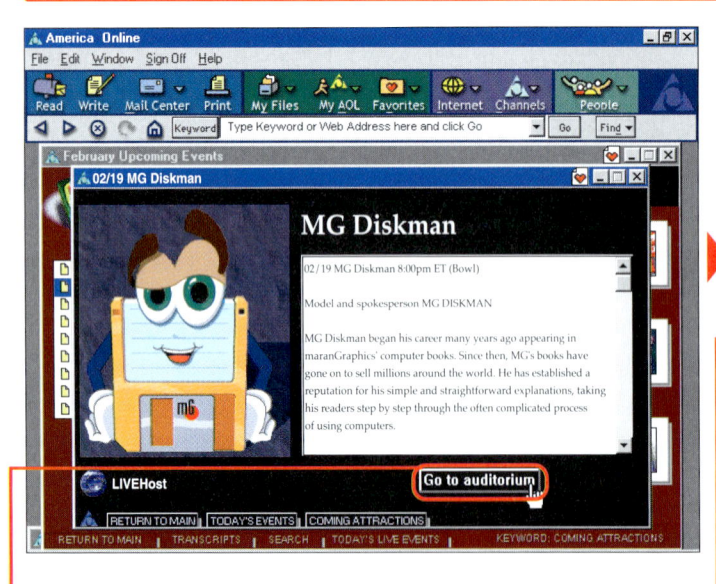

1 When viewing information about an event, click **Go to auditorium** to attend the event.

Note: To view information about an event, perform steps 1 to 4 starting on page 152.

■ A window appears.

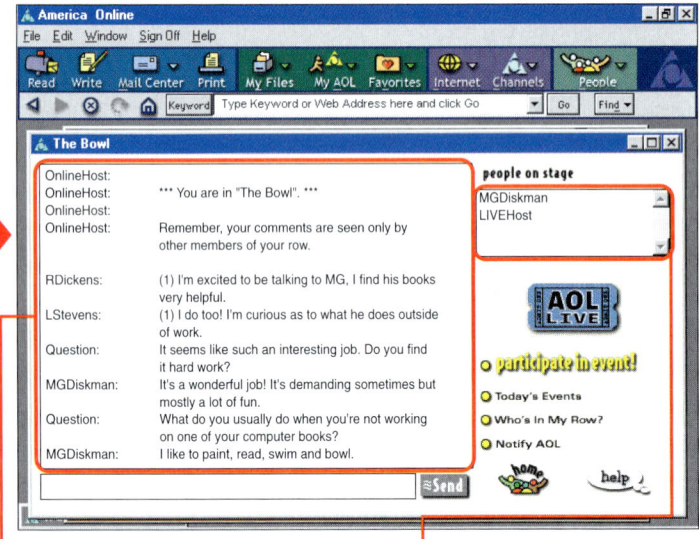

■ This area displays the ongoing conversation. You can see the text typed by the host, guests and members in your row. Comments typed by row members start with the row number in brackets.

■ This area displays the names of the host and guests.

154

TURN CHAT OFF

ATTEND LIVE EVENTS — 9

You can ignore messages sent by other members in your row. This allows you to view only the text typed by the host and guests.

Turning off the chat feature allows you to remove distractions so you can concentrate on the event.

TURN CHAT OFF

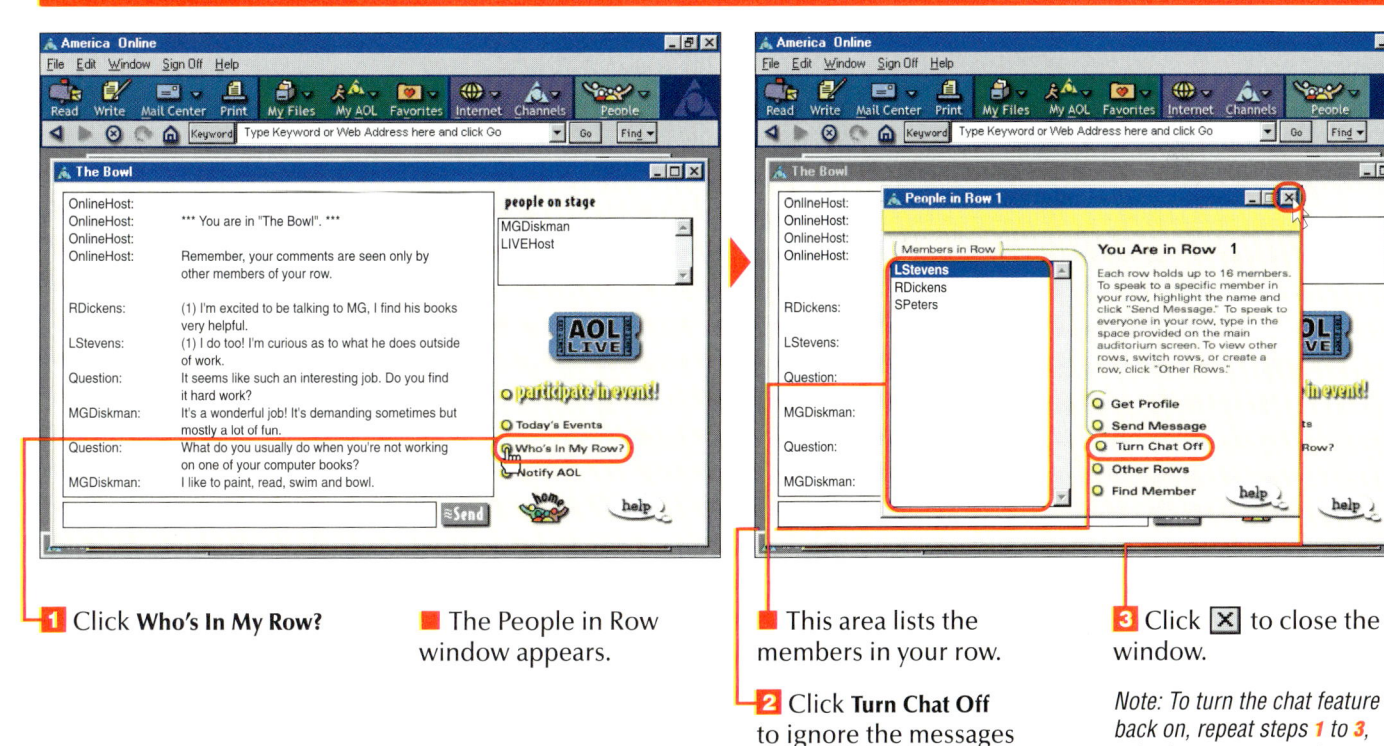

1 Click **Who's In My Row?**

■ The People in Row window appears.

■ This area lists the members in your row.

2 Click **Turn Chat Off** to ignore the messages sent by other members in your row.

3 Click ⊠ to close the window.

*Note: To turn the chat feature back on, repeat steps 1 to 3, selecting **Turn Chat On** in step 2.*

155

SEND MESSAGES

While attending an event, you can exchange messages with other members in your row.

Messages you send are seen only by the other members in your row.

SEND MESSAGE TO OTHER ROW MEMBERS

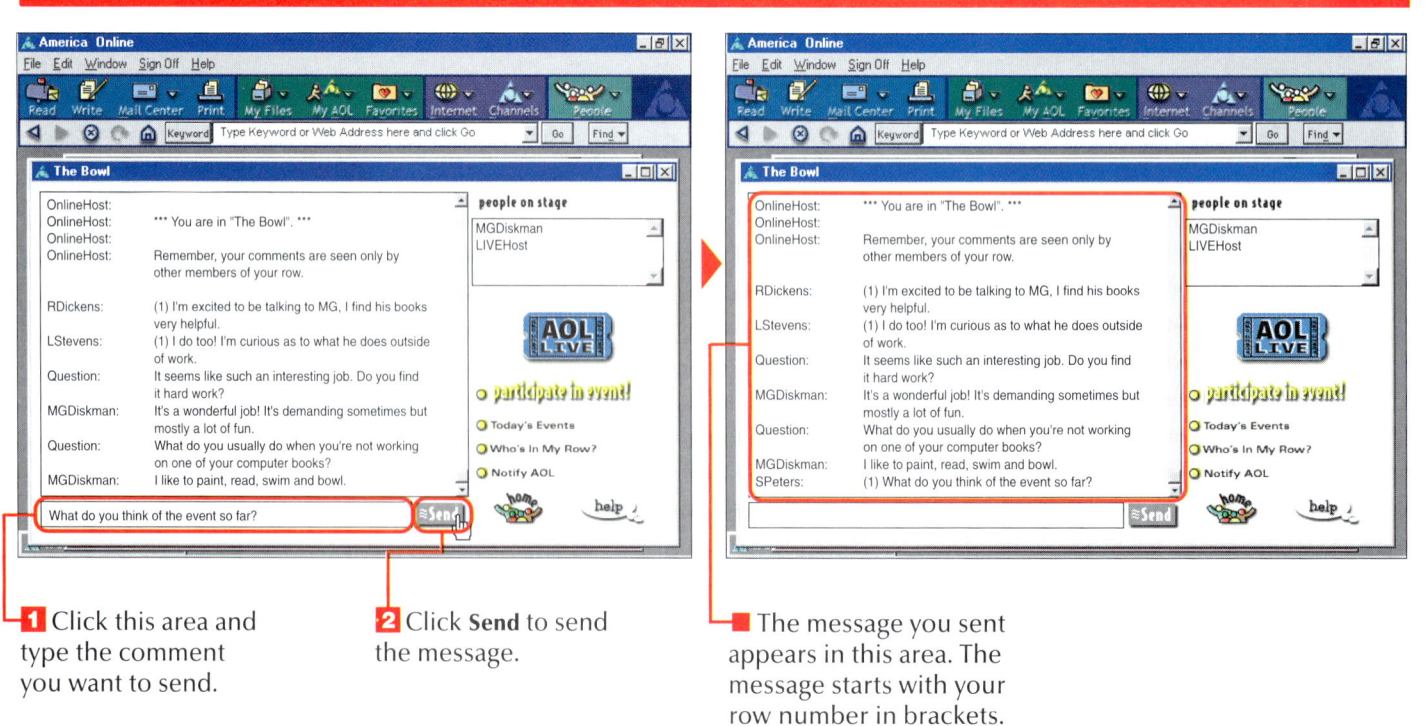

1 Click this area and type the comment you want to send.

2 Click **Send** to send the message.

■ The message you sent appears in this area. The message starts with your row number in brackets.

ATTEND LIVE EVENTS

You can send questions or comments to the guest.

If you have a question for the guest, make sure you enter the auditorium early. The host asks questions in the order they arrive.

SEND MESSAGE TO GUEST

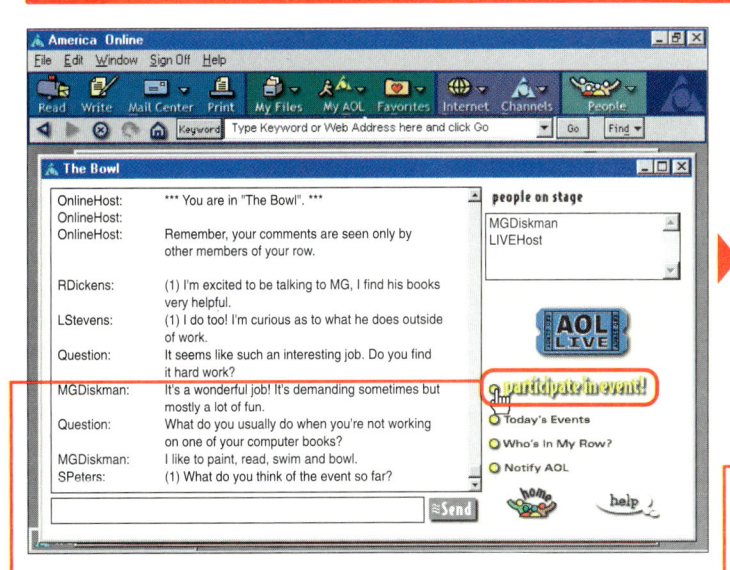

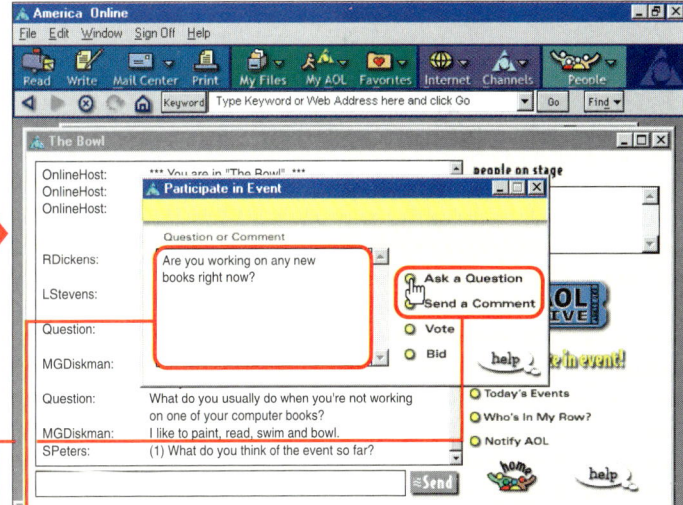

1 Click **participate in event!**

■ The Participate in Event window appears.

2 Type your question or comment.

3 Click an option to specify if the text you typed is a question or a comment.

■ A dialog box appears, confirming that your message was received. Click **OK** to close the dialog box.

157

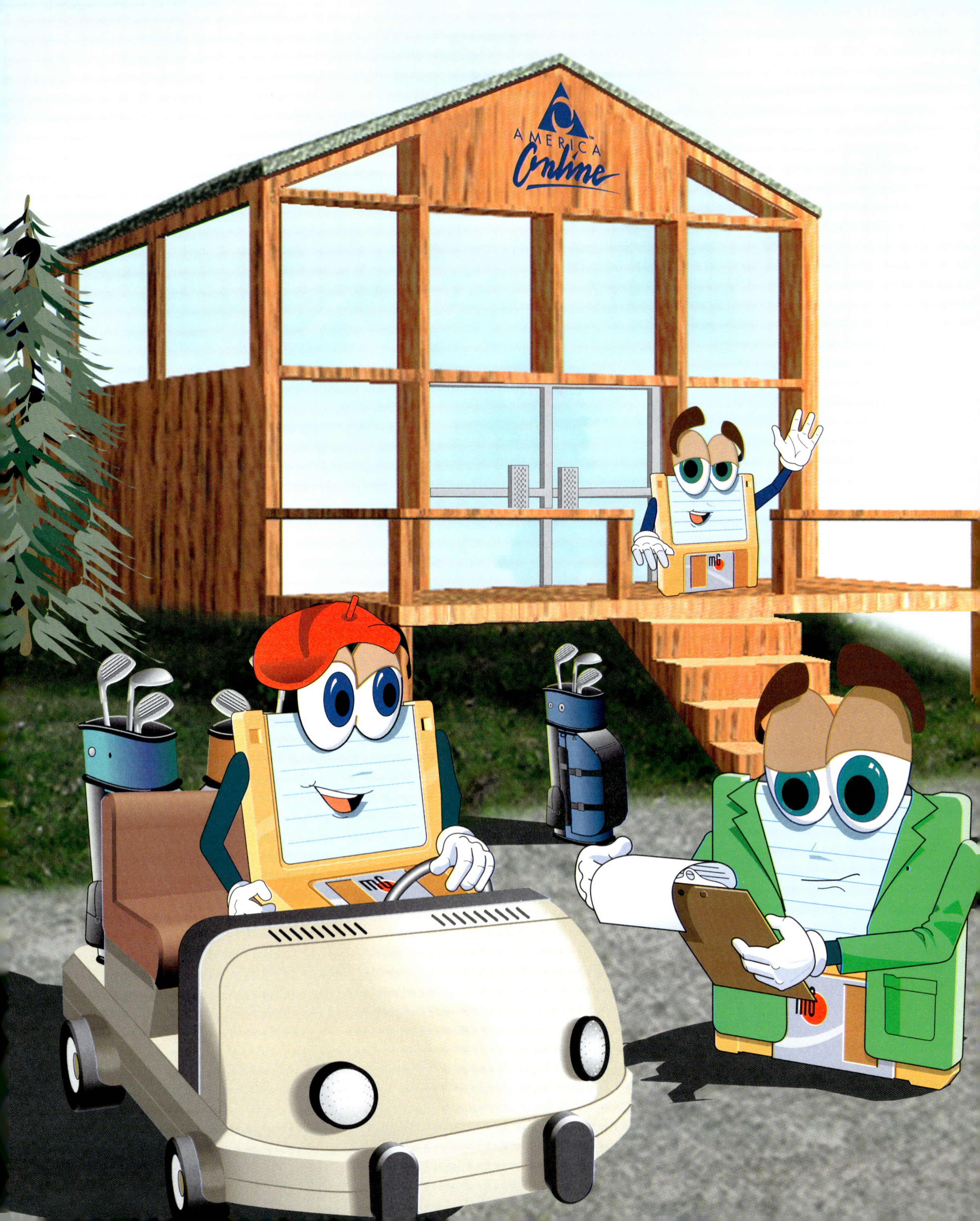
AMERICA
Online

CHAPTER 10

FIND AOL MEMBERS

Do you have friends, family members or co-workers who are AOL members? If so, this chapter will show you how to locate them online and much more.

Search the Member Directory 160

Enter Member Profile Information 162

Locate an AOL Member 164

Add Members to a Buddy List 166

View Buddy Lists 168

SEARCH THE MEMBER DIRECTORY

You can search the Member Directory to find members based on their name, location, interests or other information.

Finding a member allows you to determine the screen names of family, friends and people who share similar interests. You may want to know a member's screen name so you can send the member an e-mail message or an instant message.

SEARCH THE MEMBER DIRECTORY

1 Click **People**.

2 Click **Search AOL Member Directory**.

■ The Member Directory window appears.

3 Type the information you want to search for.

4 Click **Search** to start the search.

■ A window appears, listing each member who matches the information you entered.

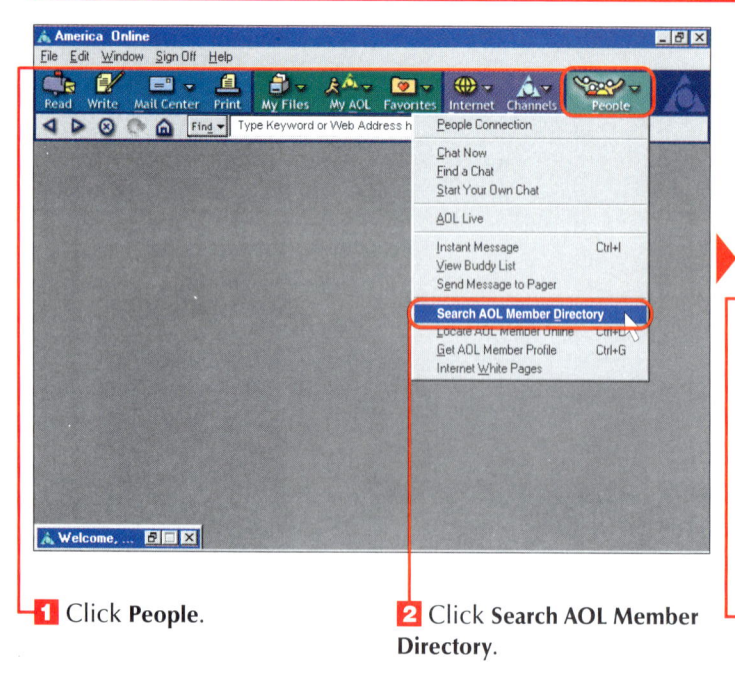

160

FIND AOL MEMBERS

Why can't I find a member in the Member Directory?

AOL members who do not create member profiles will not be found when searching the Member Directory. Some people choose not to enter member profile information. To create your own member profile, see page 162.

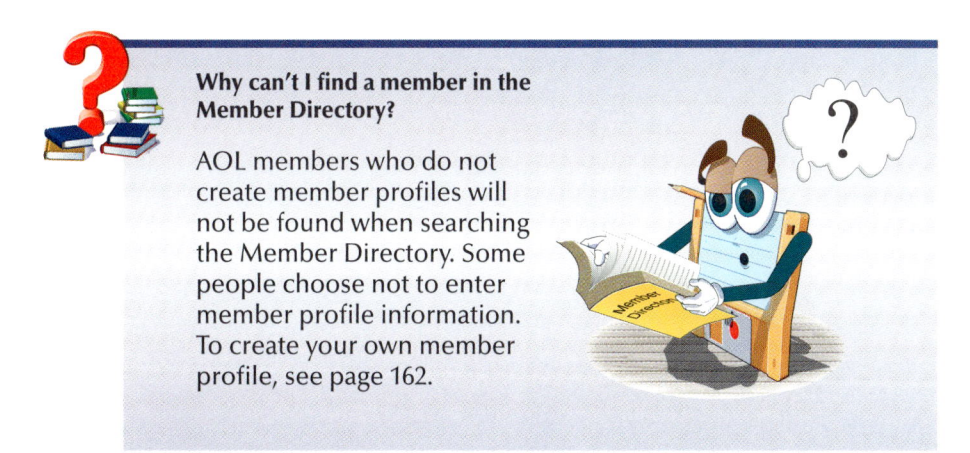

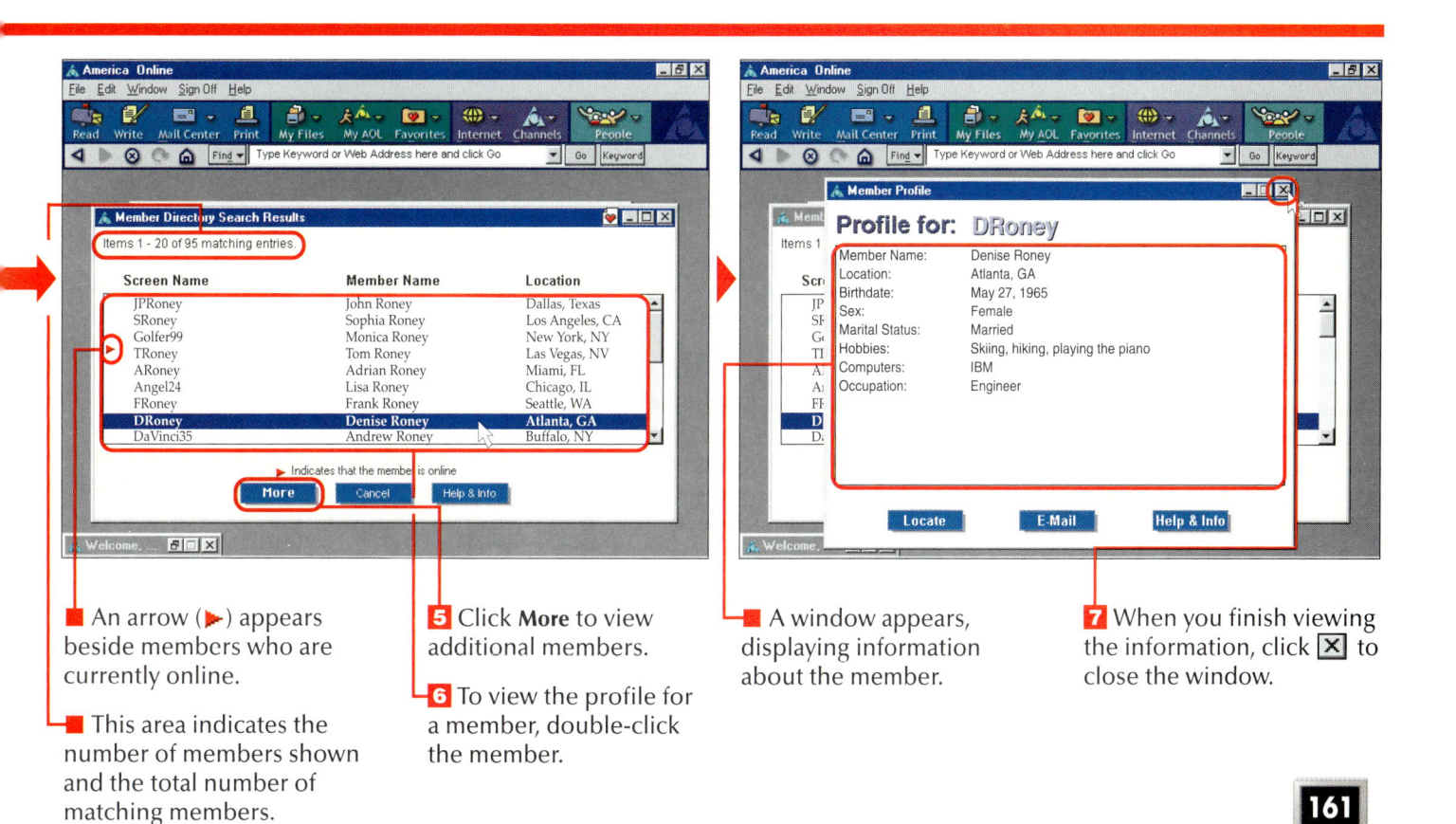

■ An arrow (▶) appears beside members who are currently online.

■ This area indicates the number of members shown and the total number of matching members.

5 Click **More** to view additional members.

6 To view the profile for a member, double-click the member.

■ A window appears, displaying information about the member.

7 When you finish viewing the information, click ⊠ to close the window.

161

ENTER MEMBER PROFILE INFORMATION

You can provide information about yourself that other AOL members can view. Entering your member profile information is optional.

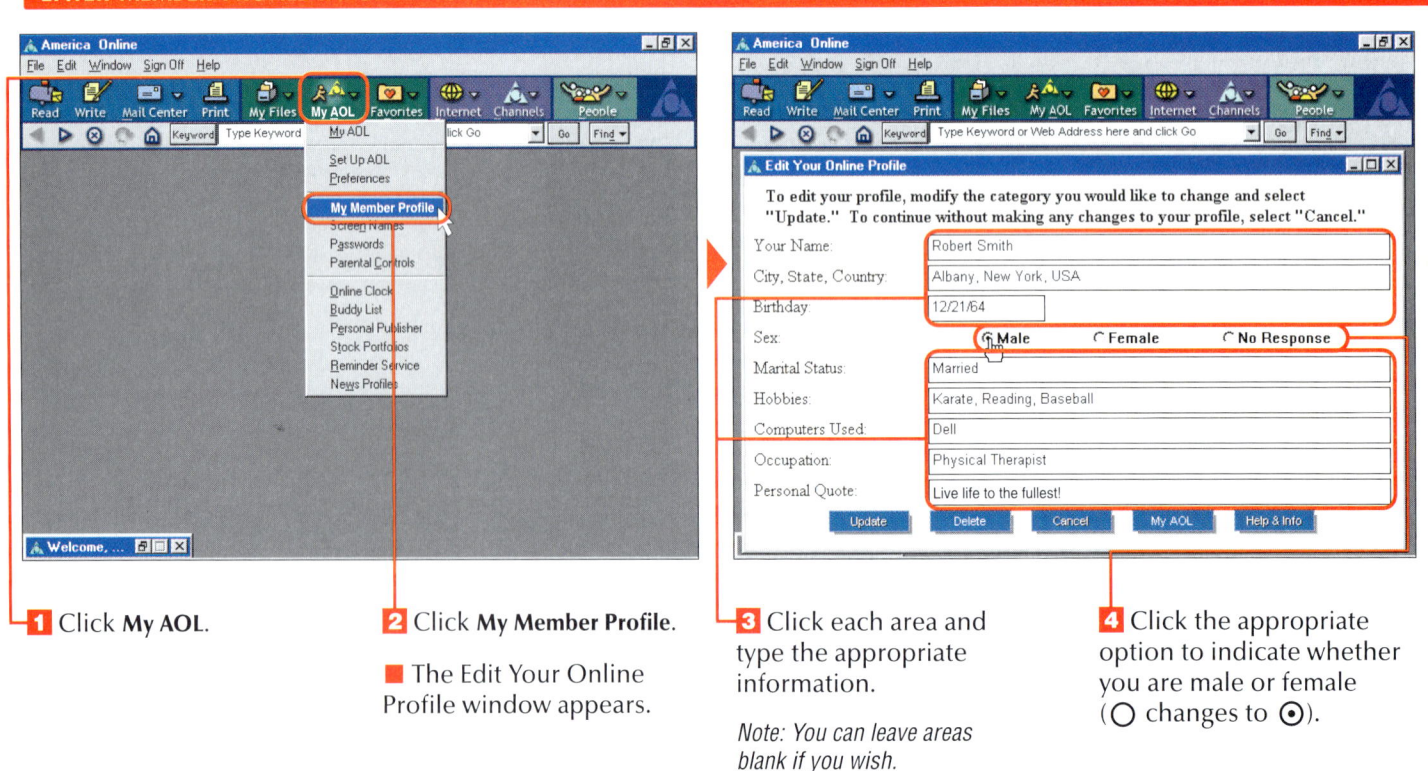

ENTER MEMBER PROFILE INFORMATION

1 Click **My AOL**.

2 Click **My Member Profile**.

■ The Edit Your Online Profile window appears.

3 Click each area and type the appropriate information.

Note: You can leave areas blank if you wish.

4 Click the appropriate option to indicate whether you are male or female (○ changes to ⊙).

FIND AOL MEMBERS

How can I see another member's profile?

When chatting in a chat room, you may want to see another member's profile to get more information about the member. See page 142.

Member Profile

Member Name:
Disk Guy

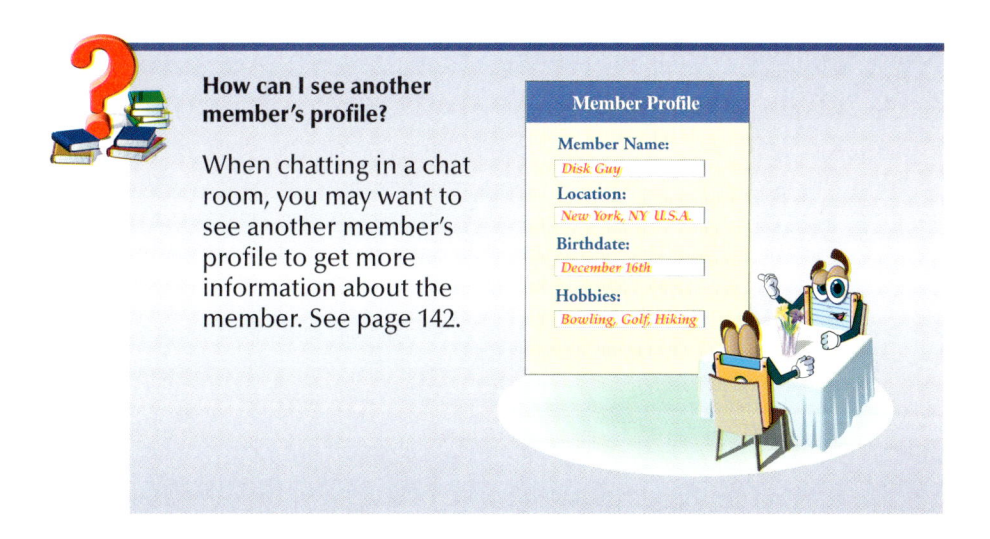

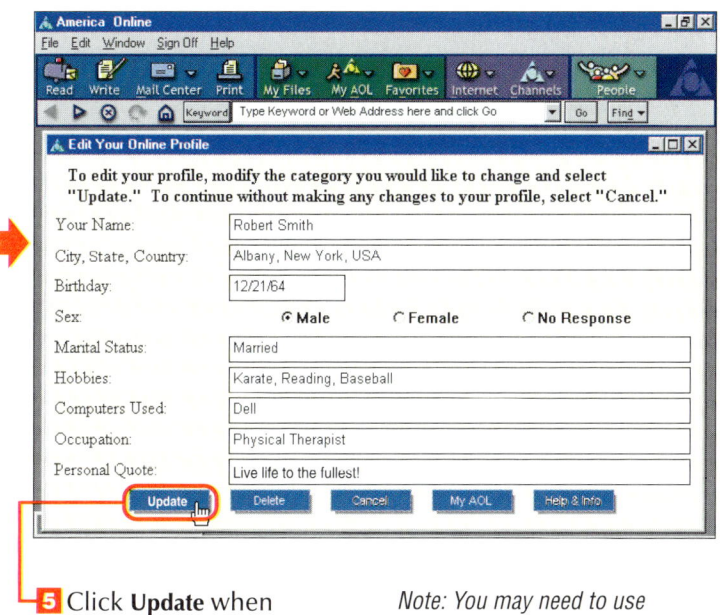

Location:
New York, NY U.S.A.

Birthdate:
December 16th

Hobbies:
Bowling, Golf, Hiking

---

5 Click **Update** when you finish entering the information.

*Note: You may need to use the scroll bar to display the **Update** button.*

■ A confirmation dialog box appears, indicating that your profile has been created or updated.

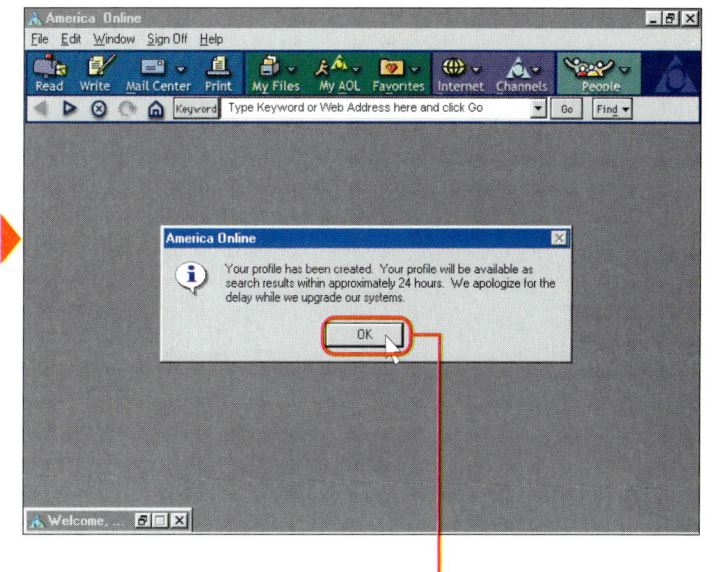

6 Click **OK** to close the dialog box.

163

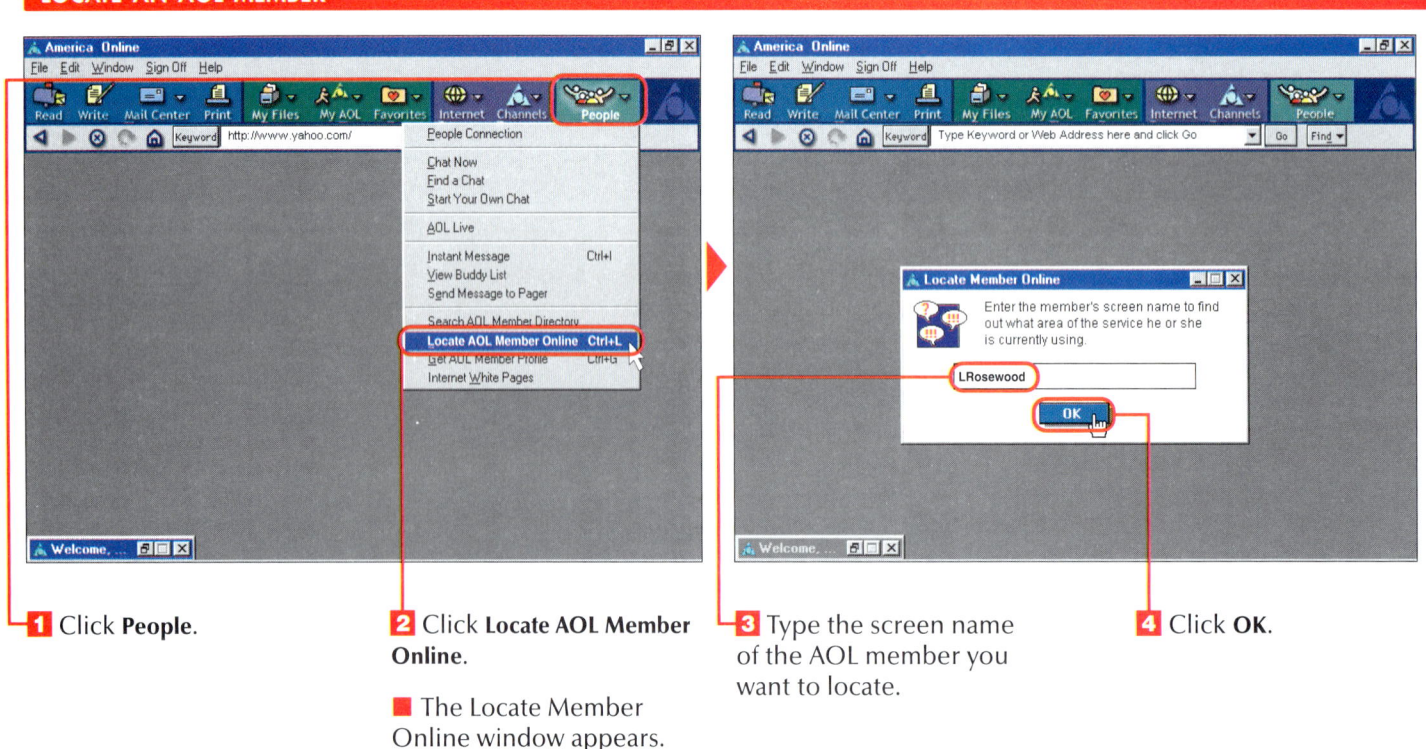

LOCATE AN AOL MEMBER

If an AOL member is online and in a chat room, you can locate and join the member in the chat room.

LOCATE AN AOL MEMBER

1 Click **People**.

2 Click **Locate AOL Member Online**.

■ The Locate Member Online window appears.

3 Type the screen name of the AOL member you want to locate.

4 Click **OK**.

164

FIND AOL MEMBERS

How can I quickly locate a member on my Buddy List?

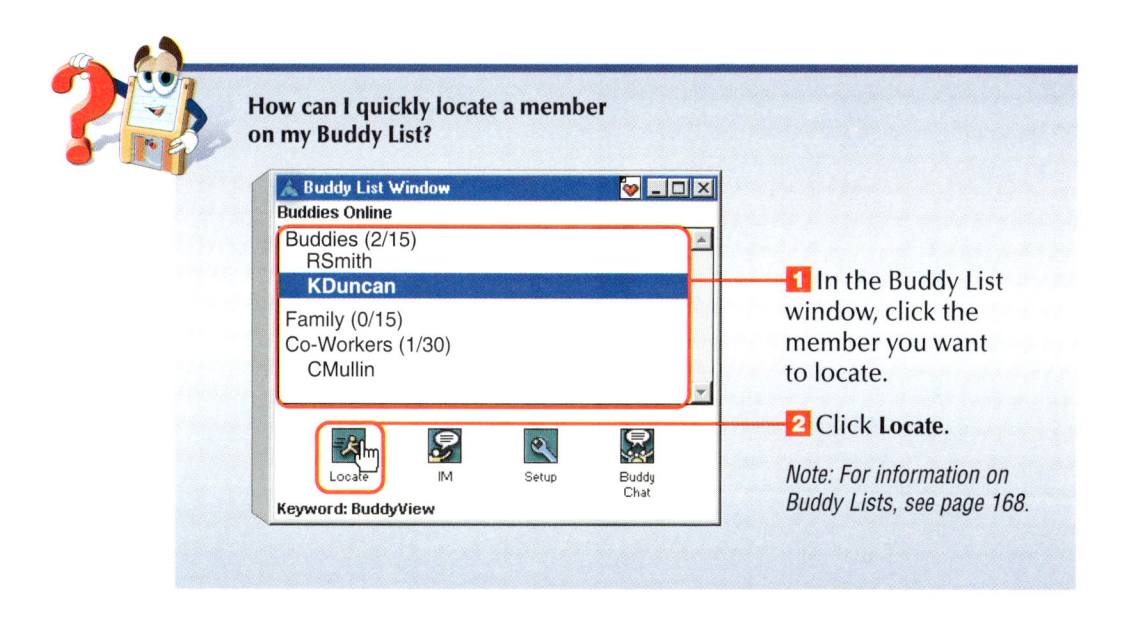

1 In the Buddy List window, click the member you want to locate.

2 Click **Locate**.

Note: For information on Buddy Lists, see page 168.

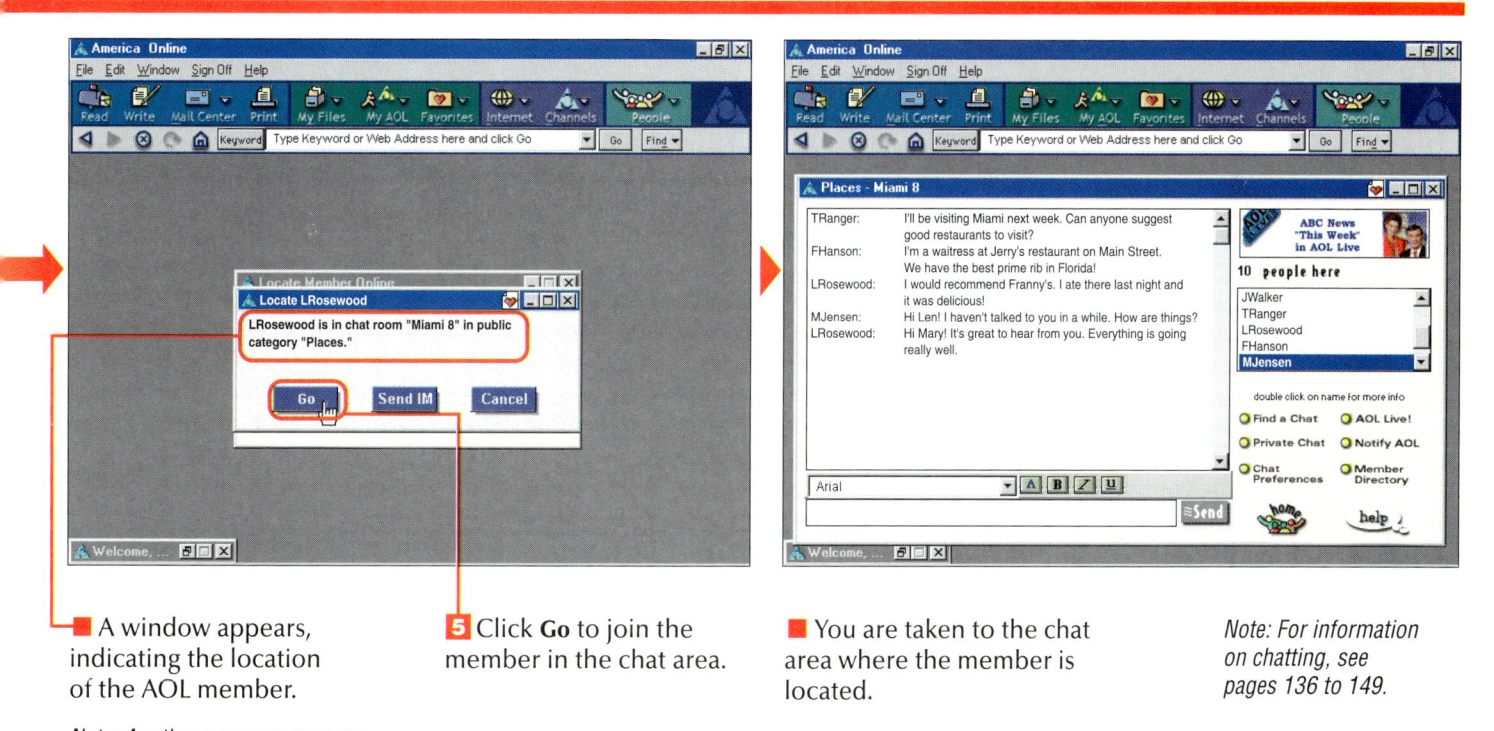

■ A window appears, indicating the location of the AOL member.

Note: Another message appears if the member is not in a chat area or is not currently online.

5 Click **Go** to join the member in the chat area.

■ You are taken to the chat area where the member is located.

Note: For information on chatting, see pages 136 to 149.

165

ADD MEMBERS TO A BUDDY LIST

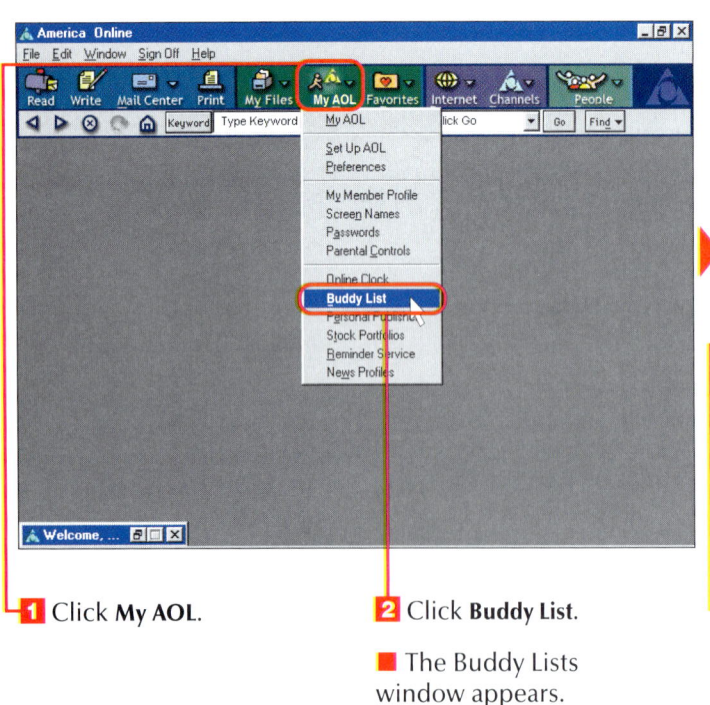

You can use Buddy Lists to keep track of friends, colleagues and family members you frequently communicate with. Buddy Lists allow you to see who is currently online.

AOL automatically creates the Buddies, Family and Co-Workers Buddy Lists for you. You can add or remove members on these lists at any time.

ADD MEMBERS TO A BUDDY LIST

1 Click **My AOL**.

2 Click **Buddy List**.

■ The Buddy Lists window appears.

■ This area displays the names of your Buddy Lists and the number of members in each list. AOL automatically created three Buddy Lists for you.

3 To add members to a Buddy List, double-click the list.

■ The Edit List window appears.

166

FIND AOL MEMBERS

How do I remove a member from a Buddy List?

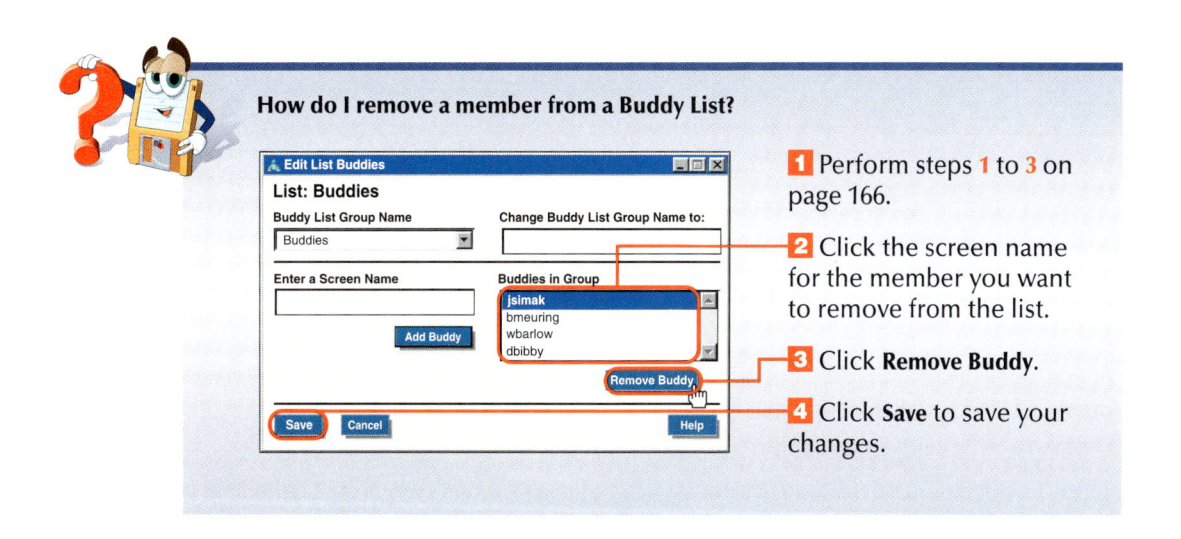

1 Perform steps **1** to **3** on page 166.

2 Click the screen name for the member you want to remove from the list.

3 Click **Remove Buddy**.

4 Click **Save** to save your changes.

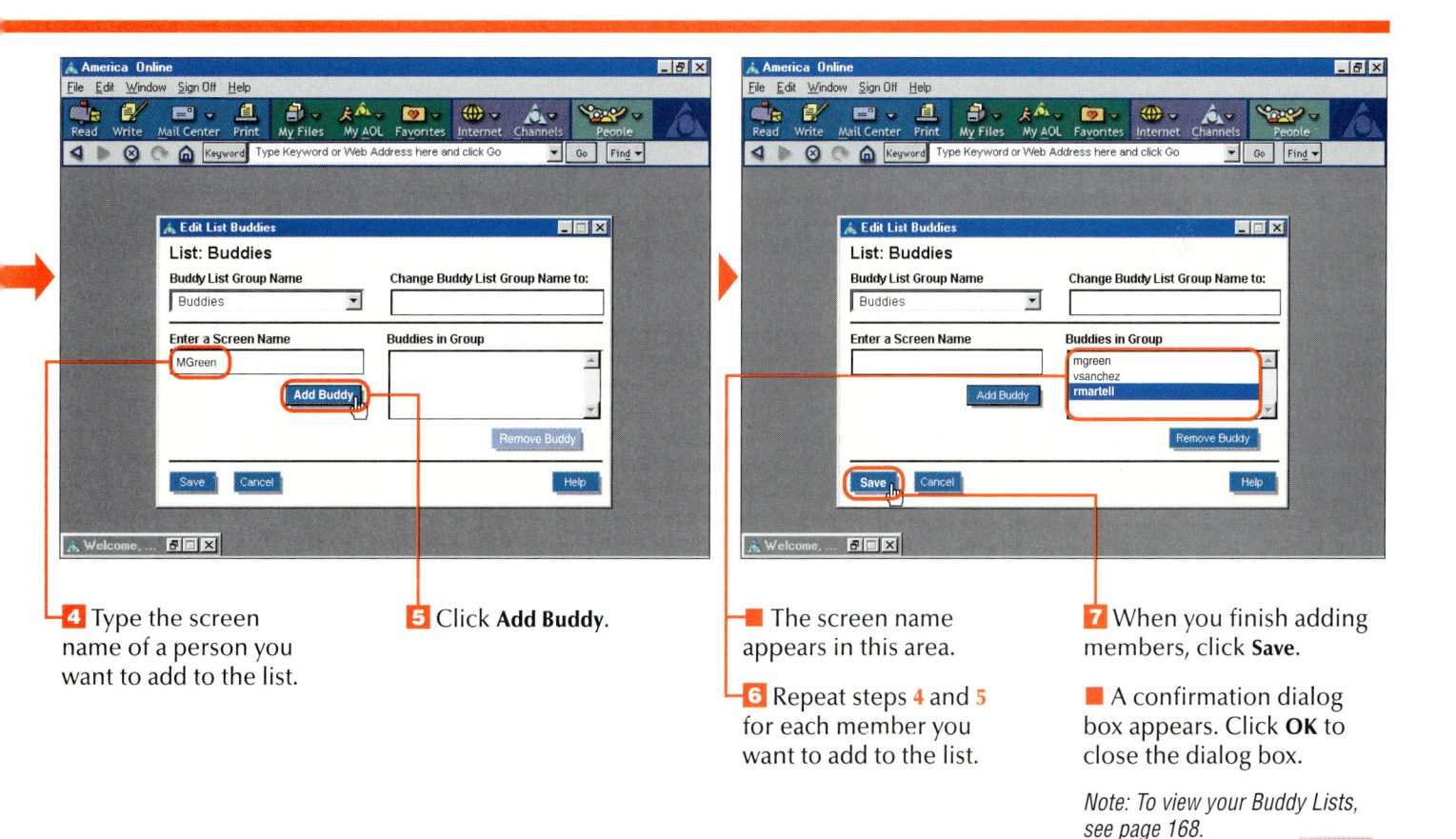

---

4 Type the screen name of a person you want to add to the list.

5 Click **Add Buddy**.

■ The screen name appears in this area.

6 Repeat steps **4** and **5** for each member you want to add to the list.

7 When you finish adding members, click **Save**.

■ A confirmation dialog box appears. Click **OK** to close the dialog box.

Note: To view your Buddy Lists, see page 168.

167

VIEW BUDDY LISTS

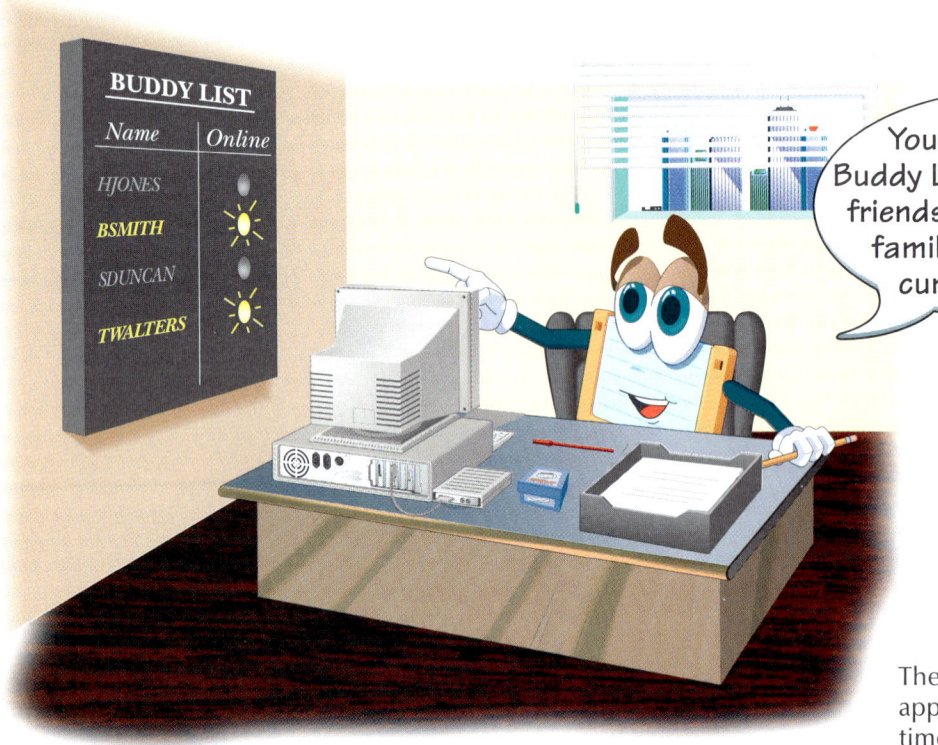

You can view your Buddy Lists to see which friends, colleagues and family members are currently online.

The Buddy List window appears automatically each time you sign on to AOL.

VIEW BUDDY LISTS

1 Click **People**.

2 Click **View Buddy List**.

■ The Buddy List window appears.

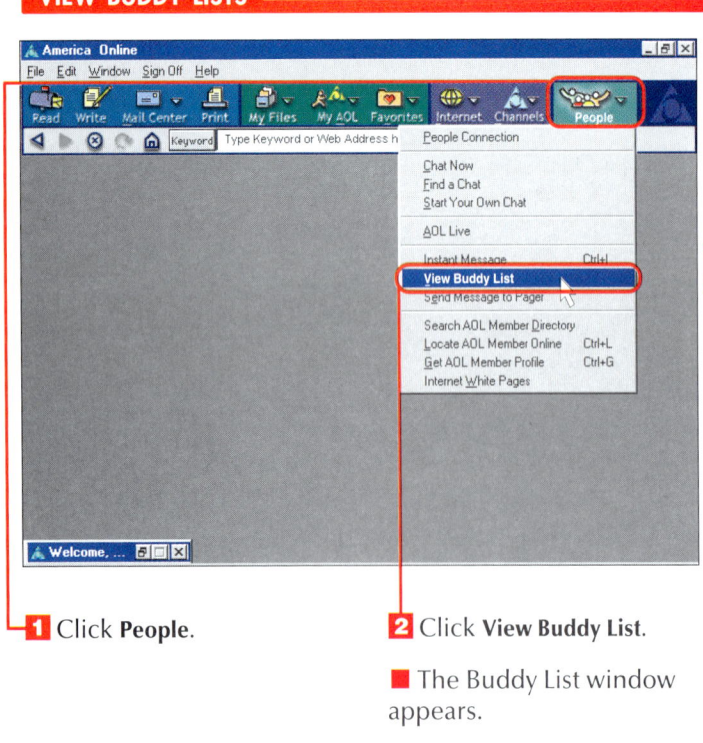

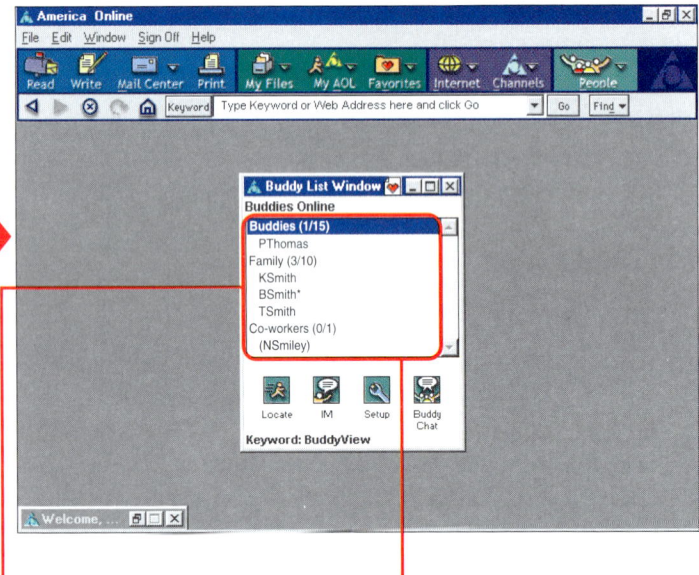

■ This area displays your Buddy Lists. Each member that is online appears below the appropriate list name.

■ The numbers in brackets beside each list name indicate how many members on the list are online and the total number of members on the list.

168

FIND AOL MEMBERS

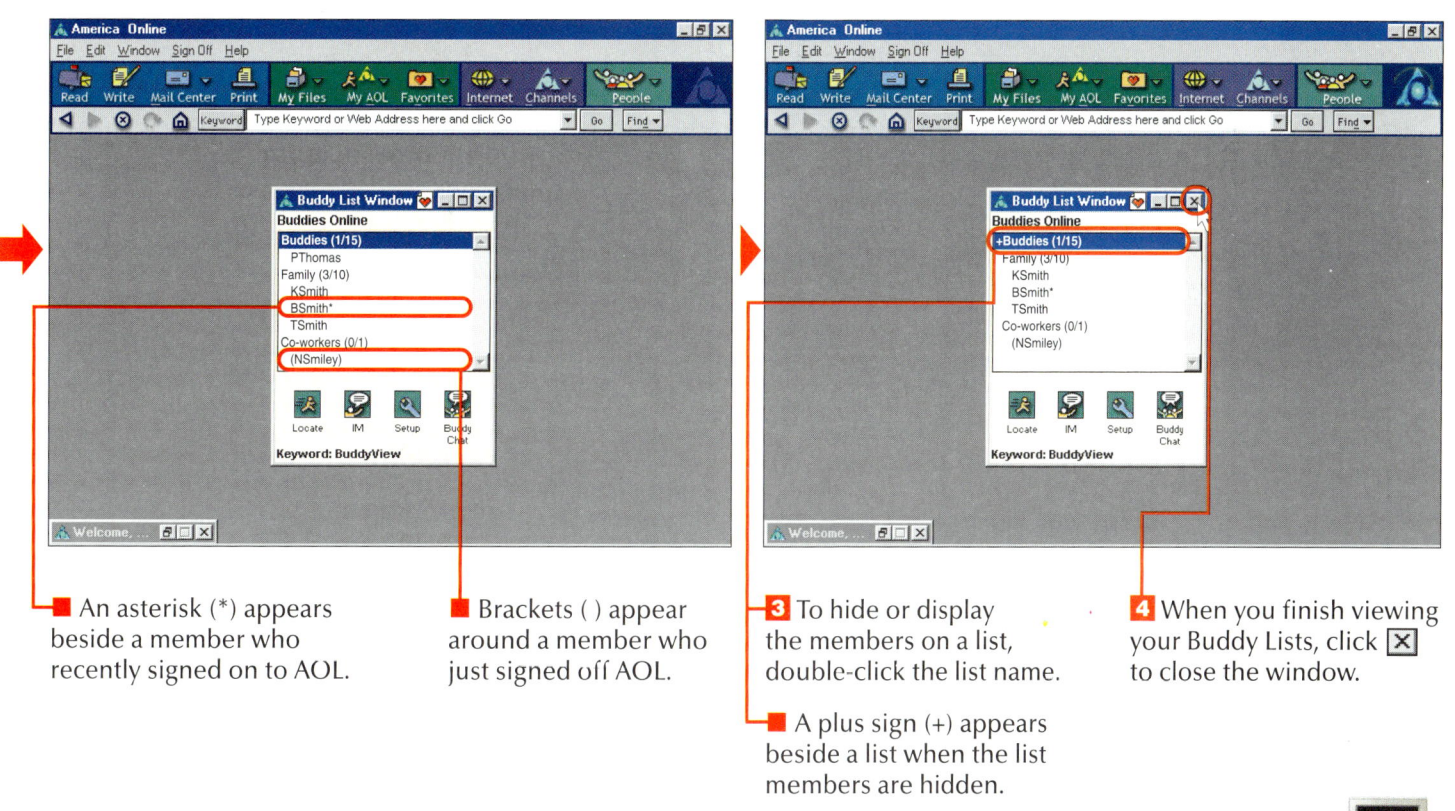

What can I do when I discover a buddy is online?

When you discover that a friend or colleague is online, you may want to send an instant message or join the friend in a private chat room. See page 146 to send an instant message. See page 144 to create a private chat room.

■ An asterisk (*) appears beside a member who recently signed on to AOL.

■ Brackets ( ) appear around a member who just signed off AOL.

3 To hide or display the members on a list, double-click the list name.

■ A plus sign (+) appears beside a list when the list members are hidden.

4 When you finish viewing your Buddy Lists, click ⊠ to close the window.

169

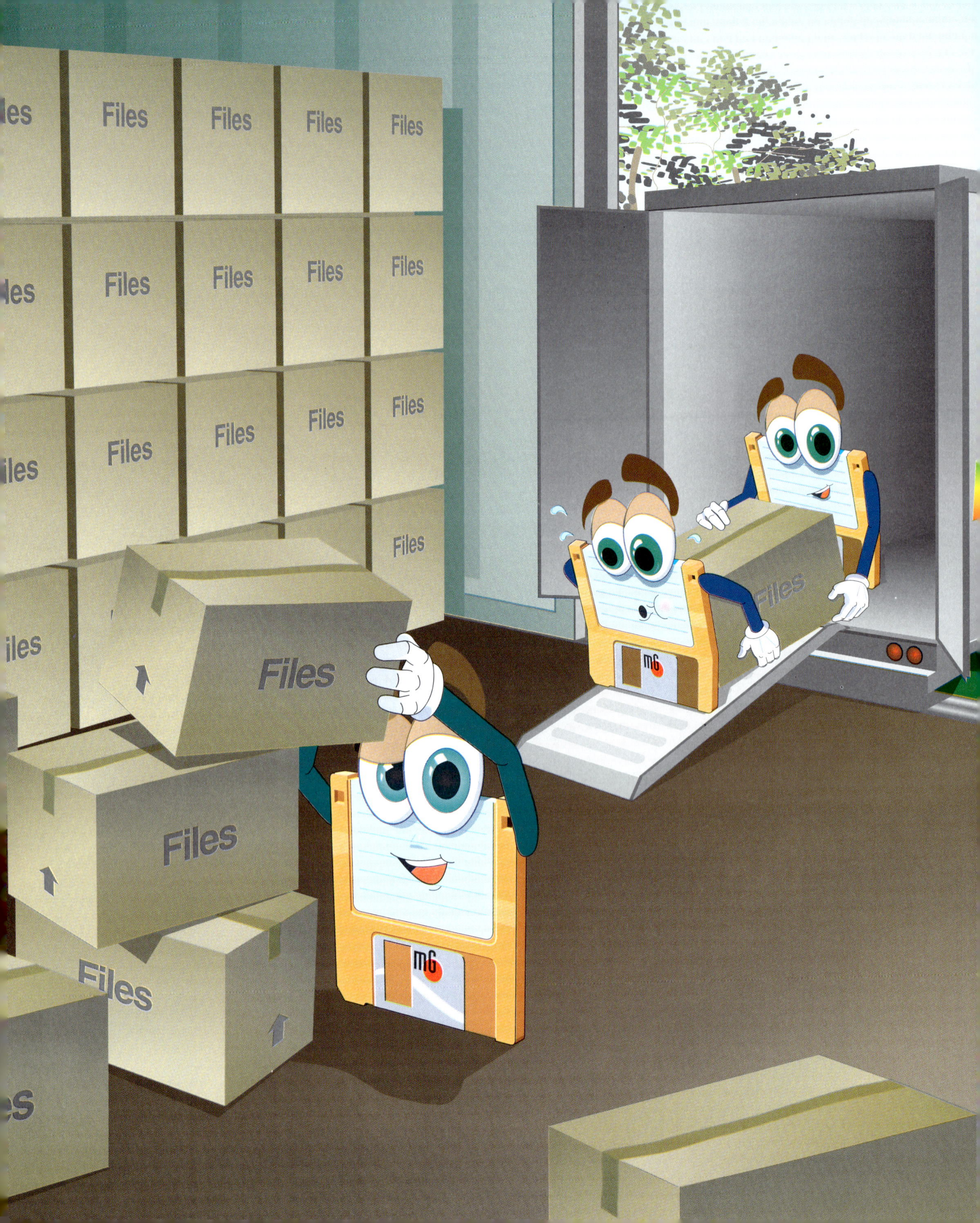

Files
mG

CHAPTER 11

DOWNLOAD FILES

Do you want to learn how to download games, pictures and movie clips? In this chapter, you will find out how to transfer many different types of files to your computer using AOL.

Introduction to Downloading Files 172

Find Files to Download 174

Download a File 178

Using the Download Manager 180

INTRODUCTION TO DOWNLOADING FILES

AOL offers thousands of files that you can transfer to your computer.

When you transfer information to your computer, you are "downloading" the information.

Every file has a name and an extension, separated by a period (.). The name describes the contents of a file. The extension usually identifies the type of file.

FILE RESTRICTIONS

Public Domain
Public domain programs are free and have no copyright restrictions. You can change and distribute public domain programs as you wish.

Freeware
Freeware programs are free but have copyright restrictions. The author may require you to follow certain rules if you want to change or distribute freeware programs.

Shareware
You can try a shareware program free of charge for a limited time. If you like the program and want to continue using the program, you must pay the author.

DOWNLOAD FILES

TYPES OF FILES

Document Files
You can get documents such as books, song lyrics, recipes and templates for resumes. Look for these extensions:

.doc   .dot   .me   .txt
.wks   .wp5   .xls

Image Files
You can get images such as computer-generated art, landscapes, cartoons and movie scenes. Look for these extensions:

.art   .bmp   .eps   .gif
.jpg   .pct   .pcx   .tif

Sound Files
You can get sound clips of favorite songs, television shows, movies and animal sounds. Look for these extensions:

.mid   .mod   .snd   .wav

Video Files
You can get computer-generated animation and videos. Look for these extensions:

.avi   .mov   .mpg

Program Files
You can get programs such as word processors, spreadsheets, databases and games. Look for these extensions:

.bat   .com   .exe

Compressed Files
Many large files are compressed, or squeezed, to make them smaller. Compressed files require less storage space and transfer more quickly. Look for these extensions:

.arc   .cpt   .sea   .sit   .zip

Before you can use a compressed file, you need to decompress the file. When you exit AOL, the AOL program will automatically decompress files you downloaded.

173

FIND FILES TO DOWNLOAD

You can browse through the files available on AOL to find files of interest to you.

The files on AOL are organized into various categories, such as Animation & Video, Business & Finance and Home & Hobby.

FIND FILES TO DOWNLOAD (BY BROWSING)

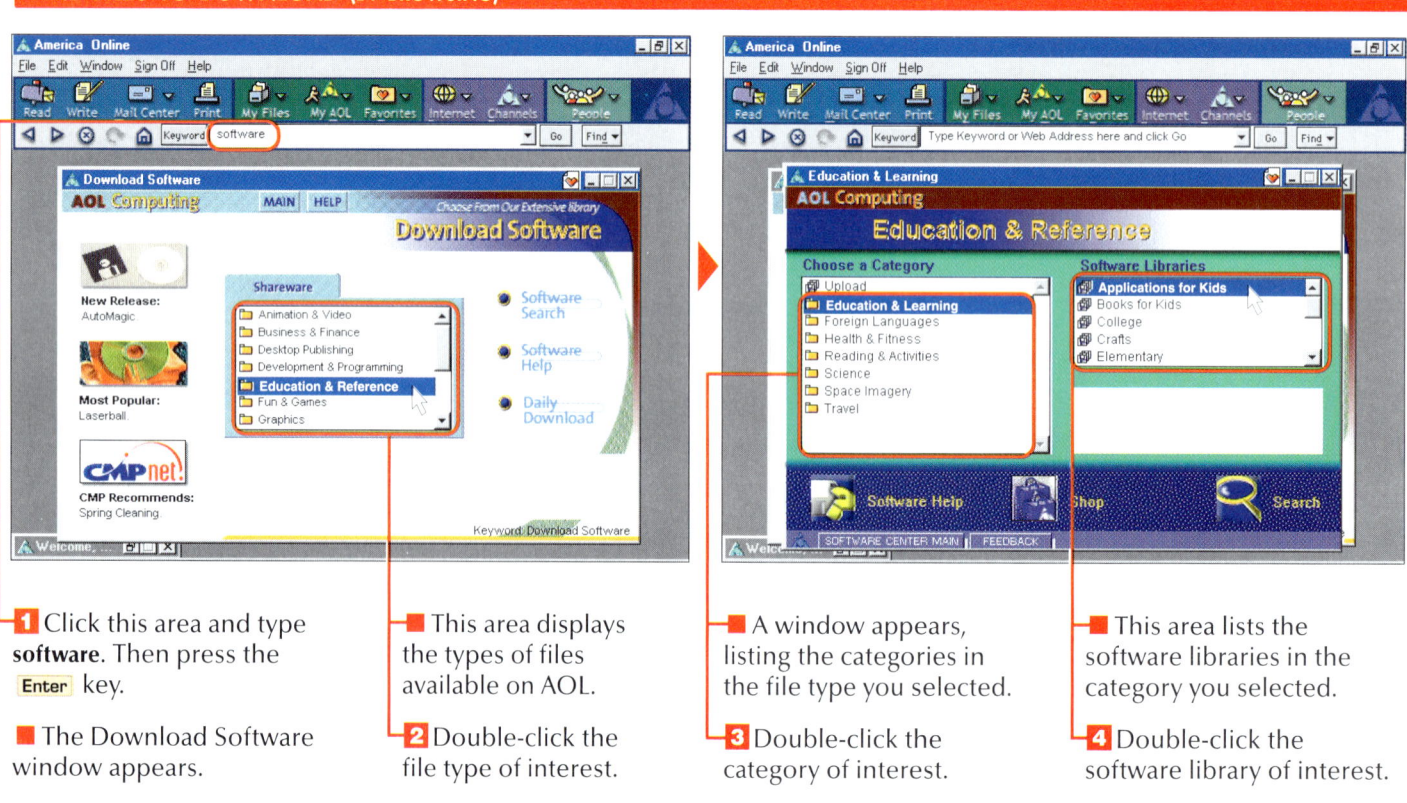

1 Click this area and type **software**. Then press the `Enter` key.

■ The Download Software window appears.

■ This area displays the types of files available on AOL.

2 Double-click the file type of interest.

■ A window appears, listing the categories in the file type you selected.

3 Double-click the category of interest.

■ This area lists the software libraries in the category you selected.

4 Double-click the software library of interest.

174

11

DOWNLOAD FILES

Are there other ways I can find files?

While browsing through the areas on AOL, you may find files you want to transfer to your computer. The floppy disk symbol (🖫) and the word "downloads" or "library" usually indicate areas on AOL that offer files you can download.

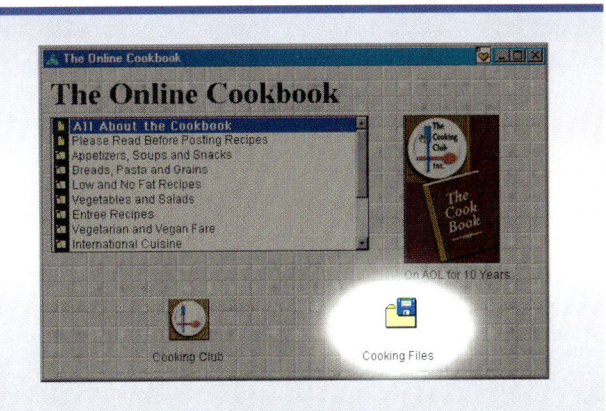

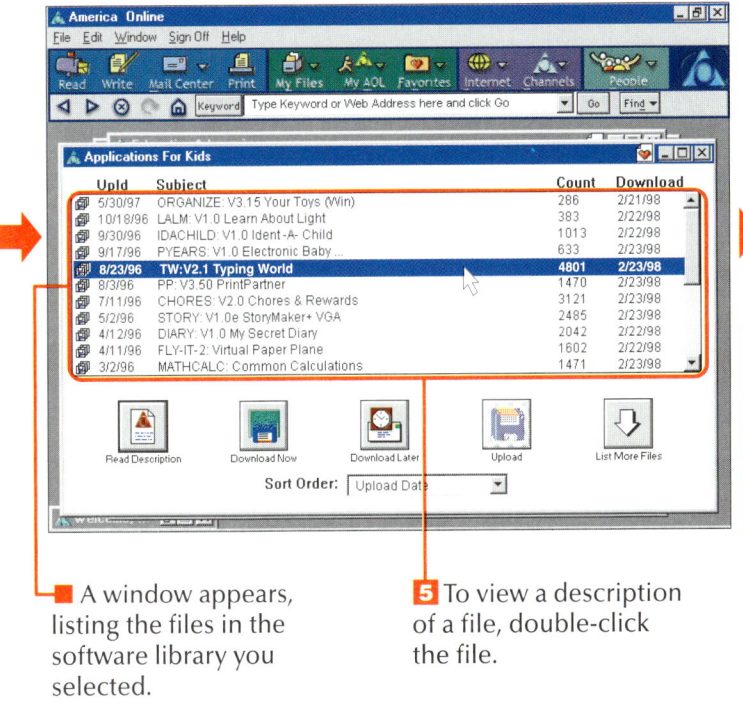

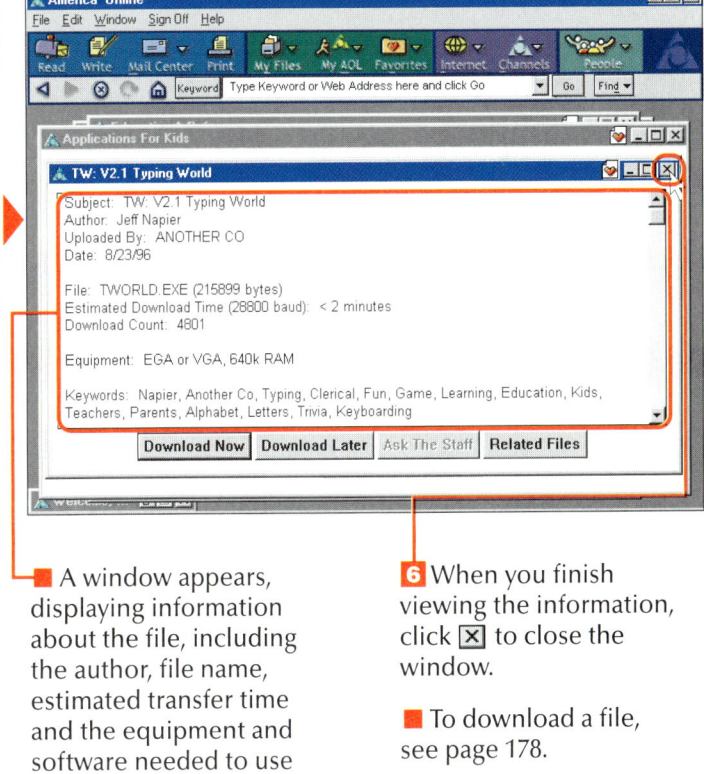

■ A window appears, listing the files in the software library you selected.

5 To view a description of a file, double-click the file.

■ A window appears, displaying information about the file, including the author, file name, estimated transfer time and the equipment and software needed to use the file.

6 When you finish viewing the information, click ☒ to close the window.

■ To download a file, see page 178.

175

FIND FILES TO DOWNLOAD

You can search through thousands of files offered on AOL to find files of interest to you.

FIND FILES TO DOWNLOAD (BY SEARCHING)

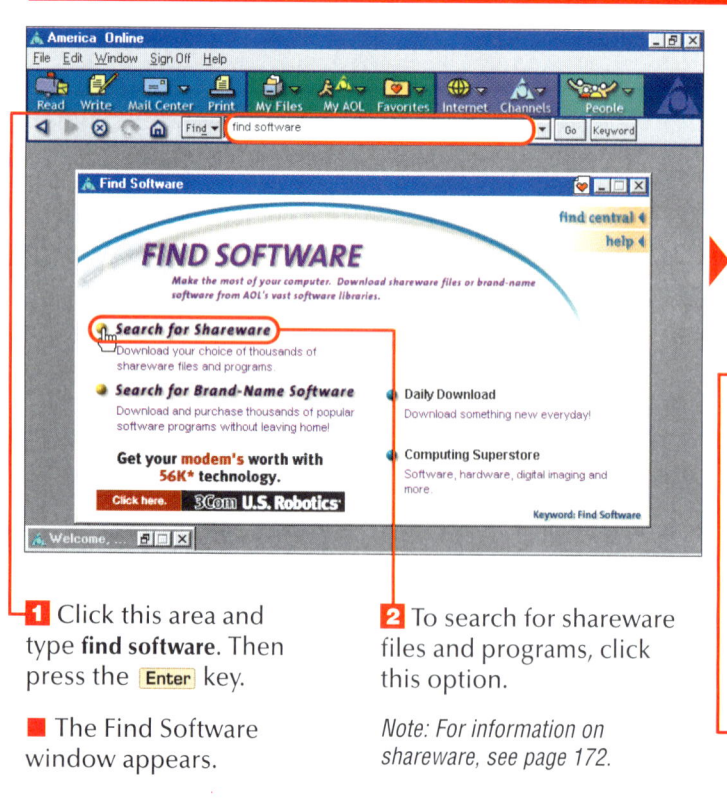

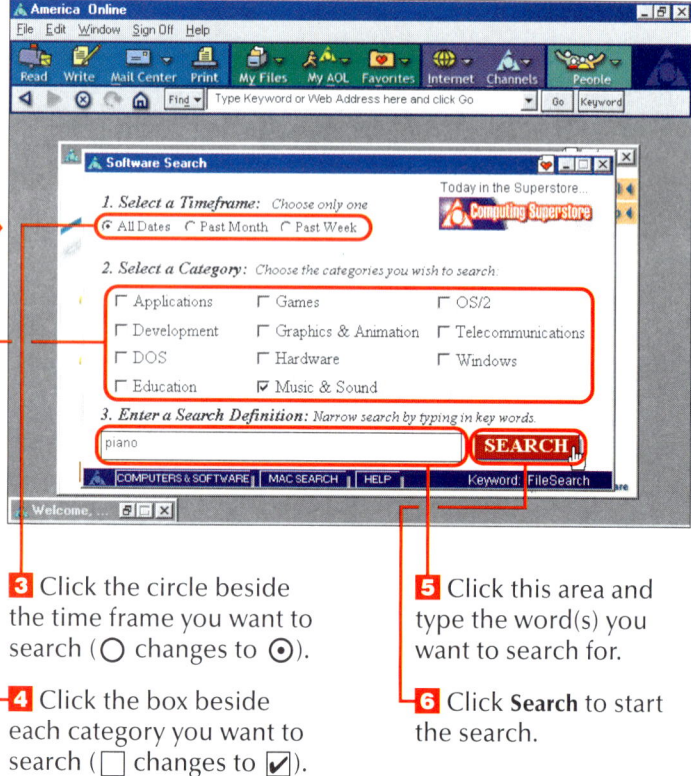

1 Click this area and type **find software**. Then press the Enter key.

■ The Find Software window appears.

2 To search for shareware files and programs, click this option.

Note: For information on shareware, see page 172.

3 Click the circle beside the time frame you want to search (○ changes to ⊙).

4 Click the box beside each category you want to search (☐ changes to ☑).

5 Click this area and type the word(s) you want to search for.

6 Click **Search** to start the search.

176

DOWNLOAD FILES

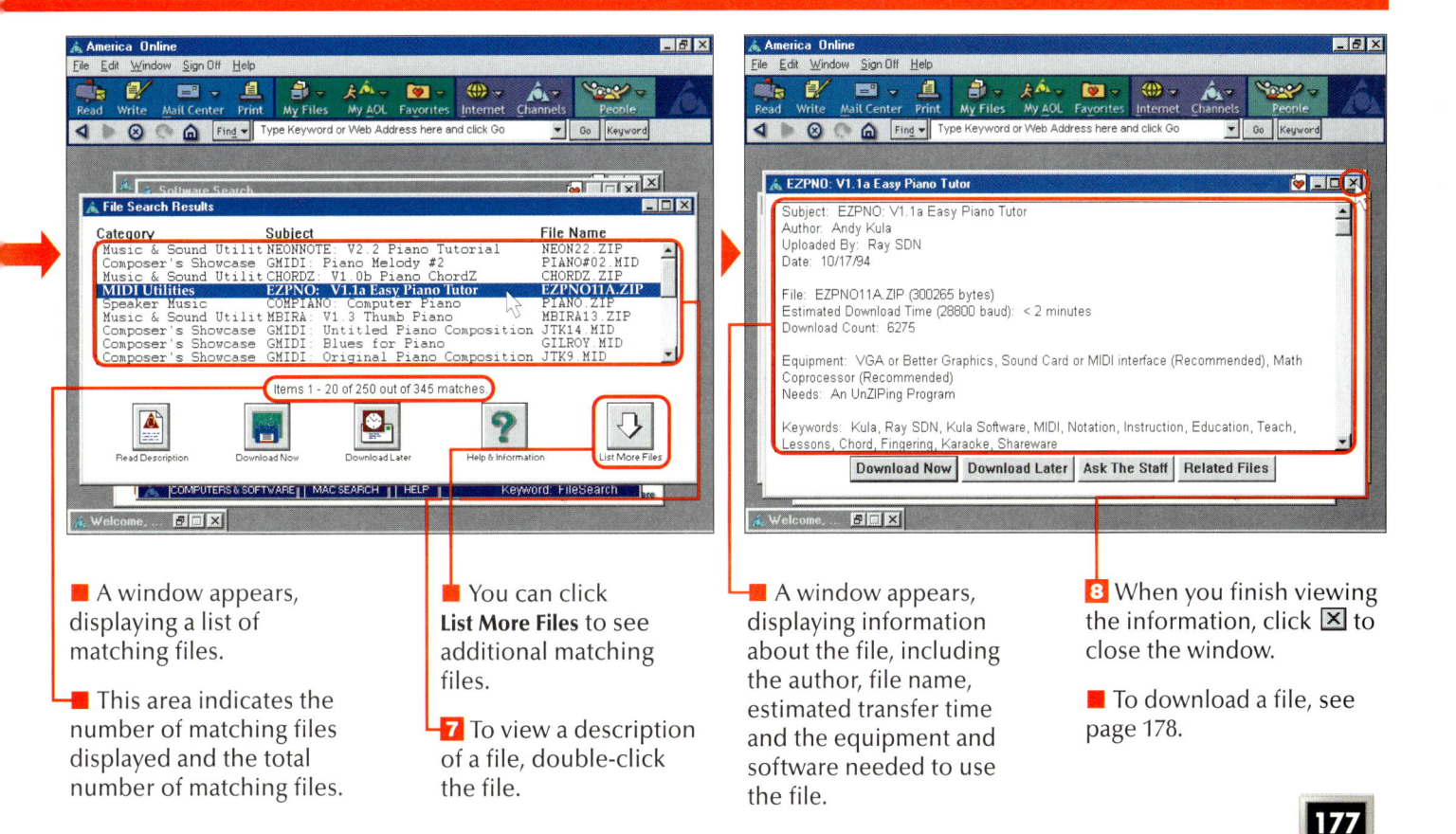

11

Will I be able to use any file I find on AOL?

You may need special hardware or software to use files you download from AOL. For example, you need a sound card and speakers to hear sound files.

■ A window appears, displaying a list of matching files.

■ This area indicates the number of matching files displayed and the total number of matching files.

■ You can click **List More Files** to see additional matching files.

7 To view a description of a file, double-click the file.

■ A window appears, displaying information about the file, including the author, file name, estimated transfer time and the equipment and software needed to use the file.

8 When you finish viewing the information, click ☒ to close the window.

■ To download a file, see page 178.

177

DOWNLOAD A FILE

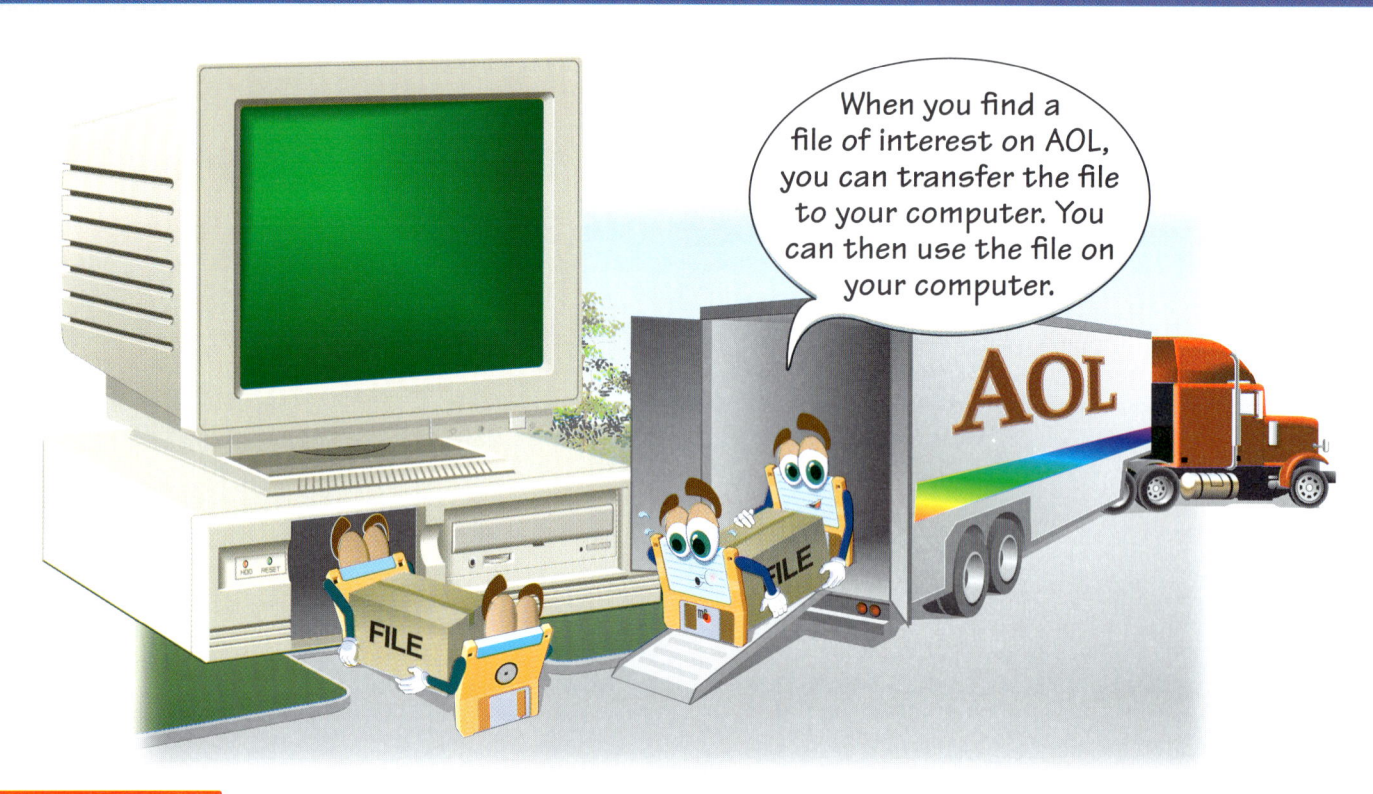

When you find a file of interest on AOL, you can transfer the file to your computer. You can then use the file on your computer.

DOWNLOAD A FILE

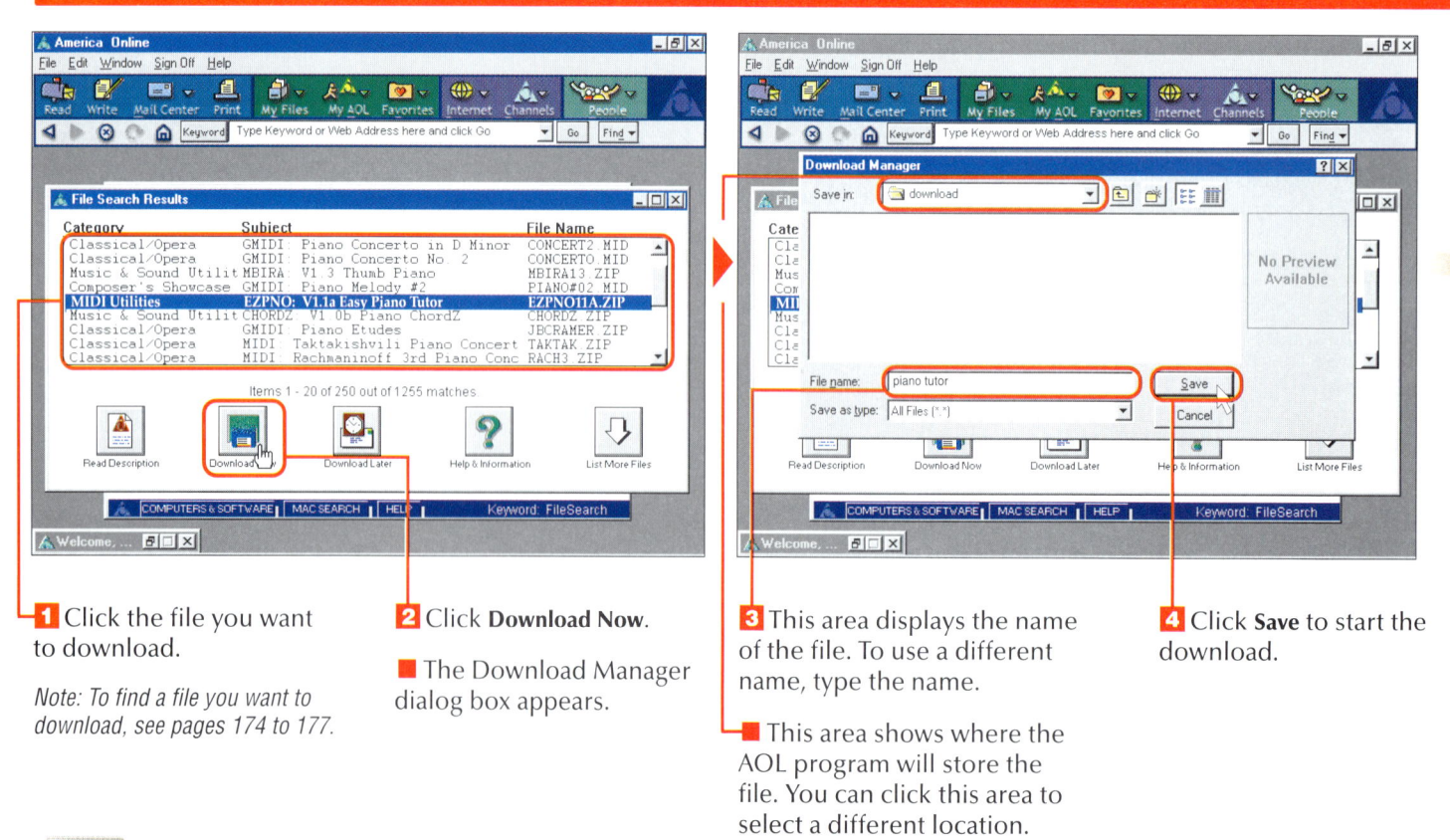

1 Click the file you want to download.

Note: To find a file you want to download, see pages 174 to 177.

2 Click **Download Now**.

■ The Download Manager dialog box appears.

3 This area displays the name of the file. To use a different name, type the name.

■ This area shows where the AOL program will store the file. You can click this area to select a different location.

4 Click **Save** to start the download.

178

DOWNLOAD FILES

Do I need to check for viruses after downloading files?

AOL checks most files for viruses before making the files available to you, but you should also use an anti-virus program to protect your information. A virus is a destructive program that can disrupt the normal operation of a computer. You can use the keyword **virus info** to read more information about viruses and get an anti-virus program. See page 32 for information on keywords.

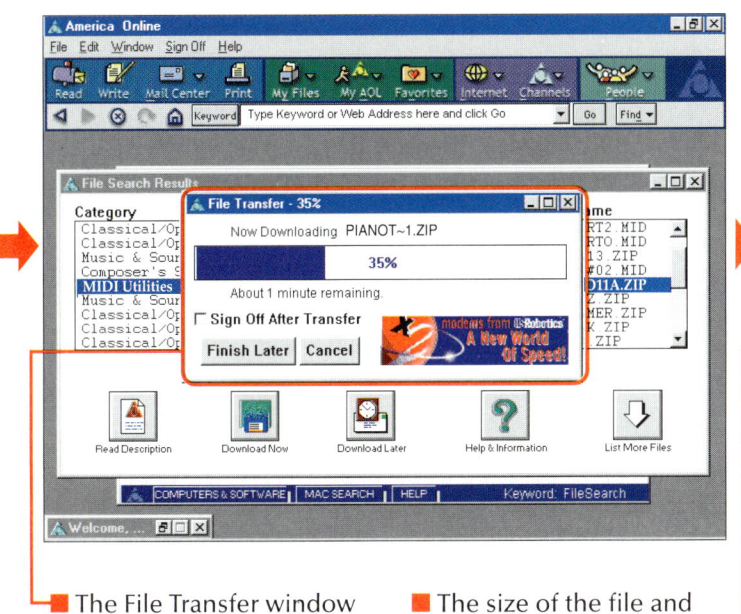

■ The File Transfer window appears, showing the progress of the transfer.

■ The size of the file and the speed of your modem determine how long a file will take to transfer.

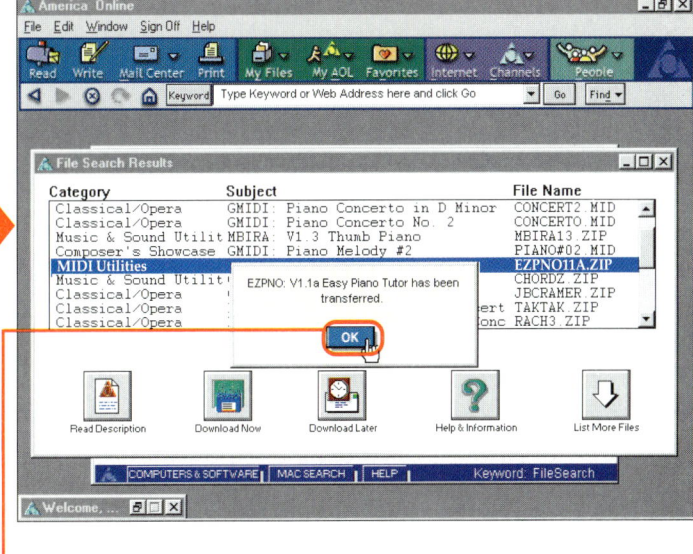

■ When the transfer is complete, a dialog box appears.

5 Click **OK** to close the dialog box.

■ You can now use the file on your computer.

Note: The contents of some files, such as images, may automatically appear on your screen.

179

USING THE DOWNLOAD MANAGER

The Download Manager keeps track of the files you have downloaded and where the files were stored on your computer.

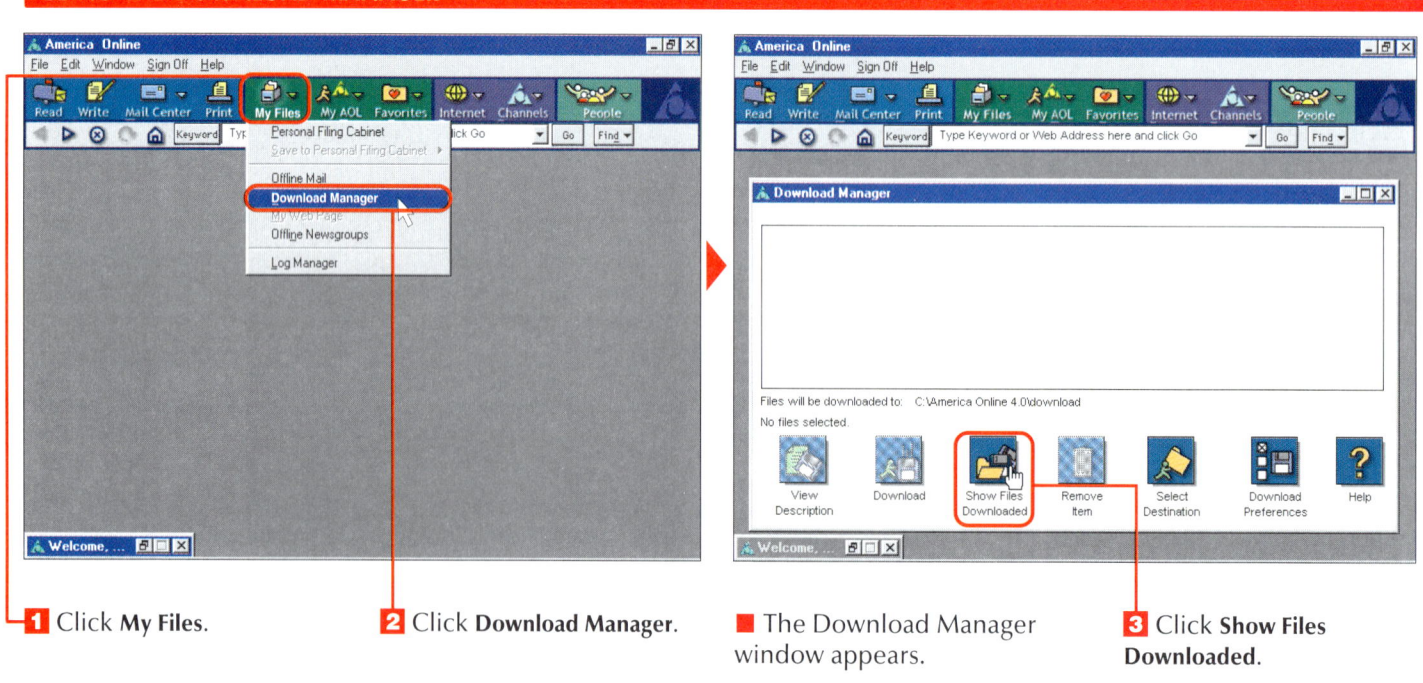

DOWNLOADED FILES

1. Name: *Mystery Game*
   Location: *download folder*
2. Name: *Blizzard Screen Saver*
   Location: *download folder*
3. Name: *The Ultimate Card Game*
   Location: *download folder*
4. Name: *Poker Version 1.0*
   Location: *download folder*

USING THE DOWNLOAD MANAGER

1 Click **My Files**.

2 Click **Download Manager**.

■ The Download Manager window appears.

3 Click **Show Files Downloaded**.

180

DOWNLOAD FILES

After I download a file, where will I find the file on my computer?

You will find most downloaded files in the download folder, located inside the America Online 4.0 folder on your hard drive (C:).

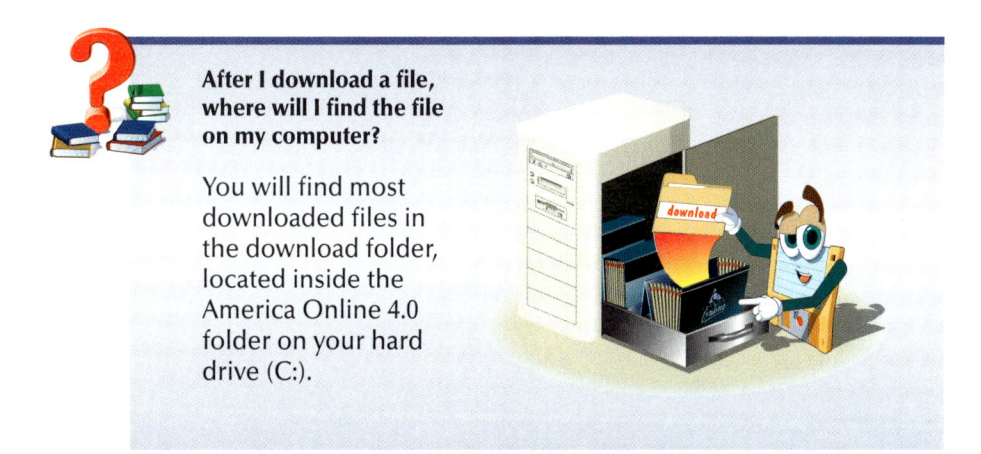

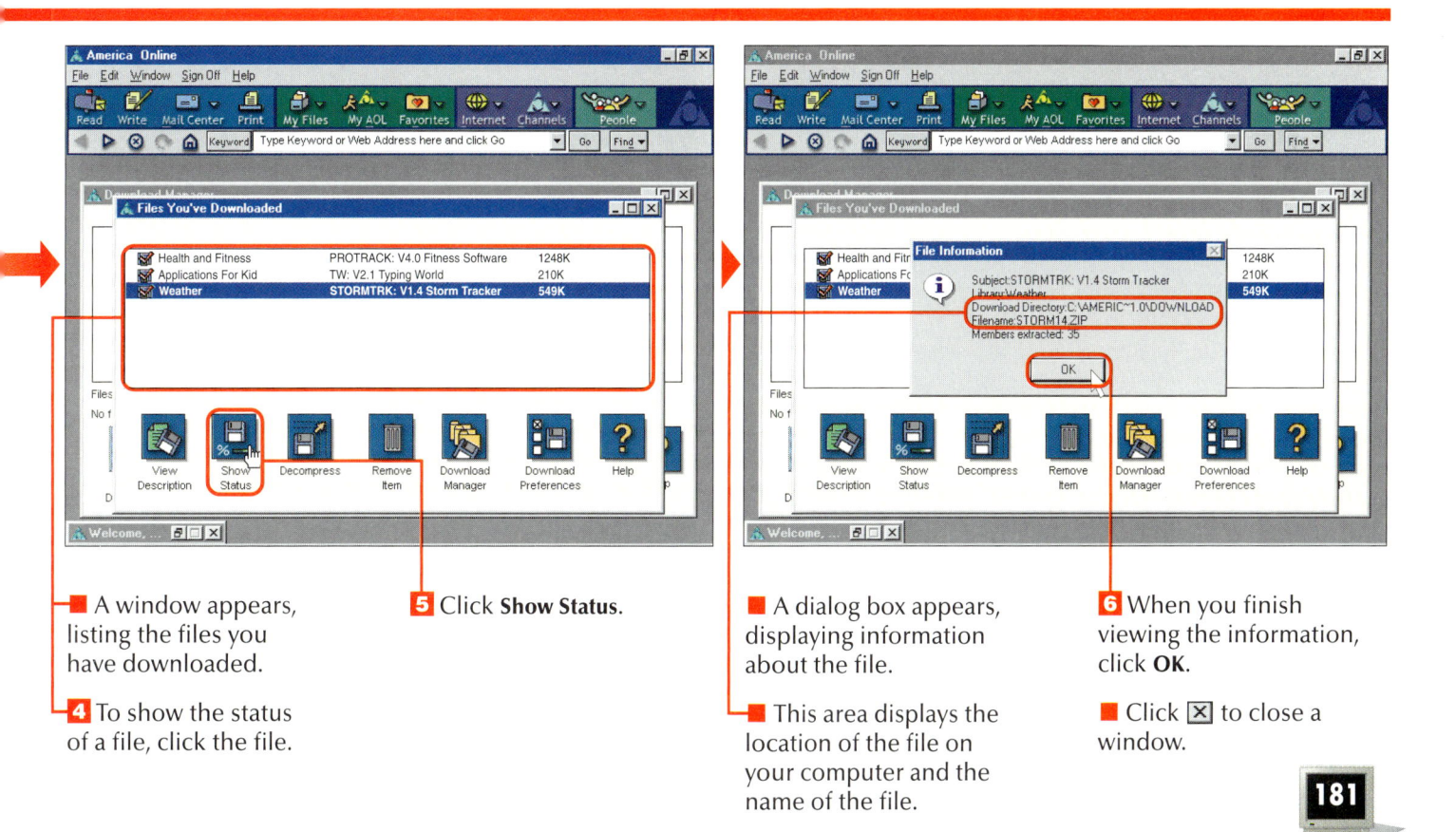

■ A window appears, listing the files you have downloaded.

4 To show the status of a file, click the file.

5 Click **Show Status**.

■ A dialog box appears, displaying information about the file.

■ This area displays the location of the file on your computer and the name of the file.

6 When you finish viewing the information, click **OK**.

■ Click ☒ to close a window.

181

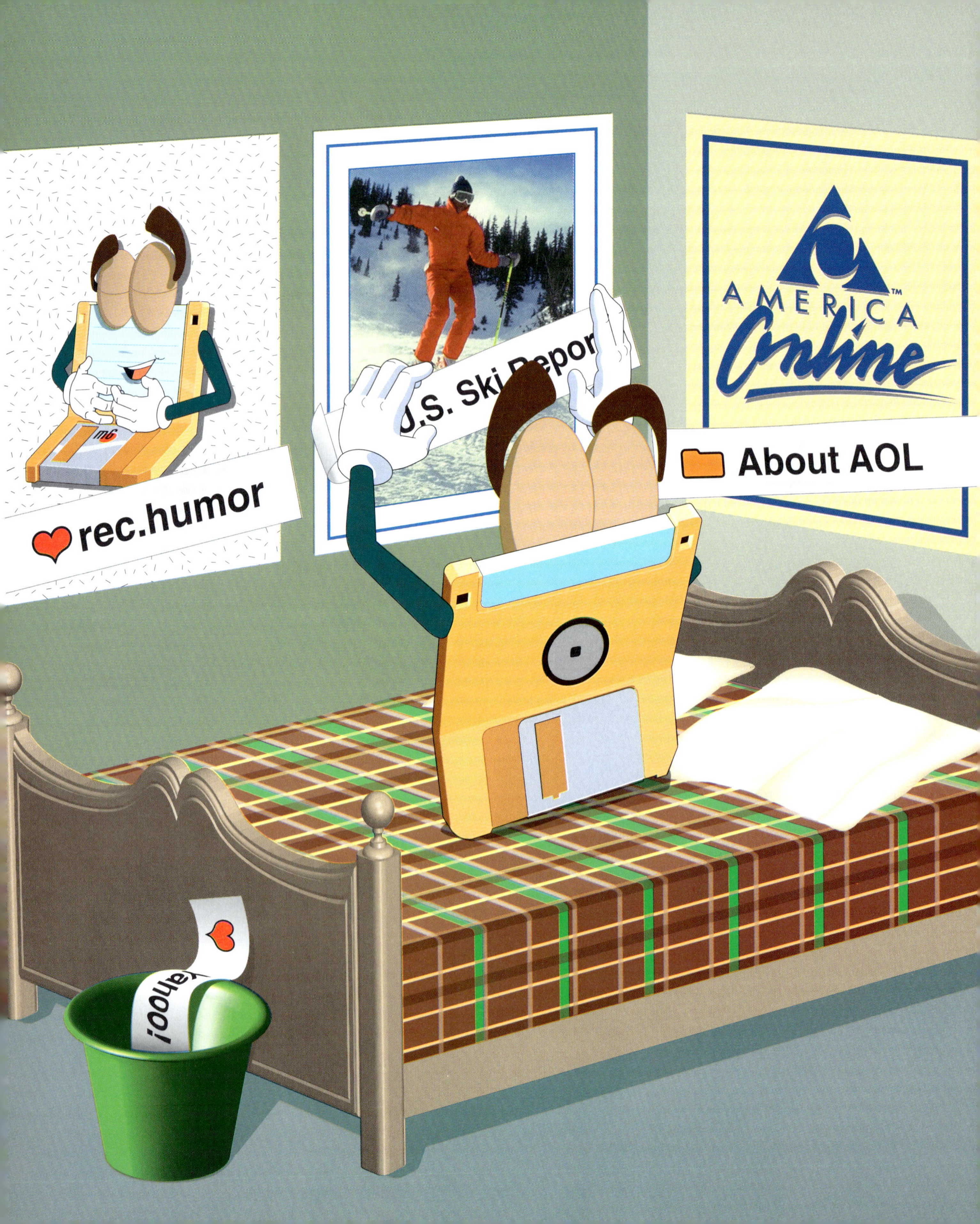
rec.humor
U.S. Ski Report
AMERICA Online
About AOL
Yahoo!

CHAPTER 12

KEEP TRACK OF FAVORITE PLACES

Do you have a favorite AOL channel or Web site? In this chapter, you will learn how to save the places you visit the most in a special folder.

Add a Favorite Place .184

Change Order of Favorite Places 186

Delete a Favorite Place 187

Add a Favorite Places Folder 188

ADD A FAVORITE PLACE

You can create a list of your favorite places on AOL so you can quickly return to those locations.

You can store places on AOL, Web pages and Internet newsgroups in your list of favorite places.

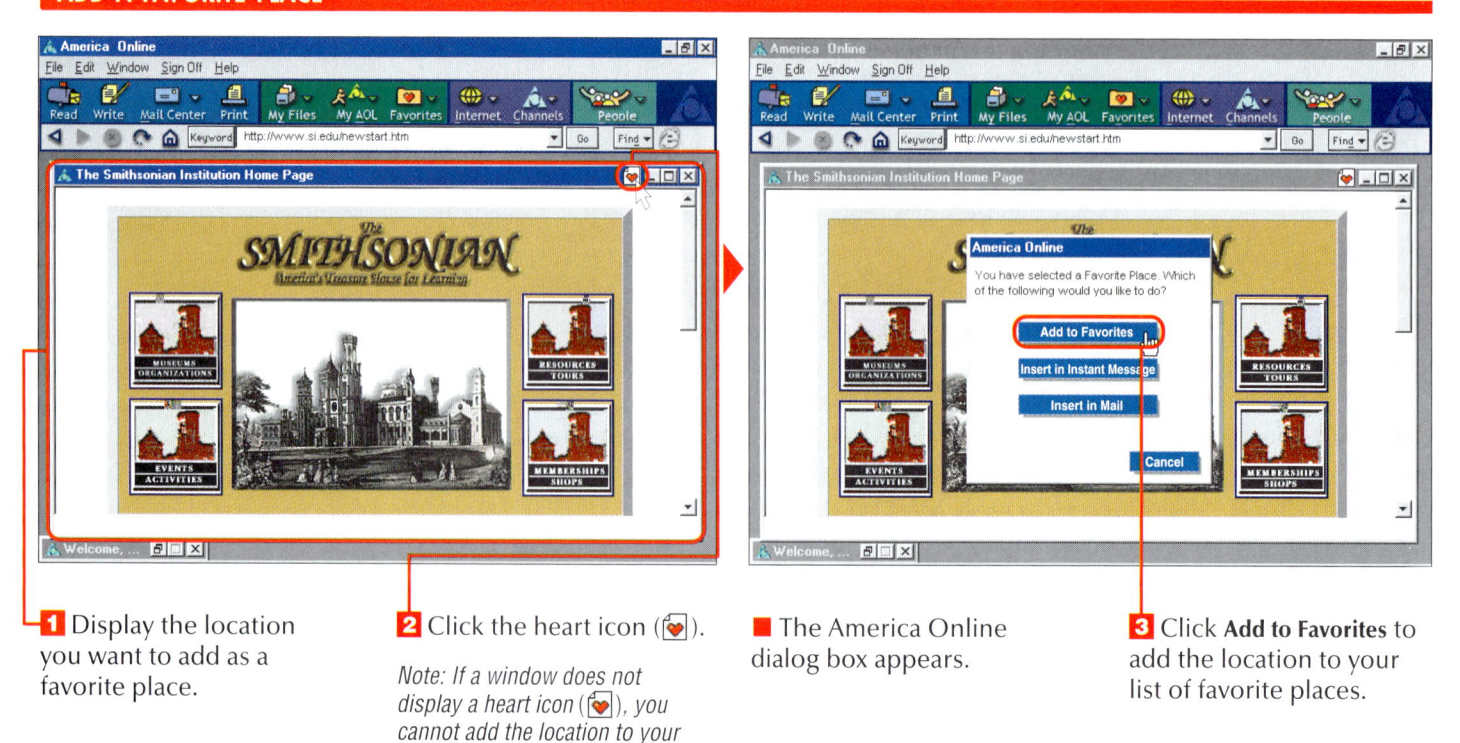

ADD A FAVORITE PLACE

1 Display the location you want to add as a favorite place.

2 Click the heart icon (♥).

Note: If a window does not display a heart icon (♥), you cannot add the location to your list of favorite places.

■ The America Online dialog box appears.

3 Click **Add to Favorites** to add the location to your list of favorite places.

KEEP TRACK OF FAVORITE PLACES

Why does the Favorites menu display items I did not add?

AOL automatically added four items to your list of favorite places. These items provide quick access to locations you may find interesting.

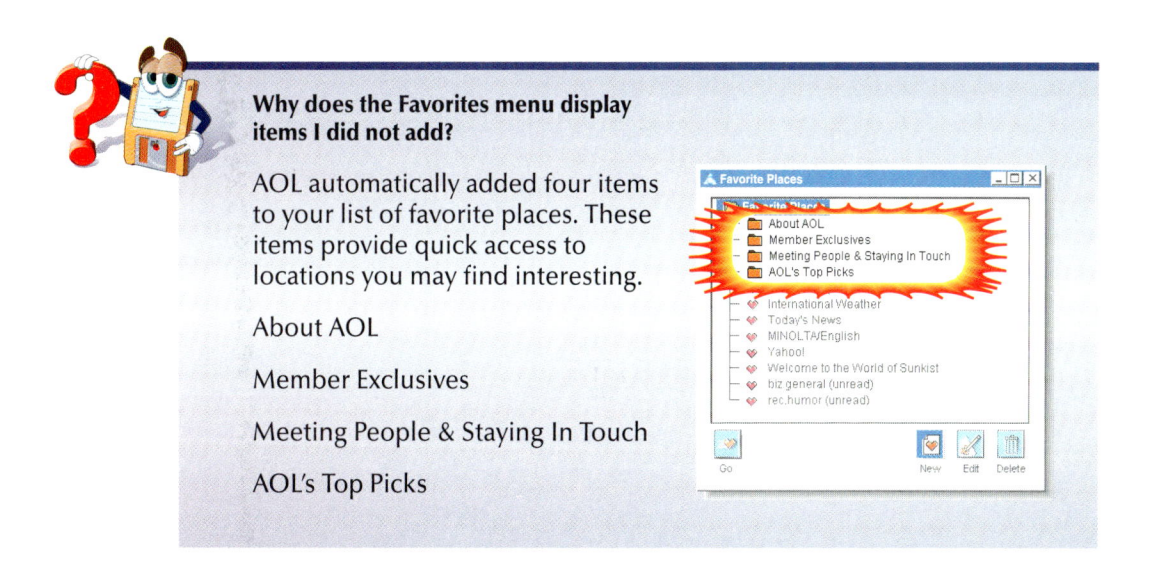

About AOL

Member Exclusives

Meeting People & Staying In Touch

AOL's Top Picks

DISPLAY A FAVORITE PLACE

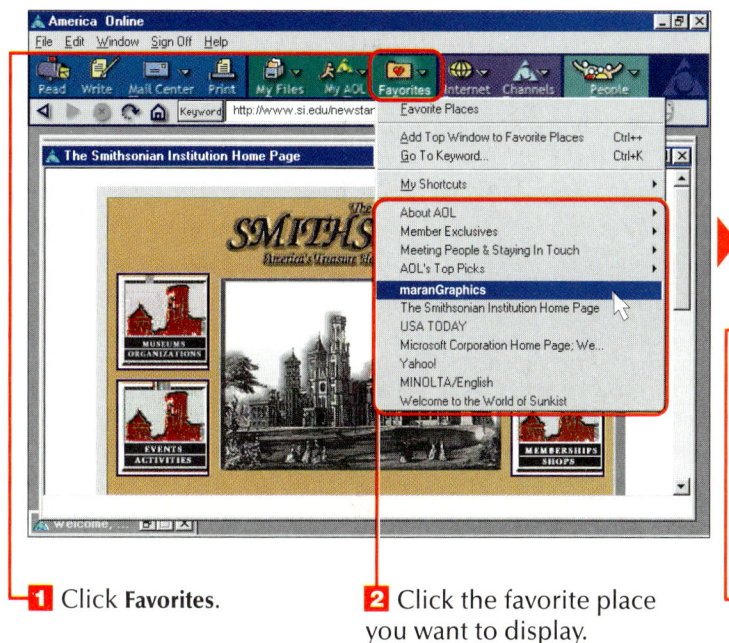

1 Click **Favorites**.

2 Click the favorite place you want to display.

Note: Menu items displaying an arrow (▶) contain favorite places that are related. To display the favorite places, move the mouse over the menu item.

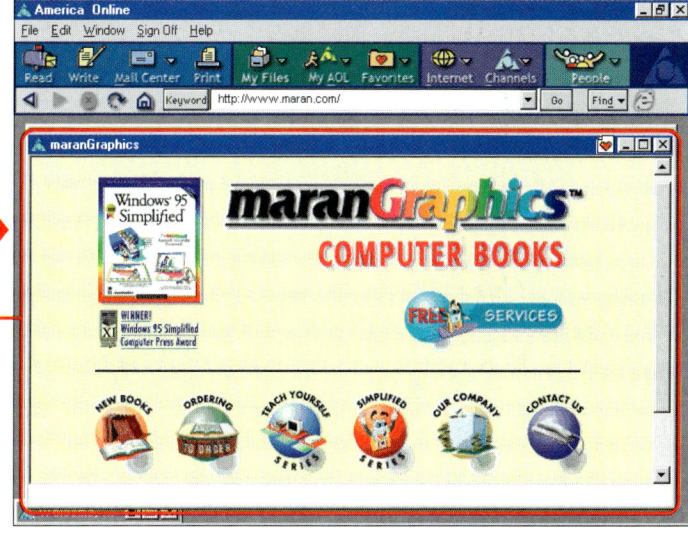

■ The favorite place appears.

185

CHANGE ORDER OF FAVORITE PLACES

You can change the order of items in your list of favorite places. You may want to move a place you frequently visit to the top of your list or move a place to a folder.

CHANGE ORDER OF FAVORITE PLACES

1 Display the Favorite Places window by performing steps 1 and 2 on page 188.

2 Position the mouse ↕ over the favorite place you want to move.

3 Drag the favorite place to a new location.

Note: The favorite place you move will appear above the favorite place that displays a border or in the folder that displays a border.

■ The favorite place appears in the new location.

■ You can double-click a folder (📁) to display the contents of the folder. Double-click the folder again to hide the folder's contents.

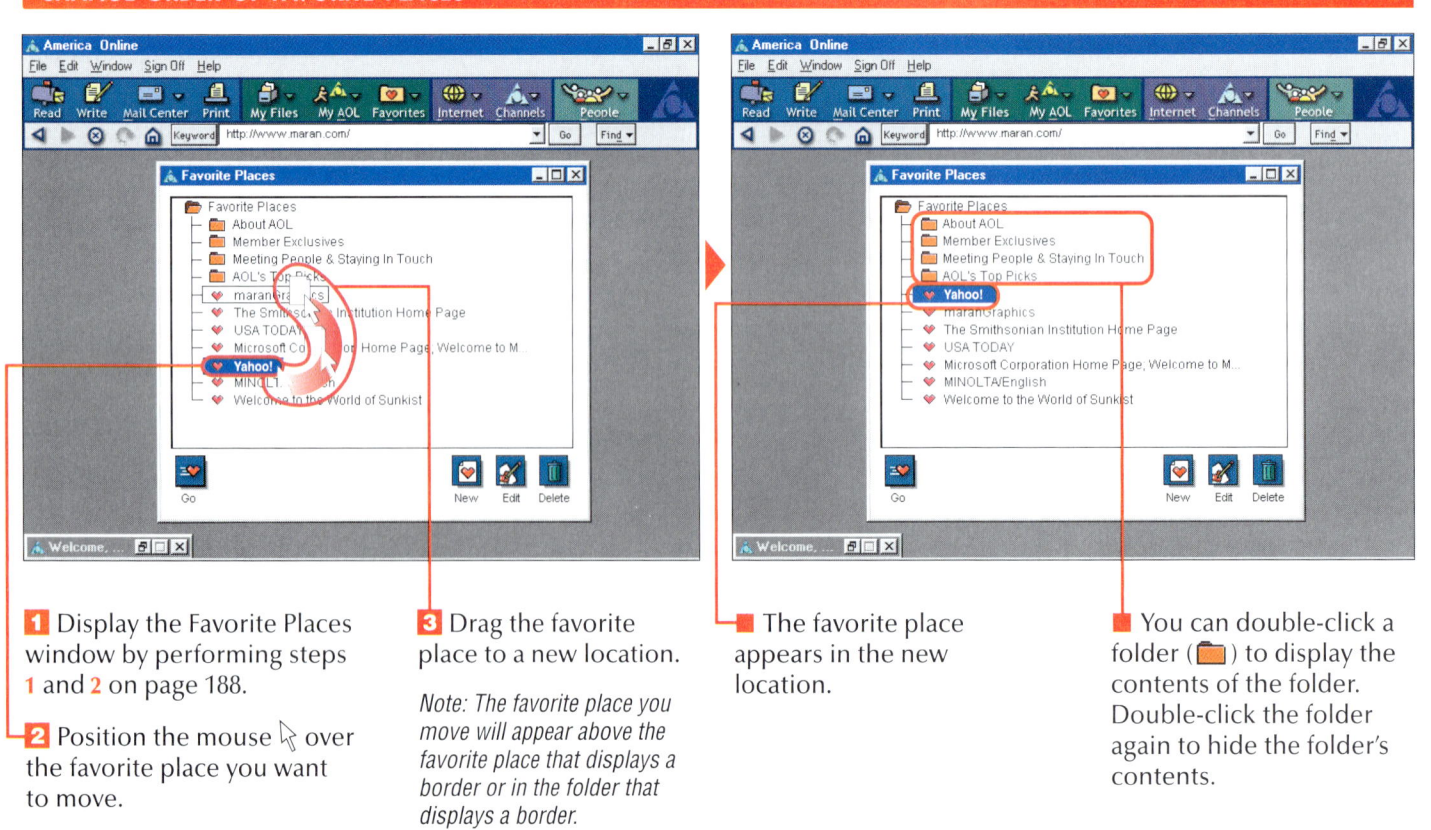

186

DELETE A FAVORITE PLACE

KEEP TRACK OF FAVORITE PLACES

> You should delete favorite places you no longer use. Deleting favorite places can help keep your list from becoming cluttered.

DELETE A FAVORITE PLACE

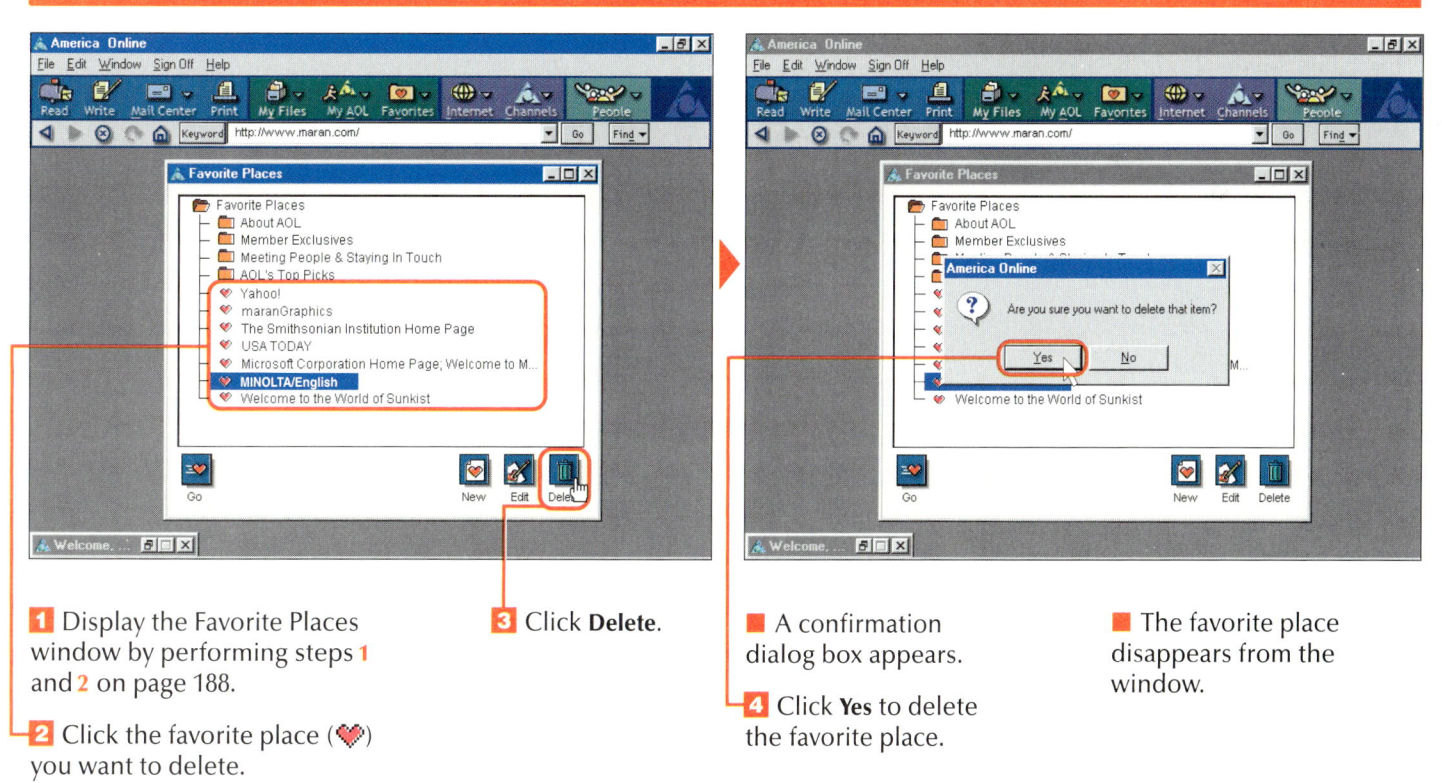

1 Display the Favorite Places window by performing steps **1** and **2** on page 188.

2 Click the favorite place (♥) you want to delete.

3 Click **Delete**.

■ A confirmation dialog box appears.

4 Click **Yes** to delete the favorite place.

■ The favorite place disappears from the window.

ADD A FAVORITE PLACES FOLDER

You can create folders to help organize your list of favorite places.

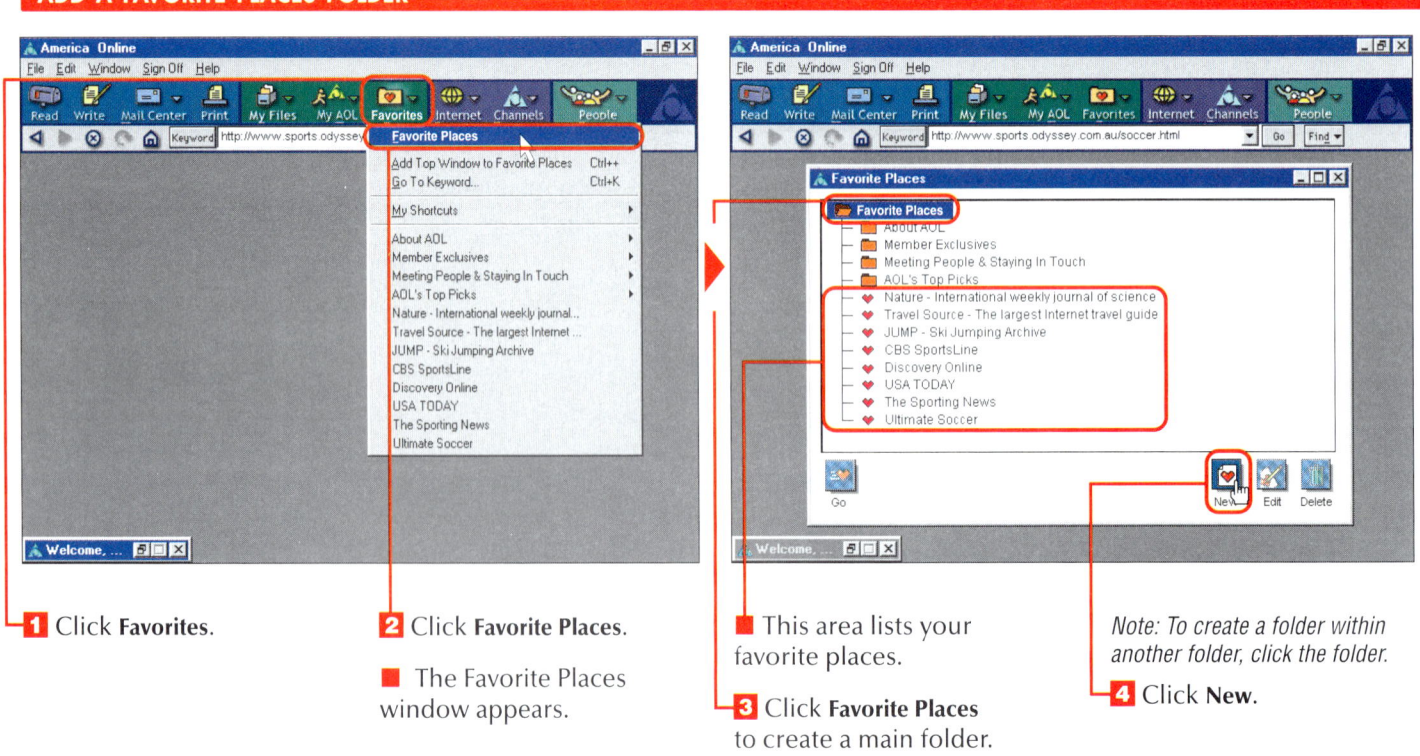

ADD A FAVORITE PLACES FOLDER

1 Click **Favorites**.

2 Click **Favorite Places**.

■ The Favorite Places window appears.

■ This area lists your favorite places.

3 Click **Favorite Places** to create a main folder.

Note: To create a folder within another folder, click the folder.

4 Click **New**.

188

KEEP TRACK OF FAVORITE PLACES

12

How can I use my new folder?

After you add a new folder in the Favorite Places window, the folder will appear on the Favorites menu. Folders on the Favorites menu display an arrow (▶). You can display the contents of a folder by positioning the mouse over the folder.

- ■ The Add New Folder window appears.

- ■ Click **New Folder** to create a new folder (○ changes to ⦿).

- ■ Type a name for the new folder.

- ■ Click **OK**.

- ■ The new folder appears.

- ■ You can double-click a folder to display the contents of the folder. Double-click the folder again to hide the contents.

- ■ You can move a favorite place to the new folder. See page 186 for information.

- ■ Click ✕ to close the Favorite Places window.

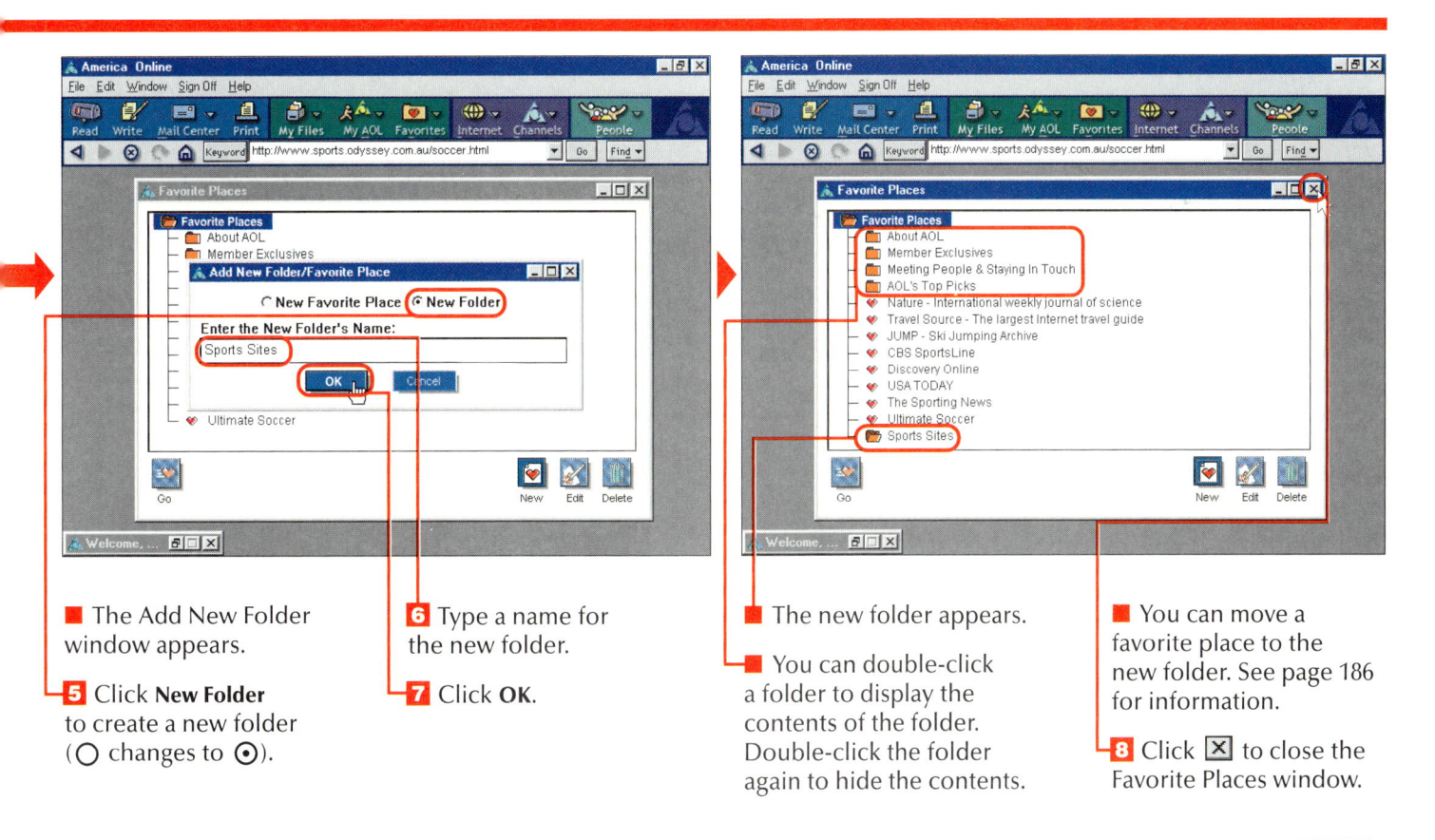

189

AMERICA Online
PASSWORD
BLUE123
Reminder Service
1 2 3 4 5 6
7 8 9 10 11 12 13
14 15 16 17 18 19 20
21 22 23 24 25 26 27
28 29 30
June 1998
15
Doctor's Appointment
Personal Filing Cabinet

CHAPTER 13

AOL FEATURES

Does AOL offer any special features? In this chapter you will learn to use AOL features such as Parental Controls, the Personal Filing Cabinet, Stock Portfolios, News Profiles and more.

Create a Screen Name 192

Change Your Password 196

Change Parental Controls 198

Switch Screen Names Without Signing Off..200

Using the Personal Filing Cabinet 202

Create a Stock Portfolio 204

Add Item to Stock Portfolio 206

Display and Print a Stock Portfolio 208

Create a News Profile 210

Manage News Profiles 214

Using the Reminder Service 216

CREATE A SCREEN NAME

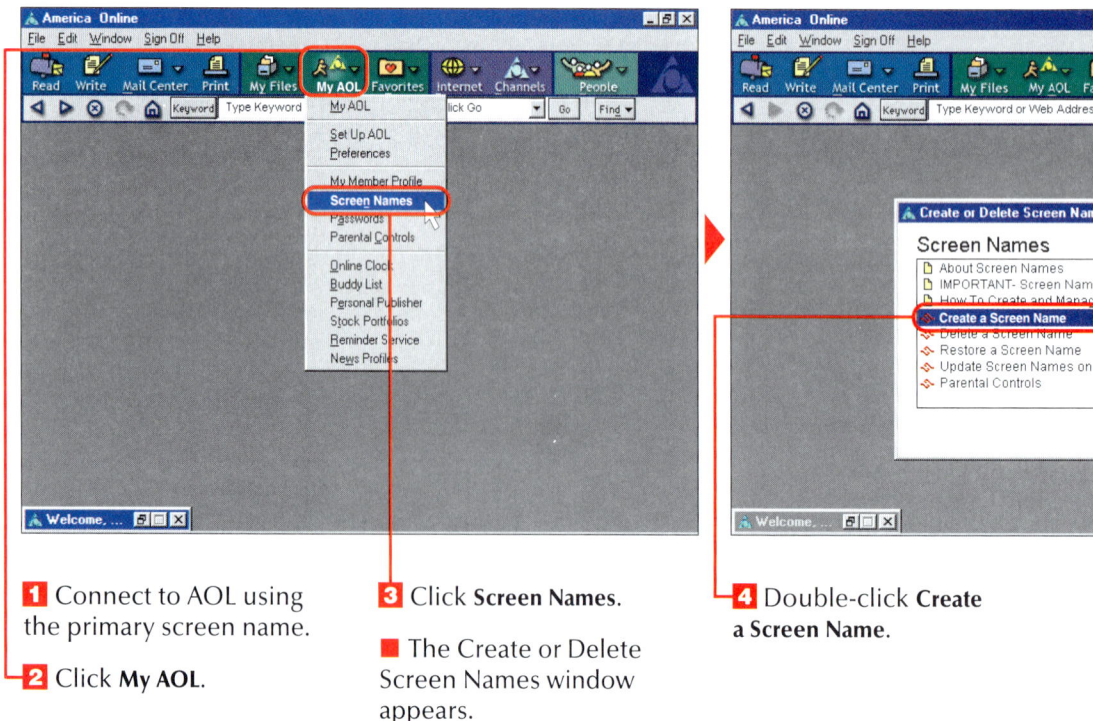

You can create up to five screen names to place different members of your family or company on one AOL account.

Screen Names

Sign up here!
1. JSMITH 4.
2. DSMITH 5.
3. KSMITH

A screen name is a name you choose that people use to identify you. Each screen name has its own password, e-mail and preferences.

To create new screen names, you must connect to AOL using the primary screen name. The primary screen name is the name you created when you first set up your AOL account.

CREATE A SCREEN NAME

1 Connect to AOL using the primary screen name.

2 Click **My AOL**.

3 Click **Screen Names**.

■ The Create or Delete Screen Names window appears.

4 Double-click **Create a Screen Name**.

■ The Create a Screen Name dialog box appears.

192

AOL FEATURES

What screen name and password should I use?

Screen Name
A screen name can be your real name or a nickname. A screen name must start with a letter and can be 3 to 10 characters long. A message will appear if the screen name you request is already in use.

Password
Do not use your first name, screen name or other obvious words as your password. Your password can be 4 to 8 characters long and can contain letters and numbers.

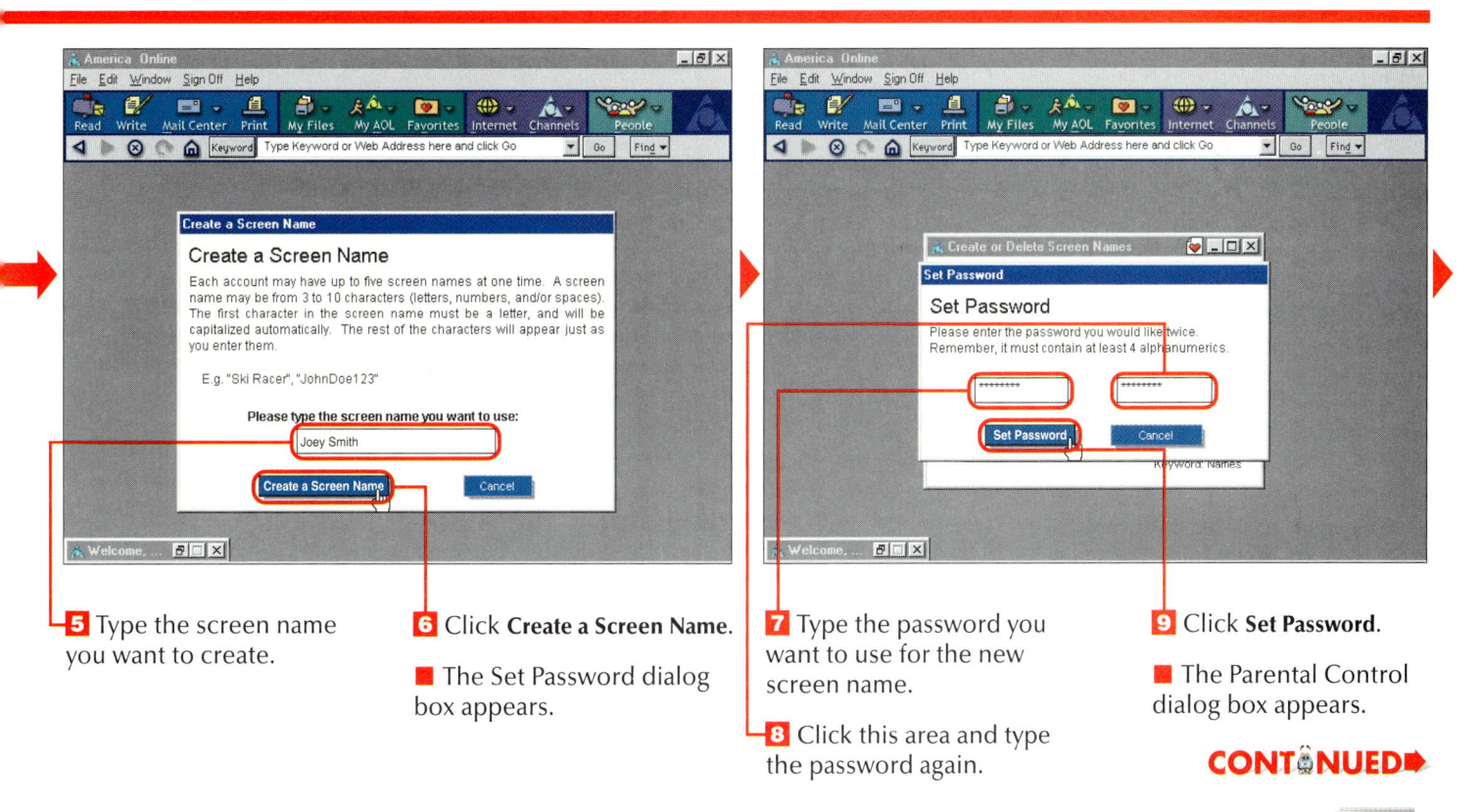

5 Type the screen name you want to create.

6 Click **Create a Screen Name**.

■ The Set Password dialog box appears.

7 Type the password you want to use for the new screen name.

8 Click this area and type the password again.

9 Click **Set Password**.

■ The Parental Control dialog box appears.

CONTINUED

193

CREATE A SCREEN NAME

When creating a screen name, you need to select the appropriate age group for the person who will use the screen name. This helps parents control the content their children can access.

CREATE A SCREEN NAME (CONTINUED)

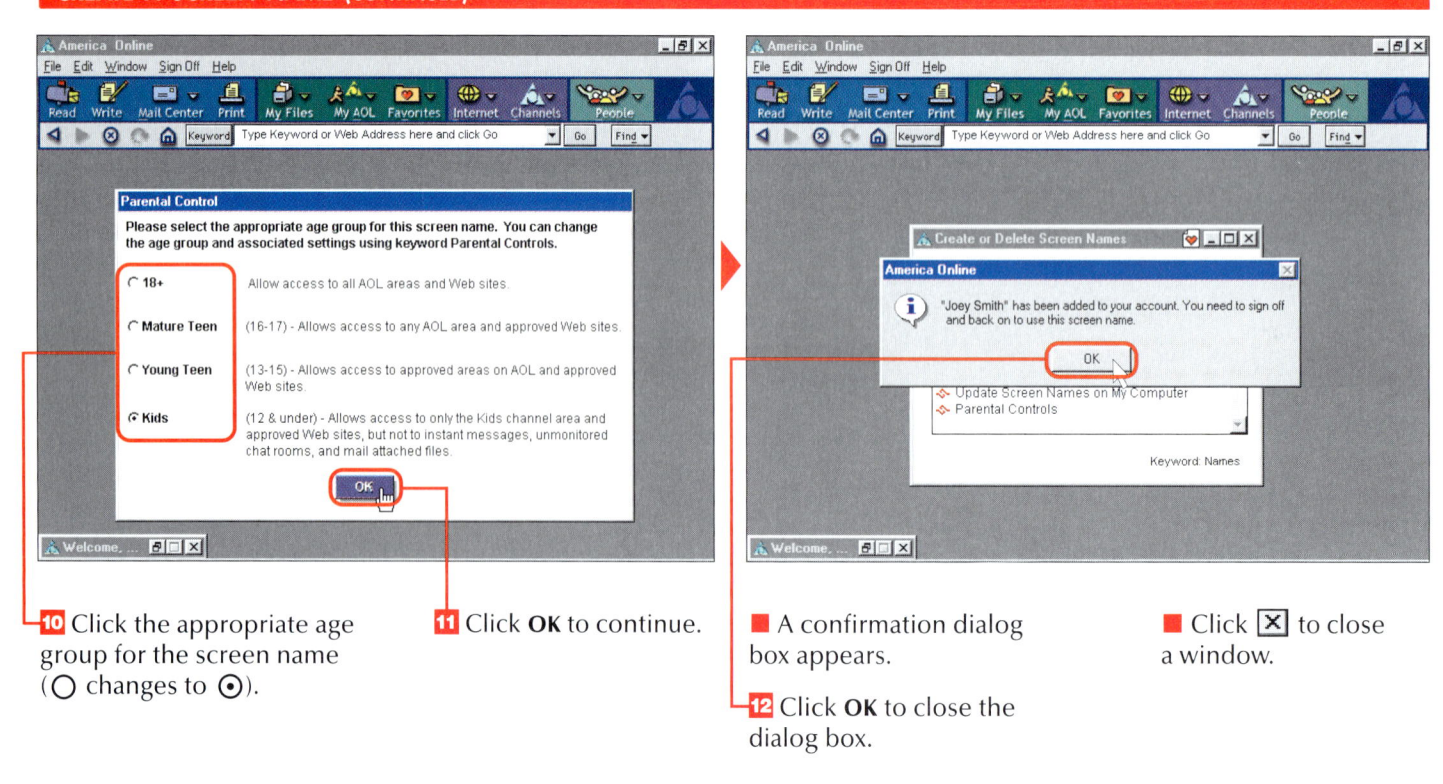

10 Click the appropriate age group for the screen name (○ changes to ⊙).

11 Click **OK** to continue.

■ A confirmation dialog box appears.

12 Click **OK** to close the dialog box.

■ Click ✖ to close a window.

AOL FEATURES

Can AOL store the password for a new screen name I created?

The next time you connect to AOL using the new screen name, a dialog box appears, asking if you want to store your password. This lets you avoid having to type your password each time you connect. To connect to AOL, see page 8.

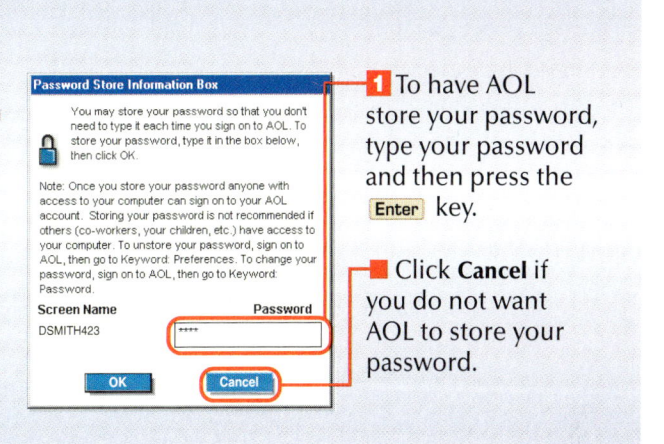

1 To have AOL store your password, type your password and then press the Enter key.

■ Click **Cancel** if you do not want AOL to store your password.

DELETE A SCREEN NAME

1 Double-click **Delete a Screen Name**.

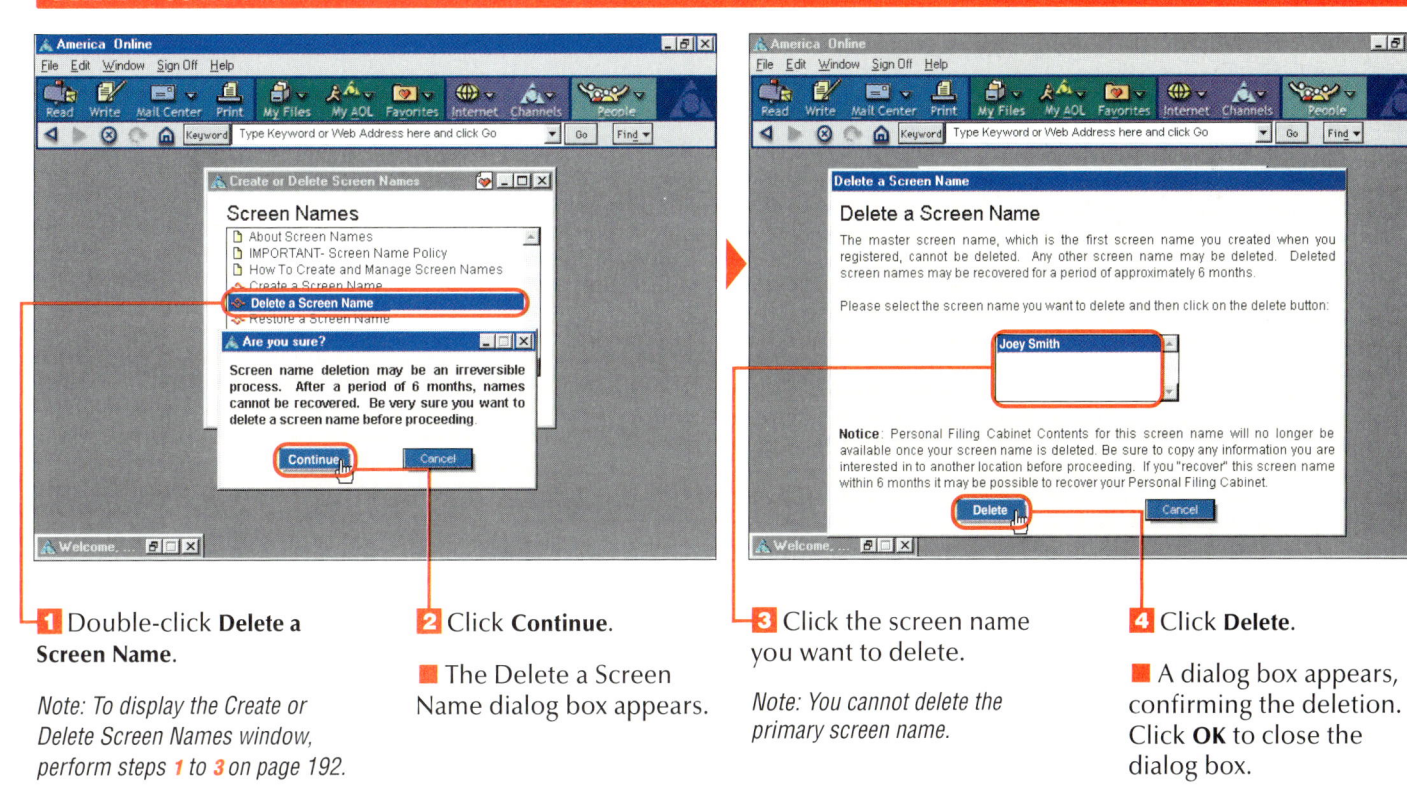

Note: To display the Create or Delete Screen Names window, perform steps **1** to **3** on page 192.

■ A confirmation window appears.

2 Click **Continue**.

■ The Delete a Screen Name dialog box appears.

3 Click the screen name you want to delete.

Note: You cannot delete the primary screen name.

4 Click **Delete**.

■ A dialog box appears, confirming the deletion. Click **OK** to close the dialog box.

195

CHANGE YOUR PASSWORD

You should change your password frequently to prevent other people from accessing your AOL account.

Do not use your first name, screen name or other obvious words as your password. Your password can be 4 to 8 characters long and can contain letters and numbers.

CHANGE YOUR PASSWORD

1 Click **My AOL**.

2 Click **Passwords**.

■ A dialog box appears.

■ This area displays information about changing your password.

3 Click **Change Password**.

■ The Change Your Password dialog box appears.

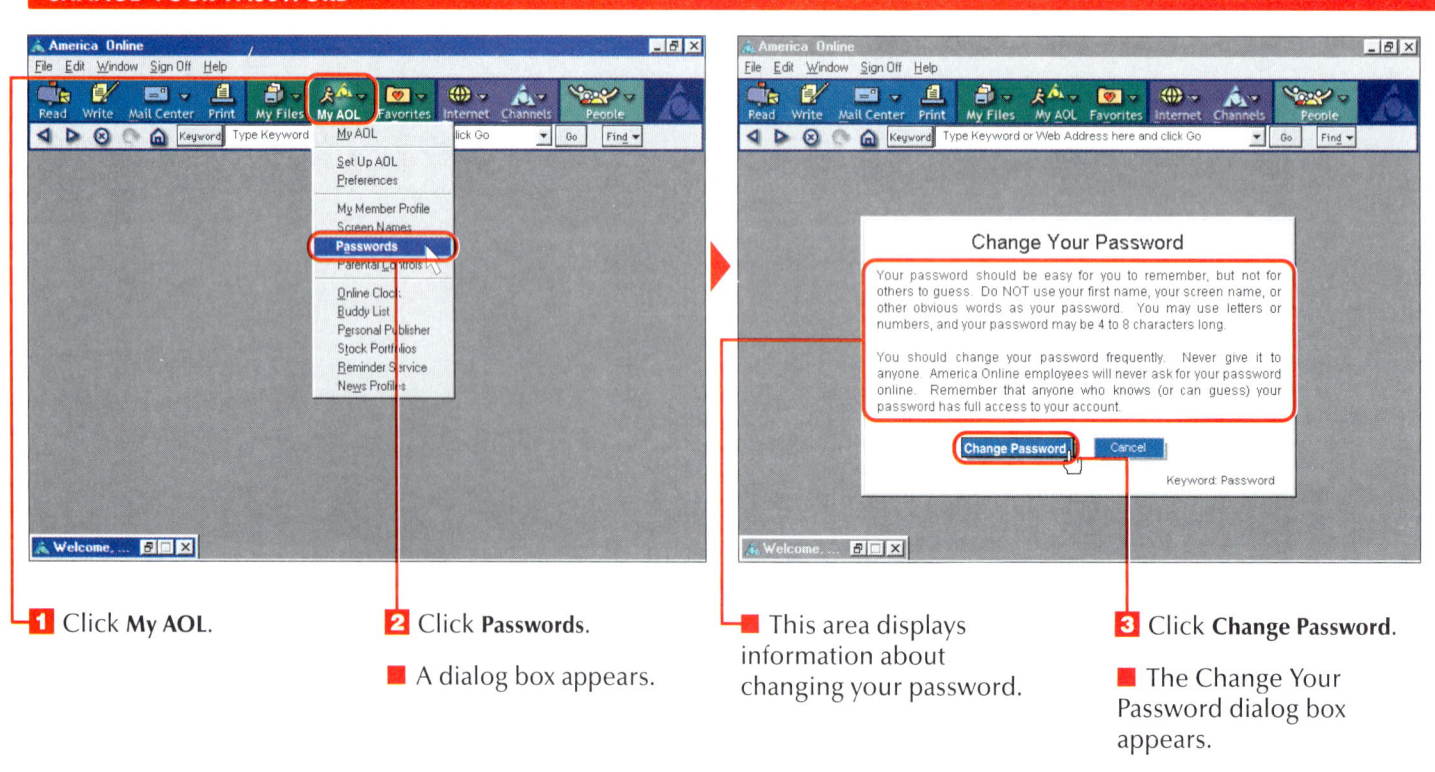

AOL FEATURES

While online, an AOL employee asked for my password. Should I give them my password?

No. An AOL employee will never ask for your password. To keep your AOL account secure, you should never give out your password to anyone. A person who knows your password has full access to your account.

■ 4 Type your current password.

■ 5 Click this area and type the new password you want to use.

■ 6 Click this area and type the new password again.

■ 7 Click **Change Password**.

■ A confirmation dialog box appears.

■ 8 Click **OK** to close the dialog box.

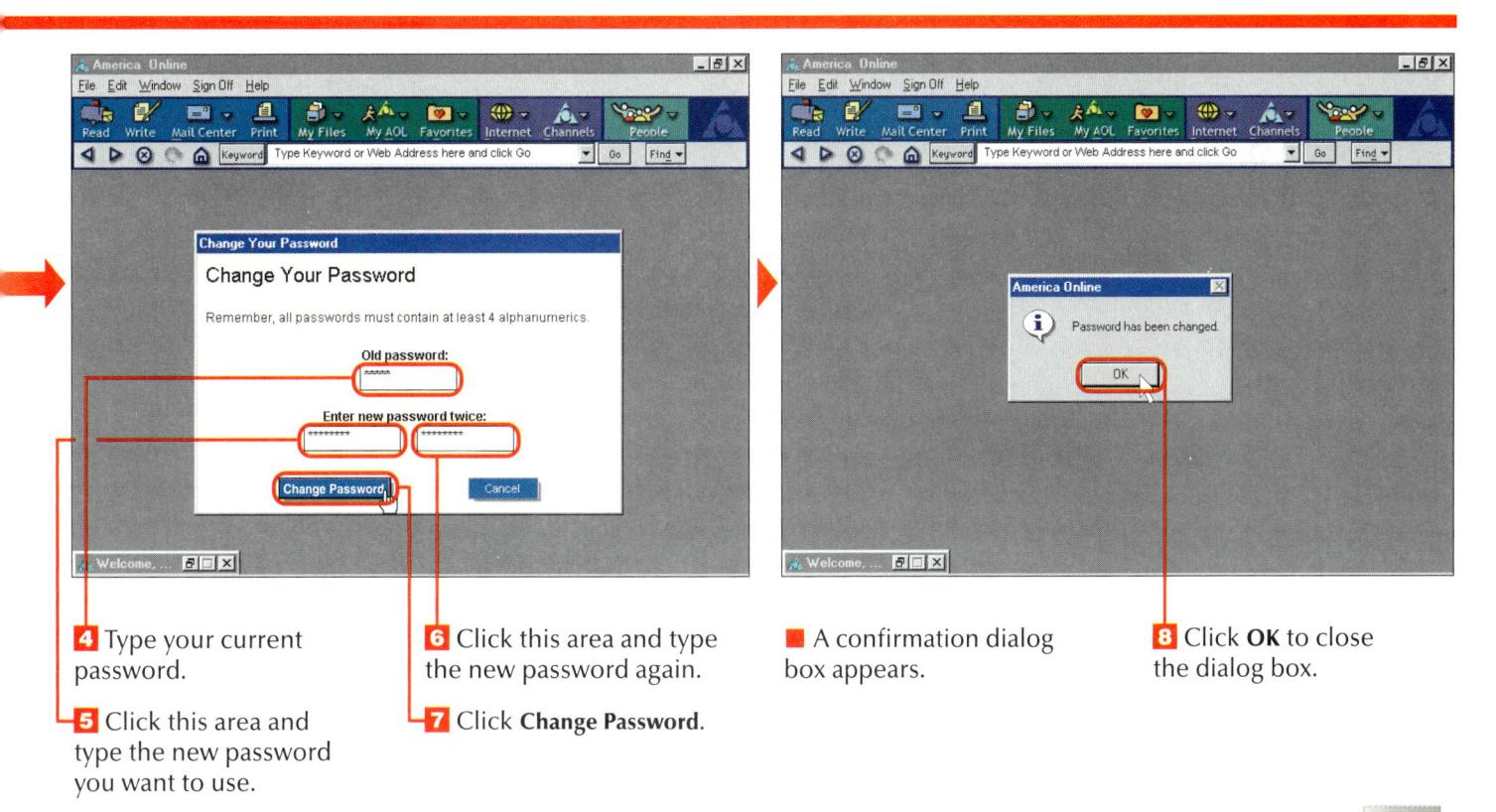

197

CHANGE PARENTAL CONTROLS

You can control what information your children can access on AOL and the Internet. As a child matures, you may want to change the type of access given to the child.

Parental controls are first set up when you create a screen name for a child you want to use your account. For information on creating screen names, see page 192.

CHANGE PARENTAL CONTROLS

1 Connect to AOL using the primary screen name.

Note: The primary screen name is the name you created when you first set up your AOL account.

2 Click **My AOL**.

3 Click **Parental Controls**.

■ The Parental Controls window appears.

4 Click **Set Parental Controls Now**.

■ A window appears, allowing you to change the parental controls.

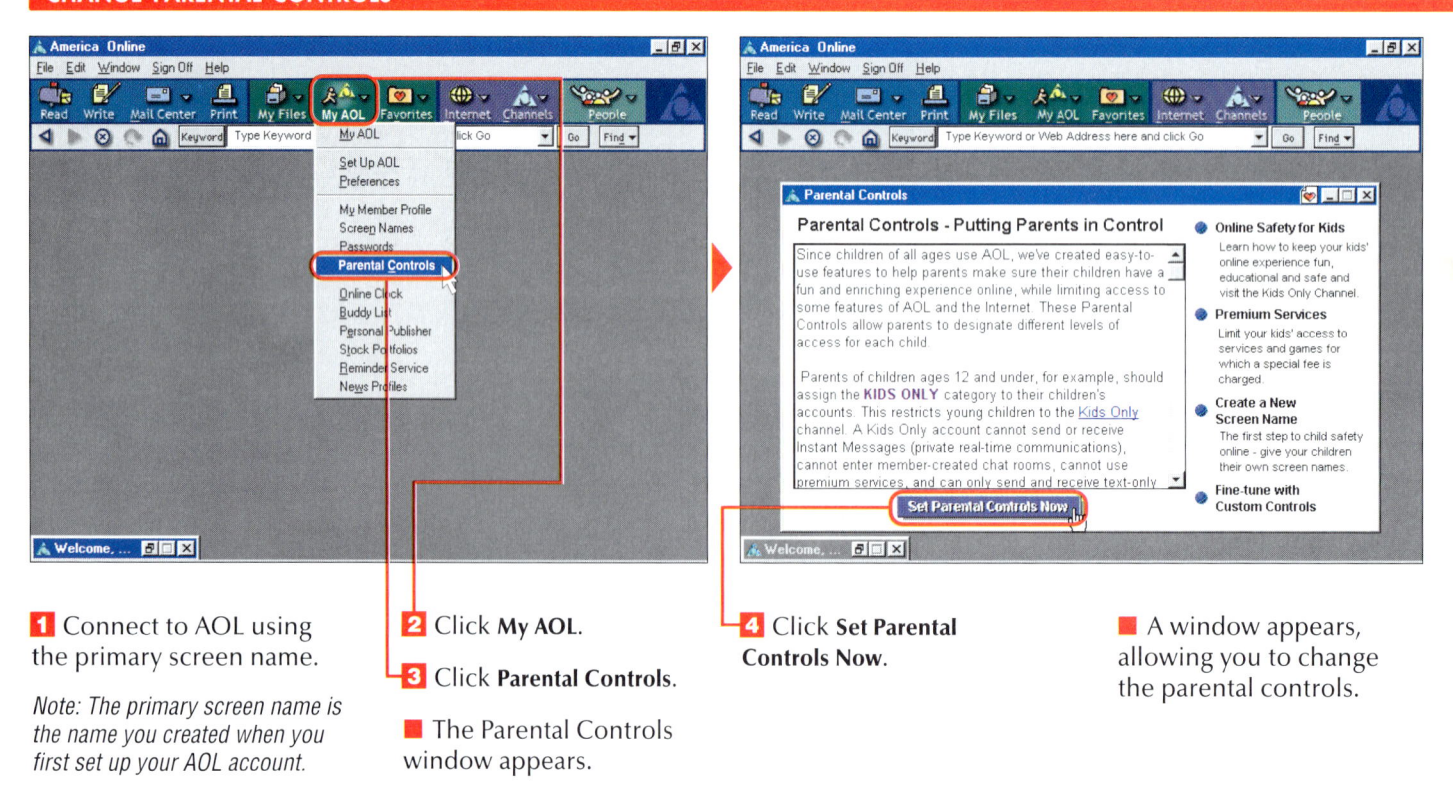

198

13
AOL FEATURES

How can I further protect my children?

In addition to using AOL's parental controls, you should supervise your children's use of AOL and the Internet. Making sure your children follow these guidelines can help keep your children safe:

• Do not give your AOL password, home address or telephone number to anyone you meet online.

• Do not agree to meet anyone in person.

• If someone makes you feel uncomfortable, tell a parent.

■ This area describes the types of access you can set for each screen name.

■ This area displays the screen names set up on your account.

5 Click the circle for the type of access you want to set for each screen name (○ changes to ⊙).

6 Click **OK** to save your changes.

■ A confirmation dialog box appears. Click **OK** to close the dialog box.

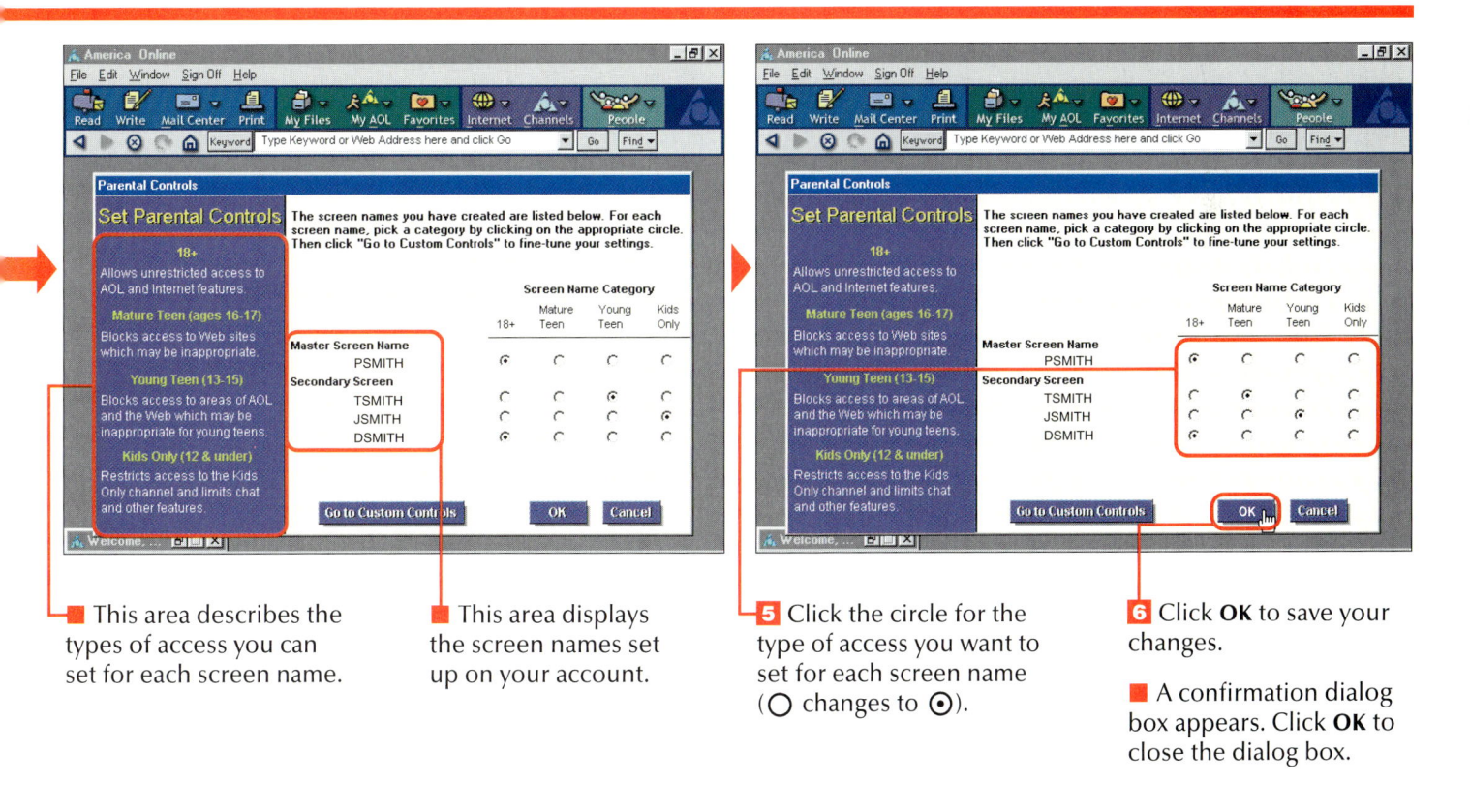

199

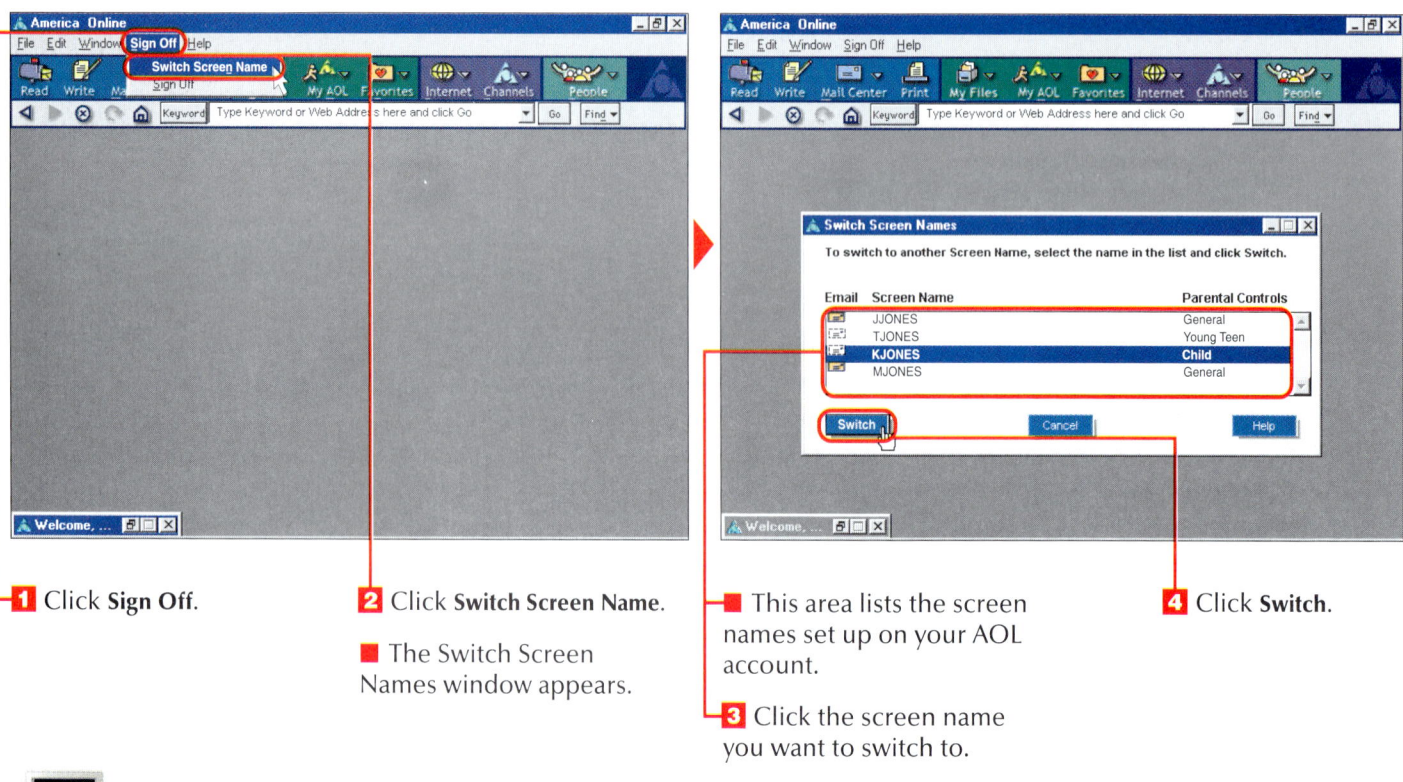

SWITCH SCREEN NAMES WITHOUT SIGNING OFF

When you finish using AOL, another family member or colleague can switch to their screen name without having to sign off AOL.

Switching screen names allows another family member or colleague to check for new messages and use AOL with their own preferences.

SWITCH SCREEN NAMES WITHOUT SIGNING OFF

1 Click **Sign Off**.

2 Click **Switch Screen Name**.

■ The Switch Screen Names window appears.

■ This area lists the screen names set up on your AOL account.

3 Click the screen name you want to switch to.

4 Click **Switch**.

200

AOL FEATURES — 13

When switching screen names, how can I determine if a screen name has new mail?

In the Switch Screen Names window, a colored envelope (📧) appears beside screen names that have new mail. Screen names that do not have new mail display a white envelope (📩).

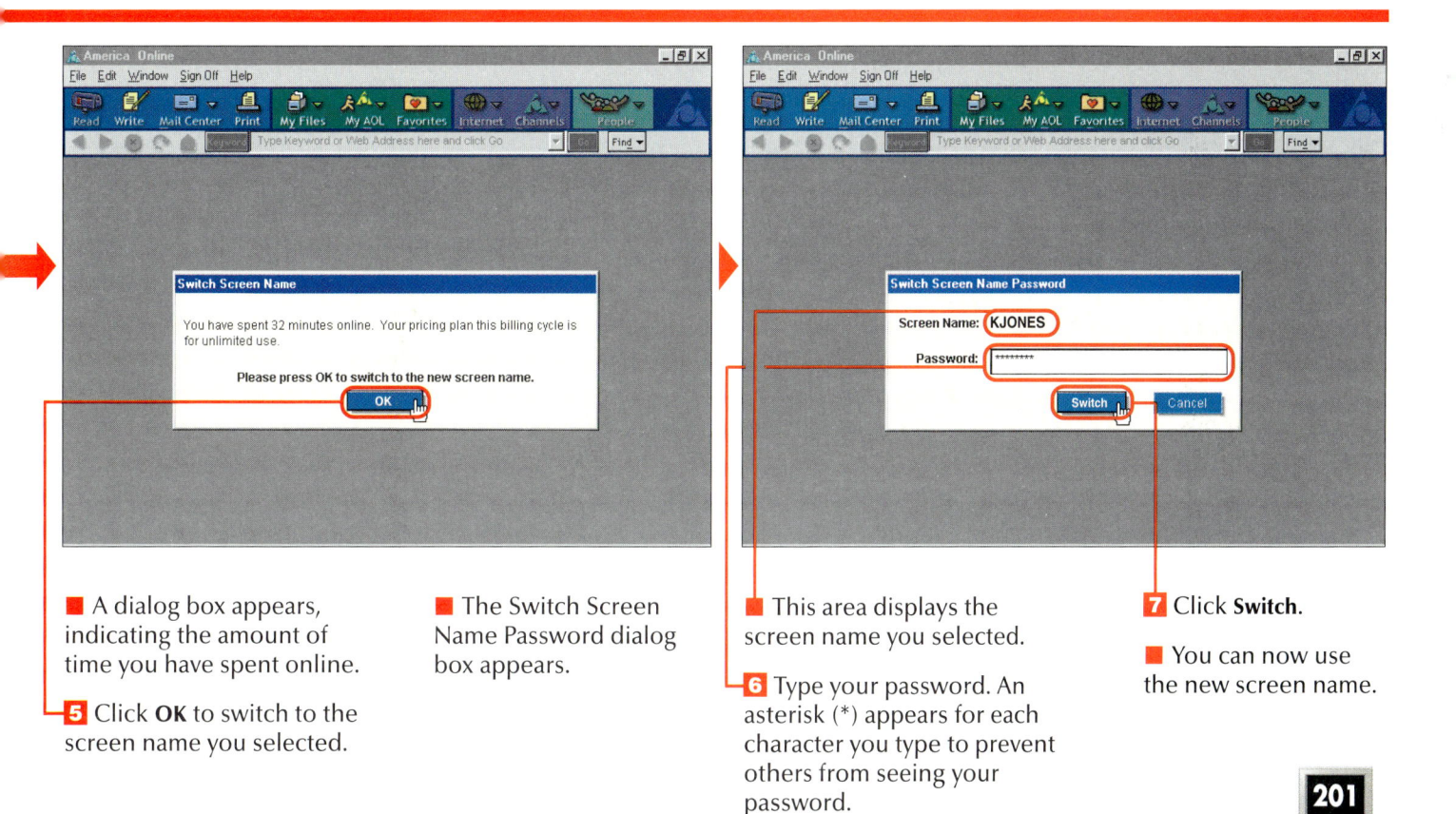

New Mail   No New Mail

■ A dialog box appears, indicating the amount of time you have spent online.

5 Click **OK** to switch to the screen name you selected.

■ The Switch Screen Name Password dialog box appears.

■ This area displays the screen name you selected.

6 Type your password. An asterisk (*) appears for each character you type to prevent others from seeing your password.

7 Click **Switch**.

■ You can now use the new screen name.

201

USING THE PERSONAL FILING CABINET

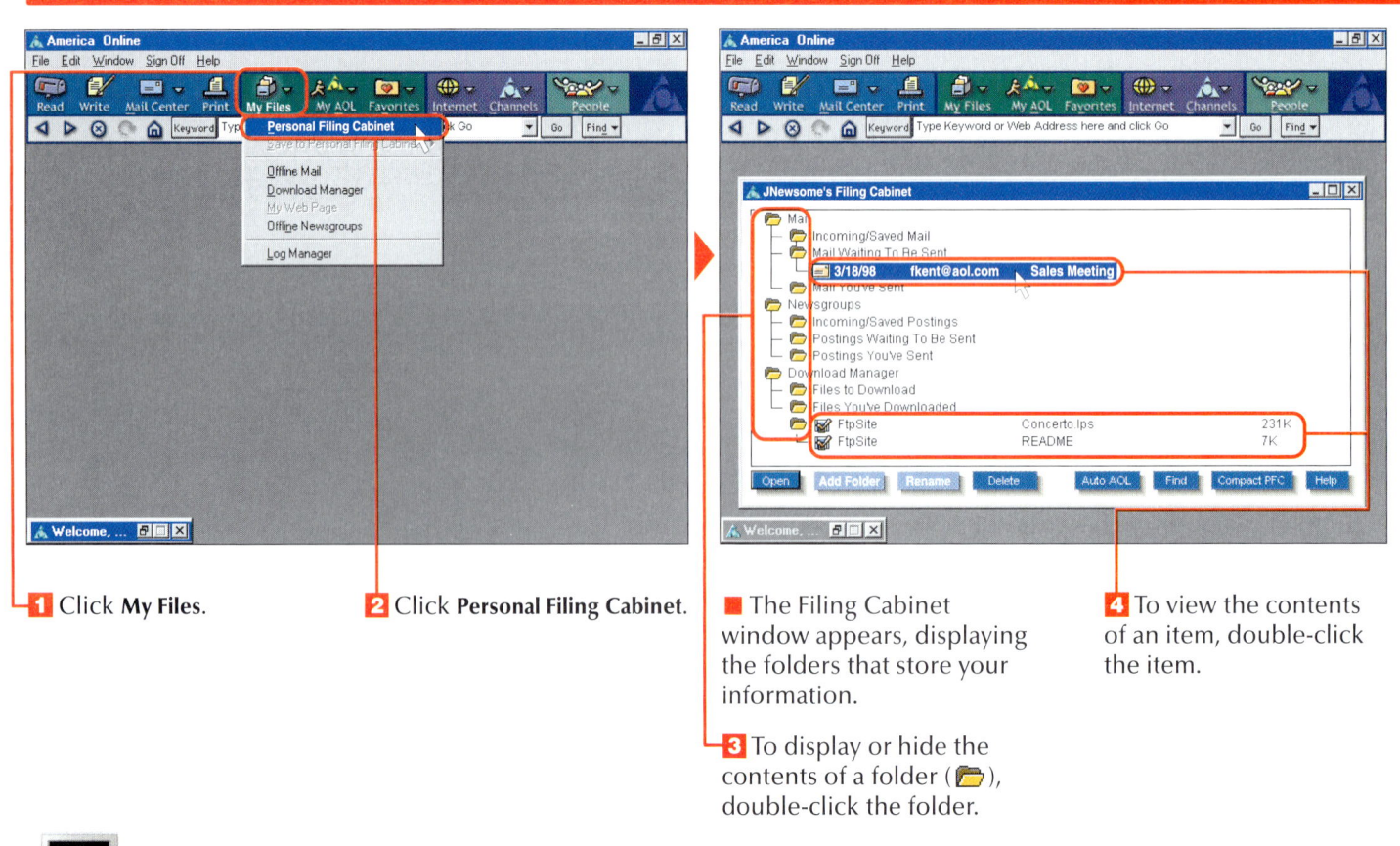

The personal filing cabinet stores and organizes information you have gathered on AOL.

Like a real filing cabinet, the personal filing cabinet uses folders to store your information.

USING THE PERSONAL FILING CABINET

1 Click **My Files**.

2 Click **Personal Filing Cabinet**.

■ The Filing Cabinet window appears, displaying the folders that store your information.

3 To display or hide the contents of a folder (📁), double-click the folder.

4 To view the contents of an item, double-click the item.

202

AOL FEATURES

What information does the personal filing cabinet store?

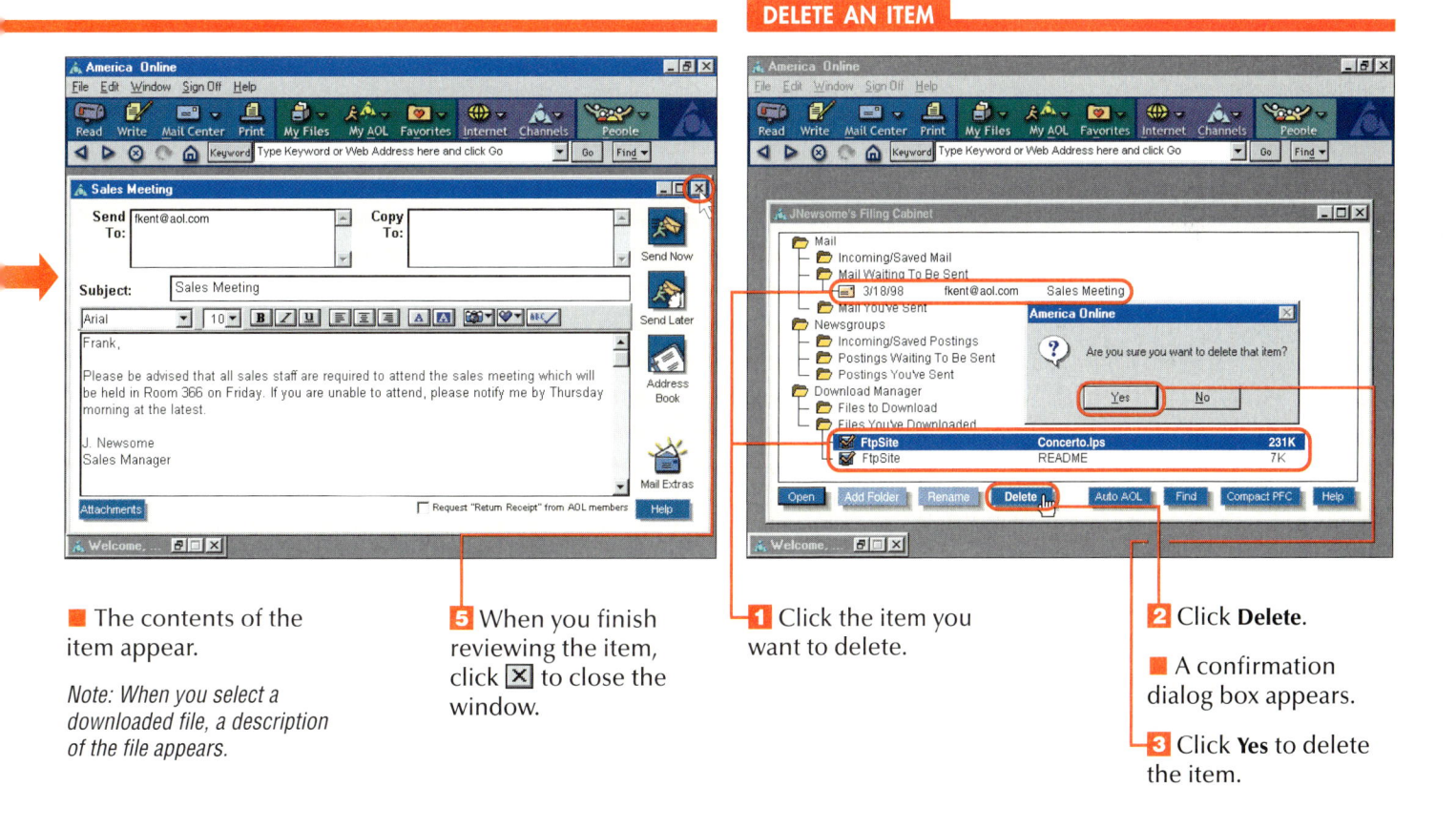

Mail
Stores e-mail messages you have saved and messages waiting to be sent.

Newsgroups
Stores newsgroup messages you have saved and messages waiting to be sent.

Download Manager
Stores files you have downloaded and files waiting to be downloaded.

DELETE AN ITEM

■ The contents of the item appear.

Note: When you select a downloaded file, a description of the file appears.

5 When you finish reviewing the item, click ☒ to close the window.

1 Click the item you want to delete.

2 Click **Delete**.

■ A confirmation dialog box appears.

3 Click **Yes** to delete the item.

203

CREATE A STOCK PORTFOLIO

You can create a portfolio to track stocks and mutual funds of interest to you.

You can create more than one portfolio. For example, one portfolio can contain stocks you own while another can contain stocks you want to monitor.

CREATE A STOCK PORTFOLIO

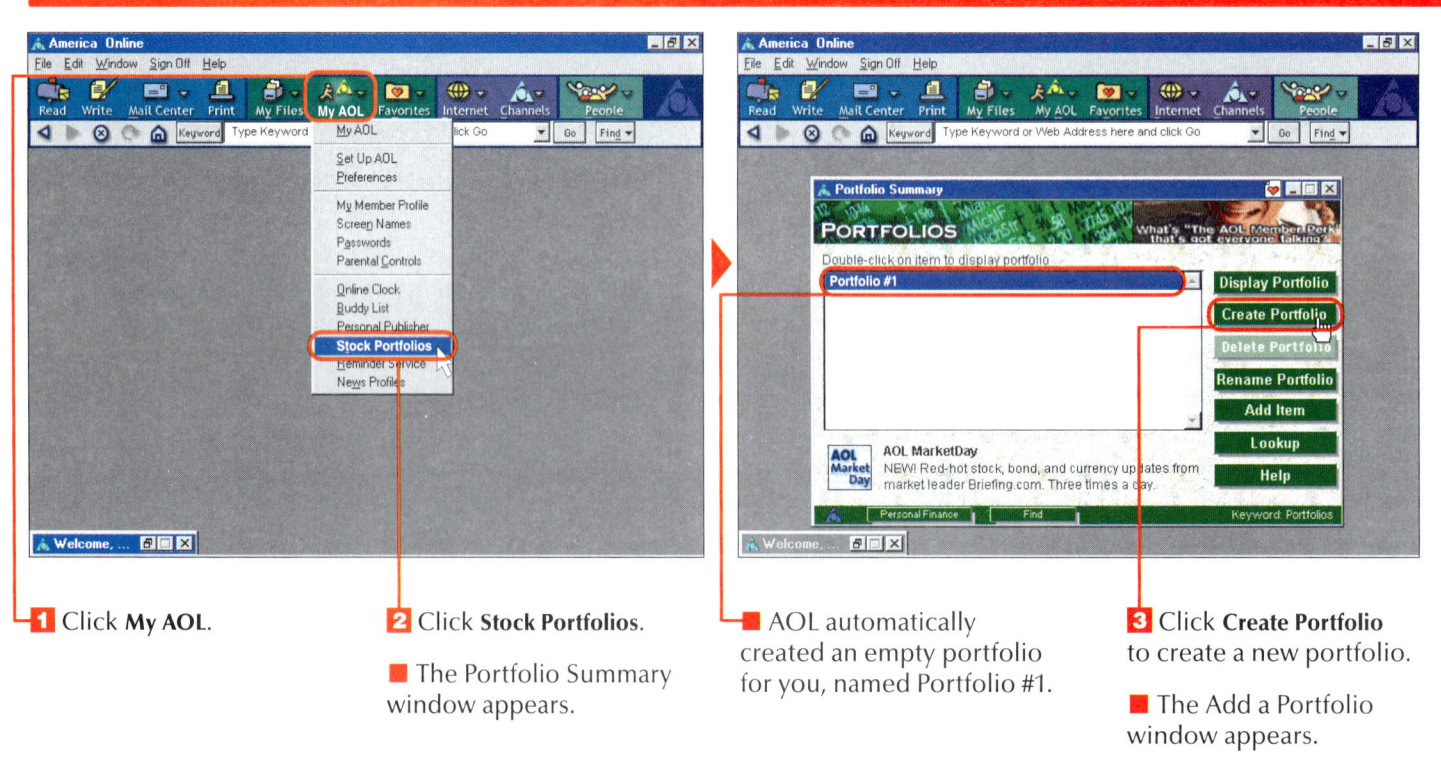

1 Click **My AOL**.

2 Click **Stock Portfolios**.

■ The Portfolio Summary window appears.

■ AOL automatically created an empty portfolio for you, named Portfolio #1.

3 Click **Create Portfolio** to create a new portfolio.

■ The Add a Portfolio window appears.

204

13

AOL FEATURES

How up-to-date is the information in my portfolio?

Unlike the newspaper, which gives you the performance of stocks for the previous day, AOL updates the performance of stocks on a regular basis. You can use AOL to get the latest stock information at any time.

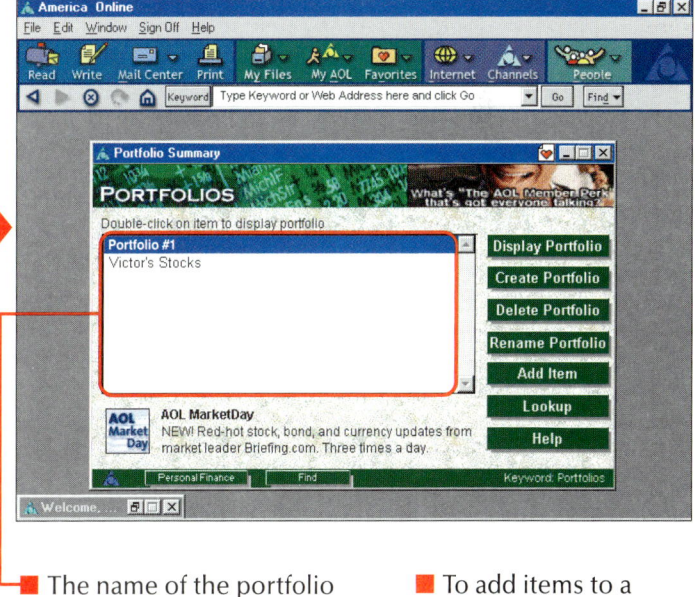

■ **4** Type a name for your portfolio.

■ **5** Click **OK** to continue.

■ The name of the portfolio appears in this area.

■ To add items to a portfolio, see page 206.

205

ADD ITEM TO STOCK PORTFOLIO

> You can add up to 100 different stocks and mutual funds to each portfolio. AOL will keep track of each item.

ADD ITEM TO STOCK PORTFOLIO

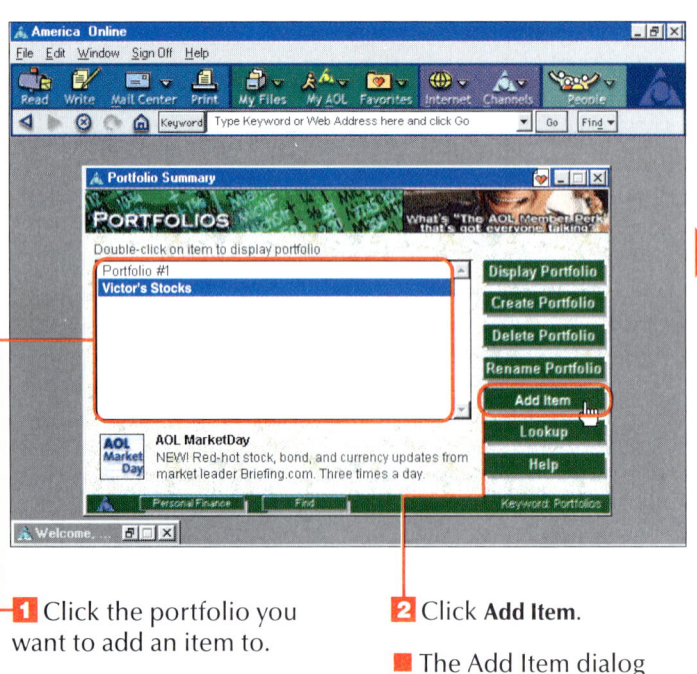

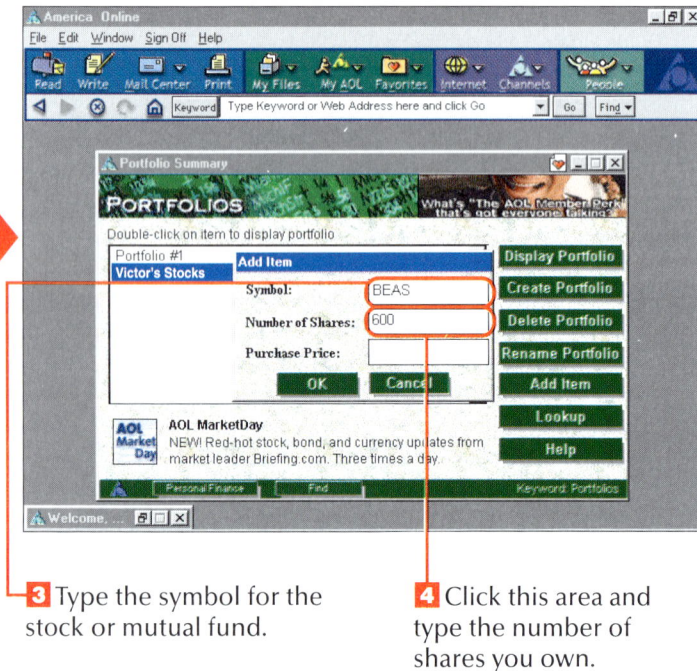

1 Click the portfolio you want to add an item to.

2 Click **Add Item**.

■ The Add Item dialog box appears.

3 Type the symbol for the stock or mutual fund.

4 Click this area and type the number of shares you own.

206

AOL FEATURES

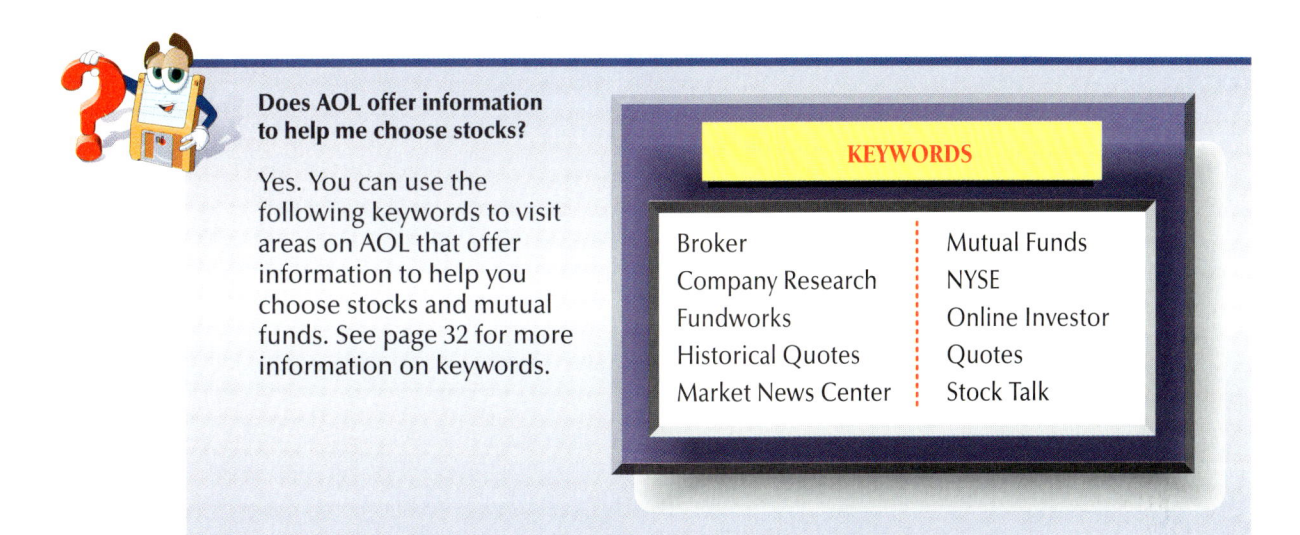

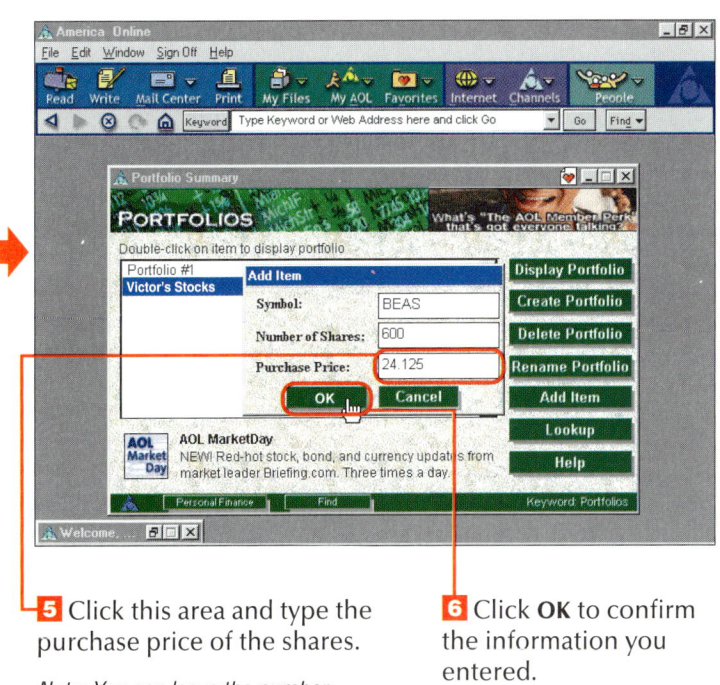

Does AOL offer information to help me choose stocks?

Yes. You can use the following keywords to visit areas on AOL that offer information to help you choose stocks and mutual funds. See page 32 for more information on keywords.

KEYWORDS

Broker	Mutual Funds
Company Research	NYSE
Fundworks	Online Investor
Historical Quotes	Quotes
Market News Center	Stock Talk

5 Click this area and type the purchase price of the shares.

Note: You can leave the number of shares and purchase price areas blank if you want to keep track of a stock you do not own.

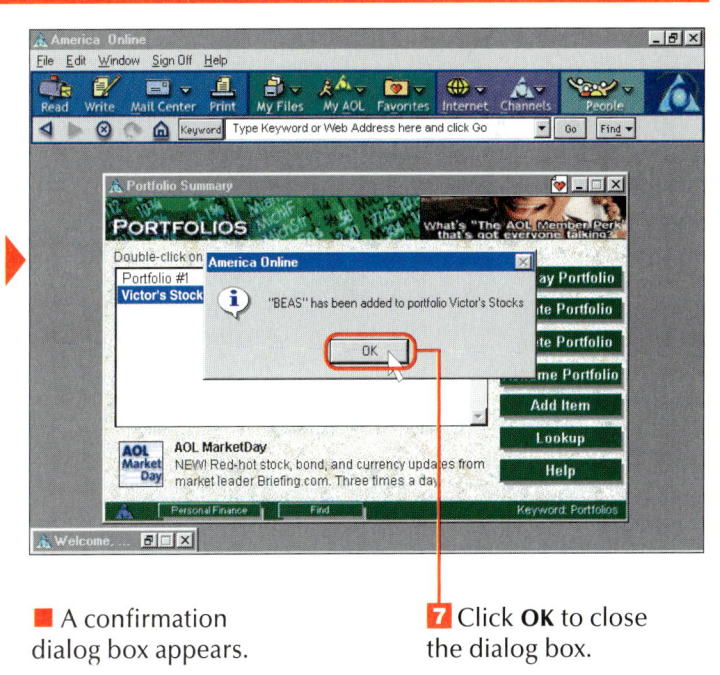

6 Click **OK** to confirm the information you entered.

■ A confirmation dialog box appears.

7 Click **OK** to close the dialog box.

207

DISPLAY AND PRINT A STOCK PORTFOLIO

You can see how your stocks are performing at any time by displaying your portfolio. You can also print information about the stocks in your portfolio.

DISPLAY A STOCK PORTFOLIO

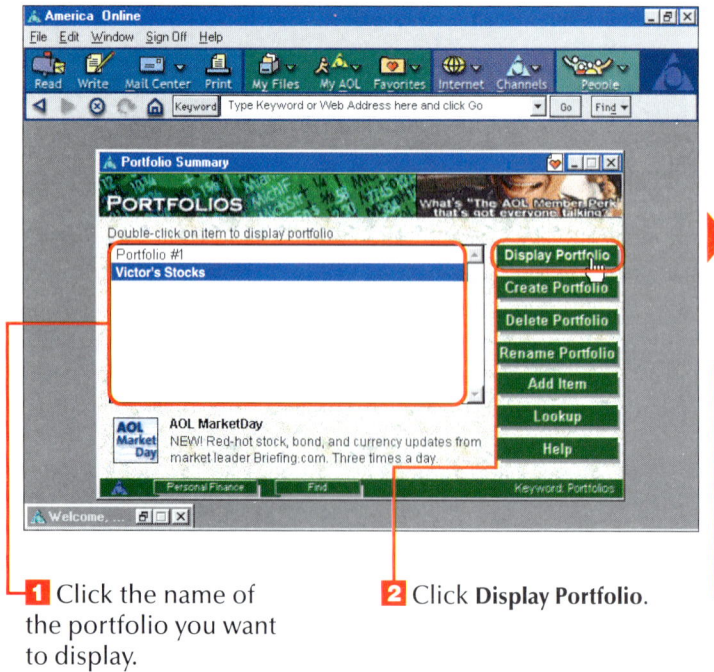

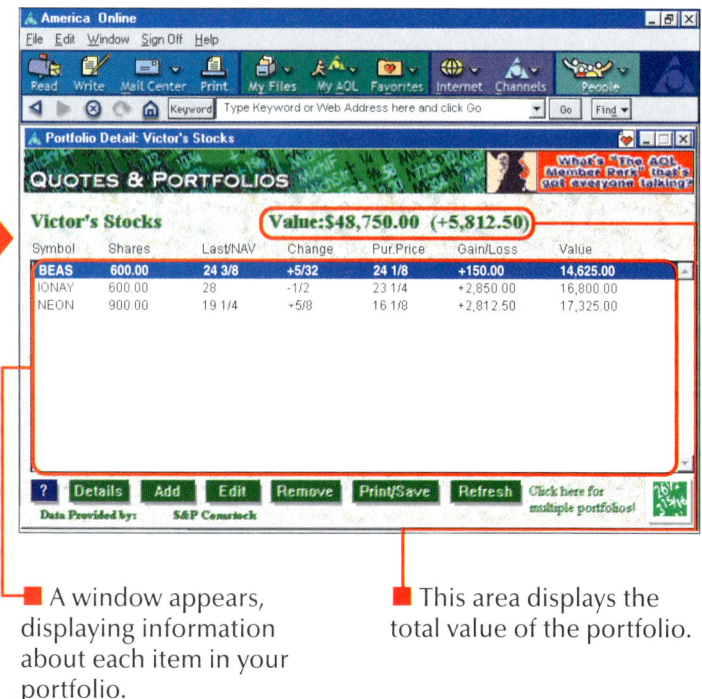

1 Click the name of the portfolio you want to display.

2 Click **Display Portfolio**.

■ A window appears, displaying information about each item in your portfolio.

■ This area displays the total value of the portfolio.

208

AOL FEATURES

How can I remove a stock from a portfolio?

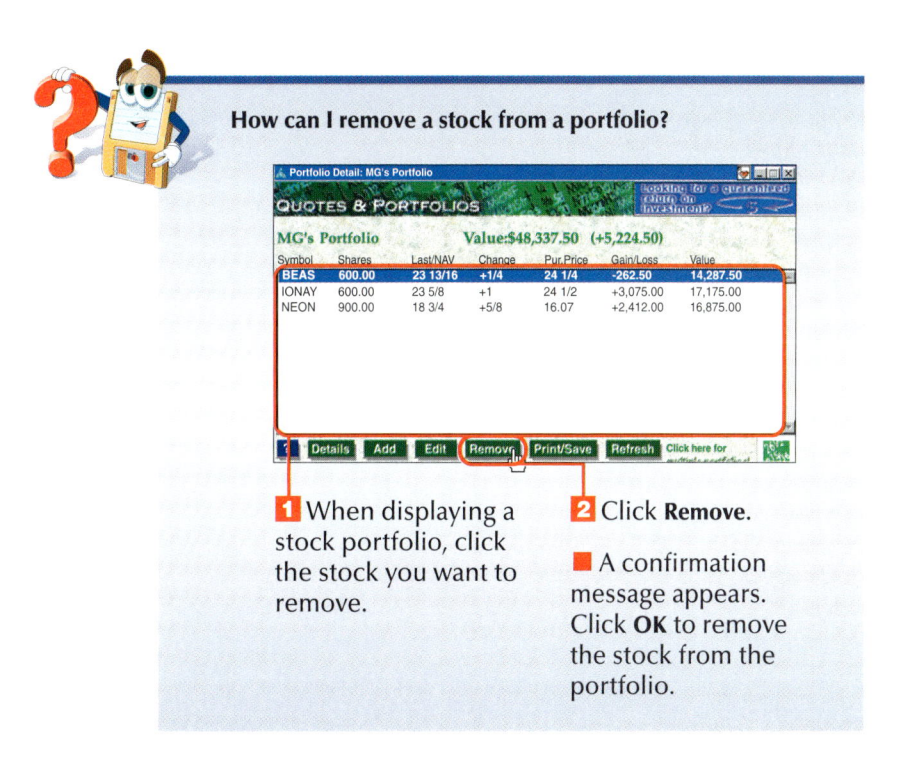

1 When displaying a stock portfolio, click the stock you want to remove.

2 Click **Remove**.

■ A confirmation message appears. Click **OK** to remove the stock from the portfolio.

PRINT A STOCK PORTFOLIO

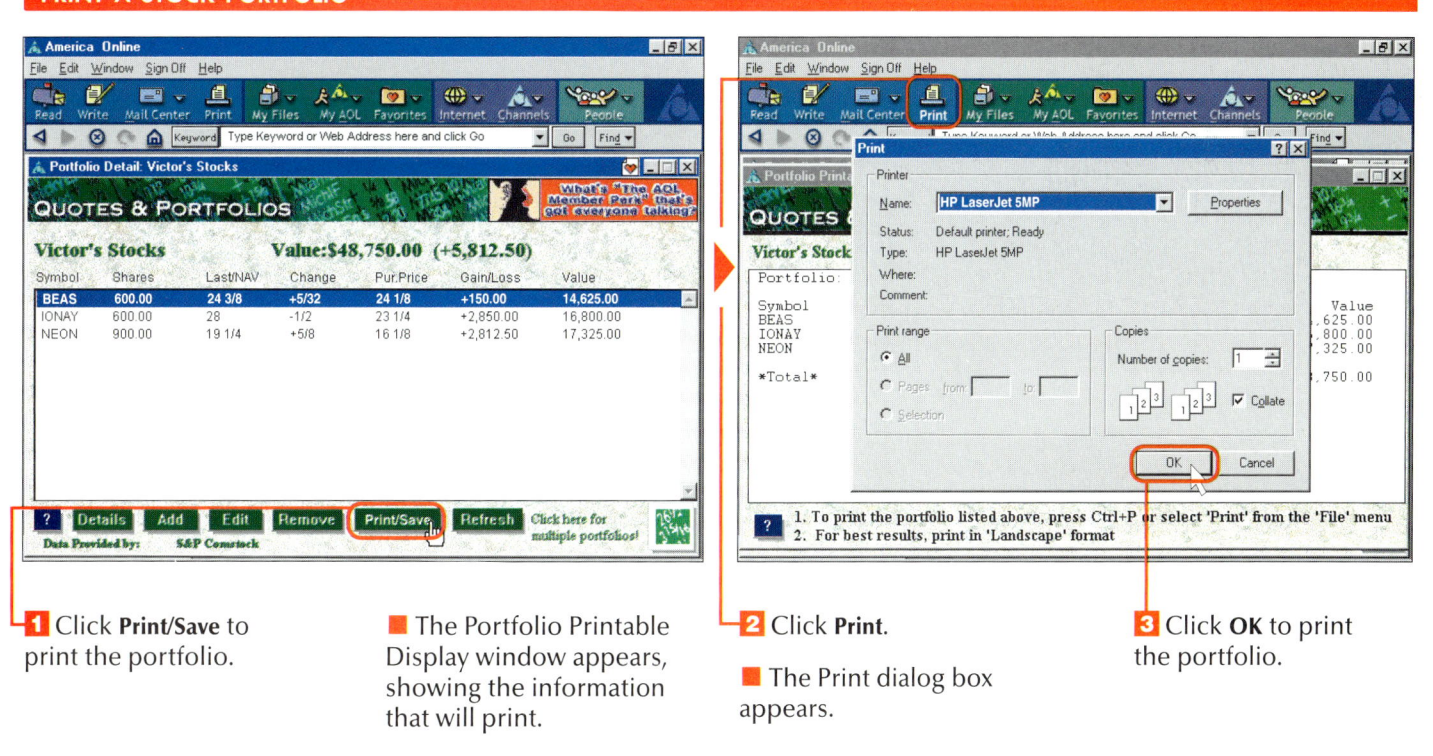

1 Click **Print/Save** to print the portfolio.

■ The Portfolio Printable Display window appears, showing the information that will print.

2 Click **Print**.

■ The Print dialog box appears.

3 Click **OK** to print the portfolio.

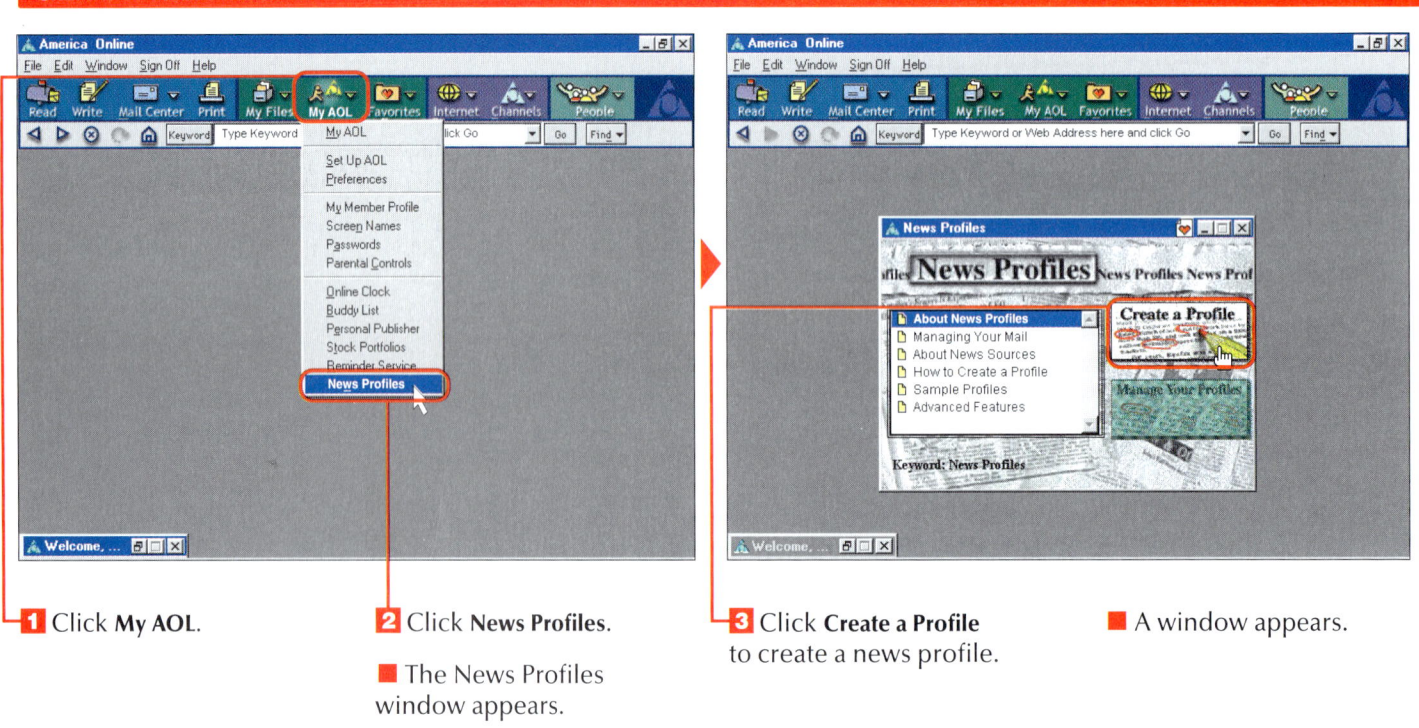

CREATE A NEWS PROFILE

> You can create a news profile to search AOL's many news sources for articles of interest to you. Articles that match your interests will be sent to your mailbox.

CREATE A NEWS PROFILE

1 Click **My AOL**.

2 Click **News Profiles**.

■ The News Profiles window appears.

3 Click **Create a Profile** to create a news profile.

■ A window appears.

210

AOL FEATURES

How many articles can I receive each day?

You can receive a maximum of 50 articles a day for a news profile. You should regularly check your mailbox for new messages since your mailbox can quickly fill up with messages.

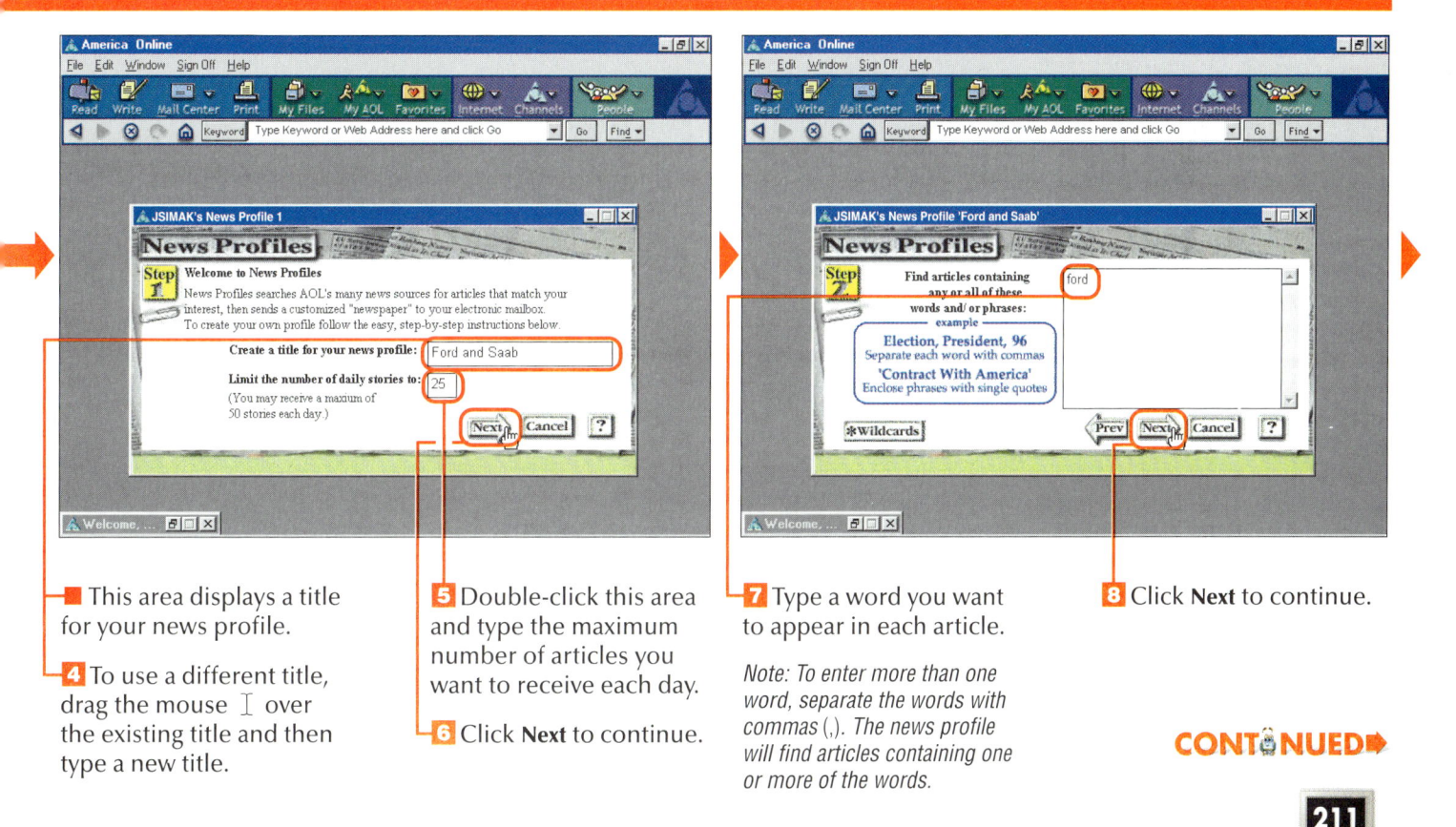

■ This area displays a title for your news profile.

4 To use a different title, drag the mouse I over the existing title and then type a new title.

5 Double-click this area and type the maximum number of articles you want to receive each day.

6 Click **Next** to continue.

7 Type a word you want to appear in each article.

Note: To enter more than one word, separate the words with commas (,). The news profile will find articles containing one or more of the words.

8 Click **Next** to continue.

CONTINUED

211

CREATE A NEWS PROFILE

After you specify what text you want to look for in news articles, you must select the news sources you want to search.

You can search general news, business, entertainment and sports sources.

CREATE A NEWS PROFILE (CONTINUED)

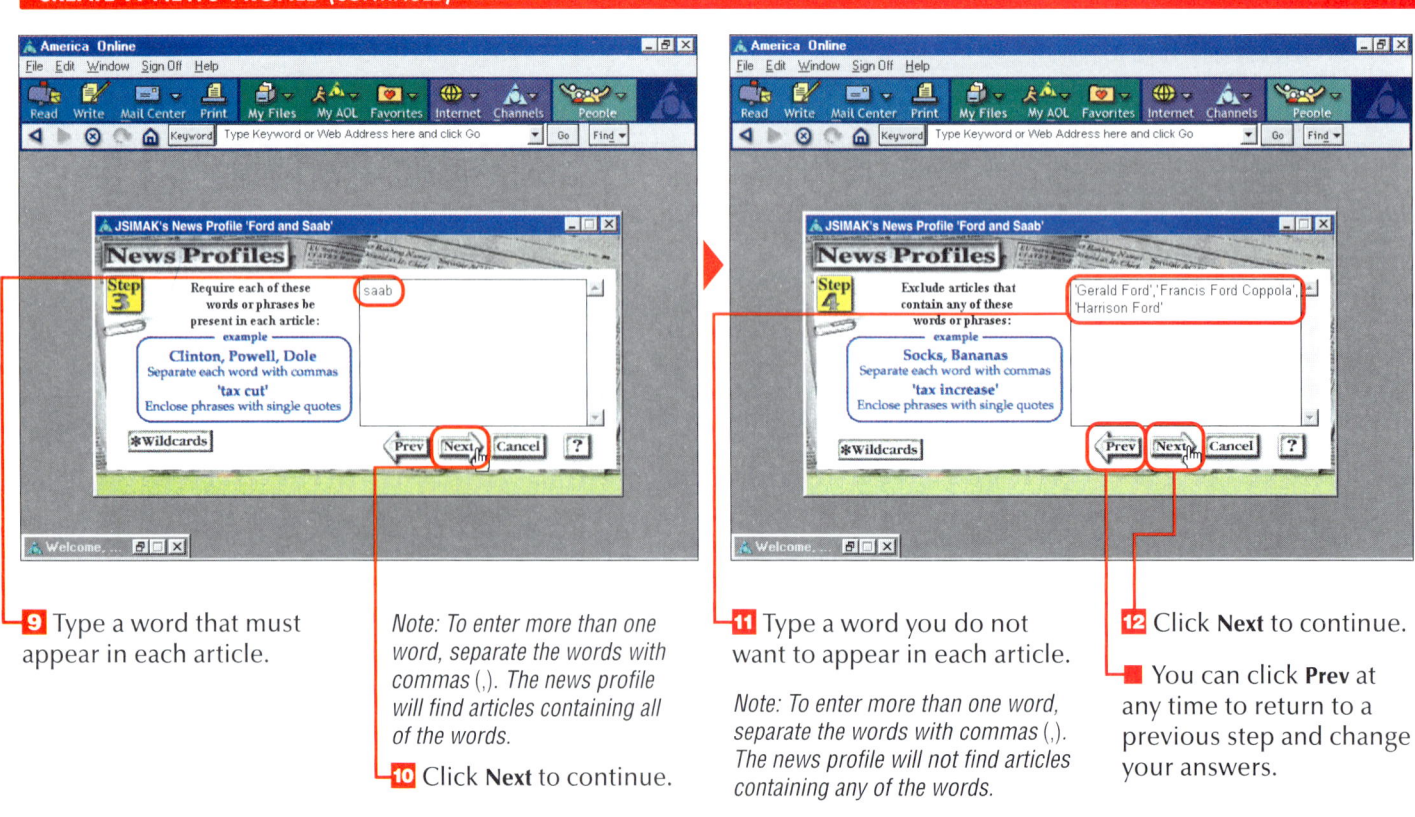

9 Type a word that must appear in each article.

Note: To enter more than one word, separate the words with commas (,). The news profile will find articles containing all of the words.

10 Click **Next** to continue.

11 Type a word you do not want to appear in each article.

Note: To enter more than one word, separate the words with commas (,). The news profile will not find articles containing any of the words.

12 Click **Next** to continue.

■ You can click **Prev** at any time to return to a previous step and change your answers.

212

AOL FEATURES

Can I search for a phrase in articles?

Yes. Enclose the phrase with single quotes, such as 'Bill Clinton'. The news profile will only find articles that contain the entire phrase.

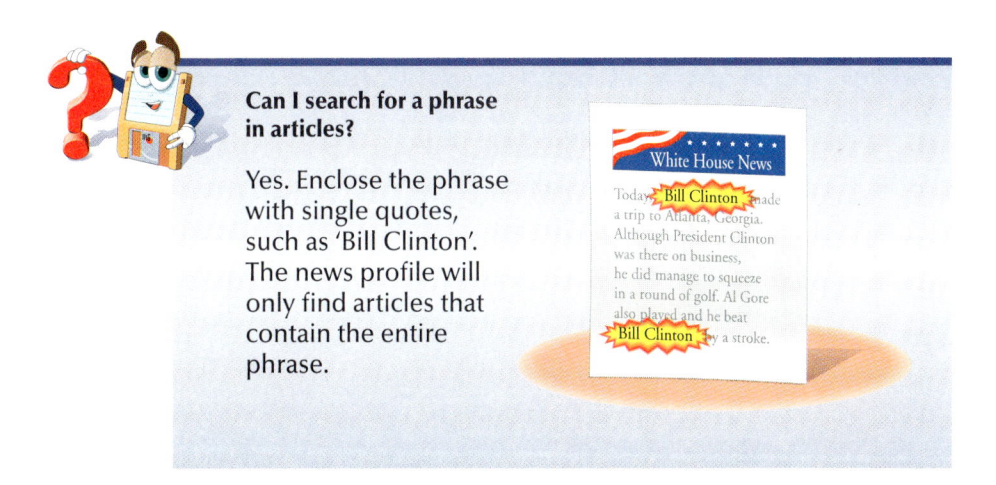

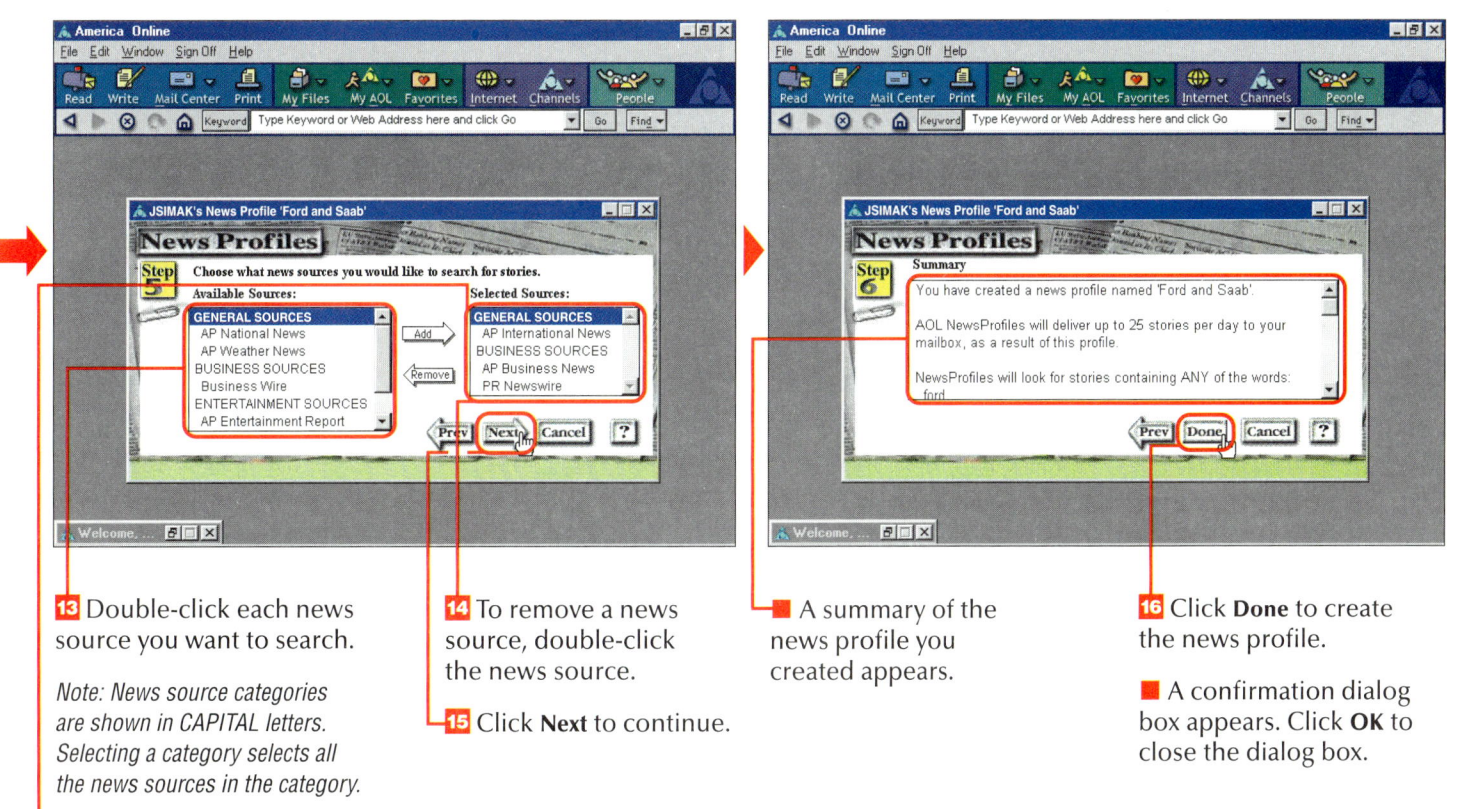

■ **13** Double-click each news source you want to search.

Note: News source categories are shown in CAPITAL letters. Selecting a category selects all the news sources in the category.

■ This area displays the news sources you selected.

■ **14** To remove a news source, double-click the news source.

■ **15** Click **Next** to continue.

■ A summary of the news profile you created appears.

■ **16** Click **Done** to create the news profile.

■ A confirmation dialog box appears. Click **OK** to close the dialog box.

213

MANAGE NEWS PROFILES

You can make changes to a news profile you have created. You may want to change the maximum number of articles you receive each day or the news sources you want to search.

MANAGE NEWS PROFILES

1 Click **Manage Your Profiles** in the News Profiles window.

Note: To display the News Profiles window, perform steps 1 and 2 on page 210.

■ A window appears, listing the news profiles you have created.

2 Click the news profile you want to change.

3 Click **Edit**.

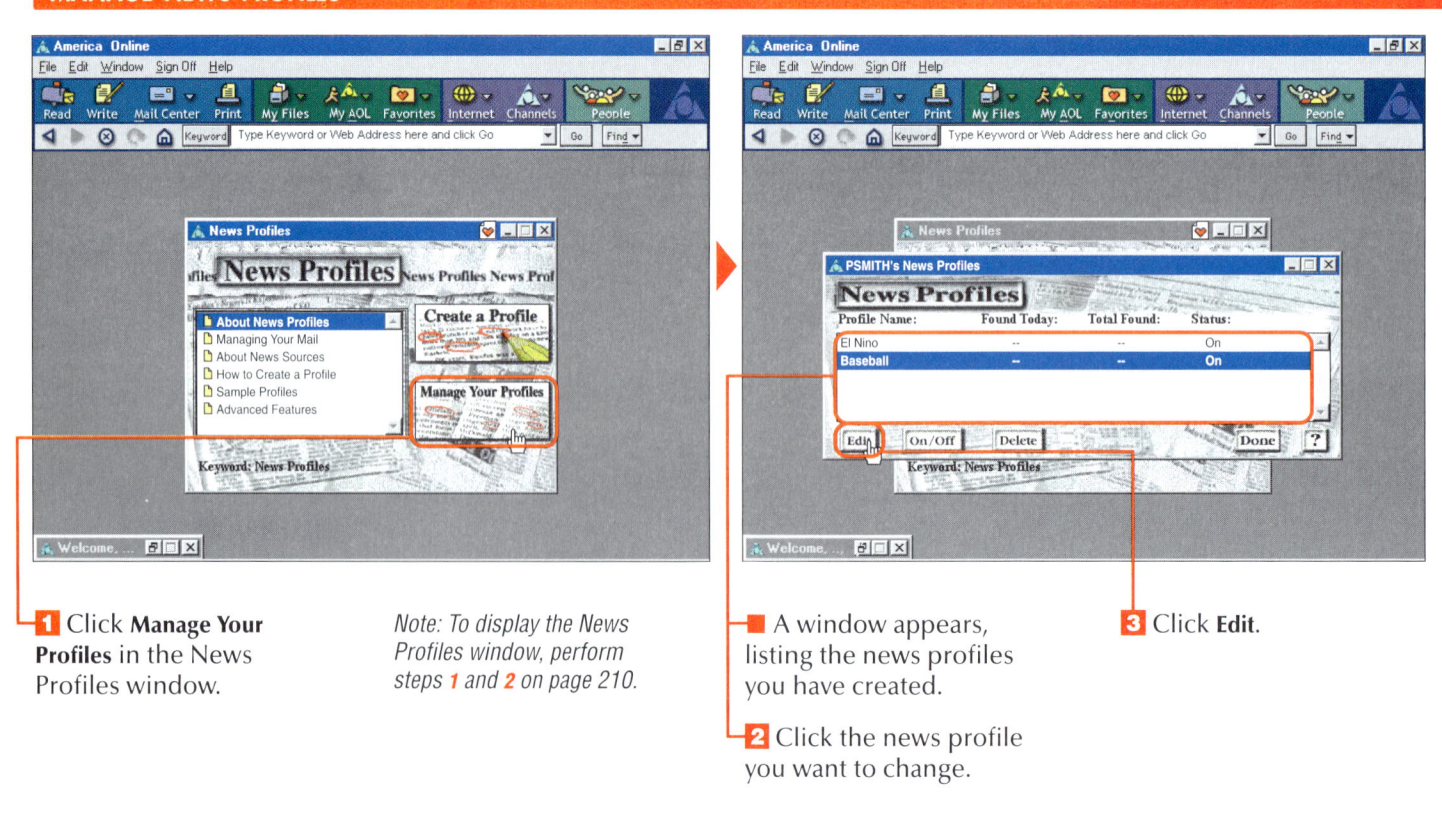

214

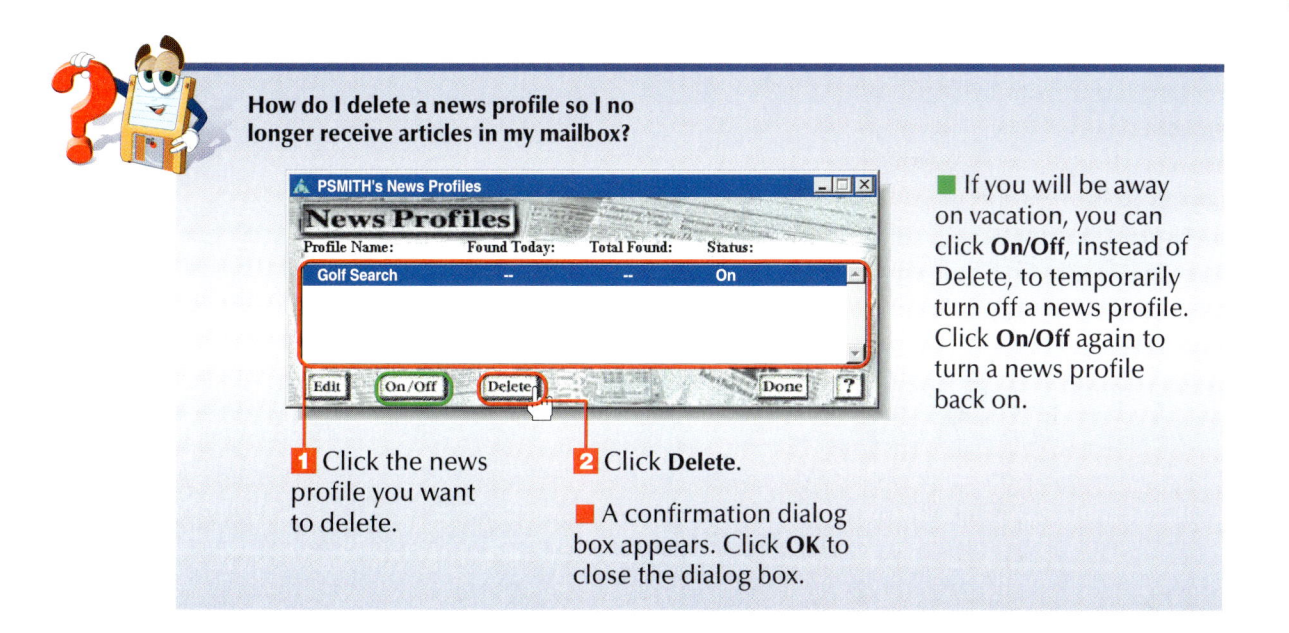

AOL FEATURES

How do I delete a news profile so I no longer receive articles in my mailbox?

■ If you will be away on vacation, you can click **On/Off**, instead of Delete, to temporarily turn off a news profile. Click **On/Off** again to turn a news profile back on.

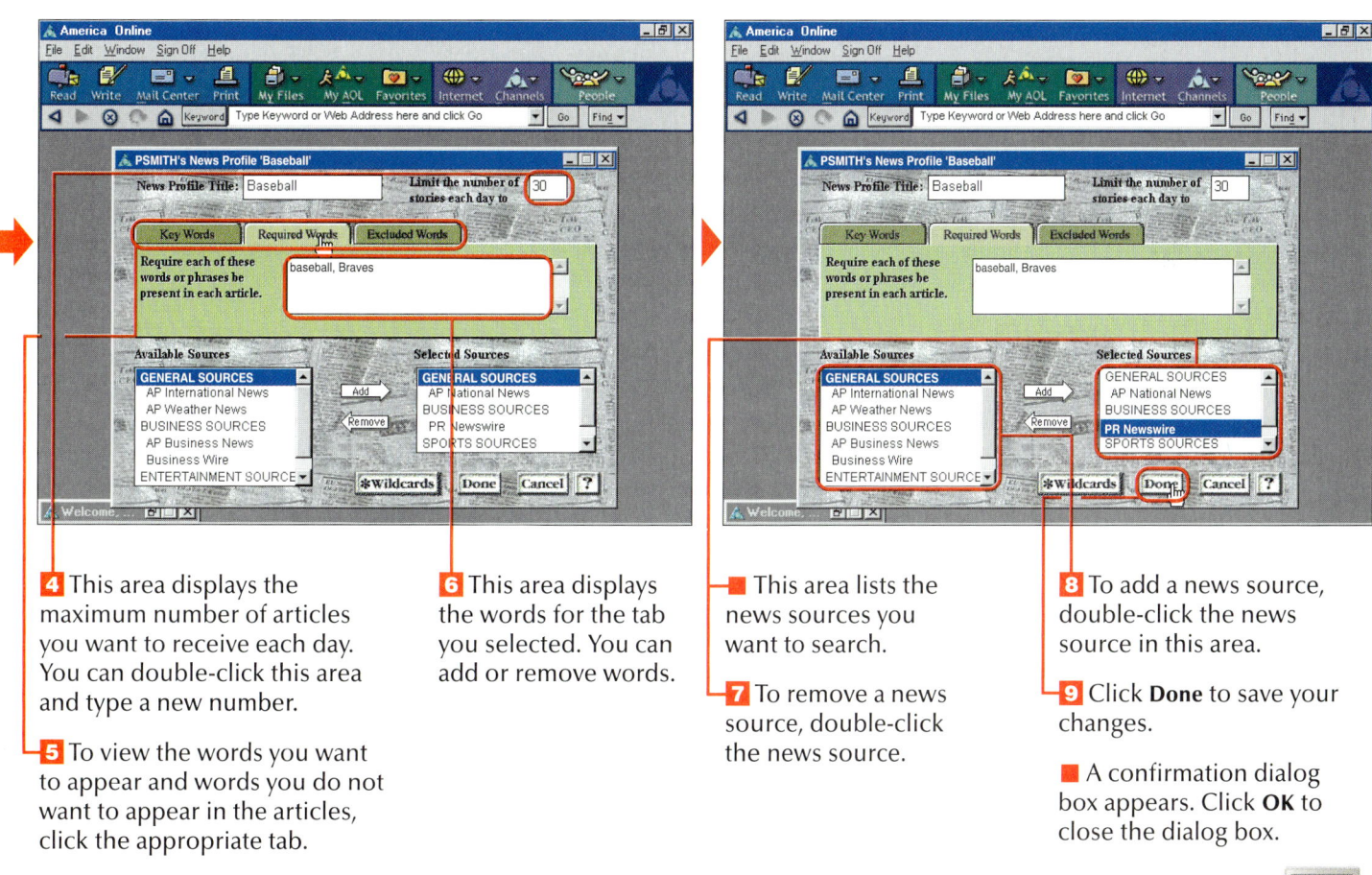

1 Click the news profile you want to delete.

2 Click **Delete**.

■ A confirmation dialog box appears. Click **OK** to close the dialog box.

4 This area displays the maximum number of articles you want to receive each day. You can double-click this area and type a new number.

5 To view the words you want to appear and words you do not want to appear in the articles, click the appropriate tab.

6 This area displays the words for the tab you selected. You can add or remove words.

■ This area lists the news sources you want to search.

7 To remove a news source, double-click the news source.

8 To add a news source, double-click the news source in this area.

9 Click **Done** to save your changes.

■ A confirmation dialog box appears. Click **OK** to close the dialog box.

215

USING THE REMINDER SERVICE

> AOL offers a free reminder service to help you remember important occasions.

You will receive a reminder message in your mailbox 14 days before the occasion.

USING THE REMINDER SERVICE

1 Click **My AOL**.

2 Click **Reminder Service**.

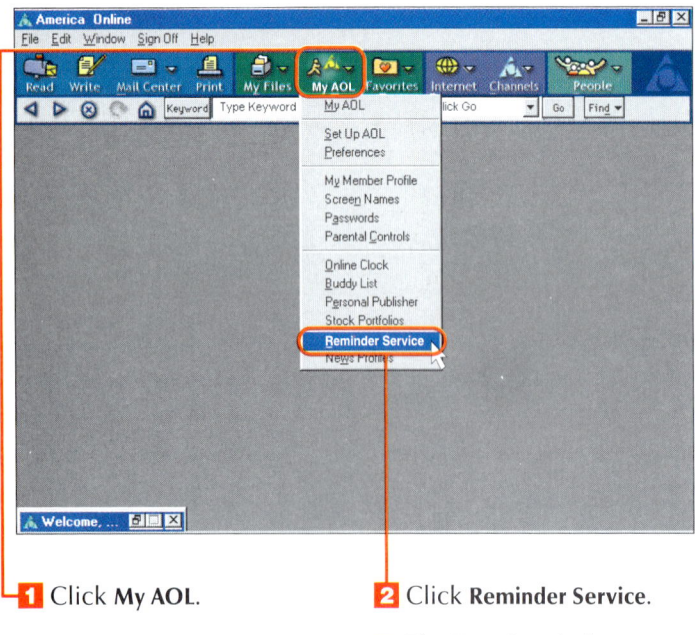

■ The Free Reminder Service window appears.

3 Click **create your reminder**.

■ A window appears, welcoming you to the Reminder Service. This window only appears the first time you use the service.

*Note: If this window does not appear, skip to step **9** on page 218.*

216

AOL FEATURES

Where can I get a list of important dates?

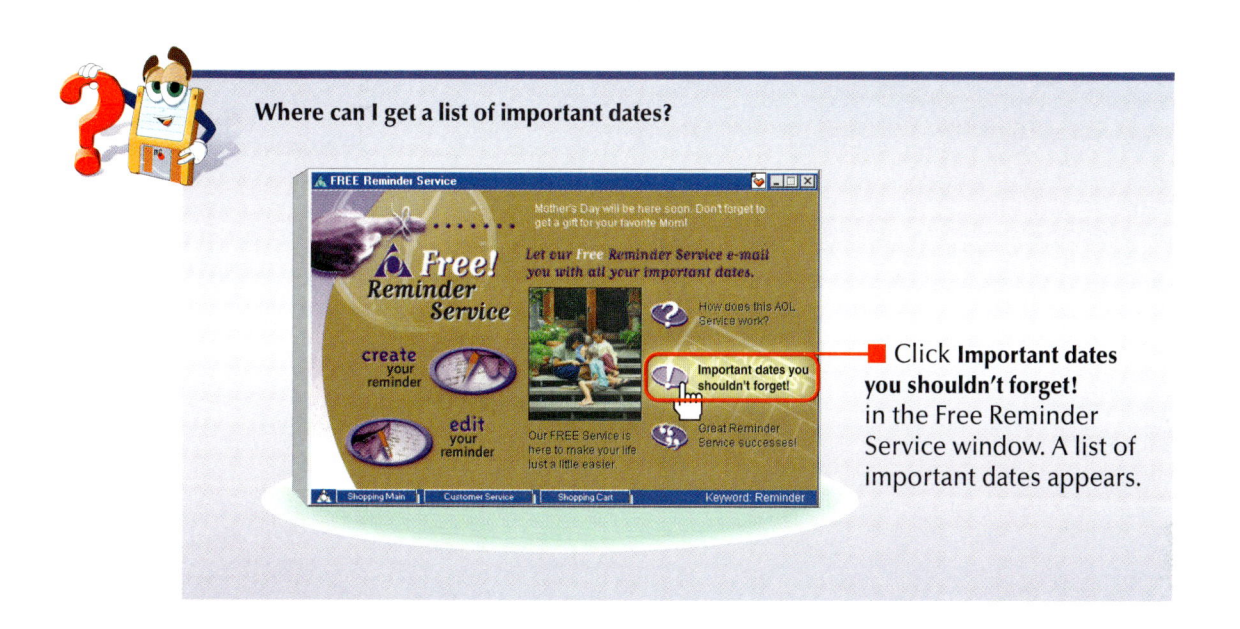

■ Click **Important dates you shouldn't forget!** in the Free Reminder Service window. A list of important dates appears.

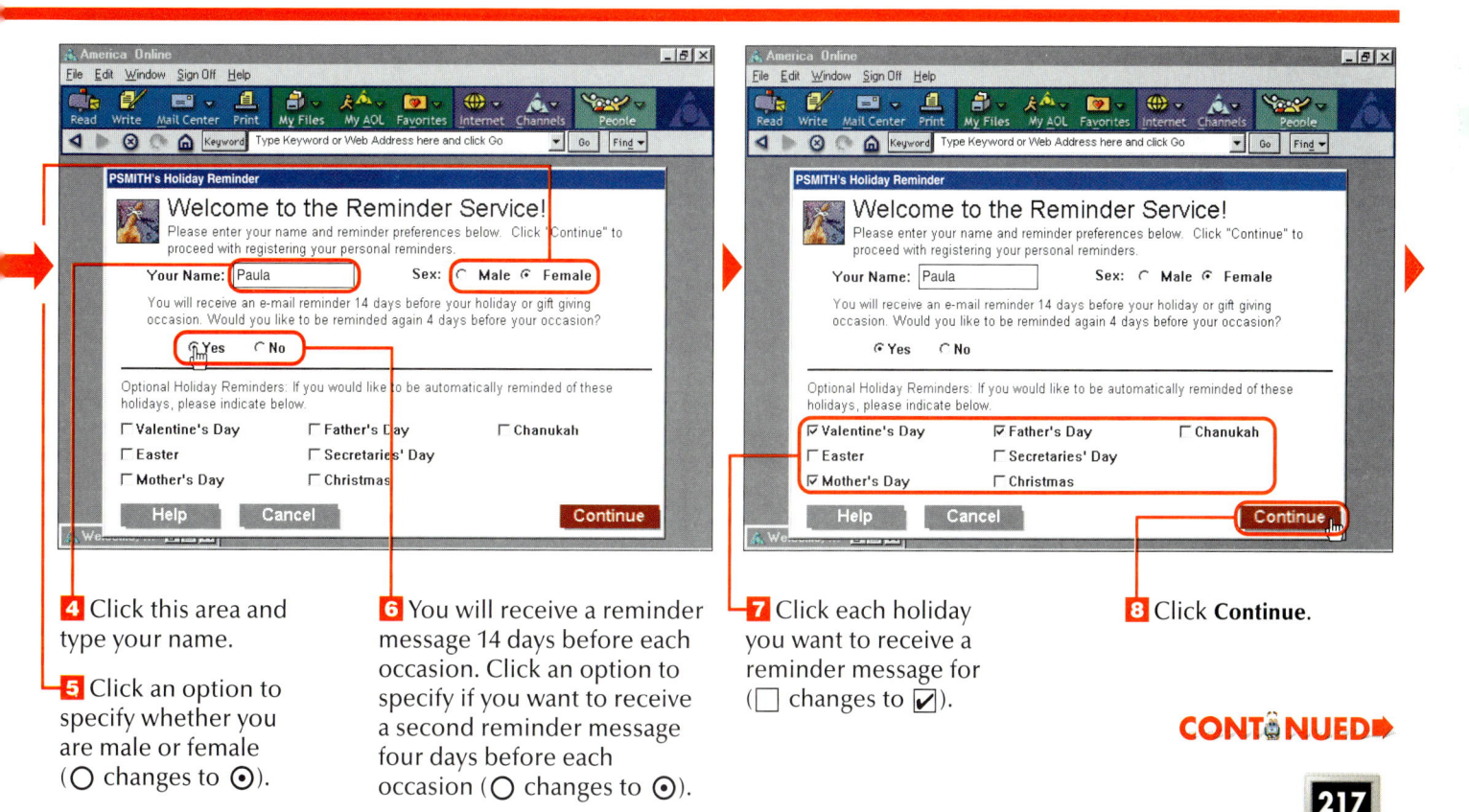

4 Click this area and type your name.

5 Click an option to specify whether you are male or female (○ changes to ⊙).

6 You will receive a reminder message 14 days before each occasion. Click an option to specify if you want to receive a second reminder message four days before each occasion (○ changes to ⊙).

7 Click each holiday you want to receive a reminder message for (☐ changes to ☑).

8 Click **Continue**.

CONTINUED

217

USING THE REMINDER SERVICE

Your Daughter's Birthday!

You can have AOL remind you of birthdays, anniversaries and other special occasions.

When adding a reminder, the information you send to AOL is completely confidential.

USING THE REMINDER SERVICE (CONTINUED)

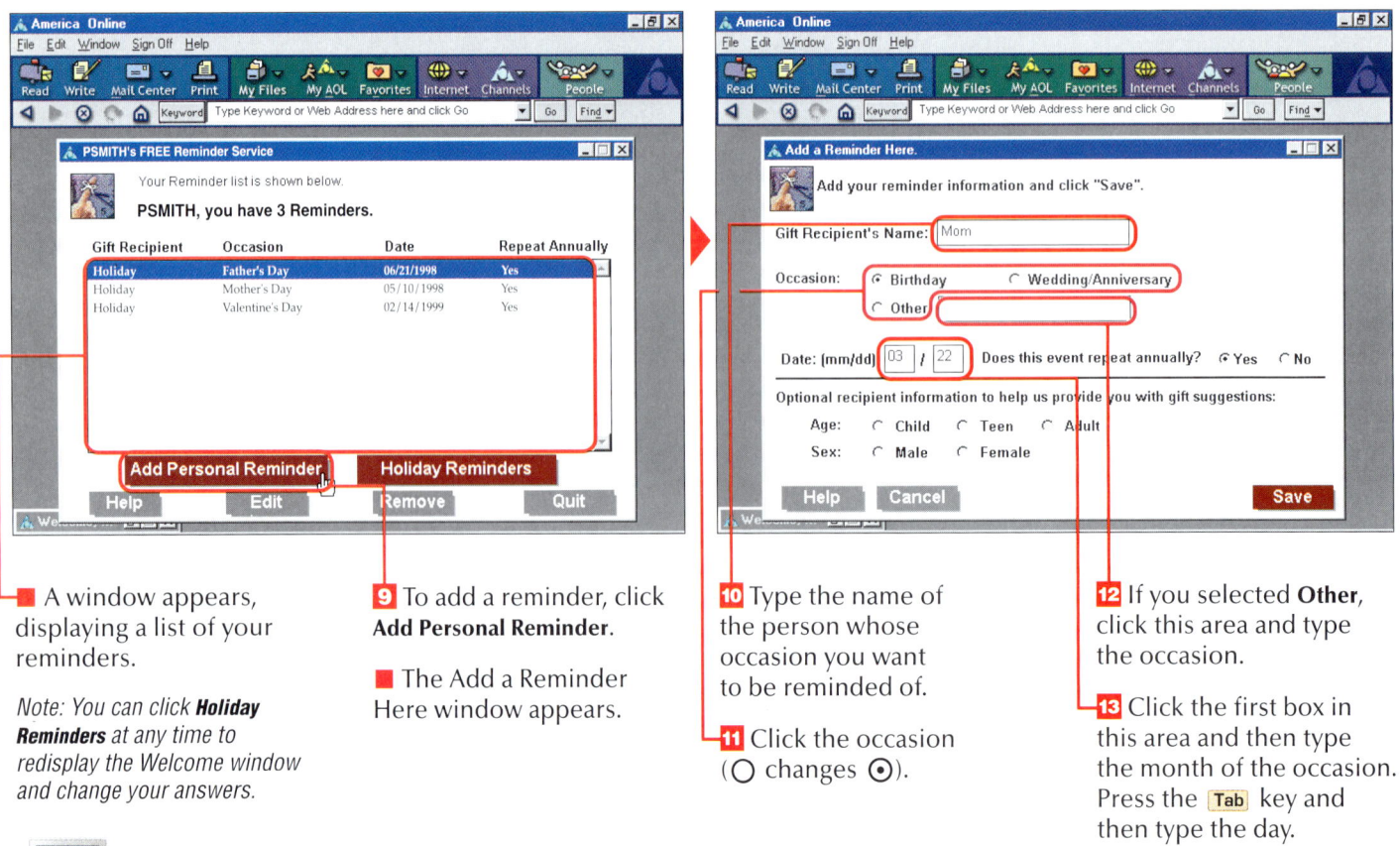

■ A window appears, displaying a list of your reminders.

*Note: You can click **Holiday Reminders** at any time to redisplay the Welcome window and change your answers.*

9 To add a reminder, click **Add Personal Reminder**.

■ The Add a Reminder Here window appears.

10 Type the name of the person whose occasion you want to be reminded of.

11 Click the occasion (○ changes ⊙).

12 If you selected **Other**, click this area and type the occasion.

13 Click the first box in this area and then type the month of the occasion. Press the **Tab** key and then type the day.

218

AOL FEATURES

How do I delete a reminder?

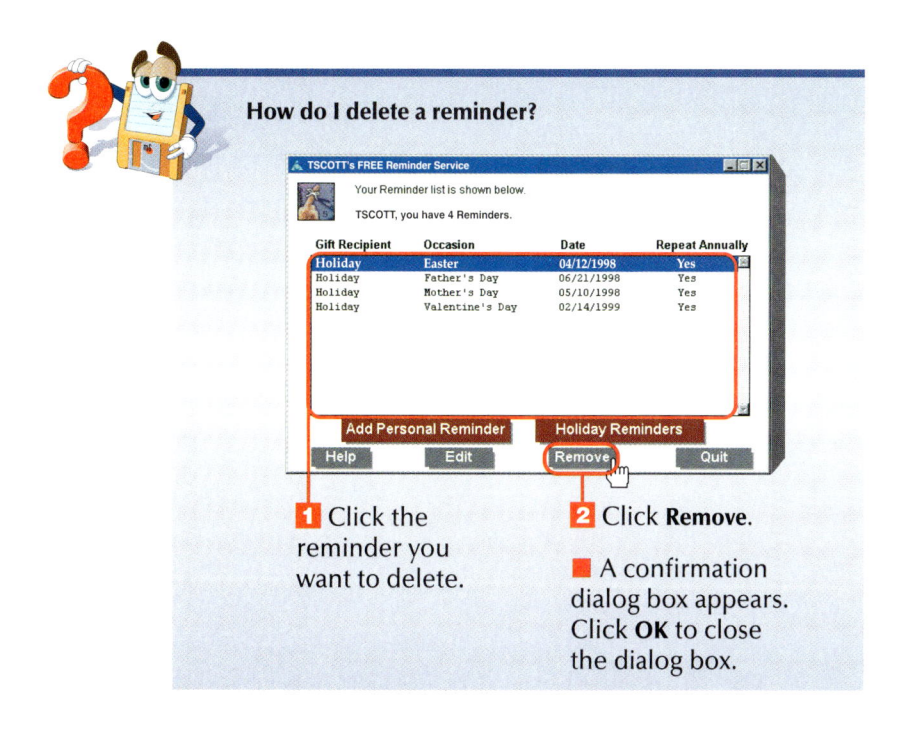

1 Click the reminder you want to delete.

2 Click **Remove**.

■ A confirmation dialog box appears. Click **OK** to close the dialog box.

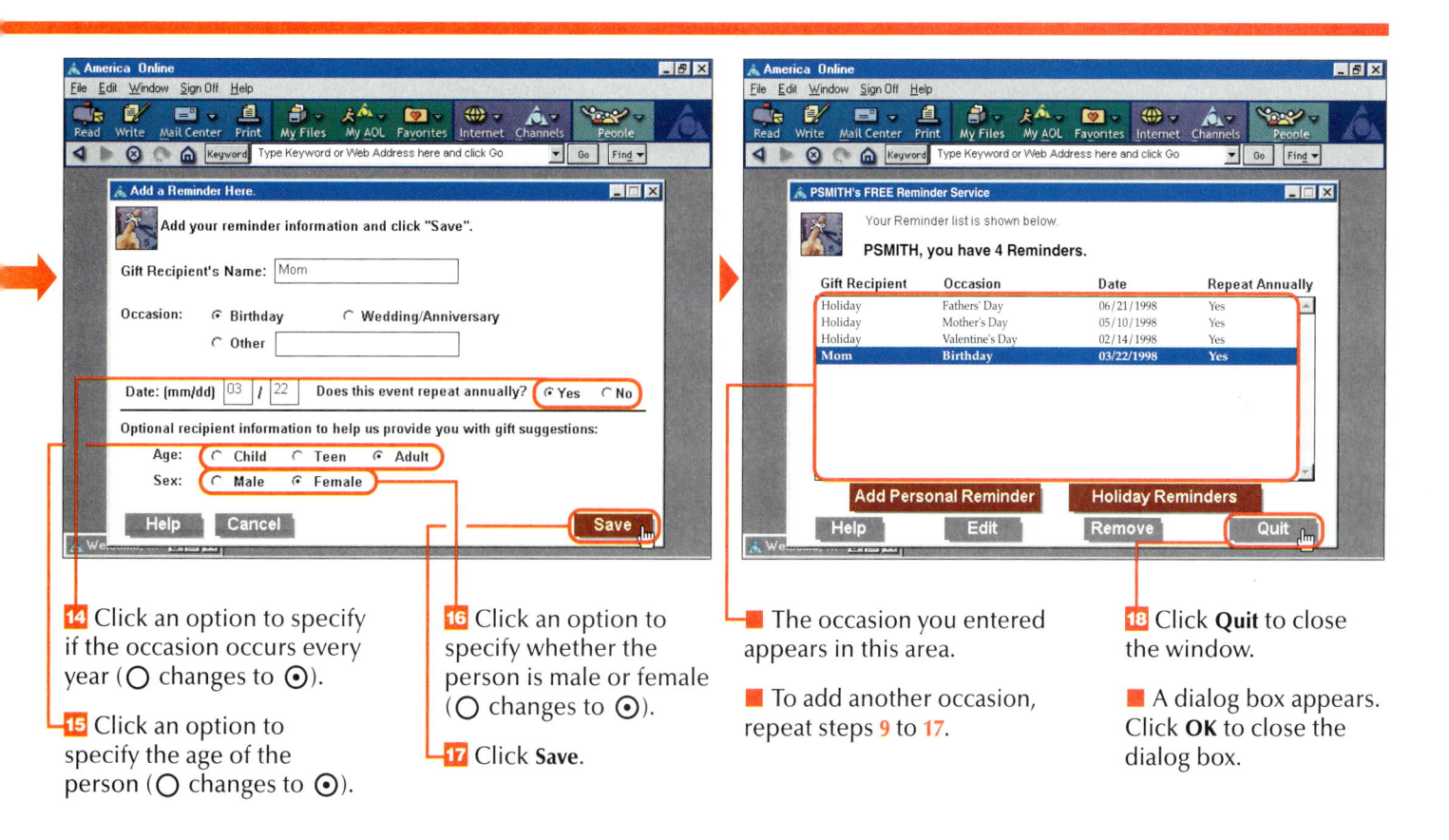

14 Click an option to specify if the occasion occurs every year (○ changes to ⦿).

15 Click an option to specify the age of the person (○ changes to ⦿).

16 Click an option to specify whether the person is male or female (○ changes to ⦿).

17 Click **Save**.

■ The occasion you entered appears in this area.

■ To add another occasion, repeat steps **9** to **17**.

18 Click **Quit** to close the window.

■ A dialog box appears. Click **OK** to close the dialog box.

219

INDEX

A

abbreviations in chat comments, 137
add
    favorite places, 184-185
        to e-mail messages, 99
    favorite places folder, 188-189
    files to e-mail messages, 86-87
    groups to address book, 74-75
    items to stock portfolios, 206-207
    members to Buddy Lists, 166-167
    messages to message boards, 114-115
    names to address book, 72-73
address book
    add
        groups, 74-75
        names, 72-73
    names
        add, 72-73
        select, 76-77
    select names from, 76-77
addresses
    e-mail
        parts, 63
        search for, 78-79
    Web pages, 44-45
align text in e-mail messages, 95
AltaVista, 51
AOL
    connect to, 8-9
    exit, 9
    features, 7
    find information on, 6, 38-39
    and Internet, 4
    keywords, 34
    NetFind, 50-51
        E-mail Finder, 78-79
    overview, 4-7
    screen, parts of, 10
    software, 5
articles
    find, using news profiles, 210-213
    number received for news profiles, 211
at (@) symbol, in e-mail addresses, 63

attach files to e-mail messages, 86-87
attached files, download, 88-89
attend live events, 152-157

B

background color of e-mail messages, change, 97
blind copies, e-mail messages, 67, 77
bold text
    in e-mail messages, 94
    in instant messages, 147
bounced e-mail messages, 73
browse
    through
        Web pages, 48
        windows, 16
    the Web, 6
Buddy Lists
    add members, 166-167
    locate members on, 165
    remove members, 167
    view, 168-169

C

Channel Guide
    areas on, 31
    using, 30-31
channels
    on AOL, 24-29
    view, 22-23
Channels window, 9
chat
    etiquette, 137
    ignore members during, 143
    member profiles, view, 142
    overview, 7, 136-137
    rooms
        comments, send, 140
        find, 138-139
        play sounds in, 141
        private
            create, 144-145
            join, 145
        types of, 136
    view member profiles, 142

chatting, 136
click, 10
close AOL, 9
colors
    background, change, in e-mail messages, 97
    text, change, in e-mail messages, 96
compressed files, download, 173
computing keywords, 34
confirmation messages, 98
connect to AOL, 8
copy to, e-mail messages, 67, 77
copyright, 107, 172
create
    chat rooms, private, 144-145
    groups in address book, 74-75
    profiles
        member, 162-163
        news, 210-213
    screen names, 192-194
    stock portfolios, 204-205

D

delete. *See also* remove
    favorite places, 187
    items from personal filing cabinet, 203
    members from Buddy Lists, 167
    messages
        e-mail, 84
    reminders, 219
    screen names, 195
    stocks from portfolios, 209
display
    AOL channels, 22-23
    contents of folders, 189
    favorite places, 185
    home pages, 52
    important dates, 217
    list of keywords, 33
    online clock, 11
    stock portfolios, 208
    Web pages, 44-45
document files, download, 173

domain names, 63
double-click, 10
download
    files, 7, 178-179
        attached to messages, 88-89
    folder, 181
Download Manager, using, 180-181
downloading, overview, 172-173
drag, 10

E

electronic mail. *See* e-mail
e-mail
    address book
        add
            groups, 74-75
            names, 72-73
        select names, 76-77
    addresses
        find, 78-79
        parts, 63
    messages
        add favorite places, 99
        address, 67, 77
        attach files, 86-87
        attached files, download, 88-89
        background color, change, 97
        bounced, 73
        delete, 84
        download attached files in, 88-89
        extra information in, 65
        format, 92-97
        forward, 70-71
        mark read as new, 85
        print, 82
        read, 64-65
        reply, 68-69
            options, 69
        return receipts, request, 98
        save, 83

INDEX

send, 66-67
    later, 100-101
spell check, 90-91
store, for later, 100
text
    alignment, change, 95
    bold, 94
    color, change, 96
        of background, 97
    font sizes, change, 93
    fonts, change, 92
    italicize, 94
    underline, 94
time stored by AOL, change, 103
unsend, 102
overview, 6, 62-63
E-mail Finder, 78-79
entertainment keywords, 34
etiquette
    chat, 137
    message boards, 106-107
exit AOL, 9

F

families keywords, 34
FAQs (Frequently Asked Questions), 119
favorite places
    add, 184
        to e-mail messages, 99
    change order, 186
    delete, 187
    display, 185
    folder
        add, 188-189
        display contents of, 189
Favorites menu, 185
files
    attach to e-mail messages, 86-87
    contents of downloaded, view, 88
    download, 178-179
        attached to e-mail messages, 88-89
    find, to download
        by browsing, 174-175
        by searching, 176-177

types,
    attached to e-mail messages, 87
    to download, 173
find. *See also* search
    AOL members, 160-161, 164-165, 168-169
    chat rooms, 138-139
    e-mail addresses, 78-79
    files to download
        by browsing, 174-175
        by searching, 176-177
    help information, 18-19
    information on AOL, 38-39
    newsgroups
        by category, 120-121
        by name, 122-123
    Web pages, 50-51
font sizes, change
    in e-mail messages, 93
    in instant messages, 147
fonts, change in e-mail messages, 92
forward e-mail messages, 70-71
freeware programs, 172
Frequently Asked Questions (FAQs), 119

G

games keywords, 35
groups, add to address book, 74-75

H

health keywords, 35
heart icon, 184
help
    button, 19
    search for, 18-19
Home button, 52
home pages
    change, 52-53
    display, 52
    set, 53
HotBot, 51
HTML (HyperText Markup Language), 43
http (HyperText Transfer Protocol), 43

I

ignore chat members, 143
image files, download, 173
influence keywords, 35
information
    find
        on AOL, 6, 38-39
        on Web, 50-51
    printed
        on e-mail messages, 82
        on message board messages, 110
        on newsgroup messages, 128
    stop transfer of, on Web, 47
Infoseek, 51
interests keywords, 35
international keywords, 35
Internet, and AOL, 4. *See also* Web
italicize text
    in e-mail messages, 94
    in instant messages, 147

J

join members
    in chat room, 164-165
    in private chat room, 145

K

keywords
    display list, 33
    examples, 34-37
    location in windows, 33
    using, 32-33
kids only keywords, 35

L

lifestyles keywords, 36
links, 43
    select, 46

live events, 7
    auditorium, enter, 154
    chat, turn off, 155
    send messages
        to guest, 157
        to row members, 156
    view
        current day, 153
        upcoming, 152-153
local keywords, 36
locate members
    on Buddy Lists, 165
    online, 164-165
lurk in newsgroups, 133

M

maximize windows, 12
Member Directory, search, 160-161
member profiles
    create, 162-163
    view, 160-161
        while chatting, 142
members
    add to Buddy Lists, 166-167
    ignore, in chat room, 143
    join
        in chat room, 164-165
        in private chat room, 145
    locate,
        on Buddy Lists, 165
        online, 164-165
    remove from Buddy Lists, 167
menu bar, 10
message boards, 6, 106-107
    messages
        add, 114
        mark as read, 111
        print, 110
        read, 108-109
        reply, 112-113
    topics, 106

INDEX

messages
  bounced, 73
  e-mail
    forward, 70-71
    print, 82
    read, 64-65
    reply, 68-69
      options, 69
    return receipts, request, 98
    save, 83
    send, 66-67
      later, 100-101
    spell check, 90-91
    text, format, 92-97
    unsend, 102
  instant
    reply to, 149
    send
      any time, 148
      while chatting, 146-148
    text
      bold, 147
      italicize, 147
      size, change, 147
      underline, 147
  at live events, ignore, 155
  message boards
    add, 114
    mark as read, 111
    print, 110
    read, 108-109
    reply, 112-113
    vs. subjects, 109
  newsgroups
    print, 128
    quoting in, 130
    read, 126-127
    reply, 130-131
      options, 131
    send, 132-133
    vs. subjects, 127

minimize windows, 13
modems, 5
mouse pointers, 10
move
  favorite places, 186
  through
    Web pages, 48
    windows, 16
  windows, 14

N

names
  address book
    add, 72-73
    select, 76-77
  e-mail
    domain, 63
    user, 63
  screen
    create, 192-194
    delete, 195
    find, 160-161
      new mail for, 201
    primary, 192
    switch, 200-201
NetFind, 50-51
news
  keywords, 36
  profiles
    create, 210-213
    delete, 215
    manage, 214-215
    search sources
      add, 215
      remove, 215
    turn off, 215
    turn on, 215
  servers, 119
  sources, search, 210-213

newsgroups, 6, 118-119
    categories, 121
    lurk in, 133
    mark as read, 129
    messages
        print, 128
        quoting in, 130
        read, 126-127
        reply, 130-131
            options, 131
        send, 132-133
        vs. subjects, 127
    names, parts, 119
    open, 118
    search for, 120-121
    subscribe, 124
    unsubscribe, 125
Norton AntiVirus, 89

O

online clock, view, 11
open. *See also* start
    AOL, 8-9
    newsgroups, 118

P

pages on Web. *See* Web, pages
parental controls
    change, 198-199
    set, 192-194
passwords
    change, 196-197
    security, 197
    set, 192-193
    store, 195
    use to access AOL, 9
personal filing cabinet
    delete items, 203
    information stored in, 203
    using, 202-203
personal finance keywords, 36

portfolios, stock
    add items, 206-207
    create, 204-205
    display, 208
    print, 208-209
    remove items, 209
primary screen names, 192
print
    messages
        e-mail, 82
        message boards, 110
        newsgroups, 128
    stock portfolios, 208-209
program files, download, 173
public domain programs, 172

Q

quote in messages
    e-mail, 68
    newsgroups, 130

R

read messages
    e-mail, 64-65
    message boards, 108-109
    newsgroups, 126-127
reminder service
    important dates, view, 217
    using, 216-219
reminders
    add, 216-219
    delete, 219
remove. *See also* delete
    favorite places, 187
    items from personal filing cabinet, 203
    members from Buddy Lists, 167
    messages, e-mail, 84
    reminders, 219
    screen names, 195
    stocks from portfolios, 209

225

INDEX

reply to messages
    e-mail, 68-69
    instant messages, 149
    message boards, 112-113
    newsgroups, 130-131
research & learn keywords, 37
return receipts, request, for e-mail messages, 98

S

save e-mail messages, 83
screen names, 4
    create, 192-195
    delete, 195
    find, 160-161
        new mail for, 201
    primary, 192
    switch, 200-201
scroll through windows, 16
search. *See also* find
    for chat rooms, 138-139
    for e-mail addresses, 78-79
    for files to download
        by browsing, 174-175
        by searching, 176-177
    for help information, 18-19
    for information on AOL, 38-39
        improve, 39
    Member Directory, 160-161
    for newsgroups, 120-121
    services, 51
    the Web, 50-51
    for Web pages, 50-51
security
    guidelines for children, 199
    passwords, 197
select
    links, 46
    names from address book, 76-77

send
    comments in chat room, 140
    messages
        during live events, 156-157
        e-mail, 66-67
            later, 100-101
        instant
            at any time, 148
            while chatting, 146-148
        to newsgroups, 132-133
send to, e-mail messages, 67, 77
shareware programs, 172
shopping keywords, 37
size windows, 15
smileys, 137
software
    AOL, 5
    download, 178-179
sound files, download, 173
sounds, 5
    play in chat room, 141
spell check e-mail messages, 90-91
sports keywords, 37
start
    AOL, 8
stocks
    find information on, 207
    portfolios
        add items, 206-207
        create, 204-205
        display, 208
        print, 208-209
        remove items, 209
stop
    ignoring chat members, 143
    transfer of Web pages, 47
subjects vs. messages
    on message boards, 109
    in newsgroups, 127
subscribe to newsgroups, 124
switch between windows, 17

T

text
- align in e-mail messages, 95
- bold
  - in e-mail messages, 94
  - in instant messages, 147
- color, change, in e-mail messages, 96
  - of background, 97
- font sizes, change
  - in e-mail messages, 93
  - in instant messages, 147
- fonts, change, in e-mail messages, 92
- italicize
  - in e-mail messages, 94
  - in instant messages, 147
- underline
  - in e-mail messages, 94
  - in instant messages, 147

toolbars, 10
transfer
- files, 178-179
  - attached to e-mail messages, 88-89
- of Web pages, stop, 47

travel keywords, 37

U

underline text
- in e-mail messages, 94
- in instant messages, 147

unsend e-mail messages, 102
unsubscribe from newsgroups, 125
update Web pages, 49
URLs (Uniform Resource Locators), 43
user names, 63

V

video files, download, 173
view
- AOL channels, 22-23
- Buddy Lists, 168-169
- files, attached, 88-89
- home pages, 52
- live events, 152-153
- member profiles, 160-161
  - while chatting, 142
- online clock, 11
- Web pages, 44-45
  - recently visited, 45

viruses, check for in downloaded files, 89, 179

W

Web
- browse, overview, 6, 43
- pages, 42
  - addresses, 44-45
    - save time when typing, 45
  - display, 44-45
    - recently viewed, 45
  - examples, 54-59
  - find, 50-51
  - home pages
    - change, 52-53
    - display, 52
    - set, 53
  - links, 43
    - select, 46
  - move through, 48
  - refresh, 49
- search services, 51
- sites, 42
- stop transfer of, 47

Welcome window, 9
windows, 10
- maximize, 12
- minimize, 13
- move, 14
- scroll through, 16
- size, change, 15
- switch between, 17

workplace keywords, 37
World Wide Web. See Web
WWW. See Web

Y

Yahoo!, 51

227

OVER 5 MILLION

OTHER 3-D Visual SERIES

SIMPLIFIED BOOKS

NOW AVAILABLE!
Windows 98 Simplified
ISBN 0-7645-6030-1
$24.99 USA/£23.99 UK

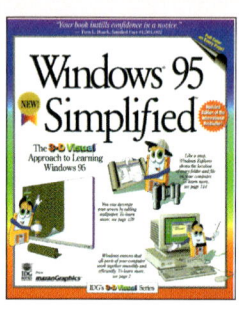

Windows 95 Simplified
ISBN 1-56884-662-2
$19.99 USA/£18.99 UK

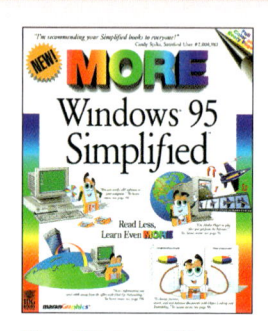

More Windows 95 Simplified
ISBN 1-56884-689-4
$19.99 USA/£18.99 UK

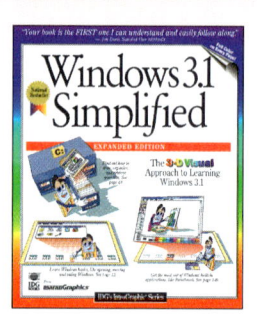

Windows 3.1 Simplified
ISBN 1-56884-654-1
$19.99 USA/£18.99 UK

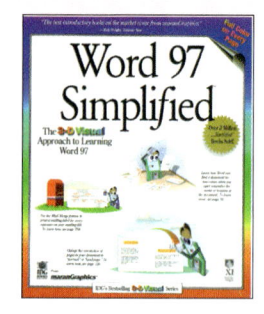

Word 97 Simplified
ISBN 1-7645-6011-5
$24.99 USA/£23.99 UK

Office 97 Simplified
ISBN 0-7645-6009-3
$29.99 USA/£28.99 UK

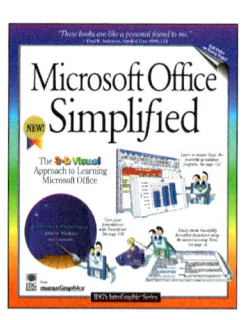

Microsoft Office 4.2 For Windows Simplified
ISBN 1-56884-673-8
$27.99 USA/£26.99 UK

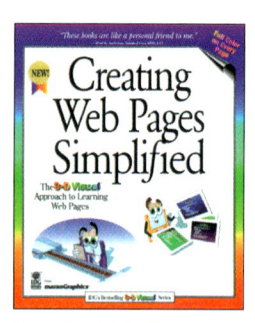

Creating Web Pages Simplified
ISBN 0-7645-6007-7
$24.99 USA/£23.99 UK

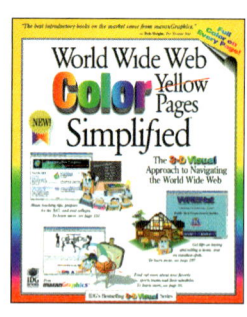

World Wide Web Color Yellow Pages Simplified
ISBN 0-7645-6005-0
$29.99 USA/£28.99 UK

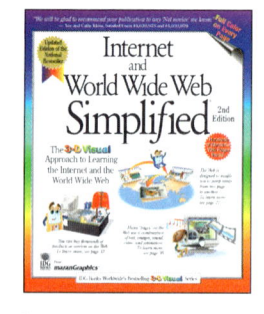

Internet and World Wide Web Simplified, 2nd Edition
ISBN 0-7645-6029-8
$24.99 USA/£23.99 UK

POCKETGUIDES

The Proven 3-D Visual Approach To Learning Computers In A Handy Pocket Size.

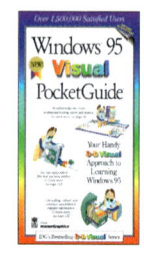

Windows 95 Visual PocketGuide
ISBN 1-56884-661-4
$14.99 USA/£13.99 UK

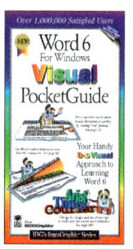

Word 6 For Windows Visual PocketGuide
ISBN 1-56884-666-5
$14.99 USA/£13.99 UK

ALSO AVAILABLE:

Windows 3.1 Visual PocketGuide
ISBN 1-56884-650-9
$14.99 USA/£13.99 UK

FOR CORPORATE ORDERS, PLEASE CALL: **800-469-6616**

SATISFIED USERS!

maranGraphics & IDG BOOKS

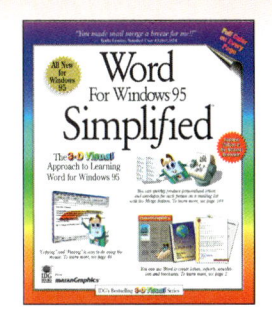

Word For Windows 95 Simplified
ISBN 1-56884-681-9
$19.99 USA/£18.99 UK

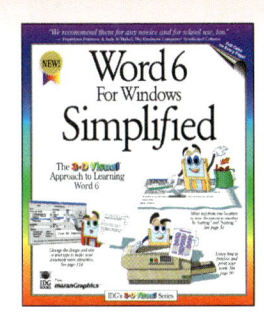

Word 6 For Windows Simplified
ISBN 1-56884-660-6
$19.99 USA/£18.99 UK

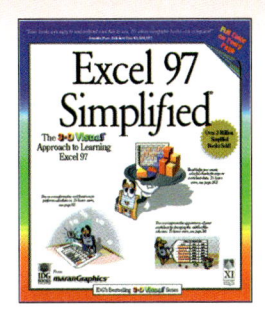

Excel 97 Simplified
ISBN 1-7645-6022-0
$24.99 USA/£23.99 UK

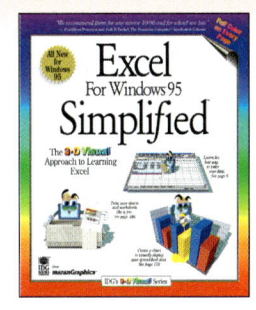

Excel For Windows 95 Simplified
ISBN 1-56884-682-7
$19.99 USA/£18.99 UK

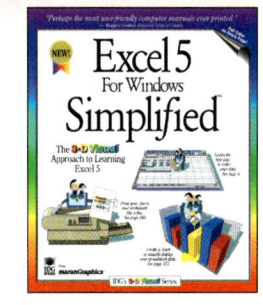

Excel 5 For Windows Simplified
ISBN 1-56884-664-9
$19.99 USA/£18.99 UK

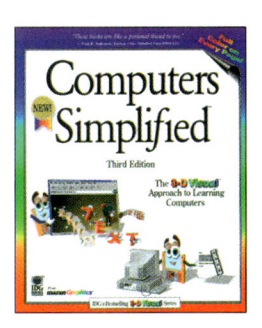

Computers Simplified, Third Edition
ISBN 0-7645-6008-5
$24.99 USA/£23.99 UK

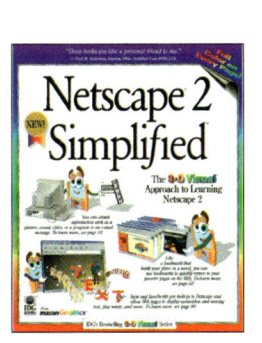

Netscape 2 Simplified
ISBN 0-7645-6000-X
$19.99 USA/£18.99 UK

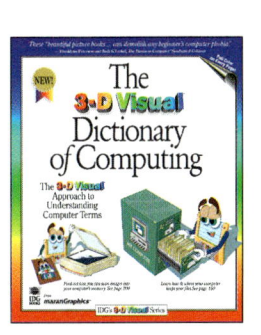

The 3-D Visual Dictionary of Computing
ISBN 1-56884-678-9
$19.99 USA/£18.99 UK

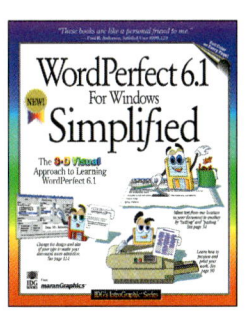

WordPerfect 6.1 For Windows Simplified
ISBN 1-56884-665-7
$19.99 USA/£18.99 UK

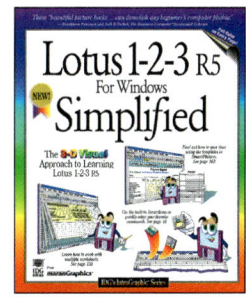

Lotus 1-2-3 R5 For Windows Simplified
ISBN 1-56884-670-3
$19.99 USA/£18.99 UK

Excel 5 For Windows Visual PocketGuide
ISBN 1-56884-667-3
$14.99 USA/£13.99 UK

WordPerfect 6.1 For Windows Visual PocketGuide
ISBN 1-56884-668-1
$14.99 USA/£13.99 UK

Lotus 1-2-3 R5 For Windows Visual PocketGuide
ISBN 1-56884-671-1
$14.99 USA/£13.99 UK

FOR CORPORATE ORDERS, PLEASE CALL: **800-469-6616**

OVER 5 MILLION OTHER 3-D Visual SERIES

TEACH YOURSELF VISUALLY

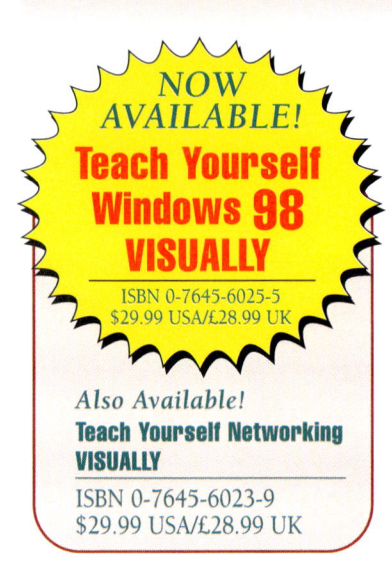

NOW AVAILABLE!
Teach Yourself Windows 98 VISUALLY
ISBN 0-7645-6025-5
$29.99 USA/£28.99 UK

Also Available!
Teach Yourself Networking VISUALLY
ISBN 0-7645-6023-9
$29.99 USA/£28.99 UK

Teach Yourself Computers and the Internet VISUALLY
ISBN 0-7645-6002-6
$29.99 USA/£28.99 UK

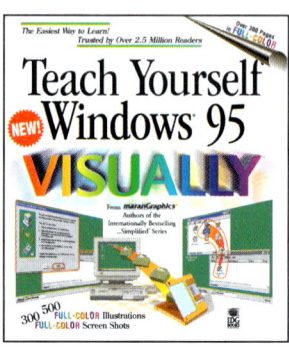

Teach Yourself Windows 95 VISUALLY
ISBN 0-7645-6001-8
$29.99 USA/£28.99 UK

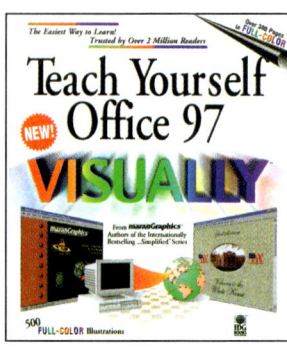

Teach Yourself Office 97 VISUALLY
ISBN 0-7645-6018-2
$29.99 USA/£28.99 UK

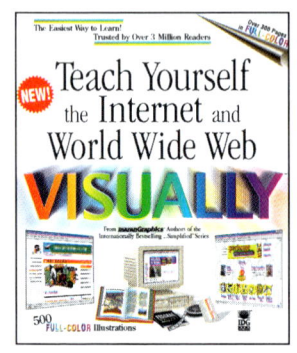

Teach Yourself the Internet and World Wide Web VISUALLY
ISBN 0-7645-6020-4
$29.99 USA/£28.99 UK

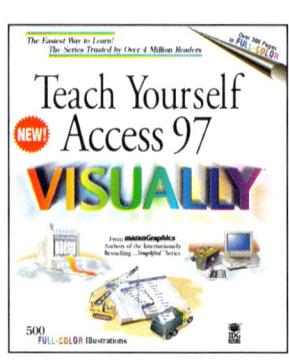

Teach Yourself Access 97 VISUALLY
ISBN 0-7645-6026-3
$29.99 USA/£28.99 UK

Teach Yourself Netscape Navigator 4 VISUALLY
ISBN 0-7645-6028-X
$29.99 USA/£28.99 UK

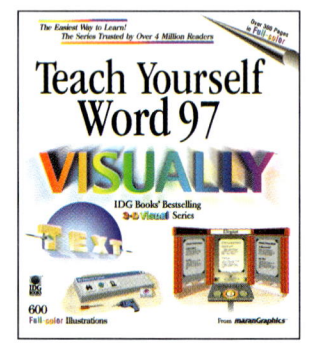

Teach Yourself Word 97 VISUALLY
ISBN 0-7645-6032-8
$29.99 USA/£28.99 UK

FOR CORPORATE ORDERS, PLEASE CALL: 800-469-6616

SATISFIED USERS!

maranGraphics & IDG BOOKS

MASTER VISUALLY SERIES

The Complete Visual Reference

MASTER Windows 95 VISUALLY

- Step-by-Step Instructions
- 1200 Screenshots
- The Revolutionary Way to Learn

- Totally searchable onscreen version of the book on CD!
- PLUS CleanSweep, Paint Shop Pro, First Aid, and more

by maranGraphics

Master Windows 95 VISUALLY
ISBN 0-7645-6024-7
$39.99 USA/£36.99 UK

Visit our Web site at:
http://www.maran.com

NOW AVAILABLE!
Master Windows 98 VISUALLY
ISBN 0-7645-6034-4
$39.99 USA/£36.99 UK

This is what people are saying about our books...

"This book was so easy to understand that it did everything except punch the keys."
—Charles Ray Greene, Rincon, Georgia

"This series is written for people on planet Earth."
—M. Klappenberger, Elkridge, Maryland

"Your expertise in presenting information logically, understandably and completely is absolutely beyond compare."
—Rey Archambault, Phoenix, Arizona

"Beautifully illustrated. Crystal clear. Excellent for beginner to expert."
—Henry Conn, Athens, Alabama

"I have learned more since I bought your book than I did in the last 6 months on my own. Best purchase I ever made."
—Helene Jacobs, St. Petersburg, Florida

"For the first time, a book I can really understand. I can't imagine anyone not being able to learn from this book."
—Charles Kline, Catskill, New York

FOR CORPORATE ORDERS, PLEASE CALL: 800-469-6616

ORDER FORM

IDG BOOKS®

TRADE & INDIVIDUAL ORDERS
Phone: **(800) 762-2974**
or **(317) 895-5200**
(8 a.m.–6 p.m., CST, weekdays)
FAX : **(317) 895-5298**

EDUCATIONAL ORDERS & DISCOUNTS
Phone: **(800) 434-2086**
(8:30 a.m.–5:00 p.m., CST, weekdays)
FAX : **(817) 251-8174**

CORPORATE ORDERS FOR 3-D VISUAL™ SERIES
Phone: **(800) 469-6616**
(8 a.m.–5 p.m., EST, weekdays)
FAX : **(905) 890-9434**

Qty	ISBN	Title	Price	Total

Shipping & Handling Charges

	Description	First book	Each add'l. book	Total
Domestic	Normal	$4.50	$1.50	$
	Two Day Air	$8.50	$2.50	$
	Overnight	$18.00	$3.00	$
International	Surface	$8.00	$8.00	$
	Airmail	$16.00	$16.00	$
	DHL Air	$17.00	$17.00	$

Subtotal _____

CA residents add applicable sales tax _____

IN, MA and MD residents add 5% sales tax _____

IL residents add 6.25% sales tax _____

RI residents add 7% sales tax _____

TX residents add 8.25% sales tax _____

Shipping _____

Total _____

Ship to:

Name_____

Address_____

Company_____

City/State/Zip_____

Daytime Phone_____

Payment: ☐ Check to IDG Books (US Funds Only)
☐ Visa ☐ Mastercard ☐ American Express

Card #_____ Exp. _____ Signature_____

maranGraphics™